Lucretia Mott
Speaks

WOMEN, GENDER, AND SEXUALITY
IN AMERICAN HISTORY

Editorial Advisors:
Susan K. Cahn
Wanda A. Hendricks
Deborah Gray White

Anne Firor Scott,
   Founding Editor Emerita

*A list of books in the series appears
   at the end of this book.*

collection supported by
Figure Foundation

to script surely

Figure 1. "Discourse on Woman," delivered in 1849, Mott's most widely published speech. (Courtesy of the Friends Historical Library, Swarthmore College)

Lucretia Mott Speaks

Speaks

The Essential Speeches and Sermons

Edited by
Christopher Densmore,
Carol Faulkner,
Nancy Hewitt, and
Beverly Wilson Palmer

UNIVERSITY OF ILLINOIS PRESS
Urbana, Chicago, and Springfield

© 2017 by the Board of Trustees
of the University of Illinois
All rights reserved
Manufactured in the United States of America
C 5 4 3 2 1
♾ This book is printed on acid-free paper.

Library of Congress Control Number: 2016962070
ISBN 978-0-252-04079-5 (hardcover)
ISBN 978-0-252-09925-0 (e-book)

Contents

Introduction   xi

Editorial Policies   xxix

LUCRETIA MOTT SPEAKS: THE ESSENTIAL SPEECHES AND SERMONS

Twelfth Street Meeting, Philadelphia, 1818   3

Pennsylvania Hall, Philadelphia, May 16 and 17, 1838   3

New England Non-Resistance Society, Chardon Street Chapel, Boston, September 25–27, 1839   4

Unitarian Chapel, August 9, 1840, Glasgow, Scotland   6

Marlboro Chapel, Boston, September 23, 1841   8

Rose Street Meeting, New York City, September 29, 1841   14

Manhattan Society, Asbury Church, New York City, September 29, 1841   15

Unitarian Church, Washington, D.C., January 15, 1843   16

Hicksite Meetinghouse, Rochester, New York, July 21, 1844   27

Unitarian Christians Convention, First Unitarian Church, Philadelphia, October 22, 1846   28

Anti-Sabbath Convention, The Melodeon, Boston, March 24, 1848   30

American Anti-Slavery Society, Broadway Tabernacle, New York City, May 9, 1848   39

Women's Rights Convention, Wesleyan Chapel, Seneca Falls, New York, July 19–20, 1848   44

Women's Rights Convention, Unitarian Church,
   Rochester, New York, August 2, 1848   45
"Sermon to the Medical Students," Cherry Street
   Meeting, Philadelphia, February 11, 1849   48
American Anti-Slavery Society, Minerva Rooms,
   New York City, May 8, 1849   55
Cherry Street Meeting, Philadelphia, November 4, 1849   56
Cherry Street Meeting, Philadelphia, November 6, 1849   64
"Discourse on Woman," Assembly Buildings,
   Philadelphia, December 17, 1849   68
Cherry Street Meeting, Philadelphia, March 31, 1850   81
Women's Rights Convention, Brinley Hall, Worcester,
   Massachusetts, October 23–24, 1850   87
Isaac T. Hopper Memorial Service, Broadway
   Tabernacle, New York City, May 12, 1852   92
Women's Rights Convention, Horticultural Hall, West
   Chester, Pennsylvania, June 2–3, 1852   93
Women's Rights Convention, City Hall, Syracuse,
   New York, September 8–10, 1852   95
Pennsylvania Anti-Slavery Society, Horticultural Hall, West
   Chester, Pennsylvania, October 25–26, 1852   100
Pennsylvania Anti-Slavery Society, Assembly Buildings,
   Philadelphia, December 15–16, 1852   102
Women's Rights Convention, Broadway Tabernacle,
   New York City, September 6–7, 1853   104
Women's Rights Convention, Melodeon Hall,
   Cleveland, October 5 and 7, 1853   110
Rose Street Meeting, New York City, November 11, 1855   120
Women's Rights Convention, Broadway Tabernacle,
   New York City, November 25–26, 1856   122
Yardleyville, Pennsylvania, September 26, 1858   127
American Anti-Slavery Society, Assembly Rooms,
   New York City, May 11, 1859   137
Anti-Slavery Sympathy Meeting, Assembly Buildings,
   Philadelphia, December 16, 1859   138
Pennsylvania Anti-Slavery Society, Town-Hall,
   Kennett Square, October 25–26, 1860   139
Fifteenth Street Meeting, New York City, June 1, 1862   142

30th Anniversary of the American Anti-Slavery Society,
    Concert Hall, Philadelphia, December 3–4, 1863   144
American Anti-Slavery Society, Church of the Puritans and
    Cooper Institute, New York City, May 10–11, 1864   148
Women's Rights Convention, Church of the Puritans,
    New York City, May 10, 1866   151
Fifteenth Street Meeting, New York City, November 11, 1866   153
Pennsylvania Anti-Slavery Society, Franklin Institute,
    Philadelphia, November 22–23, 1866   160
American Equal Rights Association, Church of the
    Puritans, New York City, May 9–10, 1867   163
Free Religious Association, Horticultural
    Hall, Boston, May 30, 1867   166
Second Unitarian Church, Brooklyn, New
    York, November 24, 1867   171
Pennsylvania Peace Society, Assembly Buildings,
    Philadelphia, November 17–18, 1868   178
Race Street Meeting, Philadelphia, March 14, 1869   180
Women's Suffrage Meeting, Academy of Music,
    Brooklyn, New York, May 14, 1869   189
Pennsylvania Peace Society, Friends' Meeting House,
    Abington, Pennsylvania, September 19, 1869   191
Opening of Swarthmore College, Swarthmore,
    Pennsylvania, November 10, 1869   195
Philadelphia Female Anti-Slavery Society, Assembly
    Buildings, March 24, 1870   196
American Anti-Slavery Society, Apollo Hall,
    New York City, April 9, 1870   197
Reform League, Steinway Hall, New York City, May 9, 1871   199
Fifteenth Street Meeting, New York City, May 26, 1872   199
Funeral of Mary Ann W. Johnson, Home of Oliver
    Johnson, New York City, June 10, 1872   201
Free Religious Association, Tremont Temple,
    Boston, May 30, 1873   203
Philadelphia Quarterly Meeting, Race Street,
    November 4, 1873   205
Pennsylvania Society for Promoting the Abolition of Slavery,
    Concert Hall, Philadelphia, April 14, 1875   207

Free Religious Association, Beethoven Hall, Boston,
    May 28, 1875   207
Women's Peace Festival, Institute Hall, Philadelphia,
    June 2, 1875   209
Women's Peace Festival, Mercantile Hall,
    Philadelphia, June 2, 1876   211
30th Anniversary of the Seneca Falls Convention, Unitarian
    Church, Rochester, New York, July 19, 1878   214

Acknowledgments   217

Index   219

Introduction

Carol Faulkner and Nancy Hewitt

Lucretia Mott, the Quaker minister, abolitionist, and women's rights activist, was as famous for her inspiring and provocative words as for her principled and courageous actions. A gifted orator, she spoke before thousands of people over the course of her sixty-year career. In 1848 alone, the year Mott became the "moving spirit" of the first women's rights convention in Seneca Falls, she also attended an Anti-Sabbath Convention, the annual meeting of the American Anti-Slavery Society, Philadelphia Yearly Meeting, Genesee Yearly Meeting, the annual Strawberry Festival on the Cattaraugus (Seneca Nation) reservation, a second women's rights convention in Rochester, a "Colored" Convention in Philadelphia, monthly meetings of the Philadelphia Female Anti-Slavery Society, and the annual meeting of the Pennsylvania Anti-Slavery Society. That same year, Mott made several joint appearances with the former slave and writer William Wells Brown, and she preached to diverse audiences, including prisoners, fugitives, Universalists, and Quakers.[1] Mott did not write down any of these speeches or sermons. As a Friend, she believed in speaking spontaneously on a subject that moved her. To capture Mott's witty, moving, and reasoned arguments, as well as her sometimes tart tongue, subsequent generations must rely on the journalists, stenographers, Quakers, and co-workers who recorded her words.

When she spoke, Lucretia Mott addressed a wide array of issues that confronted the United States and the world: the abolition of slavery and racism, feminism, religious freedom, international peace and cooperation, education, and democracy. *Lucretia Mott Speaks* is an authoritative selection of her abundant but scattered speeches, many of which readers will find relevant today. The editors have identified approximately 190 lectures by Mott in archives, newspapers, and other printed sources. Some of these appear in Dana Greene's *Lucretia Mott: Her Complete Speeches and Sermons* (1980), but this volume includes significant additional speeches as well as fuller versions of those previously published.[2] The sixty selected speeches present critical themes and important events in Mott's long and distinguished public life. The annotations provide the vibrant context for her words and actions, identifying Mott's intellectual engagement with allies and opponents, as well as with transatlantic religious and political debates across the nineteenth century.

This volume complements Beverly Wilson Palmer's *Selected Letters of Lucretia Coffin Mott*. Letters and oratory were two of the most important forms of communication in the nineteenth century, circulating information and opinions within circles of family and friends as well as to broad and diverse publics. Although letters were often read aloud and sometimes published in newspapers, and a speech or sermon might be described in personal correspondence, these genres spoke to distinct audiences and offered distinct perspectives. Thus a different Lucretia Mott appears in these pages than in the *Selected Letters*. While Mott's letters contain trenchant observations about friends and enemies in the transatlantic Quaker, antislavery, and women's rights movements, the letters also focus on the details of her extended family, many friends, and bustling household. Even though Mott's private and public lives were intertwined, readers of this volume will find little mention of her husband James, her children and grandchildren, or her daily life in these orations (for wonderful exceptions, see pp. 5 and 161). Instead, Mott's speeches and sermons illuminate the engaged, tireless, and often controversial public figure.

While Mott is notable for the breadth and depth of her radicalism, she participated in a larger movement of reformers. This introduction places Mott in that expansive activist milieu. Though Mott does not always mention her co-workers, they formed an important part of her audience, attending the same meetings and conventions, and listening and responding to her words. Many of them supported Mott's view that "all these subjects of reform are kindred in their nature; and giving to each its proper consideration, will tend to strengthen and nerve the mind for all."[3] And, like Mott, many were or had been Hicksite Quakers. The Society of Friends experienced multiple fractures over Mott's lifetime, and these debates had a lasting impact on both the antislavery and women's rights movements. While many of her allies left the Society of Friends, Mott did not. Neither, however, did she stop agitating for change—within the Society of Friends and in other religious institutions, reform organizations, and society at large.

Mott used her persuasive powers to challenge the authority of social customs, laws, and organized religion. Speaking to activists at the Syracuse women's rights convention, she proclaimed her faith in "agitation—in the wisdom of not keeping still" (97). Though Mott was a Quaker and a pacifist, she refused to be quiet. In fact, her friend Robert Purvis, a wealthy free black activist, called her the most "belligerent Non-Resistant he ever saw" (141). Fearless and outspoken, Mott became the target of attacks by her opponents. At times, even her allies objected to her unwavering principles. In her speeches and sermons, Mott critiqued ministers, politicians, writers, and slaveholders, whose social position, rather than the truth of their arguments, gave them power over the lives of religious dissenters, African Americans, and women. Yet she maintained a boundless optimism in the potential of these ordinary Americans to create a new egalitarian society.

The career of the most influential female activist in the nineteenth century began in the Society of Friends. In 1818 Mott delivered her first public remarks at Twelfth Street Monthly Meeting in Philadelphia. She prayed for the power to resist worldly temptations so that she and other Quakers might devote themselves to "Thy glorious cause" (3). At this point, Mott was a twenty-five-year-old wife and mother, still grieving over the recent death of her two-year-old son Thomas. Over the next few years, Mott explored her religious calling, and, in 1821, the Society of Friends recorded her name as an approved minister, the only formal recognition that the denomination offered.[4] Quakers opposed social hierarchies, including what they termed "hireling" ministers, or the educated, salaried professionals of other churches. While her prayer might seem unremarkable, Mott presaged issues that soon divided the Society of Friends. For the next few decades, Quakers debated whether it was best to ally with non-Quakers in reform or to remain apart from "the world." Although Friends had officially ended direct involvement with slavery before the American Revolution, their disputes centered in part on how best to challenge the massive economic and geographic expansion of slavery.[5] Quakers also disagreed about the authority of the Scriptures, the power of the meeting, and whether the select meetings of leading ministers and elders nurtured Friends or interfered with individual rights and conscience.

As a child on Nantucket, Mott absorbed Quaker opposition to slavery. Born on January 3, 1793, Lucretia was the second daughter of Thomas Coffin, a whaling captain, and his wife, Anna Folger Coffin, who, like many island women, operated a small store. In Lucretia's schoolroom, the teacher hung a copy of British abolitionist Thomas Clarkson's diagram of the ship *Brookes*, which showed almost five hundred African captives being transported to slavery in Jamaica. In many of her later speeches, Mott referred to Clarkson, as well as pioneering Quaker activists such as Ralph Sandiford, Benjamin Lay, and Anthony Benezet (see 40 and 145, for example). Some of Lucretia's Quaker ancestors had owned slaves, but had since abandoned the practice. New England Yearly Meeting censured involvement in the slave trade in 1727 and condemned slavery in 1760. In 1773 New England Quakers took the final step by requiring all members to free their slaves or be disowned from the Society of Friends.[6]

Lucretia's progressive education continued at Nine Partners Boarding School in Dutchess County, New York, where she also met her future husband James Mott. The Society of Friends established Nine Partners and other co-educational schools to protect their children from the materialism and religious competition of the larger society. In addition to learning Quaker principles and practice, Lucretia studied the same academic subjects as male students, receiving one of the best educations of her time. Many female Quaker activists benefited from a similar education, and at least some of their fellow male students learned to respect independent and intellectual women in this environment.

Yet when Lucretia became a teacher at Nine Partners, she discovered there were limits to Quaker egalitarianism. In 1809, twenty-one-year old James Mott, the grandson of the school's superintendent, earned more than twice as much as the head female teacher. Despite her growing affection for James, Lucretia vowed "to claim for myself all that an impartial Creator has bestowed," adding a nascent feminism to her abolitionism.[7]

In 1811, when eighteen-year-old Lucretia married James Mott in Pine Street Meeting in Philadelphia, they were no different from other young couples in the Society of Friends. According to Quaker custom, no minister presided over such ceremonies. Rather, the couple stood before the meeting and declared their mutual love and fidelity. As Lucretia later reminded audiences, Quaker unions contained no "promised *obedience* in the marriage contract" (47).[8] Other denominations included a female vow of obedience, and, in a legal doctrine known as coverture, women lost all independent political and economic rights upon marriage. In this context, Mott viewed her own and other Quaker marriages as successful egalitarian models. Following their wedding, James struggled to establish himself in business in Philadelphia, eventually becoming a successful wool merchant. Lucretia taught in a Quaker school even after the first of their six children, a daughter named Anna, was born in 1812. In 1828, when Lucretia had been a minister for seven years, she gave birth to their youngest child, Martha. Throughout Lucretia's career, James, a fellow activist though not a public speaker, was her strong supporter.

In the 1820s the Hicksite controversy split the Society of Friends in America. The term "Hicksite" referred to allies of Long Island Quaker minister Elias Hicks, a member of the Nine Partners School Committee. Hicks criticized Philadelphia's Quaker leaders for using their power to silence those who did not agree with them, for placing the authority of the Bible over the authority of the inward light, and for their continued financial connections to slavery.[9] When Philadelphia Yearly Meeting separated into Hicksite and Orthodox branches in 1827, the Motts sided with the Hicksites. This division had a lasting impact on Lucretia's religious and political views.

Both Lucretia Mott and Elias Hicks urged Friends to follow the "great fundamental" principle of the inward light, the democratic belief that every individual had access to guidance from the Divine spirit within (64). Mott used a variety of terms for this doctrine, including the "inner voice" or "inward monitor" (14 and 15); she also described it as "a religious instinct in the constitution of man" (127). Based on this foundational tenet of the Society of Friends, she shared Hicks's disapproval of the disciplinary power of the "officers and high seat occupants of this Society," who believed they had the right to judge the ideas and activities of Quaker reformers (66). Throughout her ministry, she agreed with Hicks's concern for undue "veneration" of the Bible. Mott had a detailed knowledge of Scripture, which she liberally quoted or paraphrased in her sermons. Nevertheless, she also asked, "has there not been an unworthy resort to this volume to prove the rightfulness of war and Slavery, and of crushing woman's powers, the assumption of authority over her, and indeed of all the evils under which the earth, humanity

Figure 2. Elias Hicks (1748–1830). (Courtesy of the Friends Historical Library, Swarthmore College)

has groaned from age to age?" (59). Finally, she and Hicks agreed that the Quaker abolition of slavery did not go far enough and urged Friends to cut all ties to slavery. Mott became a leading advocate of "free produce," an abolitionist strategy to boycott slavery. She and her allies recommended using alternatives like wool and maple syrup, or purchasing sugar and cotton produced by free labor.[10]

In the midst of the period of revivalism known as the Second Great Awakening, Elias Hicks and his followers promoted a rational, egalitarian, and individualistic approach to human salvation. They called their opponents "Orthodox" or "Evangelical" Quakers for their investment in social hierarchy, their reliance on the Bible, and their connections to evangelical Protestants. Hicksites dominated many meetings in rural Pennsylvania; on Long Island, where Hicks and his extended family lived; and in central and western New York, where migrants from New England and Long Island had formed new meetings in the early 1800s. These areas, like Philadelphia, nurtured significant numbers of passionate antislavery and women's rights advocates in the 1830s and 1840s, who viewed Hicks and Mott as role models.

The Hicksites did not exist in isolation, but interacted with African American abolitionists who demanded equal political and economic citizenship, newly enfranchised white working-class men who shared their anticlerical politics, and Unitarians who embraced a similar democratic faith in human nature. Over the course of her career, Mott frequently quoted Unitarian minister and abolitionist William Ellery Channing's egalitarian sermon "Honour Due to All Men" (for example, 10 and 176).[11] Increasingly, Mott argued that the inner light, which she insisted was "not a mere Quaker doctrine," justified agitation against slavery, racial prejudice, sectarianism, war, and sexual inequality (131). Mott often signed autographs with the phrase "Truth for Authority, not Authority for Truth," capturing this commitment to a higher, but accessible, spiritual power (similar phrasing can be found on 114 and 185).

Many people in these religious and social movements likewise elevated the individual conscience and human freedom over the authority of the Bible or secular laws. Mott regularly spoke against "mere forms and rituals of the Church," which she believed interfered with "practical goodness." At the 1848 Anti-Sabbath Convention, she condemned the "hallowing" of a single day as the Sabbath, asking why it should be "a greater crime to do an innocent thing on the first day of the week,—to use a needle, for instance—than to put a human being on the auction-block on the second day" (31, 33). Since the seventeenth century, Quakers had regarded Sunday as no different, or more holy, than any other day. In the early nineteenth century, as evangelical reformers campaigned for strict Sabbath laws, Quakers and Unitarians found allies among freethinkers, workers, and Jews, who viewed these laws as discriminatory.[12] Mott argued that devotion to the Sabbath resulted from fear, asking, "Why not judge ye for yourselves what is right?" And she believed that Truth, as "ever progressive," favored religious liberals over evangelicals and the orthodox (174).

In the 1830s this embrace of "Truth for Authority" helped to create an abolitionist coalition of African Americans, Hicksite Quakers, and Unitarians. Such coalitions were fragile given the racial politics and religious upheavals of the era. While many African American activists were affiliated with black Methodist and Baptist churches, they often found support for their antislavery campaign among white religious liberals. Even so, many Hicksites continued to reject participation in "worldly" (or interfaith) organizations, including those with the shared goal of abolishing slavery. However complicated the relationship, Hicksite Quakers were among the first white northerners to join forces with black abolitionists.[13]

Lucretia Mott was a leader in this effort. With her antislavery radicalism reinforced by the Hicksite schism, in December 1833 she attended the founding meeting of the American Anti-Slavery Society (AASS), which called for the immediate, unconditional emancipation of slaves. Initially, women had not been invited to the meeting, but Thomas Whitson, a Quaker who had founded the Clarkson Anti-Slavery Society, urged them to attend. Mott accepted the invitation, as did her mother, Anna; sister Martha; and oldest daughter, Anna, who had recently married Edward Hopper, the son of Hicksite abolitionist Isaac Hopper. At least three other women also attended the meeting, two of whom worked with Mott in the free produce movement. Although these women were experienced speakers and organizers, only Lucretia joined in the convention's debates.[14]

Mott endorsed the organizers' strategy of using moral suasion rather than physical or political power to end slavery (see especially 140–41 and 144–45 for Mott's views of the founding principles of the AASS). Only male abolitionists, including James Mott and Robert Purvis, signed the convention's Declaration of Sentiments, but Lucretia helped draft its language. With her guidance, for example, the declaration read, "We may be personally defeated, but our principles never."[15] Within the week, Mott, Harriet Forten Purvis (Robert Purvis's wife); Lydia White, who owned the first free produce store in the city; and other women formed the racially integrated Philadelphia Female Anti-Slavery Society (PFASS), with the interconnected goals of ending slavery and racial prejudice. PFASS became the longest-lived female antislavery society, only ending its work after the ratification of the Fifteenth Amendment in 1870 (see 145 and 196–97).[16]

Family, friendship, and Quaker networks in Philadelphia formed the bedrock of Mott's activism in this early period of interracial and interfaith organizing, allowing her sphere of influence to expand beyond the city. As Mott traveled to Quaker meetings and antislavery conventions, she connected with religious and social radicals in other parts of the country. Like eastern Pennsylvania, central and western New York was home to Quaker abolitionists as well as free blacks and fugitive slaves. In 1834 Hicksites organized the new Genesee Yearly Meeting, which included meetings in central and western New York, Upper Canada (now Ontario), and Michigan. Concerned with the threatened sale of Indian reservations in New York State, members of Genesee, Philadelphia, New York, and Baltimore Yearly Meetings formed the Joint Indian Committee and worked with Seneca leaders to fight their removal westward. Lucretia Mott periodically made the journey from Philadelphia to Farmington, New York, to attend Genesee Yearly Meeting. There, she met former Philadelphia Friends like Thomas and Mary Ann M'Clintock, who had moved to Waterloo, New York, and visited her younger sister Martha Coffin Wright, who now lived in nearby Auburn with her husband, David. The Motts also reconnected with other reformers in the region, including Amy and Isaac Post of Rochester.

Lucretia Mott's activist network extended far beyond New York and Pennsylvania, but she was not always received with enthusiasm. In the United States, a country hostile to their cause, abolitionists embraced great personal risks. In 1838 Mott's Philadelphia home narrowly missed the fate of Pennsylvania Hall, which was burned to ashes by a hostile crowd just a few days after abolitionists celebrated its opening (3–4). This episode was not her last encounter with mob violence. In February 1840 Mott tried to reason with a mob in Smyrna, Delaware, as they tarred and feathered her traveling companion, Quaker abolitionist Daniel Neall.[17] Then in May Mott traveled to London as a delegate to the World's Anti-Slavery Convention, where she was the most visible woman in the newly radicalized, but increasingly divided American antislavery movement. The subsequent controversy over Mott's official status at the World's Anti-Slavery Convention reflected strategic differences in the transatlantic abolitionist movement.

Just weeks before the London convention began, the American Anti-Slavery Society divided over the participation of women. The British organizers of the World's Anti-Slavery Convention sympathized with those American activists who opposed female officers and lecturers, preferring a less public, less controversial role for women. In addition, English Quakers had sided with the Orthodox Friends in the separation of 1827, and did not recognize Hicksites as Quakers.[18] Although the convention voted to deny the credentials of Mott and the other seven female delegates, they sat in the gallery throughout the discussions. Mott then gave a number of speeches in London and throughout Great Britain, including one in Glasgow's Unitarian Church (6–7). She also met some like-minded British abolitionists and corresponded with Irish activist Daniel O'Connell. (For Mott's recollections of the World's Anti-Slavery Convention, see especially 94 and 152.)

The contentious experience in London reinforced Mott's belief in women's right to participate equally in social movements. Although Mott continued to view slavery as the nation's most urgent moral problem, she saw it as connected to other potent forces restricting individual freedom. When she addressed the AASS's annual meeting in May 1848, Mott cited the "great principles of human freedom" articulated in the Society's Declaration, that "every man had a right to his own body, and that no man had a right to enslave or imbrute his brother." She believed abolitionists, pacifists, temperance activists, and religious reformers—women and men—were all engaged in this "work of blessing man," or embracing the equality of all humans (39, 40). As a result, in the 1840s and 1850s Mott also attended non-resistance (or non-violence), temperance, Unitarian, and anti-Sabbath conventions, where she interacted with activists like William Lloyd Garrison, Charles C. Burleigh, Lydia Maria Child, Frederick Douglass, Abby Kelley Foster, Theodore Parker, and Henry C. Wright.

At many of these conventions, she raised the question of women's status. In 1846, for example, she compared the interest of Unitarian ministers in "the relief of Hindu woman" to their authority over American women, asking, "have you, brethren, unfettered yourselves from a prejudice that is tending to immolate one half the whole human family?" Mott referred to the Unitarians' (wrong-headed) interpretation of Scripture, which had long justified the exclusion of women from the ministry. Confident in her own status as a preacher, Mott criticized the limits that most organized religions placed on women, who, due to their inferior educations, became pretty, but inconsequential, ornaments to society. Despite her own experience, Mott well knew that most American women had neither the right nor training to speak "the gushings of her soul" (29).

In the summer of 1848 her wide-ranging interests brought Mott back to central and western New York. Her first destination was Genesee Yearly Meeting in Farmington. With other Hicksites, the conservatives in Genesee Yearly Meeting disapproved of Quaker involvement with non-Quakers in antislavery, temperance, and other reform societies. In the 1840s a number of activist Friends withdrew from Genesee Yearly Meeting, believing that Quaker caution hindered the work of reform. While Mott remained a Quaker, she no longer asked for a "minute" or endorsement for her "travels in the ministry" from her Cherry Street Meeting. Having postponed action for several years on questions of "worldly" activism and the right of meetings to restrict individual conscience, the 1848 Genesee Yearly Meeting would be forced to address issues central to Mott's own identity as a Quaker activist.[19]

When the conservatives continued to support the authority of ministers and elders over the "sacred rights of conscience," long-simmering tensions erupted into another schism in the Society of Friends. The radicals of Genesee Yearly Meeting walked out and formed the Yearly Meeting of Congregational Friends. Rejecting existing Quaker discipline, they organized against "War, Slavery, Intemperance, &c."[20] Thomas M'Clintock and Rhoda DeGarmo served as co-clerks of the new meeting, and Mott identified M'Clintock as the author of its "Basis of Religious Association." In the Congregational Friends, men and women would meet together for worship and business; no special authority would be granted to ministers and elders; and non-Quakers committed to peace, abolition, and other causes were invited to participate.[21]

In the late 1840s and early 1850s additional meetings of Congregational (later Progressive) Friends emerged in Michigan, Ohio, Indiana, and Pennsylvania. Mott had many friends in the original Yearly Meeting of Congregational Friends, including the M'Clintocks, the Posts, and Griffith M. Cooper, who had served with the Motts in the Friends' Joint Indian Committee. Mott also worked closely with non-Quaker activists who attended Congregational Friends meetings, most notably Frederick Douglass and Elizabeth Cady Stanton. On at least one occasion, Stanton identified herself as a member of the local Junius Monthly Meeting of the Yearly Meeting of Congregational Friends, which was renamed the Friends of Human Progress in the 1850s.[22]

After the upheavals in Farmington, Lucretia and James Mott traveled west to the Cattaraugus reservation near Buffalo. As members of the Joint Indian Committee, they had taken an interest in the Seneca since the Ogden Land Company and the United States had tried to force them out a decade earlier. Now, she and James witnessed the Seneca debating their own constitution. From there, the Motts crossed the border into Canada and visited fugitive slaves who had settled in the province of Ontario. Lucretia gave lectures in Chatham, Dawn, London, and Toronto, though no account of these speeches survives. By mid-July Mott returned to the home of her sister Martha Coffin Wright in Auburn.[23]

The presence of Mott, a speaker with an international reputation, inspired local activists to organize the first convention devoted to women's rights. The plan originated during a small party at the Waterloo home of Quakers Jane and Richard Hunt, which Mott attended with her sister. The Hunts also invited their friend and neighbor, Mary Ann M'Clintock, and perhaps her two oldest daughters, as well as Elizabeth Cady Stanton, whom Lucretia had met at the World's Anti-Slavery Convention in 1840. In the intervening years, Mott and Stanton, despite their twenty-two-year difference in age, became fast friends. The women decided to advertise a convention "to discuss the Social, Civil, and Religious Condition of Woman" in Stanton's hometown of Seneca Falls on July 19–20. Just as earlier revolutionaries expounded on the "rights of man," nineteenth-century feminists often, and rather presumptuously, used the singular "woman" to define their movement as universal, encompassing the interests of all women.

As many as three hundred people attended the meeting at Seneca Falls, with Lucretia and James Mott, Elizabeth Cady Stanton, Thomas M'Clintock, his daughter Elizabeth M'Clintock, and Frederick Douglass among the most prominent participants. Like the American Anti-Slavery Society, the convention issued its own declaration, asserting that "all men and women are created equal." For Mott, the most controversial part of the statement involved women's right "to the elective franchise." As a Quaker, Mott viewed voting—and party politics more broadly—as morally compromising. As a member of the AASS, she believed the political system to be deeply, and irreversibly, corrupted by slavery. Nevertheless, of the one hundred women and men who signed the declaration, Lucretia Mott's name was the first and was followed by those of at least two dozen other Quakers, including the M'Clintocks, Jane Hunt, and Amy Post.[24]

Lucretia Mott's remarks at the Seneca Falls Convention and those at the women's rights meeting held two weeks later in Rochester reveal the unevenness in reports of her speeches. Mott addressed the crowd at Seneca Falls more times than any other activist, but all that remains are brief summaries from two different sources. Her public "discourse" on the evening of July 19 probably echoed her speech to the AASS earlier that year (44). The published proceedings of the Rochester women's rights convention are much more detailed, and contain humorous exchanges between Mott and African American activist William C. Nell as well as more skeptical participants, like a Mr. Colton and Richard Sulley (see 46–47). This second meeting was more confrontational than the gathering at Seneca Falls, considering the "Rights of women Politically, Socially, Religiously, and Industrially." While James Mott had chaired the Seneca Falls Convention, Amy Post and other members of the Rochester organizing committee nominated a woman, Abigail Bush, to preside.[25] Of the five organizers of the Rochester convention, four were Hicksite or Congregational Quakers, and all were members of the Western New York and American Anti-Slavery Societies. Embracing Mott's vision of moral power and individual conscience as well as her universalist approach to social change, this committee invited local working-class women to speak and introduced a resolution that extended the rights they claimed for themselves to every woman "whatever her complexion," that is, race.[26]

The following year, inspired by her participation in these inaugural women's rights conventions, Mott published her most important address on the topic, the "Discourse on Woman" (68–80). Delivered in Philadelphia, her speech rebutted a recent lecture by the writer and literary critic Richard Henry Dana. The annotations that accompany this version of the speech show the interaction between Mott's arguments and Dana's "Woman and Her Influence on Society" based on his manuscript in the Massachusetts Historical Society. She rejected Dana's sentimental praise of women and endorsed "a more extended recognition of her rights, her important duties and responsibilities in life." Mott had an exceptional memory, and this lecture, like her other speeches and sermons, is filled with biblical and literary quotations (Mott was especially fond of British poet William Cowper). The discourse is unique because it contains long, almost verbatim passages from unusual (for Mott) sources, including Catharine Beecher's *Suggestions Respecting Improvements in Education* and Nathaniel Parker Willis's *Inklings of Adventure*. The discourse is also distinctive because it was "revised by the author" before publication. The editors have identified only a few instances in which Mott reviewed her lectures before publication, including her "Sermon to the Medical Students" (48–55) and her sermon at the Cherry Street Meeting on March 31, 1850 (81–87). The long, exact quotations in "Discourse on Woman" may have been inserted before printing. It is possible that for this occasion, however, she brought notes containing the relevant quotes.

Lucretia Mott's distinctive presence and speaking style often appealed to diverse audiences, including slaveholders in Maysville, Kentucky (unfortunately, no report of this speech exists),[27] and southern congressmen in Washington, D.C. (see Unitarian Church, January 15, 1843, 16–26). She was very petite, less than 5 feet tall and weighing under 100 pounds, and she wore a simple Quaker gown, shawl, and bonnet. Mott's voice was sweet and pleasant.[28] By the time she delivered "Discourse on Woman," she was a fifty-six-year-old grandmother. Her radical words offered a compelling contrast to her femininity, her outward appearance of piety, and her status as a minister. Late in her career, even the *New York Herald*, a newspaper opposed to abolition and feminism, commented on her "perfect womanliness" (200).

But not everyone was a fan, and at times Mott could be critical herself. In 1855 the *New York Times* described the beginning of her address at the Rose Street Meeting as "impassive and monotonous," and her style as "not so much sympathy-inspiring by loveliness of expression and tenderness of emotion as respect-commanding by rigid inflexibility of conviction, and all-absorbing intensity of thought." The reporter concluded one was more likely to enjoy Mott's speeches if one agreed with her.[29] In 1859, at the annual national women's rights convention in New York City, Mott's short address (not included in this volume) was interrupted by calls for "Phillips," "Lucy Stone," and "Garrison." As she wrote her sister Martha, "To be stuck up, to speak ½ an hour, with nothg. special to inspire you at the time, is an inflictn. and bore on the Audience."[30] As sectional hostilities increased, some northerners blamed Mott and her allies for the tensions. For example, the *Philadelphia Sunday Dispatch* described a Quaker "attack" on southern medical students trying to leave the city. Mott was their "Amazonian leader" who felled students with "a carboy of vitriol" and "a well-armed blow from a bundle of anti-slavery tracts."[31]

The coming of the Civil War presented a dilemma for this pacifist abolitionist, as it did for others. Many abolitionists admired the assault on slavery launched at Harper's Ferry, Virginia, but Lucretia Mott urged them to praise "John Brown the moral hero" not "John Brown the soldier." She reminded abolitionists that their most effective "weapons" were "faith and hope and love" (141). Orthodox, Hicksite, and Progressive Quakers all debated how they should react to a war against the slave South. Some Quaker men volunteered for military service, including Mott's son-in-law Edward M. Davis, while others refused to take up arms. Female Friends had more choices as the war progressed, providing bandages, clothing, and other goods for needy soldiers or for slaves escaping behind Union lines.

Slaves increasingly emancipated themselves. When the war commenced, many seized the opportunity to flee to Union lines, forcing the military and the government to recognize their freedom. On January 1, 1863, Mott and other abolitionists rejoiced at President Abraham Lincoln's Emancipation Proclamation freeing slaves in rebellious states. To ensure that the proclamation had the effect of ending slavery permanently, Elizabeth Cady Stanton and Susan B. Anthony organized the Women's Loyal National League in May 1863. They launched a massive petition campaign urging Congress to act on behalf of emancipation and called on the Philadelphia Female Anti-Slavery Society and similar groups to gather signatures. The Philadelphia women returned one hundred copies of the petition. They also worked to improve the treatment of black soldiers—those training near Philadelphia and those fighting in the South. And both abolitionist and Quaker women dedicated themselves to helping former slaves in Union-occupied areas, sending teachers and aid workers as well as clothing, books, and medical supplies to the South Carolina Sea Islands, Virginia, and elsewhere (161).[32]

Despite abolitionist hopes that a victory would eradicate slavery, Mott remained a critic of the war and of Lincoln. At a speech to the American Anti-Slavery Society in 1864, Mott stated that "war, being of evil, must produce evil, and that continually"; and she told abolitionists it was their duty "to present the errors and short-comings of the Administration." At the same time, she celebrated the "moral warfare" of the AASS, which had the potential to transform "the great heart of the people" (148–49; see also 178). But she was disappointed in 1865 when, following the passage of the Thirteenth Amendment abolishing slavery, William Lloyd Garrison retired from the Society he had founded. The Pennsylvania Anti-Slavery Society had closed its business office a year earlier, its male leaders absorbed with that fall's presidential election and focused on political issues and tactics. Other abolitionists, however, including Wendell Phillips, Mott, Douglass, and other radical Quaker and black activists, vowed to continue fighting for the equal political and civil rights that would give meaning to emancipation (see Mott's speech to the Pennsylvania Anti-Slavery Society, 160–62).[33]

The Civil War prompted feminists as well as abolitionists to rethink their strategies. From 1848 to 1860 women's rights activists met at regular conventions, but they formed no official organization beyond these national meetings (96). After suspending their conventions for the duration of the war, and mobilizing on behalf of the Thirteenth Amendment, they formed the American Equal Rights Association (AERA) to advocate for universal suffrage, or voting rights for all men and women. In 1867 the seventy-four-year-old Mott told the AERA that "her age and feeble health" prevented her from becoming too involved, but the organization appointed her president anyway (163). The following year, however, she resigned from the organization, dismayed that members increasingly placed voting rights for women and African Americans in competition.[34] Some of her old allies, including Elizabeth Cady Stanton and Susan B. Anthony, believed the organization should oppose the Fifteenth Amendment because it did not enfranchise women. In 1869 Mott skipped the last, angry meeting of the AERA. She no doubt cringed when she heard that Elizabeth Stanton had invoked her name to question the political rights of "Patrick and Sambo and Hans and Yung Tung, who do not know the difference between a monarchy and a republic, who cannot read the Declaration of Independence or Webster's Spelling book."[35] Still, she did not break her ties completely with Stanton or women's rights. Although their racism had caused Mott to resign, she attended a meeting held the day after the AERA's final convention, at which activists discussed forming a new organization devoted to women's voting rights. In contrast to her usual optimism, Mott's discouragement was evident. As she told her old friends and colleagues, "I desire much that this cause may be advocated on the true ground. We must understand the great needs of the human race; we must have such clear insight as to be prepared to speak more from the inspiration of the time" (190). The following day, she did not attend a smaller, more exclusive meeting, at which Stanton and Anthony formed the National Woman Suffrage Association.

The factionalism of the postwar women's rights movement, so similar to earlier schisms in the Society of Friends and American Anti-Slavery Society, alienated Mott. Other advocates of universal suffrage also found themselves caught between abolitionists who used the advocacy of black male suffrage to denigrate women's political demands and advocates of women's suffrage who demeaned people of color. These reformers were also caught between the National Woman Suffrage Association and its rival organization, the American Woman Suffrage

Association, founded soon after by Lucy Stone and her husband Henry Blackwell. Many antebellum activists, including Mott, Amy Post, and Sojourner Truth, had long admired Stone's passionate pleas for abolition and women's rights but also recognized the importance of Stanton and Anthony's insistence that women be included in the postwar struggle for full citizenship. All three women maintained ties with both suffrage organizations.[36] While Mott continued to attend suffrage meetings, including the thirtieth anniversary of the Seneca Falls Convention in 1878 (214–15), she focused her attention on other causes.

Most immediately, Lucretia Mott responded to the violence of the Civil War by advocating for peace. In 1866, with fellow Quaker Alfred Love, she founded the Pennsylvania Peace Society, a branch of the Universal Peace Union. Other longtime Quaker and Unitarian activists, such as Julia Ward Howe, joined in this work as well. In her speeches, Mott criticized the culture of war that had emerged in the United States. The American government, in her view, "was based upon war" and had made the "paraphernalia of war" appealing. Ongoing wars with American Indians served as one example. Capital punishment, she believed, was another element of this violence, fueled by the spirit of revenge rather than the "spirit of forgiveness." She opposed corporal punishment and lamented that some public schools offered instruction in military training. Mott believed that pacifists owed it to "our children, to our State and to the world" to denounce the centrality of violence in American society (178 and 191). In place of war, she favored international arbitration, citing the 1871 Treaty of Washington, which had resolved U.S. grievances regarding Britain's material support of the Confederacy, as a successful example (200).

Mott's involvement in the non-sectarian free religious movement served as a culmination of her longstanding commitment to individual rather than institutional spiritual authority. In 1867 she attended the founding meeting of the Free Religious Association, an organization that welcomed Unitarians, Quakers, Jews, and Spiritualists as well as religious liberals of any faith. The organization also attracted former abolitionists and Progressive Friends, including Oliver Johnson, past editor of the *Pennsylvania Freeman*. The Free Religious Association devoted itself to "pure religion," "the scientific study of theology," and "fellowship in the spirit."[37] Mott had long been skeptical of theology, which she distinguished from religion, so she hoped the organization would advocate "so enlarged an idea of religion, and of the proper cultivation of the religious nature and element in man, as to be able to bear all things" (169). The organization must have lived up to these expectations because Mott returned to Boston to participate in its annual meetings. In 1875 she attended her last Free Religious Association convention at age 82.

Throughout Mott's life, the Society of Friends was a constant. She viewed the Quaker inward light as an organizing principle as well as a fundamental insight into the religious nature of humankind. Mott also defined the inner light as inclusive. As she told the Free Religious Association, "Let it be called the Great Spirit of the Indian . . . the 'Blessed Mary, mother of Jesus,' of the Catholics, or Brahma, the Hindoo's God—they will all be one" (204). Her openness to other people and ideas made Mott "a kind of outlaw in my own society" (169). Despite her conflicts with other Quakers, and unlike some of her co-workers in the antislavery movement, Mott had avoided disownment. She remained a member because, as she wrote, "I know of no religious association I would prefer."[38] True, or pure, religion, in Mott's view, was not about denominations or doctrines, but about "every day practice" and "good works" (169).

The fundamental link between individual conscience, human equality, and direct action defined Mott's career. She formed close bonds with Quakers and other allies who embraced the same vision of change. They, in turn, influenced her views and priorities. Although these activists were raised in the Society of Friends, many—including her sister Martha Coffin Wright, who had married outside the faith, as well as Isaac Hopper and the Posts—were disowned or embraced Progressive Quakerism, Spiritualism, or Unitarianism. Other allies came from the ranks of free blacks and fugitive slaves. Robert and Harriet Purvis, Frederick Douglass, and the Reverend Henry Highland Garnet shared little of Mott's background but brought similar commitments to practical Christianity, personal morality, and democratic ideals to their activism. Unitarians, like William Ellery Channing, also shaped Mott's understanding of faith and shared her dedication to abolition. Her network of friends and co-workers extended to Ireland and Great Britain as well, and she exchanged lengthy letters with reformers such as phrenologist George Combe.[39]

Lucretia Mott Speaks illuminates these multiple, overlapping religious and political commitments. Mott's speeches extended the Quaker inward light, and its radical possibilities for equality and freedom, to all humanity. Remembered for her advocacy of equal rights for women and African Americans, as well as for peace, Mott's radical voice also promoted religious tolerance, prison reform, economic equality, temperance, and respectful treatment of American Indians. For nineteenth-century audiences, filled with allies as well as critics, Mott offered an optimistic assessment of the potential for social change. Even as her speeches criticized the current social and political order, she also portrayed the end of slavery, racism, religious bigotry, sexual inequality, and war as possible and even immanent. Reformers, Mott urged, just had to keep agitating.

Notes

See page xxxi for a list of short citations used in the notes.

1. For Mott as the "moving spirit," see Palmer, 236; Gordon, 1:76. For Mott's activities in 1848, see Faulkner, chapter 8; *Pennsylvania Freeman*, April 13, June 8, September 14, November 2, 9, 16, and December 7, 1848. For a chronology of Mott's life, see Palmer, xxxix–xliv.

2. Dana Greene, ed., *Lucretia Mott: Her Complete Speeches and Sermons* (New York: Edwin Mellen, 1980). The dates and locations of these full text speeches, along with brief references to Mott's appearances, are on the Friends Historical Society website, http://www.swarthmore.edu/library/friends/Mott/timeline/ .

3. Palmer, 167.

4. Palmer includes a useful guide to Quaker terms (liii–liv).

5. For Quaker struggles over the issue of slavery, see Thomas E. Drake, *Quakers and Slavery in America* (New Haven, Conn.: Yale University Press, 1950); and Brycchan Carey and Geoffrey Plank, eds., *Quakers and Abolition* (Urbana: University of Illinois Press, 2014).

6. *The Old Discipline: Nineteenth-Century Friends' Disciplines in America* (Glenside, Pa.: Quaker Heritage Press, 1999), 192.

7. Notes on the Life of Lucretia Mott, as given in an interview to Sarah J. Hale, Box 6, Mott Manuscripts, Friends Historical Library, quoted in Faulkner, 34.

8. See also Mott's "Discourse on Woman," especially 74–77, as well as 114–15 and 163–65.

9. On the Hicksite schism, see Faulkner, chapter 3; Bruce Dorsey, "Friends Becoming Enemies: Philadelphia Benevolence and the Neglected Era of American Quaker History," *Journal of the Early Republic*, vol. 18, no. 3 (Fall 1998), 395–428; H. Larry Ingle, *Quakers in Conflict: The Hicksite Reformation* (Wallingford, Pa.: Pendle Hill, 1986, 1998).

10. Carol Faulkner, "The Root of the Evil: Free Produce and Radical Antislavery, 1820–1860," *Journal of the Early Republic*, vol. 27 (Fall 2007), 377–405.

11. See also Faulkner, 57.

12. Kyle G. Volk, *Moral Minorities and the Making of American Democracy* (New York: Oxford University Press, 2014), 2.

13. Christopher Densmore, "Aim for a Free State and Settle Among Quakers: African American and Quaker Parallel Communities in Pennsylvania and New Jersey," in Brycchan Carey and Geoffrey Plank, eds., *Quakers and Abolition* (Urbana: University of Illinois Press, 2014), 120–34.

14. In her remarks at the 30th Anniversary of the American Anti-Slavery Society, Mott remembered being invited by Thomas Whitson (144). See also Faulkner, 64–65.

15. "Declaration of the Anti-Slavery Convention," *Liberator*, January 4, 1834.

16. Beth A. Salerno, *Sister Societies: Women's Anti-Slavery Organizations in Antebellum America* (DeKalb: Northern Illinois University Press, 2005).

17. Faulkner, 85–86; Palmer, 75–76.

18. See Faulkner, chapter 6; Kathryn Kish Sklar, "'Women Who Speak for An Entire Nation': American and British Women at the World Anti-Slavery Convention, London, 1840," in Jean Fagan Yellin and John C. Van Horne, eds., *The Abolitionist Sisterhood: Women's Political Culture in Antebellum America* (Ithaca, N.Y.: Cornell University Press, 1994), 301–33; Kathryn Kish Sklar, *Women's Rights Emerges within the Antislavery Movement, 1830–1870* (Boston: Bedford/St. Martin's, 2000).

19. Faulkner, 120–26.

20. Quoted in Faulkner, 132–33. See also Nancy A. Hewitt, *Women's Activism and Social Change: Rochester, New York, 1822–1872* (Ithaca, N.Y.: Cornell University Press, 1984), 135; Judith Wellman, *The Road to Seneca Falls: Elizabeth Cady Stanton and the First Woman's Rights Convention* (Urbana: University of Illinois Press, 2004), 178–81.

21. *Proceedings of the Yearly Meeting of Congregational Friends, Held at Waterloo, New York, 1849* (Auburn, N.Y.: Oliphant's Press, 1849), 6.

22. Wellman, *The Road to Seneca Falls*, 215.

23. For Mott's description of these travels, see Palmer, 165–67; Nancy Hewitt, "'Seeking a Larger Liberty': Remapping First Wave Feminism," in Kathryn Kish Sklar and James Brewer Stewart, eds., *Women's Rights and Transatlantic Antislavery in the Era of Emancipation* (New Haven, Conn.: Yale University Press, 2007), 266–78.

24. Gordon, 1:75–83; Faulkner, 138–42; Wellman, *The Road to Seneca* Falls, chapter 8.

25. Hewitt, *Women's Activism and Social Change*, 131–35; Nancy Hewitt, "Feminist Friends: Agrarian Quakers and the Emergence of Woman's Rights in America," *Feminist Studies*, vol. 12, no. 1 (Spring 1986), 33.

26. Hewitt, "'Seeking a Larger Liberty,'" 273.

27. For reaction to her speech in Maysville, see Palmer, 229.

28. For a description of her speaking voice as "clear, sweet, and musical," see the *New York Tribune*'s coverage of the New England Anti-Slavery Convention, reprinted in the *Pennsylvania Freeman*, June 3, 1847.

29. "Lucretia Mott in New-York," *New York Times*, November 12, 1855.

30. Faulkner, 159; Palmer, 288, 289n3; *Proceedings of the National Woman's Rights Convention, Held in New York City, Thursday, May 12, 1859, With a Phonographic Report of the Speech of Wendell Phillips, by J. M. W. Yerrinton* (Rochester, N.Y.: Steam Press of A. Strong and Co., 1859), 4–5, available as a full text source in Kathryn Kish Sklar and Thomas Dublin, eds., *Women and Social Movements in the United States, 1600–2000*, http://asp6new.alexanderstreet.com.libezproxy2.syr.edu/was2/was2.object.details.aspx?dorpid=1000636136, accessed through Syracuse University Libraries on June 9, 2015.

31. This account from the *Philadelphia Sunday Dispatch* is described in Palmer, 293–94.

32. Faulkner, 180–82.

33. For these political and strategic debates among abolitionists, see W. Caleb McDaniel, *The Problem of Democracy in the Age of Slavery: Garrisonian Abolitionists and Transatlantic Reform* (Baton Rouge: Louisiana State University Press, 2013).

34. Palmer, 407.

35. Faulkner, 195. For the women's movement in this period, see especially Faye Dudden, *Fighting Chance: The Struggle over Woman Suffrage and Black Suffrage in Reconstruction America* (New York: Oxford University Press, 2011).

36. Palmer, 437–38; Faulkner, 204–7. On women's rights advocates who refused to choose sides, see Nell Painter, *Sojourner Truth, A Life, A Symbol* (New York: W. W. Norton, 1996), chapter 15.

37. *Free Religion: Report of Addresses at a Meeting Held in Boston, May 30, 1867* (Boston: Adams and Co., 1867), 54.

38. Palmer, 106.

39. Many of LM's letters to Combe and other allies are included in Palmer.

Editorial Policies

Selection

In her long speaking career, Lucretia Mott traveled to ten states, Washington, D.C., as well as Canada, England, Ireland, and Scotland. Many of the speeches and sermons she delivered were collected in Greene's *Lucretia Mott: Her Complete Speeches and Sermons* (1980). Some of these have appeared in anthologies such as Michael Warner, ed., *American Sermons: The Pilgrims to Martin Luther King, Jr.* (New York: Library of America, 1999). A few are available online, including in the *Women and Social Movements* database. Palmer's *Selected Letters of Lucretia Coffin Mott* (2002) and Faulkner's *Lucretia Mott's Heresy* (2011) summarize and occasionally quote speeches not included in the Greene edition. A search of contemporary newspapers, such as the *Anti-Slavery Bugle*, the *Liberator*, and the *Pennsylvania Freeman*, have yielded even more texts, summaries, and mentions of Mott's speaking engagements. In addition, the Mott manuscript collection at the Friends Historical Library includes shorthand recordings of many of Mott's sermons. These, recently acquired by the Friends Historical Library, have been converted into conventional English by LaJean Pursell Carruth.

Building on Greene's selections, our edition includes new and definitive examples of Mott's speeches. For those addresses that appeared in Greene's volume, we add annotations as well as debates and procedural comments, for example, the 1852 Syracuse Women's Rights Convention, over which Mott presided. Further, we remove all titles added by Greene. Except in the rare instances when Mott's speeches had titles (for example, "Discourse on Woman") we identify the speech by event, venue, location, and date whenever possible. Since the full titles of the event are often found in the annotations, we use shorter versions with contemporary language, such as "Women's Rights Convention" for "Eleventh National Woman's Rights Convention." After reviewing all the known speeches drawn from contemporary newspapers, journals, the archives at Friends Historical Library, Swarthmore College, and Special Collections, Haverford College, as well as other printed sources, we have selected sixty speeches and sermons for this edition.

We excluded addresses with repetitious topics and themes. With the support of Friends Historical Library, Swarthmore College, and the assistance of Patricia C. O'Donnell, we provide a timeline of all of Mott's known utterances, at http://www.swarthmore.edu/library/friends/Mott/timeline/.

No handwritten copies of Mott's speeches have been discovered. As a Quaker, Lucretia Mott did not speak from a prepared text, but was guided by the inner light. As she wrote her sister Martha, "I have great faith in the Quaker creed, 'to speak, as the Spirit giveth utterance' . . . Fixed speeches on such occasions are not to be compared to spontaneous discussion" (to Martha Coffin Wright, May 31, 1859, in Palmer, 288). However, Mott approved several of the printed texts, such as her "Discourse on Woman." We have used these approved texts when available, along with other printed or transcribed versions.

Transcription

All speeches have been carefully proofread and checked against the original sources, which are cited at the end of each document. Nineteenth-century spelling and punctuation standards have been retained, for example, "intreat" for "entreat." Material from printed sources is transcribed as it appears in those sources, often resulting in inconsistencies from speech to speech and within speeches. Thus, capitalization ("Church," "Scripture," even lowercase "christian") will vary as will names (sometimes indicated as "MOTT," sometimes "Lucretia Mott") and terms (for example, "woman" and "women"). Additions to the printed texts, such as audience reaction, interruptions, and asterisks, are preserved. Obvious typographical errors ("batchelor" for "bachelor") are silently corrected. Other typographical errors such as "petition" instead of the correct "partition" are transcribed as "[*partition*]." Words added for clarification, for example [*as*] or [*Morning Session*], are noted in the same way. Punctuation, especially commas, semicolons, quotation marks, and question marks, is silently included or corrected at times for clarification. Asterisks (* * * *) indicate intervals between Mott's remarks, most often occurring at the women's rights conventions.

Four of Mott's sermons included in our edition have been transcribed from the original nineteenth-century phonographic reports, at the FHL at Swarthmore. In these instances some punctuation is added, "and" is substituted for the handwritten "&," and capitalization within each document is regularized, for example, "Bible" for "bible."

Annotation

1. Persons, events, and quotations, from figures such as William Cowper and Isaac Watt, are identified briefly, using contemporary sources and other documentary editions when possible. No citations are supplied for major reference works such as *American National Biography*, *Notable American Women*, and electronic re-

sources that are readily available. We do not add a note when people, events, or allusions cannot be identified. Persons mentioned only in the notes are not fully identified.
2. Mott's sermons and speeches contain frequent quotations, paraphrases, and allusions to biblical verses. To reduce the number of annotations, we have not noted these biblical references. Readers can easily locate these online or in the many reference guides.
3. Persons, events, and non-biblical quotations are fully identified. When a person's name occurs after she or he has been identified, the first names will appear, italicized and in brackets, for example [*William Ellery*] Channing.

Short Citations

Bacon:	Margaret Hope Bacon, *Valiant Friend: The Life of Lucretia Mott*, 2nd ed. (Philadelphia: Friends General Conference, 1999)
Faulkner:	Carol Faulkner, *Lucretia Mott's Heresy: Abolition and Women's Rights in Nineteenth Century America* (Philadelphia: University of Pennsylvania Press, 2011)
Gordon:	Ann Gordon, ed., vol. 1, *The Selected Papers of Elizabeth Cady Stanton and Susan B. Anthony: In the School of Anti-Slavery*; vol. 2, *Against an Aristocracy of Sex*; vol. 6, *An Awful Hush* (New Brunswick, N.J.: Rutgers University Press, 1997, 2000, 2013)
Hallowell:	Anna Davis Hallowell, ed., *James and Lucretia Mott: Their Life and Letters* (Boston: Houghton Mifflin, 1884)
Palmer:	Beverly Wilson Palmer, ed., *Selected Letters of Lucretia Coffin Mott* (Urbana: University of Illinois Press), 2002
WASM:	*Women and Social Movements in the United States 1600–2000*, ed. Kathryn Kish Sklar and Thomas Dublin, Alexander Street Press, accessed via Syracuse University Libraries and the Claremont Colleges Library, http://asp6new.alexanderstreet.com.libezproxy2.syr.edu/was2/was2.help.aspx?dorpID=1001007951 and http://libraries.claremont.edu/research/databases/dbredirect/wasm.asp
WLG *Letters*:	Louis Ruchames and Walter Merrill, eds., *Letters of William Lloyd Garrison*, 5 vols. (Cambridge, Mass.: Harvard University Press, 1971–81)

Abbreviations

ADS	Autograph Document Signed
AASS	American Anti-Slavery Society
FHL	Friends Historical Library, Swarthmore College
LM	Lucretia Mott
JM	James Mott

PD   Printed Document
PASS   Pennsylvania Anti-Slavery Society
PFASS Philadelphia Female Anti-Slavery Society
WLG   William Lloyd Garrison
WR   Women's Rights

Lucretia Mott Speaks:
The Essential Speeches and Sermons

Figure 3. Lucretia Mott, ca. 1842. (Courtesy of the Friends Historical Library, Swarthmore College)

Twelfth Street Meeting, Philadelphia, 1818

"As all our efforts to resist temptation, and overcome the world prove fruitless unless aided by Thy Holy Spirit, enable us to approach Thy Throne, and ask of Thee the blessing of Thy preservation from *all* evil, that we may be wholly devoted to Thee and Thy glorious cause."

Lucretia Mott.
1879.
5/10[1]

ADS Mott Manuscripts, FHL

1. Although the date on the document indicates "5/10," a note accompanying it states that the holograph copy was presented to LM on May 12, 1879, "with the information that they were the first words she had expressed in public" (Mott Manuscripts, FHL; Hallowell, 62; Faulkner, 41).

Pennsylvania Hall, Philadelphia, May 16 and 17, 1838

[*May 16, Evening Session*]

A FEW remarks were then made by LUCRETIA MOTT, of Philadelphia, stating that the present was not a meeting of the Anti-Slavery Convention of American Women, as was supposed by some, and explaining the reason why their meetings were confined to females—to wit, that many of the members of that Convention considered it improper for women to address promiscuous assemblies.[1] She expressed the "hope that such false notions of delicacy and propriety would not long obtain in this enlightened country."

* * * *

[*May 17, Morning Session*]
Lucretia Mott made some impressive remarks respecting the riot of the preceding evening, and exhorted the members of the Convention to be steadfast and solemn in the prosecution of the business for which they were assembled.[2]

PD *History of Pennsylvania Hall, that was Destroyed by a Mob, on the 17th of May, 1838* (Philadelphia: Merrihew and Gunn, 1838), 127, 130

1. The opening celebrations for the hall, which had been built by abolitionists, began on May 14 and featured a variety of antislavery speakers and organizations. For background on the construction of and controversy surrounding Pennsylvania Hall, see Faulkner, 75–78. LM addressed the concern of some female abolitionists about the presence of both men and women in the audience (*History of Pennsylvania Hall*, 6, 117, 127).
2. The second Anti-Slavery Convention of American Women, a national gathering that first met in New York City the previous year, had opened on May 15, with LM serving as vice-president. Protests outside Pennsylvania Hall continued, and after convention delegates left on May 17, a mob set it on fire. For LM's reaction, see Palmer, 42–43, 46–47; Faulkner, 78–79; also, *Pennsylvania Freeman*, May 24, 1838; *Liberator*, May 25, 1838.

New England Non-Resistance Society, Chardon Street Chapel, Boston, September 25–27, 1839

[*September 25 Session*]
Lucretia Mott of Philadelphia, thought the resolution[1] referred not to opinions, but to the right of opinion. The right we cannot deny, and ought to respect, though the opinion may be such as we disapprove.

* * * *

Lucretia Mott hoped this resolution would be well and thoroughly considered before its passage, as it seemed to her to strike at the root of the religious opinions entertained by some of us. Once let it be laid down that an *opinion* is necessary to salvation, and toleration becomes inconsistent. But I dislike the word toleration. It does not convey the right idea. Is it not yielded in the most orthodox sects, that the members may adopt various opinions as to the mode of being, in a future state of existence? So it might be with regard to other differences of opinion; and it is a most important thing that it should be so in our present association. This resolution, if heartily adopted, will bring good out of all our discussions. It will, like the philosopher's stone, transmute base metal into gold.

* * * *

Lucretia Mott said, I think my brother[2] again confuses opinion with the right of opinion. The ninety-nine hundredths can adopt such resolutions as they choose, in this spirit of love and freedom. But it forbids them to require of the one in the minority to adopt them, under penalty of disgrace.

* * * *

Lucretia Mott. This resolution[3] opens a broad field for discussion; and while it would be well that nothing should be done to foreclose it, I would offer a caution to my brethren in the ministry, not to take advantage of the fluency of speech, or, it may be, the powers of oratory which the exercise of their profession gives them, to occupy so much time that those who have less facility in speaking, may not have opportunity to bring forward their views. On the levelling principle which has brought us together, I would suggest that those who are greatest among us should serve—thus giving opportunity to the least.

[*September 26 Session*]

Lucretia Mott. Let us be slow in the adoption of theories, for we are religiously bound to follow in action the theories that we adopt.[4] Let us examine, let us discuss—let us aid one another in comprehending every dictate of the law of peace and love, and then let us fervently pray for strength to act in accordance with our convictions. My conviction is that penalty is ineffectual, and that there is a readier and better way of securing a willing obedience than by resorting to it. Some little incident in our own family will often illustrate truth to us, in a way that nothing else could do. One of our little girls when told to go to bed, felt disinclined to obey, and some time after, she was discovered hid under the table, thinking it a good piece of fun. No notice was taken of it, and she took her own time. We had forgotten the affair, when she came running down the stairs with her little bare feet, saying, 'do mother forgive me!' It was abundantly more efficacious, than the theory of penalty carried into practice could have been. I could wish this resolution to pass if we are prepared for it.

* * * *

Lucretia Mott. The extreme cases which may be brought to demand corporeal punishment, are like the extreme cases brought to nullify so many other arguments. The reason why such extreme cases occur is, I believe, because parents are not prepared. They overlook the fact that a child, like all human beings, has inalienable rights. It is the master that is not prepared for emancipation, and it is the parent that is not prepared to give up punishment.

[*September 27 Session*]

Lucretia Mott. As this resolution[5] does not pertain to that particular branch of righteousness under the consideration of this society, I think it would be well if there could be a convention of persons engaged in trade, before whom it might come appropriately—a mercantile convention, for the examination of the principles on which the business of the world is conducted, that they may be made to conform to the principles of right and justice.[6]

PD *The Non-Resistant*, Boston, November 2, 1839; November 16, 1839; *Liberator*, October 11, 1839

1. Offered by Samuel J. May (1797–1871), Unitarian clergyman and a vice-president of the Society, the resolution read, "the only basis upon which a reformatory Society can stand and effect its work in the hearts of men, is a sacred respect for the right of opinion." Edwin Burnham, delegate from Boston, asked whether the Society needed to respect pro-war views (*Liberator*, October 11, 1839).

2. Stephen S. Foster (1809–81), antislavery lecturer from New Hampshire, worried about resolutions that might conflict with one's beliefs. As an example he cited a report

that almost all members of the Massachusetts Anti-Slavery Society did not believe in non-resistance, and thus, in the case of the resolution now under consideration, could not "pass a resolution expressing what they did think" (*Liberator*, October 11, 1839).

3. The resolution stated that "all human penal codes . . . [*that*] necessarily involve an armed and bloody resistance to evil . . . are a nullification of the precepts and example of Christ, and cannot innocently be sustained by any of his disciples" (*The Non-Resistant*, November 2, 1839).

4. The resolution stated that the principles the Society was "applying to civil government" should also pertain to its individual members and families (*The Non-Resistant*, November 16, 1839).

5. This resolution stated that members "with delight forego the pleasures and luxuries of life, to alleviate human suffering in any form" (*The Non-Resistant*, November 16, 1839).

6. All resolutions were adopted (*Liberator*, November 1, 1839). See also Palmer, 67, 69; Faulkner, 82–83.

Unitarian Chapel, August 9, 1840, Glasgow, Scotland

On Sunday evening, August 9, the chapel was crowded to hear her.[1] Mr. [*James*] Mott first addressed the meeting, stating who they were, their object in visiting this country, their difference in religious views from the Society of Friends in Britain; and reading, in corroboration of his statements, certificates from the Monthly Meeting of Friends in Philadelphia, and of Abolition Societies.[2] Mrs. Mott then spoke, and for nearly two hours held a delighted audience in breathless attention. She began by saying, that she was glad of the opportunity which the generous offer of that pulpit had given her of addressing them; that she had been denied a hearing elsewhere because she was a woman,[3] and by her own body in this country, because she differed from them in her views of religion; that the body of Friends with whom they were connected, were looked upon with the same dislike by the other party, as the Unitarians were by those calling themselves Orthodox; she regretted this bigotry, as she wished the enlarged, and beautiful, and exalted views which she and the Unitarian brethren entertained, could be embraced and felt by all; and she was happy in believing that such views were spreading and would continue to spread, till all mankind, from their holy influence, would become like one large family, living in love and harmony together as the children of one common Father. Mrs. Mott called on the Unitarians to exert themselves to the utmost to bring about this happy state of things; to let no fear of man, or any worldly motive, deter them from openly avowing their convictions, and acting up to them; that there were too many mammon-worshippers in the world, and she feared a great lack of moral courage also. She said, her address might perhaps be thought desultory, but as it was the only opportunity she should have of speaking to them, she felt it necessary to direct their attention to many topics worthy of thoughtful contemplation. She defended, on Scriptural grounds, the right of woman to speak in public; spoke of the imperfect education which women too commonly received, which consequently debarred them from occupying their proper places in society; called upon her sisters to look to this, and embrace every opportunity of gaining knowledge on every subject; not to be content with a little reading, a little writing, and a little sewing; to brush away the silken fetters which had so long bound them—no longer to be content with being the mere toy or plaything of man's leisure hours, but to fit themselves for assuming their proper position, in being the rational companions, the friends, the instructors of their race. Better views, she rejoiced to know, were beginning to be entertained on this and kindred subjects. War, too, was looked on in a different light from what it was once wont to be; and highly gratified had she been at being present and listening to a powerful address on Capital Punishments, by the pastor of the congregation, when in Birmingham. Slavery also was calling forth those efforts for its extermination, which it behooved humanity and Christian principle to make; and deliverance to the captives of every clime would be the result. Having depicted in glowing colors the evils and abominations of slavery as it existed in America, and roused the best and holiest feelings of her audience to sympathy with the wrongs of the oppressed, and in resolutions for their extinction, Mrs. Mott burst forth into a beautiful and fervent prayer, and concluded.[4]

PD *London Christian Pioneer*, reprinted in *Liberator*, July 30, 1841

1. The Motts had traveled to Great Britain to attend the World's Anti-Slavery Convention in London, held June 12–23. Called by the British and Foreign Anti-Slavery Society, the convention promoted "the universal Abolition of Slavery and the Slave Trade." Since their arrival, the Motts and their fellow Hicksite Quakers had encountered considerable hostility from British Friends (Faulkner, 91; for details on the 1827 Hicksite/Orthodox split, see Faulkner, 44–52, 58). British Quakers and Calvinists regarded Hicksites as bearing "a taint of heresy" and an invitation for Mott to address the Glasgow Emancipation Society on August 1, 1840, was rescinded. George Harris (1794–1859), pastor of the Glasgow Unitarian Chapel, whom the Motts had met earlier, then invited LM to address his church at her convenience (Hallowell, 170–71; Faulkner, 94–95, 103–4; James Mott, *Three Months in Great Britain* [Philadelphia, 1841], 64–69; *Liberator*, September 25, 1840).

2. On April 22 Philadelphia Monthly Meeting (Hicksite) issued a letter affirming that JM and LM, respectively, as elder and minister were in "full unity with this Monthly Meeting" (Philadelphia Monthly Meeting [Hicksite] Minutes, April 22, 1840, FHL); the Association of Friends for promoting the Abolition of Slavery also recommended the Motts to the "kind regards and Christian sympathies of British Philanthropists" (May 1, 1840, Mott Manuscripts, FHL). The AASS, the PFASS, and the American Free Produce Association also sponsored LM (Faulkner, 92).

3. On June 12 LM and the other seven women delegates from the United States were refused official seats at the World's Anti-Slavery Convention (see Palmer, 77–80; Faulkner, 94–97).

4. Subsequently, members of the Glasgow Society of Friends wrote a letter on August 12 to the *Glasgow Argus* stating that "we hold no religious fellowship with Lucretia Mott, nor with the body in the United States (called Hicksites), to which she belongs; they not being recognized by the Society of Friends in the United Kingdom." Thus the Society disclaimed "any sentiments that Lucretia Mott may have uttered at the meeting." This statement prompted a lengthy reply from JM from Liverpool, August 24, stating that at the August 9 gathering he had carefully laid out the differences between Hicksite and

Orthodox Quakers in the United States (letters reprinted in *Liberator*, October 9, 1840; see also Hallowell, 175–79; Faulkner, 103–4).

Marlboro Chapel, Boston, September 23, 1841

It is highly satisfactory to me, my friends, to meet you. I rejoice to see so many fellow-beings without the usual distinctions which prevail in professing Christendom.[1] I believe that when they are so brought together, they may hear, every man in his own tongue, the truths that may be spoken; inasmuch as all truth is from 'the sempiternal source of light divine.' There is no change in its principles. They are, and they have been, and will be, from everlasting to everlasting: in their origin, divine—in their nature, eternal.

All who are believers in the truth of God, and in the righteousness of God, must come to understand, that this alone can set us free. But have we fully understood and comprehended, how it is that only the truth can make free indeed? In order to do so, educational prejudices and sectarian predilections should be laid aside; though to convince men of the necessity of doing so, might require as notable a miracle as it did to convince men in a former age, that in all nations, those who 'fear God, and work righteousness, are accepted of him.'

But what is it to fear God? and what is it to work righteousness? It is as necessary now, as when the great apostle uttered it, to say to men, 'Let no man deceive you. He that doeth righteousness, is righteous.' But what is the situation of most sects? What is their standard of righteousness? What evidence do they require of the fear of God? Is it not the acknowledgment of some scheme of salvation, or some plan of redemption, as insisted on in theological systems, and taught in theological schools? Is it not a confession of some creed, or a joining of some denomination? And have not many thus blended the fear of God and the working of righteousness with outward and ceremonial rites, till the result has been a lowering of the standard of peace and righteousness, and of common honesty?

It becomes us to inquire, whether the plain precepts and principles, which find a response in the soul of every human being, and are confirmed by the inner sense which all possess, and which have not their origin in any sect, or body, or division, have not thereby been thought of less importance than forms and ordinances. If this is so, and if all see it in our various denominations, may we not all profitably come together in the acknowledgment of principles and practices not dependent upon the reception of any abstract doctrine, or form of worship? We may all feel here in thus considering the principles and working of righteousness—the willing and the doing good—not as strangers, but as much at home as in the town in which we were born: for these principles are common to all, and are understood by all. This is not presented by me as a Quaker tenet. I desire not to stand before you as a sectarian, but to hold up principles of universal obligation.

I have seen that there is an objection, which seems reasonable to many minds, against woman's stepping forth to advocate what is right. Let me endeavor to remove these prejudices and these objections; for I have often been made sensibly to feel how hard it is to 'do the work of the Lord, where there is unbelief.'

I know that many claim high apostolic authority against this action of women. I am aware that the apostle Paul recommended to the women of Corinth, when they wanted information, to 'ask their husbands at home.' I am not disposed to deny, that under the circumstances of the case, he did it wisely. But do we find him saying, that they were not to preach or prophesy? So far from it, that he has expressly given them directions how to preach and prophesy. And what this preaching and prophesying were, is defined by the same apostle as 'speaking unto *men* to edification, and exhortation, and comfort.' Anyone will, I think, see, that to make a standing rule of the apostle's directions to the ignorant Corinthian women, is to make him inconsistent with himself, not only to those same Corinthian women, but in his declaration to the Galatians, that, to as many of them as had put on Christ, there was neither Jew nor Greek, male nor female; and also in his expressions of gratitude to the women helpers in the gospel.

Again, we find in the records of the evangelist, the fact that four daughters of one man became public advocates of the truth, and 'honorable women not a few' are also stated to have done the same thing. We read, also, of the woman of Samaria going to the men of the city; and of Huldah, the prophetess. In the history of earlier times, we read that the villages were in ruins through the land of the Hebrews, and the highways unoccupied, till 'Deborah arose—till she arose, an other in Israel.'

This evening's opportunity would be far too short to present the Bible argument, and I therefore refer you to this volume itself, as its paramount authority is so generally acknowledged among you, to see whether there is not far more plentiful testimony to the rightfulness of woman's directly laboring for the gospel, than you had supposed from perusing it without reference to this question.

Was it not one of the first acts of the apostles, to announce, in the words of the prophet Joel, that the spirit of the Lord was poured out upon *all flesh*;—and was not this quoted to convince the people, that the prophesying and preaching of both sexes was in fulfillment of ancient prophecy? In the phrase in which 'Phebe, the servant of the church,' is mentioned; those who are familiar with the original have found, that the same word, which is, in her case, translated *servant*, is, in the case of men, translated *minister*. And has not conscious evidence been afforded by this translation, of the priest-craft and monopoly of the pulpit, which have so long held women bound? I ask the sticklers for Bible authority, where they find the silence of women enjoined as a standing obligation. I find no such passage. These objectors are bound to show that these injunctions which on one side they quote in favor of the silence of woman, command an obligation, binding on the church in all ages. But we find them assuming the right to choose what they will consider such. When the apostle recommends that widows shall not marry, they do not agree with him, and therefore they explain it as applicable only to those times of trouble and persecution; and do not consider it as a standing rule.

I long for the time when my sisters will rise, and occupy the sphere to which they are called by their high nature and destiny. What a change would then appear in the character of woman! We should no longer find her the mere plaything of man, and a frivolous appendage of society. We should not find her so easily satisfied with a *little* domestic duty—with embroidering the light device on muslin and lace, or with reading the sentimental novel. When I look at the 'Ladies Department' in our newspapers and magazines, I blush for my sex, and for the low sphere of action they are content with. I believe that if woman would but look seriously at herself, she would learn how great an evil her nature suffers in being prevented from the exercise of her highest faculties. What a different race would be brought forth—what a different and nobler generation should we behold in the next, from that which preceded it, if the high duties of women were all fulfilled! I believe the tendency of truth, on this subject, is to equalize the sexes; and that, when truth directs us, there will be no longer assumed authority on one side, or admitted inferiority on the other; but that as we advance in the cultivation of all our powers, physical as well as intellectual and moral, we shall see that our independence is equal, our dependence mutual, and our obligations reciprocal.

It is this perception, my friends, that I long for. I feel bound, when in company with my sisters who have thought it improper or sinful to exercise their highest powers of mind on the most important subjects, to beseech them to think so no longer, and to come forth into that noble and becoming freedom which they, in common with man, have received:—so useful will they then be in their own day, and so happy will be their influence upon generations yet to come.

I am aware that the imaginations of many have become so depraved, and their minds so enervated, by appeals to the passions and the imagination, from the inferior literature of the novelist, that it needs not only strong effort to arouse them from the lethargy in which they live, to true and noble activity; but a tender care is needed to preserve them from the evils consequent upon their long inactivity. I am willing to incur ridicule—to become a spectacle to angels and to men—if I thereby awaken any to a sense of what the times demand of them. This is a day that requires the active cooperation of spiritually minded men and women. This is a day of overturning and of change. Many are asking, 'Who will show us any good?' Theories and abstractions will not satisfy them—outward observances will not be sufficient. The multitude who are seeking, cannot attain what they desire, but through the knowledge of themselves. I would speak to you in the spirit of the gospel of the blessed God, of that unerring guide which shall direct you. I shall use in characterizing it the language of a writer of your own: 'All mysteries of science and theology fade away before the simple impressions of duty on the mind of a little child.'[2]

I come not here to controvert the creeds or confessions of any—I am no polemic—I know very little of metaphysical theology—I love not controversy—I have no scientific theory. But I appeal to you all, if there is not this intimate knowledge of right and wrong in each of your breasts; and I appeal to the Scriptures, whether in them there is not a wide difference made between doing good, and a performance of outward rites. We find that these were never made substitutes for righteousness. They were, when performed by the oppressor and the unjust man, an abomination to God. He is in such cases 'weary to bear them'; and whatever may have been the exactness with which these things were performed, he condemned the performer, 'because,' he says, 'you grind the faces of the poor.' And again: 'Woe unto him who buildeth his house by unrighteousness, and his chambers by wrong; who taketh his neighbor's service without wages, and who giveth him not for his work.'

We have each our different theories with regard to creeds and forms; but let us not put them on a level with what is of so much greater moment. While we tolerate (if that can ever be a proper word to use in such a connection), while we acknowledge the right of opinion, as regards the various creeds and forms, let us not place these above the pure and practical fruits of righteousness.

Is not this the reason why these fruits are so few in the world? Look at the low state of public morals; look at the prevalence and the general justification of war, and slavery, and oppression; look at all the vices of society, and see how the greatest abundance of creeds, and the utmost exactitude in forms, co-exist with them all; and judge ye, whether these are not held up, rather than doing justice and loving mercy.

What a field of labor does society now present! I rejoice to see the field white to the harvest. I rejoice in a belief that the members of society are beginning to take a practical view of its wants; and have, in some instances at least, found that they cannot be satisfied with a mere outward routine, but that something more efficacious is demanded by the present age. These are gathering themselves together in the support of what is right; and let us bid them God speed. Who can look at the crimes and sufferings of men, and not labor for reformation? Let us put our own souls in their souls' stead, who are in slavery, and let us labor for their liberation as bound with them. Let us look at the souls who are led away into hopeless captivity, deprived of every right, and sundered from every happy association—the parents separated from their children, and all the relations of life outraged; and then let us obey the dictates of sympathy.

I cannot but rejoice in the efforts that they are making to arrest the progress of war. The offering of a prize for the best essay on the best mode of settling international disputes, and the thousands of persons who thronged to hear the addresses of George Harris at Birmingham on capital punishment, afford a cheering indication of an enquiring state of the public mind in England. As enquiry proceeds, men will discover the principle of forgiveness, and will feel the power of the spirit of love. They will then become more consistent with the Christianity they profess, and will find that they must no longer indulge the spirit of retaliation. In the course of our progress in the application of these principles, we shall have to put this sentiment in practice. We shall then understand the true spirit of forgiveness, and conform our lives to its requisitions. How is it that high professors of the Christian name can forget the precepts of the blessed Jesus—'Love your enemies—bless them that curse you—do good to them that hate you—pray for them that despitefully use you and persecute you.' Did not the apostle acknowledge the truth of this principle of forgiveness, when he said, 'Being defamed, we entreat—being reviled, we bless'?

The time will not permit me to enlarge, or I would turn your attention to further applications of gospel principles, and remind you, as we examined them together, that 'he that doeth righteous is righteous,' of whatever sect or clime.

I am aware that, in this city, the appeal has often been made to you in behalf of the suffering slave. I am sensible that most able appeals have been frequent here; but the time has come for you, not merely to listen to them, but to seek for the means of aiding in the working of this righteousness. Whether you should act in organized societies, or as individuals, it is not for me to decide for any; but we all have a part of the work to perform, for we are all implicated in the transgression. Let us examine our own clothing—the furniture of our houses—the conducting of trade—the affairs of commerce—and then ask ourselves, whether we have not each, as individuals, a duty which, in some way or other, we are bound to perform.

When I look only over professing Christendom, my soul mourns over the doom to perpetual and unrequited toil, the entire deprivation of rights, the outrage of human affections, and the absence of all that makes life desirable, which all unite to weigh down the lives of so many millions, while so few are ready to raise the cry of justice and mercy on their behalf. Are there not men and women here, whom these things shall yet constrain to exertion, that they may be remedied? In how many ways may you not exercise your various powers for the alleviation of the miseries of those whose sufferings we have contemplated! You have pens and voices to commend their cause to others, and to portray their miseries so as to gain sympathy. To how many towns you might go, and awaken their inhabitants to the relief of these sufferings!

We are too apt to be discouraged, and to be impressed with a sense of the difficulty of the work of reform: but when we examine into the progress it makes, and behold the effects of Temperance, and Peace, and Anti-Slavery, we may be greatly encouraged, and bid each other God speed, in full confidence that, in due time, we shall reap, if we faint not. We have sure evidence, from the success of past efforts, that the same will be the effect in future. Hard as was the labor at first, there are now far less difficulties. Many hearts are now touched, and only need the word of encouragement to come forth in aid of those who so long struggled with so many disadvantages, under a load of odium and opposition, to commence the work now so happily advancing. Let me encourage the awakening soul to enter into the work. When the question arises as to the manner of doing so, I can only say that what we sincerely desire to do, we seldom lack means to accomplish. I know there is in the community a growing dislike of organizations; but those who adopt this view must remember, that it will not do for them to do nothing. 'Herein is my Heavenly Father glorified, that ye bear much fruit.'

It is too generally understood by men, that their labors must be connected with missionary and church efforts, under submission to church-tests, and church-forms:

but it is time we made a proper distinction between those who merely cry, 'Lord, Lord,' and do not his righteous will, and those who are bent on faithful obedience. I am aware that in this day of judging by verbal and ceremonial standards, that such as have not submitted to the forms and rituals of any church are obligated to suffer on that account in the opinion of their fellow-men. But those feel that they are accountable to a higher power, and that 'it is a small matter to be judged of any man's judgment.' They look for guidance to their inner sense of right and wrong; and this is coming more and more to be acknowledged as the voice of God and his most intimate presence in the soul. Let me urge all, then, to be faithful to these manifestations of His will. It will then bring upon the reproach of high professors. But if they are faithful, they will be instant at all times in raising high the standard of righteous action, and they will, by their practice, do more to recommend the faith of God, than those who are denouncing them. Those who have regarded these good works more than plain dress, or formal speech, or observance of times, or stated reasons of vocal prayer, will be ready to proclaim that the gospel is not in these outward things, while some, who make high professions, are ignorant both of the scriptures and of the power of the gospel. Let us be faithful to the word lying in the heart, and there is no need to doubt but we shall be brought to love every good word and work, to promote the progress of righteousness, temperance, and peace and to keep ourselves unspotted from the world.

How often have I mourned, that so many in the cities depart from the plain path of integrity! How much selfishness and deception is there in trade! 'It is naught, it is naught, saith the buyer; but when he hath gone his way, then he boasteth.' How many look not on the things of Jesus Christ! But, do we not see that the principles of our holy religion would reform commerce and trade, and lead every man to do justly? Surely the cry of the oppressed is entering into the ears of the Lord of Sabaoth. Many who look at other lands, and witness the sufferings of their people, and see how the poor are crushed by oppression and taxation, to maintain the existence and the prerogatives of an aristocracy, turn with delight to the hope of a reform coextensive with the earth. They realize that true republicanism is true Christian democracy. But it is because they see not how reform is to be obtained, that they are slow of heart to believe in its possibility. Let them not participate in the wrong they acknowledge. 'If thy right hand offend thee, cut it off.' If we applied the precepts of Jesus to the direction of our own lives, how many that are now rich would become poor! I believe that the principles of righteousness can be carried out through the land, and that we show our reverence for God by the respect we pay His children. We do not sufficiently exercise our high moral nature. We resist the benevolent principles and feelings that would lead us forth into lanes and by-ways, that we might comfort and save the outcast and afflicted. We forget that this is true religion and undefiled, and to keep ourselves unspotted from the world. We may, after the manner that some call heresy, worship the God of our fathers; but if we wish to serve Him in the way prescribed by His dear Son, we shall carry out the principles of righteousness in the service of our brethren and of society; nothing doubting that if we do so, it will be well with us hereafter.

Further we need not too curiously inquire, but be content with the evidence of God's peace in our souls, after having done His will.

PD "Lucretia Mott at the Marlboro Chapel, Boston, September 23, 1841," *Liberator*, October 15, 1841

    1. Erected by the "Free Church" of Boston, the Marlboro Chapel was the frequent site of antislavery, temperance, and peace meetings (*Pennsylvania Freeman*, June 7, 1838).
    2. The quotation is adapted from "Honour Due to All Men" by William Ellery Channing (1780–1842), Unitarian minister: "All mysteries of science and theology fade away before the grandeur of the simple perception of duty, which dawns on the mind of the little child."

Rose Street Meeting, New York City, September 29, 1841

On Wednesday last, this beloved sister addressed the Friends meeting in Rose Street[1] . . . With much earnestness of feeling, she alluded to the early testimonies of Friends, and besought them to examine well whether the present proceedings of Quakers were in unison with those testimonies. She appealed to those in trade, whether they did not conform to many practices sanctioned by custom, but condemned by the inner voice. Of what avail was the repetition of their hereditary testimony against slavery, so long as they dealt without scruple in southern cotton, produced by unpaid labor? Was their testimony against war consistent and effective, so long as they took an [*active?*] interest in political parties and partisans, who were ready at any moment to become the agents and actors in a war? She warned them against a sectarian attachment to forms, to the neglect of vital principles; and strongly urged the impossibility of receiving opinions as a birthright. But above all, she pleaded for the sacredness of individual freedom,— the necessity of leaving others to judge for themselves concerning their line of duty; and here she alluded to existing divisions in the society, with great feeling and tenderness. She feared that many were now manifesting the same spirit of persecution of which they had complained during the controversy which divided Friends into two branches. There was the same unwillingness to allow a brother to think and act freely, according to the dictates of his own conscience. She feared, too, there was something of the same spirit of proscription and persecution. Where the waters were so bitter, there must be some impurity in the fountain. All these considerations she urged them to lay to heart; acknowledging her own need of the same humble, self-examination. She glanced with hearty approval at the more prominent reforms of the day, not naming them, but evidently referring to Temperance, Anti-Slavery, and Non-resistance.

    She earnestly deprecated the tendency to disparage all good works, not done within the enclosure of our own particular sect. "Master, we found men casting out devils in thy name, and we forbade them. But Jesus answered, forbid them not; for whosoever is not against me is with me."

PD L[*ydia*]. M[*aria*]. C[*hild*]., "Lucretia Mott," *National Anti-Slavery Standard*, October 7, 1841

1. Rose Street Meeting was part of the Hicksite New York Yearly Meeting (Hugh Barbour, Christopher Densmore, et al., eds., *Quaker Crosscurrents: 300 Years of Friends in the New York Yearly Meetings* [Syracuse, N.Y.: Syracuse University Press, 1995], 125, 128–29).

Manhattan Society, Asbury Church, New York City, September 29, 1841

In the evening, our friend addressed a meeting of the Manhattan Society, called mainly with reference to the continuance of a school for colored people, established by "The New-York Association of Friends."[1] Lucretia spoke very encouragingly of the state of colored schools in Philadelphia; and among other good indications, told with warm approval, of a society, formed by intelligent colored persons,[2] to visit the lowest haunts of dissipation, and seek to obtain a good influence upon the young, who were growing up in the midst of ignorance and vice, almost unconscious of a better teacher. These self-elected missionaries drew together an audience in any yard or court where they could collect them; and as the means they used consisted altogether of kindness and encouragement, they had been wonderfully blessed.

The wise and gentle speaker urged upon the colored people of New-York, the duty and policy of following this and other similar examples. She said, truly, that they could in no way so effectually assist their own race, and thereby aid the abolitionists, as by earnestly seeking moral and intellectual improvement for themselves and their children. She expressed deep regret at signs of disunion among them;[3] and she entreated them mutually to concede and forbear, for the sake of the common good of their proscribed class. She trusted that the baneful warfare of sects and parties would be entirely laid aside. It was true, the white man, with all his superior advantages, set them a poor example in this respect; but he might serve as a warning; and it must not be forgotten that the colored people had much more need to stand united. The obstacles in their path were too numerous, and prejudice had too much limited their resources, for them to afford the diminished strength attendant upon division.

While pleading with them to listen reverently to the voice within, which never left any violation of duty unrebuked, she told a pleasant anecdote of a little boy, in Boston, who was angry with his older brother. In answer to his mother's exhortations, he maintained that he had good reason to be offended. "But," said she, "do you not feel as if you could forgive your brother, even if he has done wrong?" "Why," replied he, "I feel some as if I could, and some as if I couldn't." His mother advised him to reflect upon it a short time, and she would come to him again, before she slept. When she again inquired concerning his state of mind, he answered cheerfully, "I have concluded to do what is right." The inward monitor told him plainly enough, that his resentful feelings had all been wrong.

Lucretia spoke with hearty admiration of Douglass, the eloquent lecturer, who was once a slave. She repeated two incidents related by him, the last of which is a more shocking perversion of scripture than we have heard of yet. A minister, preaching to the slaves, called their attention to the wonderful adaptation of things to their appropriate use, as manifested in the Creator's works.—"The white man," said he, "has a soft and slender hand; but you, who are made to labor for him, have large and horny hands, that enable you to do his work." The poor ignorant creatures had had no opportunity to learn that cessation from labor would make their hands likewise soft; and some of them went home, saying, "What a nice preacher that was! Every word he spoke was true.—How kind it was of God to make our hands so hard! How they *would* blister, if they were as soft as the white man's."

The other story was of a Methodist class leader, who tied up a slave woman, and flogged her till the blood streamed down her back; and when he had finished his brutal task, he quoted to her the text, "He that knoweth his master's will and doeth it not, shall be beaten with many stripes."[4]

PD L[ydia]. M[aria]. C[hild]., "Lucretia Mott," *National Anti-Slavery Standard*, October 7, 1841

1. The Manhattan Anti-Slavery Society had been founded in 1840. Although most members were African American, Hicksite abolitionist Isaac Hopper (1771–1852), the father of LM's son-in-law Edward Hopper, was one of the founders (Daniel E. Meanders, ed., *Kidnappers in Philadelphia: Isaac Hopper's Tales of Oppression, 1780–1843* [Cherry Hill, N.J.: Africana Homestead Legacy Publishers, 2009], 61–65; Margaret Hope Bacon, *Abby Hopper Gibbons, Prison Reformer and Social Activist* [New York: State University of New York Press, 2000], 33, 64). The New York Association of Friends for the Relief of Those Held in Slavery and the Improvement of Free People of Color was founded by Hicksite Quakers in 1839 (Hugh Barbour, Christopher Densmore, et al., eds., *Quaker Crosscurrents: 300 Years of Friends in the New York Yearly Meetings* [Syracuse, N.Y.: Syracuse University Press, 1995], 188).

2. LM may be referring to the American Moral Reform Society, founded in 1836 by James Forten and others (Faulkner, 112; Julie Winch, *Philadelphia's Black Elite* [Philadelphia: Temple University Press, 1988], 103–7).

3. In 1840 black abolitionists had held two competing national conventions, one that favored working with white activists and one that promoted African American efforts (Graham Russell Hodges, *David Ruggles* [Chapel Hill: University of North Carolina Press, 2010], 159–61).

4. Frederick Douglass (1818–95) recounted these incidents in a lecture to the Plymouth County Anti-Slavery Society on November 4, 1841 (John W. Blassingame, ed., *The Frederick Douglass Papers, Series I: Speeches, Debates and Interviews*, vol. 1, *1841–1846* [New Haven, Conn.: Yale University Press, 1979], 9–13).

Unitarian Church, Washington, D.C., January 15, 1843[1]

"Righteousness exalteth a Nation, but sin is a reproach to any People."

I doubt not but that this scripture truth will be readily assented to by this congregation, for there is a universal admission of the truth, that righteousness gives respect to its possessor. It is equally true of individuals as of nations; and it is a fact worthy of our observation, that throughout all the scripture, through all the dispensation of which that scripture gives us an account, that religion, justice, mercy, and all the principles of righteousness are highly exalted above the various forms of worship—the speculative doctrines of the age. But we are prone to forget this in our zeal for sectarian theology; in our earnest endeavor to exalt our favorite forms and rituals, and in the idea that has prevailed to a considerable extent, that we are the favorites of Heaven, we come to regard our sect or our professions of religion more than the practice of righteousness, of goodness, of truth. We confound truth with our sectarian forms, our systems of faith and our theology. We should duly discriminate between that which has its origin in the schools of science, and theology, and those principles which are divine in their origin and eternal in their nature. Righteousness exalteth all who love it, and God in his gracious condescension to the children of men, has caused them to be exalted in proportion as they have adhered to it through the variety of the forms of worship, and through gross misrepresentation they have received the censure of devoted worshippers. Those only are true worshippers who walk uprightly, and love righteousness—who despise the gains of oppression—those who do not close their eyes and shut themselves out from their own flesh.

Such has ever been accepted with God. It is no new doctrine. When Jesus and his apostles preached it, they declared it was of God and was good. The people imagined that he and his disciples had some new doctrine, but they declared it was that which was from the beginning; it was the same in all ages. The Jews, it is true, and Israel of old, were so sunk in their forms and ceremonies that they imagined they were the people of the Lord. They supposed they must go forth with the rounds of ceremonies—go to the temple of the Lord and even go forth unto the holy place called by this name, so that their prophets declared against them, "ye still burn incense and work after other gods whom ye know not." And, "ye say the way of the Lord is not equal." This has been the cry down to this day, that we are so constituted that we must live in sin—that we are more prone to evil than to good and we must depend on a vicarious atonement for our salvation; and this is called a mysterious operation to cleanse us from our iniquity. It proceeds from an unworthy examination of the scriptures, "ye err, not knowing the scripture or the power of God"—perverting the letter to your own destruction.

In no other way can I account for the great strength of sin in professing christendom than for the long prevalence of this doctrine. Men have been taught that they were more prone to evil than to good; hence they early fall into temptation and yield to the sins that beset them, from the very circumstances of being thus taught. "Oh House of Israel is not my way equal? Are not your ways unequal? When a righteous man turneth away from his righteousness, and committeth iniquity, and dieth in them, for his iniquity that he hath done shall he die?" Again, "when the wicked man turneth away from his wickedness that he hath committed, and doeth that which is lawful and right, he shall save his soul alive," "he shall surely live, he shall not die," " the soul that sinneth, it shall die."

It is time the noble dignity of man was elevated to a higher standard of goodness and truth—to that elevation which God designed us to occupy. I believe it to be high time there was more christian boldness, more moral courage, amongst mankind to speak to the sentiment of their hearts, whether they be in accordance with the popular doctrines of the day or not. And there is already a bursting forth of more independence of expression, of opinion among men—a greater freedom in their declaration of thought and of belief; they are becoming dissatisfied with the dogmas and theologies that they have been taught. If we take a child and teach him that he has a wicked heart, will he not be more likely to fall into evil practices? Teach him that he is necessarily, and unavoidably corrupt, and will he not feel discouraged? But instead of this, instruct him in the way he should go, then will conviction be daily implanted in his breast, and he will feel the dignity of his nature and the responsibility of his elevated station among created beings, and consequently be encouraged to works of righteousness. There is something in a child of heavenly nature, which only needs to be cultivated; and well might Jesus have held up the child in the midst of an assembly, and declare "of such was the kingdom of heaven."—How far does this go to disprove the doctrine which has been taught! Think ye that this child would have been held up as a fit emblem of the kingdom of heaven if it had not been pure and innocent? The doctrine of natural depravity which has obtained so long in the world, does not appear to have any connexion with the subject of righteousness, having no effect upon the conduct calculated to promote practical religion. But it would be a waste of time for me, at present, to undertake to controvert this doctrine.

We all have a right to our own sentiments, we claim this as a right, but when we find sentiments to effect the *conduct* of men—when we find such opinions fastened upon the community as the essential doctrine of christianity and made a test of the christian character, and when this standard is regarded as more holy than the standard of practical righteousness in order to elevate the faith, then would it be well if there were more who would examine the subject and declare what were their convictions upon it, even though they should thereby subject themselves to the charge of heresy or infidelity. Let us come to the disposition of the apostle when he said, "it is after that manner that the world calls heresy that I worship the father." Jesus taught the heresy of that age, and it was his opposition to the cherished forms and creeds of that day that constituted his greatest offence. We do not regard this heresy in its true light—we are disposed to adhere to the systems we have been taught, and to consider it heresy to call them in question, or even to endeavor to test their truth by the evidences of light and reason. As to the miracles which were performed in that day, it is not a matter for us to dispute, they were adapted to the age in which they were wrought, and were performed to answer a great end; instead of questioning them, ought we not rather endeavor to approach the Divinity by that purity of this life, which is emphatically said to have been created for the glory of God? Thus will we come to be the children of God. Let us love that Divinity of Christ that is conformable to man's intelligence and reason, and not be led by that construction of it which is tending to divest him of some of the noblest feelings of his nature, and to lower him in the scale of creative existence. The objector may ask, does not this conflict with the doctrine of the new birth? I think not. I think I understand the scriptures. The new birth is not placed upon the principle of the first birth being impure or wicked. We have a natural and a spiritual nature—that which partakes of the animal and that which partakes of the divine nature, and as we receive more of the Divinity dwelling upon the spiritual part we come to have our first nature brought out, and our feelings exalted with the operation of the love of God upon the soul. "That was not first which is spiritual." The spiritual is one, the natural another. The carnal mind is not subject to the law of God.—But when he speaks of the carnal mind, it is as men have given up to their propensities and yielded to the lust of the flesh.

But this Divine Goodness which is in every child, if cherished and adhered to old age, will enable us to realize all the christian enjoyments of communion with God and his dear Son. Oh this kingdom, were it but understood—divested of all the gloom and mysticism by which it is surrounded, how beautiful would religion appear, and how readily would it be embraced!

I come before you to preach no other righteousness, no other gospel, but the righteousness of God, that which is a spiritual righteousness—Let that gloom which has been connected with it be removed; divest it of this, and of the complicated system of theology, and I believe it will meet conviction in every breast. Divest it of this, and men will not reject the truth, let it come from what source it may. But the minds of the people are instructed not to receive truth except it come through the channel of certain rituals and ordeals, and thus are their sectarian preferences prepared. These forms and rituals though they may have been used in the days of the Apostles are but the shadow of things to come—so with washing and other outward ordinances.—Yet these are all to pass away—they are but a schoolmaster to bring us up to Christ. Do they contain any of the real substances of religion? I ask you not with any desire to shock the prejudices of any, but are these forms not taking the place of the reality—of the principle? are they not exalted to a higher estimate than the real practical duties of life? has Jesus given any forms of worship? His Prophets declared that these things were to pass away, and that a new heaven and a new earth were to be created. I know that speculative religionists have removed this to the millennial day, and referred us to that day which should bring about that glorious period when righteousness should cover the earth as the waters cover the sea; but theology is removing far the day instead of bringing it home close to our doors. This is a state of things to be brought about only when men prepare themselves to meet it, when men shall have executed their nature and subdued their evil propensities. Then may we look for the fulfillment of that prophetic declaration that "the kingdoms of this world shall become the kingdoms of our Lord and of his Christ." But those forms of worship and those opinions and doctrines, may be suited to those who practice them, and far be it from me to judge anyone for practicing such things.—But we may be teaching certain modes of speech, of observances, or peculiarities—no matter of what form—it may be music, it may be vocal or silent exercise, any, or all of these may be the gods we may be found worshipping; and while others may appear as idlers, performing none of these ceremonies, yet we may be found to be as far off the true God as they, or even they who are worshipping a heathen god; they worship heathen gods, and we verbal ones. Now let us inquire as regards the professors of the christian name in our strict adherence to the rituals of our respective churches—are we not in as much danger now of building up some images, as were those who were denounced for such things in former days, as guilty of the grossest idolatry? And how shall we appear before the Lord? No matter what were the customs in the Jewish church—no matter what their offerings were—whether a lamb, an ox or whether incense—they were not the rule for us. "It is shown unto thee, Oh man, what is good, and what the Lord thy God doth require of thee." "Who among us shall dwell with everlasting burnings? He that walketh righteously and speaketh uprightly; he that despiseth the gain of oppressions, that shaketh his hands from holding of bribes, that stoppeth his ears from hearing of blood, and shutteth his eyes from seeing evil: He shall dwell on high, his place of defense shall be the munition of rocks, bread shall be given him, his water shall be sure." It was against those who ground the face of the poor and practiced unrighteousness, that complaint was made. And we should contrast our professions with our practices, and I think we will perceive that the charge of neglecting our christian duties, is as applicable to us as it was to those formerly, and that they would be a reproach to any people. Does not christianity enjoin upon us to bring our principles to the practice of everyday life? Did not Jesus Christ come immediately in contact with the forms and customs of that day? It would have been an easy thing for him to wash his hands before he ate, and it would be of small consequence, or appear so, for him to conform in this respect; but it was his mission to break down these forms and ceremonies, and institute a practical religion. He was almost daily brought up before the Jews of his day for offenses against their laws and regulations. We have the account and it would be well for us to compare it with the institutions of our day, and see whether the effect would not likely be the same, were anyone to rise up in the present age against prevailing practices, and proclaim among the assemblies of the people the truths which he did in those days; would he not have to offer up his life.

I am glad there are a few who have ventured to come forward and declare the whole truth of God—who are placing these things in their true light; and the consequence of their labors I verily believe, will be to place the standard of true practical righteousness higher. For when we live out the practical christian, and show by our love for our brethren, and our consistent walkings, that we are the followers of Christ, we shall elevate the standard of righteousness, though we shall manifest no tenacity for our forms and creeds.

But as a community of christians, are we endeavoring to preach to the poor— to plead for the widow, and striving to promote that righteousness which exalteth a nation? are we endeavoring to remove the great evils which beset us as a nation? If this were the case would these great sins which blight this country be suffered to remain? would war still be slaying its thousands in our land? would slavery be crushing its millions? would intemperance, and vice, and wickedness in its various forms, continue to oppress the weak, and harass the poor, and corrupt the morals of our citizens? Would the name or the depth of the purse, intelligence, or literary attainments be the criterion of respectability? would the principles of right be made subservient to notions of honor or rank, and the standard of true piety and virtue be thus lowered?

We see righteousness with many is nothing in comparison to an adherence to the church ceremonies; the creeds of faith and to the fashion and usage of society. They consider this *faith* essential and that no one can enter into the kingdom of Heaven without it, at the same time vice and wrong are suffered to remain unrebuked, and teachers of religion may glide along in the popular current with a faith without works. It is considered a delicate subject to speak of the slave-holder, and it is forbidden; and are there not things done in secret of which it is a shame to speak and must be passed over in silence? Is there not a fear as regards the question of slavery, a fear to permit it to be examined? I ask the question, not in the spirit of reproach; I do not wish to injure the feelings of a single individual. If we could come together in a christian spirit, and with a right estimate of the true dignity of man, we would calmly and profitably discuss our best interests; the [*partition*] walls of prejudice, of sectarian and sectional jealousies would be broken down; universal righteousness would be the standard which we would seek to erect, and although we should retain many of our peculiar views, we might enjoy them without enforcing them upon others. When we come to understand thoroughly, our duties as christians, we will not judge a brother, though we may warn one another. We will be bound together in love without regard to denomination or sex. We shall then come to find our [*partition*] walls will be broken down. The schoolmaster which was to lead us unto Christ will no longer be needed, for we shall then have attained to the substance of which the old Jewish ceremonies were but the shadow.

I come before you this evening, my friends, with all the disadvantages of a woman breaking through the proscribed customs of the times, to endeavor to elevate the standard of righteousness and to promote the common well being of mankind; and I desire to be received in that spirit which has induced me thus to appear before you. There has been a great advancement among the people with regard to woman. Her condition is destined to become improved and elevated— she is already regarded in a very different light from that assigned to her from the dark ages; and she should come also to appreciate herself and be seeking to something higher than she has formerly done. She has already entered into many of the scientific and literary subjects of the age, and is enjoying the benefits of lyceums, and lectures and literary associations. Joining in these enjoyments, go to prove she is aspiring to something higher than the mere accomplishments and amusements of the day. Woman has long been excluded from the privilege of speaking to the people, and the Bible has been applied to for a sanction of this exclusion of her right to speak, even to the men of the cities. But the Bible has been quoted to authorize nearly every wrong in which the people have been found. The example of darker times is considered a sufficient authority for the present age; but is an unworthy application of the scriptures.

[A few sentences were here uttered which were not distinctly heard by the reporter, the import of which seemed to be the incompatibility of the exclusion of females from ministerial services, with the spirit of christianity—that in Christ Jesus male and female were one, and though it might be considered as transcending the modesty of her sex, for a woman to speak in public she did not understand Christ so. She hoped to see a better use made of the scriptures in this respect than had been done. She alluded to the announcement of the disciples on the day of Pentecost, that the prophecy of Joel was fulfilled—that daughters as well as sons should prophesy—that Philip had four daughters who did prophesy which was defined [as] "speaking to men in edification, and exhortation and comfort"—that Tryphena and Tryphosa were acknowledged co-laborers with Paul, as well as Phebe the servant of Christ, which meant minister, &c.]

And I believe it is important that we should endeavor to disabuse the christian mind with regard to this subject. This idea has obtained to a great extent in the christian world but will yet present itself in its true light through the singleness of woman.

It is then under these disadvantages that I am constrained to appear before you, and to urge upon your consideration the plain principle of right that we should all in our various sects and denominations, and those who are of no denomination, contribute what we can to the advancement of practical righteousness in the earth. I feel for those who are called non professors, and many who are called infidels, for those of this age who are thus stigmatized and denounced because they have not been willing to receive the orders and ceremonies that have been imposed upon them—for some of these my feelings have often been enlisted; that they may be faithful to that which they have seen, which will prove to them to be their Saviour; that which was with them in their youth, and was their comforter in their hour of affliction.

Oh ye who are not of any denomination, whose aspirations to God do nevertheless ascend with a confidence in the impartiality of the arm of his protecting power, it will not be by your outward profession but by your works of righteousness that you will show forth your faith; if you yield yourselves to him, and are willing to know his ability—his glorious attributes—he will know you also—he will set you above all the scoffs and frowns of the world.

There are thousands who have stepped out of the common round whose virtues will be admired by ages yet unborn. He who is now gone, but whose benevolence even in other lands has commanded respect & admiration; he who acknowledged the universal brotherhood of man, and secured the love of all, and that respect which gives evidence that righteousness exalteth—yes, the name of [*William Ellery*] CHANNING will be long remembered and revered; he was willing so far to lose his popularity for the time being as to tread upon what is considered one of the most unpopular topics of the day; he ventured to speak to the slaveholder—he was willing to forego the small consideration of present popularity, for the sake of lending the influence of his powerful mind to the work of disenthralling this guilty nation.

The language in which he uttered his sentiments will be felt, though his name will be no more heard among us. His appeals to the intelligence of the people in this country in behalf of the African bondman—engraven upon the imperishable pages of history, will be transmitted to posterity to be commended and admired. Though *he* is gone, the labor of his pen is still doing its work, and his appeals are not made in vain. There is in this nation an awakening up—there is an increasing disposition to hear, not on one subject only, but upon all.

I am aware of the place I stand; I know there are many who will not allow anything to be said in behalf of the slave. But I believe it to be my duty to plead the cause of the poor and of the oppressed whether they will hear or whether they will forbear. I have long believed that an obedience to christian duty required that more mouths should be opened upon this subject. Yet I do not regard this as an evil resting upon any particular part of the country; but "we are all verily guilty concerning our brother"; the manufacturers of the north, the consumers of the various commodities of southern productions, are implicated in this matter, and while the sweets of this system are found upon our tables we are partakers of other men's sins. I remember one of your great statesmen of South Carolina, how he showed that the north and east were deeply implicated in this subject; that we received as great profits as the immediate agent in this unlawful, this unjust business.[2] So regard me not as coming here with vituperative language against any particular part of the country; but let me implore you in the name of justice and humanity, to examine, and not fear an investigation of this subject. Oh ye statesmen! if such be present, fear not to speak aloud, fear not to discuss this subject in your public councils, fear not to speak of it by the way; let no apology, no plea of justification, deter you from hastening the liberation of the bondman. The only remedy is to break the bonds and let the oppressed go free. Let no considerations of interest or expediency divert you from the performance of this high and important duty. Oh if we would but agree that this evil should be removed from our land, would we not apply the rightful remedy? What would this nation be—of what could not this country boast, if she were free from this enormous system of injustice! Nations that are subjecting their people to wrong, might then admire our free institutions and the prosperity and happiness of our land. We ought to feel for the poor of our mother country, but we can never act effectively in their behalf, till we have removed this blot from our country. I have seen thousands, if not tens of thousands, on the other side of the water, ground down with poverty, their children with garments worn out and could scarcely dress themselves—I felt that they were objects of compassion and mercy: again I have seen the poor peasantry of Ireland calling upon the passenger by the way for aid; yea I have beheld this, and the poor of England also who are borne down by the proud hierarchy and the lordly aristocracy that have gained the ascendancy there. And when I beheld things how was my soul pained—how was my heart moved within me for the oppressed of that land. But when I turned my eyes to this country, what do I behold here? What kind of an example do we set? The eyes of that nation are upon us, and she compares our professions with our practices. This country which professes to be one of universal liberty, the asylum for the oppressed of every nation, and has not only proclaimed it to the world, but inscribed upon her parchments the principles of the inalienable rights of all men to the enjoyment of liberty. And from these high professions of equality, we have led strangers to suppose that this government would be the last to encourage monopolies—that it would do any thing but oppress its own subjects; but when they look abroad in our land, and behold how we carry out these principles they are ready to justify their own system of aristocracy.

I was ready to inquire whether the oppression of the peasantry was not equal in atrocity to that which existed in our own land. But they have the right to plead for themselves, the most oppressed and indigent laborer in that country, in his fustian jacket, can thrust himself into the public meeting—he can retire to his home where he cannot be invaded in his rights, and his domestic enjoyments; he cannot be severed from his family forever, and have their ties of affection riven asunder and sold to the merciless taskmaster—he has the command of his own children, and as they rise in education and usefulness, they are respected and encouraged. And even in Ireland the poor children may enter the public schools. But how is it here? We have laws expressly enacted to perpetuate the ignorance of the oppressed of our land! There is not only the *first* great injustice of taking from them their liberty, but all the concomitants of slavery are so many obstacles to their elevation. Oh look at it! I speak as to wise men. Look at the subject. I would not unnecessarily endeavor to awaken your sympathies; but I consider that the subject demands it. There may be many here who would point to the comparative humanity of slaveholders. But I would ask you whether there are not necessarily connected with the system, those evils of which I have spoken, and whether the humane masters do not go to give sanction to the whole system. I would entreat them, to examine the history of emancipation in the West Indies;[3] the glorious result of that noble enterprise, and hesitate not to strike off the fetters from our bondmen; and so we may secure the republican principles of our country. Oh bear with me when I speak for those who may not speak for themselves. Those who go forth with the single purpose of doing good, under the influence of the power of the living God, will ever find it their duty, "to cry aloud and spare not, to lift up their voice like a trumpet, and show the people their transgressions and the house of Jacob their sins." Righteousness exalteth a nation but sin is a lasting reproach. Let us then not hesitate to wipe from our escutcheon, this disgrace—this foulest blot. And is this the only crime in our land? Look at the Aborigines of our country; what an amount has it cost this government to drive them from their homes and from the graves of their fathers! Millions have been expended in wars with this much injured people. Alas, what little progress has christianity yet made! The intelligent mind is however beginning to behold the enormity of the crime of war. Is it not more difficult than formerly to involve a nation in this great evil? There is an obviously increasing love of right, and I believe there are measures to which nations may resort for a pacific adjudication of national difficulties. In England I know there are means, not a few, resorted to, to prevent the preparation for war—an evil which has disgraced the land from age to age. In this country now, there are appeals made to the public in behalf of peace principles, and they are beginning to claim considerable attention.[4] I regard all these things as favorable to the idea, that that desirable period is approaching when "nation shall not lift up sword against nation and shall learn war no more." Let us not think of waiting till the millennium shall arrive, but even now, we ought to know better and might *do* better. Oh have your minds cultivated and your hearts enlightened, hesitate not to speak of the evils which surround you—it may be unpopular for a time, but it is diffusing itself over the nation, and I rejoice that the time may come when violence and war will cease to crimson the land. I cannot but look forward to that time when we shall understand the true character of righteousness, and shall bring the great principles of christianity to bear upon the conduct of our every day life. In how many ways are we in our social and commercial intercourse, striving to take the advantage of one another—how we are oppressing, not only the slave, but the poor laborer? Yes, bring our christianity to our everyday practices, let our fruits test the purity of our professions, and when we are making these contracts by which we are enriching ourselves, let us look whether we are not indulging ourselves in extravagance in life to such an extent as to bring misery and woe upon others. Let us not be looking to the political arrangement which can only bring about a temporary relief until the *morals* of the people are changed; until we bring our christianity to our everyday life; until this comes to be the case, all our efforts, all our political arrangements, can afford no permanent good. May we my friends, see what part we have taken in the general oppression of the laboring classes, by our indulgences in fashionable life. I do not design to debar any from their enjoyments so far as true christianity will admit. We should remember the poor, call in to see them in their abodes of want and distress; call not in to see your rich acquaintances in preference to those who are objects of compassion and charity—it is to the poor, the maimed and the blind, that we are to administer. This is the principle which must go to reform the world—to hasten the day when the glory of the Lord will cover the earth as the waters cover the sea.

I am aware I am lengthening out to an extent beyond what might be agreeable to some, but I have but one opportunity, and this must be my apology.

[The speaker here alluded to the different customs of opening and closing meetings and that in these respects she might not accede to what was customary here. She knew she was not in these respects adhering to the taste of age—she spoke of the organs used in many churches, their singing &c., and explained that the essence of true worship consisted in the aspirations of the heart, and not in the *words* of a prayer or the *forms* of worship. She approved of vocal prayer, but not as a regular ordinance to be performed at stated periods.]

And I ardently desire that that which has been offered in much humility and sincerity this evening, may be received in the spirit in which it is tendered, and that it may be blessed and sanctified: and I believe God will bless all who are sincerely approaching unto him, whether in the secret of their hearts or in the rounds of ceremony, so that their hearts are filled with love to him and to their fellow creatures. He knoweth their hearts and he is full of mercy. Oh that we understood the attributes of deity! We should not be speculating upon abstract theory and contending about abstruse doctrines. Would that we understood the attributes of his goodness. He is ever unfolding himself to men, and as they obey his voice, they will be led by his spirit of which all men are endowed with a portion; and as we are thus taught, and cease to look unto man for that instruction which God alone can impart, he will give us an earnest of a better inheritance. Then shall we know that we are all upon equal grounds as regards what we shall do. Let us seek then to secure unto ourselves that which passeth the understanding of man, an inheritance that fadeth not away, even an earnestness of the rock of the glorious covenant where the Lord God enlighteneth the peaceful spirit in the highest is the light thereof.

Let me now my friends express in tenderness of spirit the obligation I feel, not only for the grant of this house, but the respectful attention with which I have been heard, and desiring the present and eternal welfare of you all, I bid you adieu.

[*On the reverse of the title page the stenographer wrote*:] "The following discourse, delivered at the Capitol of the United States, by a woman, touching as it does, upon topics not usually heard from the pulpits of that fashionable City, and listened to as it was by many members of the National Legislature, and other public officers, and clergymen, and many strangers, constituting a very large and promiscuous audience—naturally elicited much attention and inquiry.

The report I have given of it is believed to be substantially, if not literally correct, though the author has had no opportunity of revising it.

BENJAMIN B. DAVIS.[5]
Salem, O. 12th mo. 1843"

PD "A Sermon Delivered in the Unitarian Church in the City of Washington," B. B. Davis, Stenographer (Salem, Ohio: Davis and Pound Printers, 1843)

1. To Nathaniel Barney, LM wrote on February 14, 1843, "We applied for the Hall of Congress, but that being granted on condition of silence on slavery, we of course could not accept it." To Cecilia and George Combe she added on March 24, "a large Mg. was held—many members of Congress—some from the far South present. Their courtesy led them to bear from a woman what they would probably have resisted in a man" (Palmer, 121, 128; see also Faulkner, 111–12).
2. Most likely U.S. Senator John C. Calhoun (1782–1850), who argued that southern slaves were no worse off than many northern laborers.
3. In 1833 the British declared slavery illegal in all its colonies and established a period of apprenticeship. In 1838 they emancipated all slaves.
4. The first of a series of International Peace Congresses was held in 1843 in London, and LM continued to be active in the Non-Resistance Society.
5. Benjamin B. Davis (1811–fl. 1880) was a Hicksite abolitionist from Prairie Home, Ohio, who also advocated non-resistance (Thomas Hamm, *God's Government Begun: The Society for Universal Inquiry and Reform* [Bloomington: University of Indiana Press, 1995], 167, 111–12).

Hicksite Meetinghouse, Rochester, New York, July 21, 1844

July 21, 1844

 To day heard the celebrated Lucretia Mott preach at the Hicksite Meetinghouse.[1] She opened her discourse in the following beautiful manner. "How simple is the religion of Jesus! How plain is the Christian religion when divested of the appendages of man! When stripped of the forms & ceremonies which are its accompaniments & too often its substitute." She then proceeded to denounce the manners & customs of churches of the present day & seemed to think that all conformity to their doctrines & creeds was the result of servile fear & a want of independence on the part of the conformist. "Sabbath Day Observances" were classed among other "dogmas" of the "churches." In short, the first part of her discourse was as much opposed to the received doctrines of the Christian religion as any thing *Elias Hicks himself* could wish to hear.[2] She is a fine speaker, but her discourse so far was more like a *lecture* than a *sermon*. She insisted upon *morality as the great thing to be attained*, but not a word had she to say *about faith & repentance*.

 But after this came the truly *admirable* part of her discourse. Her views in relation to the "*mental & spiritual degradation* of *women*," *Peace, Temperance*, & *Anti Slavery* were given in a very happy manner. She hails with delight those symptoms of the *unpopularity* of *war* which governments have lately manifested in various instances. The Temperance cause she considers as the great, the glorious reform of the day. Its unparalleled success should be the beacon star to encourage us in the promotion of the other great reforms of the day. Abolitionists, especially should take courage from its success & let it cheer them onward. She cannot conceive how any benevolent persons can hesitate to *act* in these causes, but that they do so refuse she well knows, and that her *own society* are as deficient as any other in this respect she is also well aware. She spoke *very* plainly to them & probably to the dissatisfaction of many members who have hitherto been much opposed to *acting* in any way for the promotion of these causes. She accused them of being guilty of joining in the hue & cry of "going forward without being sent," of "disturbing the quiet," etc. The effect[s] of this preaching were very apparent, some being very much disturbed, others, were evidently highly delighted at the approbation of their own proceedings, for this society has some members who are *very* active in these reforms.[3]

AD Julia Wilbur Diaries, Special Collections, Haverford College, Haverford, Pennsylvania, Box 3, 1844–1865

 1. Orthodox Quaker and abolitionist Julia Wilbur (1815–95) began keeping a diary in 1844. She was then living in Rochester, where she worked as a teacher.
 2. Elias Hicks (1748–1830), divisive Quaker minister from Hempstead, New York.
 3. The Rochester Hicksite Meetinghouse, built in 1817, was retained by the Hicksites in the 1828 division. Its Monthly Meeting, Farmington Quarterly Meeting, and Genesee Yearly Meeting had been embroiled in discussions about "worldly activism" and participation in mixed-faith organizations since at least the late 1830s. Several local Hicksites, including Amy Post (1802–1889), were especially active in abolitionism (Nancy Hewitt, "The Spiritual Journeys of an Abolitionist: Amy Kirby Post, 1802–1889," in Brycchan Carey and Geoffrey Plank, eds., *Quakers and Abolition* [Urbana: University of Illinois Press, 2014], 75–76).

Unitarian Christians Convention, First Unitarian Church, Philadelphia, October 22, 1846

LUCRETIA MOTT said, it was most unexpected to her, to be permitted to speak on this occasion. I am gratified in having an invitation[1] to speak out the truth without clothing it in set theological language. I liked the observation of the last speaker, (Mr. Hedge), especially in reference to this point.[2] We make the cross of Christ of no effect, by the ambiguous and deceiving phraseology we throw around his precepts and doctrines. It goes to perpetuate the erroneous views which prevail in Christendom, of the divinity of Christ and the vicarious atonement. If we could disabuse Christianity of the errors of theology, we should do much towards advancing so great and glorious a system if it can be called such. But when preachers, for fear of losing their reputation in the religious world, speak of faith in the divinity of Christianity, and the vicarious atonement, they are retarding Christian progress by their want of simplicity and frankness.

Nothing is more fitted to impede this progress, than the popular theology, the generally received systems of faith. A speaker has said (Mr. Clarke), that we ought not unwillingly to allow ourselves to be cut off from the Body of the Church.[3] But however vital that Body may be and she would not deny it much earnestness and worth, yet we must be willing to be separated from it in respect to the important doctrines. But who is there of you glorying so much in that spirit of heresy in which St. Paul boasted—heresy after the manner of men—who of you stands so fast in liberty wherewith Christ has made us free, as to acknowledge the extent of their secret suspicions of views ordinarily professed? Who is ready to hold up the purity of human nature in place of its depravity? Who will speak of the importance of becoming Christ-like, by following his example, of that which is meant when he is called, "the Son of God with power according to the spirit of holiness," and not of that greatness of his which is inexplicable, or involves mystery and miracle.

We are too prone to take our views of Christianity from some of the credulous followers of Christ, lest any departure from the early disciples should fasten upon us the suspicion of unbelief in the Bible. But should we not feel free to speak of the narratives of those who hand down the account of Christ's mission, in their true character? The importance of free thinking, and honest speech, cannot be over-estimated. Be not afraid of the reputation of Infidels, or the opprobrium of the religious world. We must be willing to be severed from it if necessary. And our fruits, and not our opinions, will finally judge us. There is but one criterion of judgment, and every body knows what love, truth, mercy are! If we seek to bring forth righteousness, exceeding the righteousness of the Scribes and Pharisees, then we need fear little, though brother deliver up brother to death! It may become a small thing to be judged of man's judgment. We ought to rejoice that we are permitted to offer a pattern of Christianity exceeding the common one. We need Saviors that shall be Saviors on our own Mount Zion. How great is the mischief those false doctrines are doing, which make man depraved and then point him to the vicarious suffering of Christ! We are too prone to begin with the spirit, and then seek to be made perfect in the flesh. We clothe our thoughts in expressions that deceive. There is too much image-worship still practiced by Christians! We are apt to proselyte to sect rather than to Christianity! It has been well said, our fathers made *graven* images, but we make *verbal* ones. God has made man after his own image, and man has made God after his image. If you have had Channing and Worcester[4] to lead you on, why are you not prepared to carry the work forward, even beyond them?

My heart was made humble and tender when I came into the Convention. I saw in the chair the son of an old friend of my father, Samuel Parkman, of Boston.[5] Looking at Calvinistic Boston as it then was, and considering how Channing rose and bore his testimony, and what results followed, we may be encouraged. But let the work advance. Lo! the field is white to the harvest!

There are some circumstances now tending to break the connection between religion and death, and to substitute a connection between religion and life. The graveyard and the church, religion and death, are not now as they were, so closely and inseparably connected. Rural cemeteries have helped to break this connection. The spirit of God has been bestowed rather to govern our lives than to gratify our curiosity! We are fast settling down into satisfaction with the general ignorance relative to the future, and are no longer content to weave together a few texts about the nature of the future state, and play upon the superstitious feelings and hopes of the people, without moving them to good works.

Religion is coming to be mingled with every-day life, with common goodness. The minister is ashamed to make such a use of the Bible as shall make it a storehouse of arguments against the most sacred causes of humanity; to quote from the sensualist Solomon texts in defense of intemperance, or to place obstacles in the way of those who are seeking to break the fetter of the slave, by quoting texts of Scripture to prove slavery a patriarchal institution!

Look, too, at woman's place in society here among ourselves. There is great zeal for the relief of Hindu woman, but let us look at home and behold worse than their funeral pile; the immolation of woman at the shrine of Priestcraft! Has she leave to speak out the gushings of her soul? Ah! have you, brethren, unfettered yourselves from a prejudice that is tending to immolate one half the whole human family? Some of us have not so read the Scriptures so to find warrant for the exclusive appropriation of the pulpit by one sex! I know where I stand, and would speak with all delicacy. But shall not the time come when you will consider, if a great deal too much of church machinery and ecclesiastical formality does not mingle with your Christianity? Are you not wiser than your teachers, in keeping up ordinances which they would suffer to decline—and will you not soon be able to see how much more affectionate Christian institutions might be, if they were not cumbered with a salaried class, how much less expensive and more universal?

I hear you speak of missionaries—I always like that name which the excellent Joseph Tuckerman chose for himself—a minister-at-large.[6] I desire to see Christianity stripped of all names and things that make it technical; the gloomy appendage of a sect. Let it be a kingdom of God in the soul—let the inward voice speak out, and it will find a response. It may not be in superstitious language of the Quaker, or that of any other sect. I feel myself to be one of you in the advocacy of great principles. Let me urge you by all that is glorious in these principles to be faithful to them. Do not seek to build up a demure piety, but a true, useful, practical life. I wish there were more extempore speech among you. Then men who work with their own hands, and labor from day to day shall pour out the gushings of their hearts upon you. If the ministry were stripped of its peculiarity and special support, there would be many preachers for one, a greater enlargement of heart in all.

Brethren—hearken to the Spirit. He dwelleth with you, though you know it not. It is he that talketh with you by the way. Are not the aspirations for truth, a proof that we have a present God with us?

Proceedings of the Regular Autumnal Convention of the Unitarian Christians: Held in the City of Philadelphia, October 20th, 1846 (Philadelphia: Richard Beresford, 1846), 54–57

1. As the convention resumed on its third and final day, local Unitarian minister William Henry Furness (1802–96) stated that an "accredited delegate from the Society of Friends was present" and he moved that LM be given a seat and allowed to speak if she desired, a motion that was unanimously approved (*Proceedings*, 51; see also Faulkner, 122–23; Bacon, 130). At Mott's funeral in 1880, Furness delivered an oration later published as *God and Immortality: A Discourse in Memory of Lucretia Mott* (Philadelphia: Office of the Journal, 1891).

2. Frederic Henry Hedge (1805–90), then a Unitarian minister in North Cambridge, Massachusetts, and later professor at the Harvard Divinity School, had stated, "Bring Christianity into immediate contact with the business world, with actual life; make it a part of nature and reality" (*Proceedings*, 54).

3. James Freeman Clarke (1810–88), Boston Unitarian minister, said, "We must not cut off ourselves from the life of the Church by willfully rejecting venerable and expressive phraseology, simply because it is in use among those from whom we differ" (*Proceedings*, 52).

4. Noah Worcester (1758–1837), a New England Congregational minister, edited the *Christian Disciple* (later the *Christian Examiner*), which had been founded by William Ellery Channing.

5. Boston Unitarian clergyman Francis Parkman (1788–1852), the son of real estate magnate Samuel Parkman (1751–1824), presided over the convention (*Proceedings*, 5).

6. Joseph Tuckerman (1778–1840), a Boston Unitarian minister, dedicated his ministry to aiding the poor.

Anti-Sabbath Convention, The Melodeon, Boston, March 24, 1848

[*Morning Session*]

I have little to add to what has been already said upon this subject. Much that I could not have spoken so well, has been said for me by others. I am glad to be here, to have an opportunity of hearing the discussions, and also to give countenance to this important movement for the progress of the religious world.

The distinction has been clearly and ably drawn, between mere forms and rituals of the Church, and practical goodness; between the consecration of man, and the consecration of days, the dedication of the Church, and the dedication of our lives to God.

But might we not go further, and shew that we are not to rely so much upon books, even upon the Bible itself, as upon the higher revelation within us? The time is come, and especially in New England it is come, that man should judge of his own self what is right, and that he should seek authority less from the Scriptures. It is well, however, inasmuch as the faith of a large part of the professors of Christianity rests upon this book, to shew that certain also of their own teachers bear witness to the truth we advocate.

It seemed to me that the views of the last speaker went further to sanctify the book, than his own principles would justify. I thought the same of the remarks of Theodore Parker, made yesterday, with regard to the day, and wished to allude to it in his presence, but there was no opportunity. There seemed to be a little confusion, when he spoke of not hallowing the day, and yet considered it essential that there should be this religious observance.[1] Does not such an admission lead the advocates of it into a kind of compromise? and to "build again that which they are called to destroy"? It is observable, in nearly all the advance steps in theological points, particularly when there is a reluctance to acknowledge the heresy, and a desire to appear orthodox.

Those who differ from us would care little for an Anti-Sabbath Convention, which should come to the conclusion that, after all, it would be best to have one day in seven set apart for religious purposes. Few intelligent clergymen will now admit, that they consecrate the day in any other sense, or that there is any inherent holiness in it. If you should agree that this day should be for more holy purposes than other days, you have granted much that they ask. Is not this Convention prepared to go farther than this? to dissent from this idea, and declare openly, that it is lawful to do good on the Sabbath day? That it is the consecration of all our time to God and to goodness, that is required of us? Not by demure piety; not by avoiding innocent recreation on any day of the week; but by such a distribution of time as shall give sufficient opportunity for such intellectual culture and spiritual improvement, as our mental and religious nature requires. There would not then be the necessity of a devotion of the seventh part of our time, even for the rational improvement that our friend yesterday considered so essential.

In the Scripture authority, however, as it has been cited, it might have been shown, that, even in the times of the most rigid Jewish observance, it was regarded as a shadow only of good things to come. "I gave them also my Sabbaths to be a sign unto them." The distinction was then made, by the more faithful and discerning of their people, between mere formal worship and practical goodness. "Lord, who shall abide in thy tabernacle? who shall dwell in thy holy hill? He that walketh uprightly, and worketh righteousness, and speaketh the truth in his heart." When these things were not done, even the temple-worship became an abomination; the

Sabbaths, the holy meetings, he was weary of them. Their clear-sighted prophets spoke in the name of the Highest, to those who had violated the law of right: "I hate, I despise your feast-days. The new moons and Sabbaths, the calling of assemblies, I cannot away with; it is iniquity, even the solemn meeting." They were called to amend their ways and their doings—to do justly, love mercy, and walk humbly. There is now, as there ever has been, but one test—one standard of true worship.

If we were better acquainted with the doctrines and principles of the ancients, of those who are not regarded as coming within any divine enclosure, but who are looked upon as heathen, we should find abundant recognition of practical Christianity. Who is it that tells us that the testimony of a Socrates is not equally corroborative of truth, with the testimony of a Paul? That certain authorities, bound in a certain way, are of higher credence, than that which has come through other channels? Man is man, and his rational and spiritual natures are worthy of respect. His testimony is corroborative in every age of the world, let it come from what source it may, while in accordance with truth.

It has been said here, that we are not bound by the Old Testament;[2] but are we to bind ourselves to the New Testament authority? Enough has already been quoted from that book, to prove all that we would ask, with regard to the day. There is no testimony, no evidence there found, that will authorize the consecration of one day above another. Jesus recognized no such distinction; and the Apostle Paul said, "Let every man be fully persuaded in his own mind. He that regardeth the day, unto the Lord he doth regard it; and he that regardeth not the day, unto the Lord he doth not regard it." These equally give God thanks. There is all this liberal view, and it is well to bring it before the people. But, after all, are we to take this as our sufficient authority? Suppose some of them had been so under their Jewish prejudices, as to teach the importance of the observance of the day; would that have made it obligatory on us? No, we are not called to follow implicitly any outward authority. Suppose that Jesus himself had said, with regard to the day, as he did in allusion to John's baptism, "Suffer it to be so now," would that have made it binding on us? Is the example of the ancients, whether Prophets or Apostles, or the "beloved Son of God" himself, sufficient for the entire regulation of our action at the present day? No: Jesus testified to his disciples, that when the spirit of truth was come, they should be taught all things, and should do the things which he did, and greater. The people were not then prepared for more. The time would come when that which was spoken in the ear, in closets, should be proclaimed on the house-top. He urged upon his disciples to keep their eye single, that their whole body might be full of light.

His practice, then, in any of these observances, is not sufficient authority for us. We are not required to walk in the exact path of our predecessors, in any of our steps through life. We are to conform to the spirit of the present age, to the demand of the present life. Our progress is dependent upon our acting out our convictions. New bottles for new wine now, as in days past. Let us not be ashamed of the gospel that we profess, so far as to endeavor to qualify it with any orthodox ceremonies or expressions. We must be willing to stand out in our heresy; especially, as already mentioned, when the duty of Sabbath observance is carried to such an extent, that it is regarded, too generally, a greater crime to do an innocent thing on the first day of the week,—to use the needle, for instance—than to put a human being on the auction-block on the second day;—a greater crime to engage in harmless employment on the first day, than to go into the field of battle, and slay our fellow-beings, either on that or other days of the week! While there is this palpable inconsistency, it is demanded of us, not only to speak plainly, but to act out our convictions, and not seem to harmonize with the religious world generally, when our theory is not in accordance with theirs.

Many religionists apparently believe that they are consecrating man to the truth and the right, when they convert him to their creeds—to their scheme of salvation, and plan of redemption. They, therefore, are very zealous for the tradition of their fathers, and for the observance of days; while at the same time, as already mentioned, they give countenance to war, slavery, and other evils; not because they are wholly reckless of the condition of man, but because such is their sectarian idea. Their great error is in imagining that the highest good is found in their church. Hence their zeal and proselyting spirit.

The religious world ought to be disabused of this idea, and made to understand the real consecration of time. In order to do this, not only should this Convention be held, and resolutions, urging the carrying out of our principles, be passed; but we should be prepared to issue tracts, and scatter them over the land. This has been done, to some extent. There are several copies here, of a tract published a year or two ago in Philadelphia, on this question, by one, who, not feeling qualified to write, spoke to his friend who could write, but had not the means to publish, and agreed to furnish the means.[3] This is the right kind of zeal, leading to individual labor, not mere conventional interest. The more it is called for, on account of the extraordinary efforts in holding Sabbath Conventions, &c. Men of talents and reputed religious worth are going about the country, making exertions to establish a Sabbath, to increase its obligations, and the necessity of its observance, on the part of the people.

The editors of some of the daily papers in Philadelphia, especially since the issue of the Anti-Sabbath Call, are catering to the religious sentiment, praising the labors of Edwards and others, in travelling about for this purpose.[4] In proportion as these publications go forth, should there be zeal on the part of the Anti-Sabbatarians, as they are called by way of distinction, to spread clear, intelligent, and liberal views on the subject. There should, therefore, be a generous appropriation of means and funds to circulate information, and to enlighten the people, and a reasonable portion of our time and talents devoted to the cause. The reformer should advocate a portion of every day of the week, for mental and spiritual improvement, as well as innocent recreation, rather than give sanction to the idea, that the present arrangement is a wise distribution of our time.

In the existing state of society, while the laborer is over-tasked, and has so little respite from his toil, we may indeed rejoice, that, by common consent, he has even this one day in seven of rest; when if he choose, he ought to be encouraged to go out with his family, in steamboats and railroad cars; and in the fields and woods he might offer acceptable homage and worship to the Highest. This exercise of his right need not interfere at all with the conscientious action of those, who believe they may more acceptably worship God in temples made with hands. But if we take the ground, that all should rather assemble on that day, to worship, and hear what is called religious instruction, there is danger of our yielding the very point for which we are called together.

Many of us verily believe that there is, on the whole, material harm done to the people, in these false observances, and in the dogmas which are taught as religious truth. So believing, we should endeavor to discourage this kind of devotion of the time, and correct these errors, by plain speaking and honest walking—rather than, by our example and our admissions, do that which shall go to strengthen superstition, and increase idolatry in the land.

[*Afternoon Session*]

Our friend makes a difference between calling the day Sabbath, and recognizing it as the Lord's day.[5] Is not this a distinction in terms only, but the same thing in fact? The mere change of the day from the seventh to the first of the week, does not meet all the wants of the people on this subject. We may call it Sabbath or Lord's day, and be equally in darkness as to the nature of true worship.

We may deceive ourselves, in our care not to offend our neighbors, who are Sabbatarians, or Lord's day observers. For their sakes, we will seem to observe the day; refraining from that which, on another day, would be right. We will not permit our children to play in the yard, or be seen ourselves doing that which would wound them. Upon a closer examination of our motives, it may be our own love of approbation and selfishness that is wounded. If so, there is a kind of hypocrisy in the act of seeming to be what we are not. We have need to guard ourselves against any compromise for the praise of man's sake.

For years after my mind was satisfied on this subject, if engaged in sewing, on the first day, and a domestic or other person entered the room, the work was concealed, with the plea that their feelings should not be hurt. But, on being asked, why I did not also, for the same reason, go to the communion table, or submit to baptism, I could not answer satisfactorily; and was at length convinced that more harm was done to myself and children, in the little deception practiced, than in working "openly, uncondemned, and in secret doing nothing."

As advocates of the truth, we must be willing to be "made of no reputation," to lose caste among our people. If we seek to please men, we "make the cross of Christ (to use a symbolical expression) of no effect." Let us, therefore, stand fast in the liberty wherewith the truth has made us free.

* * * *

I did not ask for the reading of these resolutions again, with the intention of speaking upon them, but that, in justice to him who presented them, they should have an intelligent hearing and understanding, and passage, if it be so judged, in this Convention.[6]

Some of them do not appear in accordance with the resolutions already passed here;[7] and the tendency of them, I fear, would be rather to strengthen the superstition that prevails on this subject, than to lessen it. The object of this Convention is to remove this superstition, as well as to take measures for the repeal of all penal enactments to enforce the observance of the day. So far, its course has been in accordance with its object, as published to the world. It is important that we should carry out consistently our principles and proposed measures.

Is it needful that reformers should ever express themselves in the manner in which some of these resolutions are expressed, with regard to any institutions that they believe might rightly pass away? Those who are prone to adhere to their cherished customs and forms, will not lightly yield them. The sectarian will not give up his Sabbath too soon.

The right has been sufficiently admitted, in the speeches made here, and the resolutions passed, that all who choose should voluntarily associate themselves in the observance of the day, for as long a time as it may yield them any profit. But it would be too much to ask of us, that we should propose to do anything to continue the sacredness of the day.

If we assert that, in the attempt to strengthen its observance by appeals to superstition and ignorance, more harm will accrue to the cause of pure religion than good. Do we fear that our devotion and piety will be called in question? I trust the reformers of this character will give practical evidence, in their everyday life, of their allegiance to God. If their fruits shall testify to their faith, they need not fear the stigma or the opprobrium of the bigoted worshipper, because of their not holding up one day above another.

There are various reasons for keeping this Convention on very simple ground—not blending it with any of the popular views of the subject, which prevail to such an extent. We shall do more, in this way, to promote the cause of practical Christianity, than by yielding to the prevailing idea, that worship is more acceptable on one day in seven, than doing right every day of the week. The character of many of these reformers—their interest in the various concerns of humanity, the sacrifices they have made for the good of their fellow-beings—all testify to their devotion to God and humanity. They feel it incumbent upon them to be exceedingly careful in their conduct on all the days of the week, so that those who speak evil of them as evil-doers may be ashamed when they falsely accuse their good conversation in Christ. Numbers of these have seen to the end of gathering together for religious worship. They understand the vision of John in the Revelations, describing the New Jerusalem, the holy city; and he "saw *no temple* therein, for the Lord God Almighty and the Lamb are the temple of it." These cultivate the religious sentiment every day. They feel in their hearts the raising of praise and hallelujah unto their God, when they go forth into the fields and groves. God's temple is there; and they no longer need to enter the outward temple to perform their vows, and make their offerings. "Let every man be fully persuaded in his own mind."

There are signs of progress in the movements of the age. The superstitions and idols in our midst are held up to the view of the people. Inquiring minds are asking, "who shall show us any good?" These are dissatisfied with the existing forms and institutions of religious sects, and are demanding a higher righteousness—uprightness in everyday life. The standard of creeds and forms must be lowered, while that of justice, peace, and love one to another, must be raised higher and higher. "The earth shall be filled with the knowledge of the glory of the Lord." We wait for no imagined millennium—no speculation or arithmetical calculation—no Bible research—to ascertain when this shall be. It only needs that the people examine for themselves—not pin their faith on ministers' sleeves, but do their own thinking, obey the truth, and be made free. The kingdom of God is nigh, even at the door. He dwelleth in your midst, though ye know it not. One of your own poets hath said —

> "All mankind are one in spirit, and an instinct bears along,
> Round the earth's electric circle, the swift clash of right or wrong."[8]

This is no longer the peculiar creed of the Quaker. It is coming to be universally acknowledged in the hearts of the people, and, if faithful, the bright day of liberty, and knowledge, and truth, shall be hastened.

Many clear views have been held out before us during this Convention, to which there has been a ready response, shewing that we are ripe for advancement—that it is of more importance to live up to our convictions of right, than to subscribe to the creed of any church. May we let our light so shine, that men may see our good works, and glorify our Father in heaven, even though our worship of him may be after the way called heresy. We may be instructed by the prayer of the Apostle Paul for his brethren: "I pray to God that ye do no evil; not that we should appear approved, but that ye should do that which is honest, though we be as reprobates; for we can do nothing against the truth, but for the truth."

Is it not indicative of great progress that here, in Boston, in Puritan New England, where the Sabbath has been so long regarded with much zeal and religious devotion,—even here, there can be a large gathering of the people from day to day, and the interest continued to the end of such a Convention as this? that they can listen and bear so much? that they can receive the resolutions read here, and passed almost unanimously? I rejoice herein; yea, and will rejoice.

Some remarks have been made, tending to discourage any appeal to the State Legislatures on this subject;[9] we have nothing to do with "the powers that be," but must trust the subject entirely to the moral sentiment of the people. But is not the very act of petitioning an appeal, and often an effective one, to the moral sense of the people? It is sometimes only by remonstrances and petitions to the rulers and statesmen of the land, that the ear of a great portion of the people is reached; and by going from house to house to obtain signers, an opportunity presents itself to scatter truth, and to enlighten the mind.

It has been so, to a great extent, in the Anti-Slavery movement. Converts have been made in this way, who are now devoting themselves to the cause of human freedom; and by reiterated appeals to the Legislatures, much has been effected for the bondman. In Pennsylvania, every facility for recovering the fugitive, and the law by which man could be held as property for six months, were removed from the statute books, last year, by the unanimous vote of both houses of the Legislature.[10]

The success attendant on these measures should encourage us to adopt similar modes of action on this subject. Let us go away impressed with the importance of making every effort, that will induce inquiry among the people. What is done here, will be limited in its extent; but if we carry the subject home with us, and act there, we may effect something.

The Abolitionists endeavored early to enlist the pulpit and the press in behalf of the suffering and dumb. They organized societies, scattered tracts, and sent forth the living agent; and, behold, the whole country is aroused to the subject. May it prove a healthful agitation, resulting in proclaiming liberty throughout the land, unto all the inhabitants thereof!

In this case, may not similar measures be resorted to, with equally good effect? Every fetter which superstition and sectarian bigotry have imposed, must be broken, before the mind of man will be free. The pulpit and the press may yet be enlisted even in this cause. There are many thinking minds. The people do not love to have their prophets prophesying so falsely as they have done; and they will demand an examination into this subject. If the reformer be faithful to his convictions, and make no compromise with the religion of the day; if he do not seem to believe that for which he has no respect; if he come not to the table of the Lord unworthily; the time will not be long, before the clergymen of the various sects will investigate this subject with other spectacles than those they have hitherto worn.

The zeal now manifested to increase the sanctity of the Sabbath, is not in accordance with the spirit of the age. In travelling through New York and Ohio, last year, I mourned the evidence of this sectarian zeal. Tracts were scattered through the length of the cars, on this subject, appealing to ignorance and credulity, and gross superstition. The judgments of Heaven, in numerous anecdotes, were stated as falling on the Sabbath-breaker. It is unworthy the age, when we have such works as Combe on the Constitution of Man, so freely circulated, as well as others, shewing the true workings of the natural laws, and their unavoidable results.[11] We must, then, do our part to counteract these injurious influences of widespread error.

This is no new subject. I am one of the older members of this Convention. I have been familiar with these views from my early days, being accustomed to hear the remarks of the venerable Elias Hicks, who bore his testimony against all penal enactments for enforcing the observance of the Sabbath. He travelled extensively through New York and Pennsylvania, and after much observation, came to the conclusion, that crime and licentious indulgence were greatly increased by the existing arrangement of society, on this subject. He remarked for himself, that he was careful on the first day of the week, as on the fourth, not to do so much work in the morning, as would unfit him for the enjoyment of his meeting; but, after meeting, on either day, if he had a field of wheat which needed cradling, he would not hesitate to do it; and the law forbidding it on the first day was oppressive on his conscience. His view was, that there should be such regulation of time as should over-tax none with labor on any day of the week—that darkness was spread over the land half the time, when man might rest; and after such devotional exercises as he might choose for himself, he should have the advantage of innocent relaxation. A person present, opposing him, stated how he observed the day—that he wished all to be quiet—no secular business, &c. Elias replied, "I consider thee as much under the effect of superstition, as thou would be in the observance of any other of the Jewish rites."[12]

During that discussion, impressions were made which I have ever remembered. They were strengthened, in after years, and I now feel the more prepared, by my feeble expression, to encourage those who have been pioneers in other labors of reform.[13]

PD *Proceedings of the Anti-Sabbath Convention* (Boston: Anti-Sabbath Convention, 1848), 94–99, 122–23, 126–31.

1. Abolitionist Henry C. Wright (1797–1870) mentioned consulting the "Christian Scriptures," where he found "a strict injunction, that we are not to enforce upon one another the observance of Sabbaths" (*Proceedings*, 87). On March 23 Unitarian theologian Theodore Parker (1810–60) had urged that Sunday be set aside for rest, to explore "religious, moral and intellectual culture," but would not allow the day to be "devoted to common work or amusements" (*Proceedings*, 49–50).

2. Wright stated, "I do not ask what the Jewish Scriptures say upon the subject [*Sabbath observance*]" (*Proceedings*, 87).

3. Abolitionist Charles C. Burleigh (1810–78), "The Sabbath Question" (Philadelphia, 1847).

4. Several speakers, including WLG and Wright, had castigated Justin Edwards, secretary of the American and Foreign Sabbath Union, an organization formed in Boston in 1843, for his efforts to prevent travel or any business on the Sabbath (*Proceedings*, 55, 93, WLG *Letters*, 3:547).

5. Unitarian minister Samuel May Jr. (1810–99) stated that when he entered the ministry he found that Sunday was a day "set apart, among Unitarians, as other sects, for religious . . . purposes; but not as time holier in itself than any other time, nor was it called the Sabbath" (*Proceedings*, 121).

6. At the conclusion of his speech on March 23, Parker had offered nine resolutions, among them setting aside one day "to rest from common work" (*Proceedings*, 49).

7. All other resolutions offered by various members of the convention, including one "to do well on every day of the week," had been approved "nearly" unanimously (*Proceedings*, 11–15, 114).

8. Adapted from "The Present Crisis" (1844) by James Russell Lowell (1819–91).

9. The convention unanimously recommended submitting petitions to legislatures in states compelling Sabbath observance (*Proceedings*, 11, 118).

10. In February 1847 the Pennsylvania legislature had abolished these laws (Palmer, 152).

11. LM's friend, the Scottish phrenologist George Combe (1788–1858), had published the *Constitution of Man* in 1835 (Palmer, 54, 169, 171).

12. In a letter to William Poole of June 15, 1817, Hicks expressed his anti-Sabbatarian views (Paul Buckley, ed., *Dear Friend: Letters and Essays of Elias Hicks* [San Francisco: Inner Light Books, 2011], 37–43).

13. Criticism of the convention included this reaction to LM from the *Boston Recorder*: "Of graceful mien, with a pleasing and benignant aspect . . . it was yet evident by almost every sentence she uttered, that her soul was rankling against the kingdom of God, and his Christ" (*Proceedings*, 152). See also Palmer, 160; Faulkner, 128–29; WLG *Letters*, 3:543–48, 605–6).

American Anti-Slavery Society, Broadway Tabernacle, New York City, May 9, 1848

There is not a more interesting object for the contemplation of the philosopher and the Christian—the lover of man, and the lover of God, than the law of progress,—the advancement from knowledge to knowledge, from obedience to obedience. The contemplation of it is beautiful, the investigation of it is exceedingly interesting, as manifested in the history of the world. We find in the earliest records, the command to advance—"to get thee from thy kindred, from thy father's house, and to come into the land which I shall show thee." And, again: "ye have encompassed this mountain long enough; speak to my people, that they go forward." In the declaration of the Prophets of old, it was men of clean hands who were to grow stronger and stronger; it was the righteous who held on his way: and in later times; we find the recommendation of the Apostles to their brethren was, "to go on unto perfection not laying again the foundation for repentance from dead works." And, indeed, was not the teaching of Jesus particularly directed to lead the people onward,—"Ye have heard that it was said by them of old time, thou shalt do thus or so"? then assailed those orders and institutions which they regarded as sacred; speaking directly in opposition to their alleged Heaven ordained law. In contradiction to this law of retaliation, he taught them to love their enemies and to do good to all, embracing all mankind in the love which he so beautifully inculcated, and so happily exemplified.

In coming down to later times, this law of progress is most emphatically marked in our day, in the great reformatory movements which have agitated the truth-loving and sincere-hearted, engaged in the work of blessing man. This may not be a fitting occasion to dwell much upon this topic; but there are those present who can look back to the early days of the great peace reformation. The first efforts were to arrest the progress of *offensive* war; while they claimed to themselves, in extreme cases, the right of a resort to self-defense. But a reformer now, the Jesus of the present age, on the Mount Zion of Peace, says: "Ye have heard that it was said by them of old, thou shall war only in self-defense, but I say unto you, take not up the sword at all." The language is not now in only prophetic vision, as of old; it does not, as the current theology has attempted, explain the prophecies of peace on earth, to refer to some future, far distant millennium, but its language now is "sheath the sword"; "render good for evil"; little children are taught to return a "kiss for a blow." Do we not see the progress that these principles have made? Was there ever a period in history when nations were so prolific of events as at the present moment, giving promise of being consummated by the ultimate realization of the higher principles of "peace on earth, and good will to man," calling into action the high moral sentiments of the people, and tending to arrest the sword of the destroyer?[1]

Truly, this law of progress is worthy of our admiration. Look at it in the temperance reformation: those interested in that cause, can remember how it was said by them of old time: "thou shalt drink wine moderately, and abstain from the unnecessary use of intoxicating liquors." What is the language now of the Savior on the Mount Zion of Temperance? "I say unto you, drink not wine at all—practice 'total abstinence' from all intoxicating liquors."

And how has it been (let me touch upon it ever so lightly) with the subject of priestcraft? It was said by them of old time, "down with your hierarchies." The Protestant reformers said, "away with your popery, away with priests of that particular church," and let us have in lieu thereof, the Protestant and dissenting priesthood. What now is the language of the reformer from among those who begin to have *God* for their *high priest*—Himself the teacher of his people? "Thou shalt judge for thine own self what is right, and God alone is, and shall be thy teacher." Look at your pulpits; they are widening; they are not the little, high, narrow, isolated boxes they were wont to be in olden time; there is room for several, and occasionally a *woman* is found to occupy a place there. (Applause.) Is not this then an evidence of progress even in the greatest and highest of Christian principles?

How is it in the Anti-Slavery cause? It is now more than ten years since it was my privilege—and a great one I esteemed it—to attend an anniversary of this kind in this city.[2] I remember the tone of the speeches, how that only the first principles of Anti-Slavery were brought into view. And, indeed, looking back to a period shortly before this, when a little handful gathered together in the city of Philadelphia [*one line illegible*] declare, not merely self-evident truths—to reiterate the simplest truisms that were ever uttered. Read the declaration of the Anti-Slavery Convention of 1833, and see what it was found necessary then to declare in Convention. The people were asleep on the subject with some few exceptions. There had been solitary individuals, such as Lundy, and Elias Hicks, and the Benezets, the Clarksons, and the Wilberforces.[3] But the labors in England for twenty years were simply to arrest the progress of the Slave Trade; and it was the work of a *woman* to declare, that "Immediate, not Gradual Abolition" was no less the duty of the master, than the right of the slave.[4] In this Convention in Philadelphia, the great principles of human freedom were uttered that every man had a right to his own body, and that no man had a right to enslave or imbrute his brother, or to hold him for a moment as his property—to put a fellow-being on the auction-block, and sell him to the highest bidder, making the most cruel separations in families. At that time these things were scarcely known; the people had scarcely considered them. It was now made known to very many in the Northern States, that there were then more than two million held in this abject bondage, who were claimed as property,—that men had this irresponsible control, this legal right to their persons. This Convention resolved what it should do: first—efficiently to organize itself, and then to seek to form other Anti-Slavery Societies throughout the country. They were to go forth and endeavor to enlist the pulpit and press in behalf of the suffering and the dumb. The work it had to do was a Herculean task; it was, to meet the priests of the Church, and to endeavor, by bringing Bible texts, to oppose them to others, in order to prove that man had no right to hold his fellow-being as a slave. What has resulted from their labors? Look at the law of progress in this particular: read this appeal of the women of Scotland to the women of America:[5] (applause;) see what they there say with regard to going to the Bible to claim authority for holding human beings in bondage. It is not sufficient now to quote the example of the ancients, on which modern slaveholders claim the rights to oppress their fellow-beings, and that to an extent greatly transcending slaveholding in ancient times.

But time is no longer occupied by Abolitionists in meeting the ministers in this way. The labors of these few pioneers have been sufficient to awake the nation to the consideration of this subject, and there is a response in the hearts of those who have not been blinded by their sectarian prejudices, by the tradition they have received, or by the god of this world which blinds the eyes of them that believe not. These have heard the truth, and having received it, gladly have come forward; and in their inmost heart there is a response to the truth as it was once uttered by a speaker of the House of Assembly in Barbadoes: that "every man knows in his heart that slaveholding is wrong."[6] It was needed that some should first come forth thus armed and give their views to the people; and may not the pioneer in this cause of immediate abolition, (turning towards Mr. Garrison,) who trod the wine press alone in the beginning of this work, say in the language of the Prophet, "with my staff I passed over this Jordan, and now I have become two bands." Look around you over the country, and see whether he spoke in vain, when he declared that he *would be heard*. (Great applause.) Observe the progress in the labors of this reform, that both the pulpit and the press are enlisted to some extent in behalf of the suffering and the dumb. Also, as has been already remarked in the legislative halls of the land, the National Assembly is engaged with it. Scarcely a Legislature in the several States but discovers at every move on the great question of American Slavery, something cheering to the Abolitionist. Even though the slaves are increasing in numbers, even though their territory is being enlarged at every circle, yet, when we look abroad and see what is now being done in other lands, when we see human freedom engaging the attention of the nations of the earth, we may take courage; and while we perceive how it is assailed in our own land, still we know how impossible it will be to separate it from the question of the freedom of the slave, in that it is inseparably connected with it in France, and is beginning to be so in other countries.

Have we not evidence of progress even in our own country on this subject? A large public meeting was called the other day to hail the events of France.[7]

Mark the difference in this from former meetings. Why it was scarcely ten years since Pennsylvania Hall was burned by a mob, because the liberty of the colored man was advocated by white and colored people intermingled.—What are now the facts with regard to this large meeting in the great public square in the same city? Not only were the movements in regard to Freedom in the French colonies hailed by the white people present, but the colored people also came forward and were helped onward; they had their stand also: and was it confined to themselves alone? No, it was an *amalgamation meeting*! (Great applause.) Was it by privilege, as women sometimes have the privilege to hold a kind of play meeting? (Laughter.) No, the white people of that large gathering left their own speakers, to go among the colored crowd, and hear their speaker.

Look also at the condition of the colored people in respect to the ridicule which was once heaped upon them. Who are *they* now who ridicule us, because colored people are mingled in this meeting?[8] It is those whose ridicule is the scorn of the intelligent and wise of the nation. (Applause.). Now we find the colored people coming forth in intelligence, in moral worth, with increasing self-respect, and are respected by their white brothers; we see them stand side by side with those who have thus cruelly treated, oppressed, and trodden them down.

These, then, are the evidences of progress. Let the Abolitionist, who should be as the Jesus of the present age on the Mount Zion of Freedom, continue to say: "Ye have heard that it was said by them of old, thou shalt treat thy slaves kindly, thou shalt prepare them for freedom at a *future* day; but I say unto you hold no slaves at all, proclaim liberty now throughout the land to all the inhabitants thereof." Let this be the loud sounding jubilee that shall be uttered. Let us no longer be blinded by the dim theology that only in the far seeing vision discovers a millennium, when violence shall no more be heard in the land—wasting nor destruction in her borders; but let us behold it now, nigh at the door—lending faith and confidence to our hopes, assuring us that even we ourselves shall be instrumental in proclaiming liberty to the captive. But let there be increasing activity on the part [*of*] Abolitionists; they must not cease their labors and fold their hands, thinking their work done, because they have effected so much: they must not be satisfied with coming to these anniversary meetings, they must continue to work at home. It is the righteous that holds on his way, it is those who are faithful to the light that obtain more light; "he that is faithful in a little, shall be made ruler over more." "But if the light that is in you be darkness, how great is that darkness?" Have we not some apostates in the cause, who give evidence of the truth of this? Are there not some of whom it may be said, "it were better they had never known the way of righteousness, than that they should have turned from the commandments delivered unto them."

Let us go on, then, and make advancement by our faithfulness. When the pulpit cannot be enlisted, nor the Church aroused, it is the duty of Abolitionists to have no longer any fellowship with those unfruitful works of darkness, but rather reprove them, by separating from them, and touching not the unclean thing. Here is the advanced step the Abolitionists [*line illegible*] [*beg*]inning of their work many of them were enlisted, as some of them still are, with the political movements of the land,—the party politics of the nation. They hoped by thus uniting with these powers, to effect their work; but they have discovered that the situation of the country, the legal enactments, the statutes that the slaveholders have made, have been altogether tending to rivet the chains of the oppressed. They have, therefore, found it their duty to declare in the progress they have been called upon to make, that they must obey the command; "get thee from thy father's house, and come into a land that I shall show thee." They have found it their duty to come out against the Constitution and Government of the country, as it is at present construed. I know little, however, how to treat this part of the subject. I am glad, however, of the progress evident in this.

Glad also, of the evidence of advancement among Abolitionists as to the commercial and manufacturing relations of the country; it being made known that these are carried on by the gain of oppression, while the North, equally with the South, is "building its house by unrighteousness, and its churches by wrong, using its neighbor's service without wages, and giving him not for his work." It is beginning to be seen that they must despise the gain of oppression, and deny themselves the blood-bought sweets and the blood-stained cotton that has come through this corrupt channel. They feel that they are called upon not to be partakers of other men's sins, and not to participate in this matter, except so far as in the general admixture of things, they are necessarily involved, while they live in the country. The fact that they are also implicated in other oppressive systems—by the use of the products of human labor, ought not to discourage them. The Abolitionists have also developed the oppression existing in other lands. They have disclosed the sufferings of those engaged in the various laborious employments in England, Scotland, Ireland, and other portions of Europe.[9] The axe was first laid at the root of the corrupt tree of human slavery, and through this their eyes have been anointed more clearly to behold what are the universal rights of man. None are more ready to assist the oppressed laborer to obtain his rights than they. Let them then be faithful to their trust, so shall their work be blest, not only to the poor slave, but to all those who are in any way wronged and injured. If they are not true to their trust, if they are not united to go on in our work, but suffer themselves to slumber at their posts, what will be the result? Will there not then be reason to fear that the language of the martyr, Charles Marriott,[10] will be fulfilled: "that America, Republican America, will be the last stronghold of slavery in the civilized world"? (Applause.)

PD "Fourteenth Annual Meeting of the American Anti-Slavery Society," *National Anti-Slavery Standard*, May 18, 1848

    1. LM refers to the ongoing democratic revolutions in European countries, including France, Germany, Hungary, and Italy.
    2. In a letter to Sidney Gay, WLG noted that LM would not agree to speak at the forthcoming meeting unless her "mind should be stirred up" (May 1, 1848, WLG *Letters*, 3:554).
    3. The AASS had been organized on December 4, 1833. Its Declaration of Sentiments called on citizens "to remove slavery by moral and political action." It resolved to establish antislavery societies, hire antislavery agents, and "enlist the PULPIT and the

PRESS" on behalf of slaves (*Liberator*, December 14, 1833, in Palmer, 24). Antislavery Quaker forerunners were the Americans Benjamin Lundy (1789–1839) and Anthony Benezet (1713–84), and the British Friends Thomas Clarkson (1760–1846) and William Wilberforce (1759–1833).

4. The British Quaker Elizabeth Heyrick (1769–1831) urged boycotting West Indian sugar and published "Immediate, not Gradual Abolition" in 1824.

5. At the meeting, a "monster remonstrance" against slavery from 40,000 women of Scotland to the women of America was displayed (*Liberator*, May 19, 1848).

6. Possibly by Samuel J. Prescod (1806–71), a delegate to the 1840 World's Anti-Slavery Convention, who was the first person of color elected to the Barbados Assembly in 1843.

7. JM chaired the May 5 meeting at Franklin Hall, which approved the French proposal to abolish slavery in its colonies (*Pennsylvania Freeman*, May 11, 1848).

8. Frederick Douglass and William Wells Brown (ca. 1814–84), author of the *Narrative of William W. Brown, A Fugitive Slave*, were among the two thousand to three thousand present ("From the Annual Meeting," Henry C. Wright to Andrew Paton, *Liberator*, May 12, 1848).

9. Since the 1820s LM had been an advocate of "free produce," or boycotting goods produced by slave labor. Not all abolitionists agreed with this strategy (see Faulkner, 52–55; Carol Faulkner, "The Root of the Evil: Free Produce and Radical Antislavery, 1820–1860," *Journal of the Early Republic* [Fall 2007], 377–405). In *Three Months in Great Britain* (Philadelphia, 1841), JM wrote about working conditions among the poor in England and especially Ireland.

10. Hicksite abolitionist Charles Marriott (d. 1843), author of a pamphlet on "the Duty of Declining the Use of the Products of Slave Labour" (1835), was disowned by New York Monthly Meeting in 1841.

Women's Rights Convention, Wesleyan Chapel, Seneca Falls, New York, July 19–20, 1848[1]

[*July 19, Evening Session*]

The chief speaker was Lucretia Mott, of Philadelphia. This lady is so well known as a pleasing and eloquent orator, that a description of her manner would be a work of supererogation. Her discourse on that evening, whatever may be thought of its doctrine, was eminently beautiful and instructive. Her theme was the Progress of Reforms.[2] In illustrating her subject, she described the gradual advancement of the causes of Temperance, Anti-Slavery, Peace, &c., briefly, but in a neat and impressive style. She then alluded to the occasion which had brought the audience together—glanced at the rights and wrongs of women—and expressed the hope and belief that the movement in which she was then participating, would soon assume a grandeur and dignity worthy of its importance. She concluded by urging some of the gentlemen to let their voices be heard on the great subject.

"WOMEN'S RIGHTS CONVENTION," *Seneca Falls (N.Y.) Courier*, July 21, 1848, reprinted in *Liberator*, August 25, 1848.

[*July 20, Evening Session*]

Thomas M'Clintock then read several extracts from Blackstone, in proof of woman's servitude to man;[3] after which Lucretia Mott offered and spoke to the following resolution:

Resolved, That the speedy success of our cause depends upon the zealous and untiring efforts of both men and women, for the overthrow of the monopoly of the pulpit, and for the securing to woman an equal participation with men in the various trades, professions and commerce.

The Resolution was adopted.

* * * *

The meeting was closed by one of Lucretia Mott's most beautiful and spiritual appeals. She commanded the earnest attention of that large audience for nearly an hour.

Report of the Woman's Rights Convention, Held at Seneca Falls, N.Y., July 19th and 20th, 1848 (Rochester, 1848); Gordon, 1:82–83; WASM

1. LM's remarks at Seneca Falls are taken from two different sources. The *Seneca Falls Courier* gave more extensive coverage of her speech on July 19 than the one sentence in the *Report*, reprinted in Gordon, 1:75–78.
2. Most likely LM drew on her May 9, 1848, address to the AASS (Gordon, 1:84).
3. Thomas M'Clintock (1792–1876), Hicksite Quaker then living in Waterloo, New York (see Faulkner, 132–33). He read from the *Commentaries on the Laws of England*, by British jurist William Blackstone (1723–80), who wrote, "the very being or legal existence of the woman is suspended during the marriage, or at least is incorporated and consolidated into that of the husband" (quoted in Gordon, 1:86). For background on the convention, see Faulkner, 138–42; Palmer, 163–67; and Judith Wellman, *The Road to Seneca Falls: Elizabeth Cady Stanton and the First Woman's Rights Convention* (Urbana: University of Illinois Press, 2004), 194–204.

Women's Rights Convention, Unitarian Church, Rochester, New York, August 2, 1848

[*Morning Session*]

LUCRETIA MOTT arose and said, that although she was grateful for the eloquent speech just given, she must be allowed to object to some portions of it; such as styling "woman the better half of creation, and man a tyrant."[1] Man had become so accustomed to speak of woman in the language of flattering compliments, that he indulges in such expressions unawares. She said that man was not a tyrant by nature, but had been made tyrannical by the power which had, by general consent, been conferred upon him; she merely wished that woman might be entitled to equal rights and *acknowledged* as the equal of man, not his superior. Woman is equally tyrannical when she has irresponsible power, and we shall never place her in a true position until we have formed a just estimate of mankind as created by God. She thought there were some evidences of improvement—instanced the reform in the literature of the day, the sickly sentimentality of the "Ladies Department," which was fast disappearing, perceiving that the mind requires more substantial food.

* * * *

LUCRETIA MOTT replied in a speech of great sarcasm and eloquence. She said that the gentleman from New Haven had objected to woman occupying the pulpit, and indeed she could scarcely see how any one educated in New Haven, Ct., could think otherwise than he did.[2] She said, we had all got our notions too much from the clergy, instead of the Bible. The Bible, she contended, had none of the prohibitions in regard to woman; and spoke of the "honorable women, not a few," etc., and desired Mr. Colton to read his Bible over again, and see if there was anything there to prohibit woman from being a religious teacher.

She then complimented the members of that church for opening their doors to a Woman's Rights Convention, and said that a few years ago, the Female Moral Reform Society of Philadelphia applied for the use of a church in that city in which to hold one of their meetings; they were only allowed the use of the basement, and on condition that none of the women should speak at the meeting. Accordingly a D.D. was called upon to preside, and another to read the ladies report of the Society.[3]

[*Afternoon Session*]

Several resolutions were then read,[4] which were presented by AMY POST to the preliminary meeting, and referred to this without discussion. LUCRETIA MOTT ably advocated them, though she pronounced them too tame; she wished to have something more stirring.

* * * *

Mrs. MOTT remarked that our aim should be to elevate the lowly and aid the weak. She compared the condition of woman, to that of the free colored population, and dwelt upon the progress *they* had made within the last few years, urging woman to imitate them in their perseverance though oppression and prejudice, and said, "while woman is regarded as an inferior being, while the Bible is brought forward to prove the right of her present position, and while she is disposed to feel satisfied with it, all these efforts can do but little. We cannot expect to do much by meeting in Conventions for these borne down by the oppressor, unless the oppressed themselves *feel* and *act*, and while so little attention is paid to her education, and so little respect for woman." She spoke of the contrast in the education of boys and girls in England. The common schools there for boys show improvement; mathematics, and many of the higher branches are being taught; while girls are taught little more than to read and write, and keep their little accounts, sewing being the principal object of attention. The teacher told her it would not do to educate them, for the reason that it would unfit them for servants.

She said that she would grant that woman's intellect may be feeble, because she had been so long crushed; but is that any reason why she should be deprived of her equal rights? Does one man have fewer rights than another because his intellect is inferior? If not, why should woman? Let woman arise and demand her rights, and in a few years we shall see a different mental development. She regarded this as the beginning of the day when woman shall rise and occupy her appropriate position in society.

[*Evening Session*]

LUCRETIA MOTT replied by asking the question, which is preferable, *ignorant* or *intelligent* differences?[5]

Mr. SULLEY further asked, When two heads disagree, who must decide? There is no Lord Chancellor to whom to apply, but does not St. Paul strictly enjoin obedience to husbands, and that man shall be head of the woman?

Our ever-able LUCRETIA MOTT replied, that in an extensive acquaintance with the Society of Friends, she had never known any difficulty to arise on account of the wife's not having promised *obedience* in the marriage contract. She had never known any other mode of decision, except a resort to argument, and an appeal to reason; and although in some of the meetings of this Society, women are placed on an equality, none of the results so much dreaded have occurred. She said that many of the opposers of Woman's Rights, who bid us to obey the bachelor, St. Paul, themselves reject his counsel—he advised them not to marry. In general answer, she would quote, "One is your master, even Christ." Although Paul enjoins silence on women in the church, yet he gives directions how they should appear when publically speaking; and we have scriptural accounts of honorable women, not a few, who were religious teachers; *viz*.; Phebe, Priscilla, Tryphena, Triphosa, and the four daughters of Phillip, and various others.

PD *Proceedings of the Woman's Rights Convention, Held at Seneca Falls & Rochester, N.Y., July & August, 1848* (New York: Robert J. Johnston, 1870), 4, 5, 11–12, 13–14, WASM

1. Black activist William C. Nell (1816–74) "read an eloquent address, highly commendatory of the energies and rare devotion of woman" (*Proceedings*, 4). On the Rochester convention, see Nancy Hewitt, *Women's Activism and Social Change: Rochester, New York, 1822–1872* (Ithaca, N.Y.: Cornell University Press, 1984), 131–35; also Faulkner, 143; Palmer, 164.

2. Mr. Colton stated that women's place was in the home and he "should deprecate exceedingly her occupying the pulpit" (*Proceedings*, 5).

3. First organized in the 1830s, female moral reform societies fought prostitution and sexual immorality; they also identified the sexual double standard as a source of women's inequality. In a letter of February 20, 1840, to Maria Weston Chapman, LM described this controversy in the short-lived Female Moral Reform Society of Philadelphia. She concluded, "I expect to withdraw from the society" (Faulkner, 141; Palmer, 72).

4. Among the resolutions introduced (and passed almost unanimously at the convention's close) were ones that women should be equally represented with men in the government, that they should have the right to vote, that any laws discriminating against women should be overturned as "they reduc[ed] her almost to the condition of a *slave*," that female servants' wages should be increased, and that it was a woman's duty "whatever her complexion" (that is, race) "to assume . . . her true position of equality" (*Proceedings*, 15–16).

5. Richard Sulley, who worked with other radical Quakers in the Western New York Anti-Slavery Society (Minutes, Rochester Woman's Rights Convention, August 2, 1848, Phebe Post Willis Papers, Rare Books and Special Collections, University of Rochester), wondered about the deleterious effect equality "would have upon families" if the parents "should differ in politics, or the education of children" (*Proceedings*, 13).

"Sermon to the Medical Students," Cherry Street Meeting, Philadelphia, February 11, 1849[1]

> "Thee we reject, unable to abide
> Thy purity, till pure as thou art pure;
> Made such by thee, we love thee for that cause,
> For which we shunned and hated thee before.
> Then we are free. Then liberty, like day,
> Breaks on the soul, and by a flash from Heaven
> Fires all the faculties with glorious joy.
> A voice is heard, which mortal ears hear not,
> Till thou hast touched them; 'tis the voice of song,
> A loud Hosanna sent from all thy works;
> Which he that hears it, with a shout repeats,
> And adds his rapture to the general praise."[2]

This inspired language of the simple and artless poet, arose in my mind, as the secret prayer was offered:

> "Oh Thou my voice inspire,
> Who touched Isaiah's hallowed lips with fire!"[3]

Aware that, to many present, the opening of a meeting of this kind, without the harmonious note—the sacred hymn, would be, to say the least, novel; if, indeed, it would not divest it of the character of a religious meeting; and the service, of the nature of divine service;—aware also, that many are accustomed to the offering of prayer on their behalf; it is due to these to say, that some of us believe we may understand the sacred harmony and melodious note, arising in the soul—singing and making melody in the heart, without a dependence upon measured lines or the music of the voice; that we may no less in the secret of the heart, offer aspirations to Him who heareth the sincerely-devoted always, and maketh them "joyful in his house of prayer" without the intervention of words, or the aid of the priest or minister.

Is not the time arrived, that intelligent, spiritually-enlightened minds, should have such free access to this throne of grace, as to render less necessary, in the assemblies of the people, the delivery of the oral prayer? The recommendation of Jesus—the beloved, the blessed of God—appears to be to this end. "Enter into thy closet, and there pray in secret." Even while he bowed before the Father in outward prayer, he said: "I knew that thou hearest me always, but because of the people which stand by, I said it, that they may believe that thou hast sent me."

My prayer is that this occasion may be blessed, both to the hearers and to the speaker. That the hearers may be impressed with the importance of coming together for the consideration of their highest and best interests; and that the speaker also may be benefitted, by the deep impression that without divine aid, no good result can be expected or received.

I have desired for months, aye, for more than a year past, this opportunity with you, my friends; those of you for whom this meeting was especially called. In walking the streets of this city, at this season of the year, and approaching the places where ye are wont to gather for your instruction, maternal desires have often flowed from a heart, touched with solicitude for young men, separated from the tender care, the cautionary admonition of parents, of a beloved mother or sister; that you may be preserved in innocence and purity, while surrounded with the allurements of this city—the many temptations to vice of almost every description. While I may not speak of the things that are done in secret—delicacy may revolt from an exposure of the "rioting and drunkenness, the chambering and wantonness," that abound in our midst; due regard to the conviction of duty to invite you hither, will not allow me to be silent, and avoid an allusion to vices, of which some may think it, "a shame to speak."

I called you not here for any theological discussion. The religion we profess—the principles of Christianity we believe it our duty to inculcate, are not wrapped in mystery, or in the theories that are dividing and sub-dividing Christendom. In the view of many, the gospel is not preached, unless it embrace a certain scheme of salvation and plan of redemption. Faith in Christ has become so involved with a belief in human depravity and a vicarious atonement, imputed sin and imputed righteousness, that a discourse is divested of the character of gospel preaching, and regarded as little other than a mere lecture, if this scheme and plan—this system or theory, be not embraced.

I confess to you, my friends, that I am a worshipper after the way called heresy—a believer after the manner which many deem infidel. While, at the same time, my faith is firm in the blessed, the eternal doctrines preached by Jesus, and by every child of God from the creation of the world; especially the great truth that God is the teacher of his people himself; the doctrine which Jesus most emphatically taught, that the kingdom of God is within man—that *there* is his sacred and divine temple. This religious doctrine is simple, because it appeals to self-evident conviction. It is divested of mystery and mysticism, for it is not necessarily connected, with anything miraculous or extraordinary.

This noble gift of God, is as legitimate a part of man's being, as the moral sense with which he is quickened, the intellectual power with which he is so abundantly endowed, or as the animal propensities which are bestowed for his pleasure, his comfort, his good. All these are equally of divine origin. The religion offered to our acceptance tends in no wise to degrade man, to lessen his proper self-respect, or lead him to undervalue any of the gifts of the great Creator. I believe man is created innately good; that his instincts are for good. It is by a perversion of these, through disobedience, that the purity of his soul becomes sullied. Rejecting, then, the doctrine of human depravity, denying that by nature we have wicked hearts, I have every confidence, every hope, in addressing an audience of unsophisticated minds, that they may be reached, because I know that the love of God has previously touched their hearts; that He has implanted there, a sense of justice and mercy, of charity and all goodness. This is the beauty and divinity of true religion, that it is universal. Wherever man is found, these great attributes of Deity are there found—a nice sense of justice, a quick perception of love, a keen apprehension of mercy, and of all the glorious attributes of God; without puzzling the mind with attempts to reconcile His imagined infinite justice, with his prescience or his infinite power.

Christianity has been lamentably marred in its glory and beauty, by the gloomy dogmas of the schools. Many, however, are now enquiring for themselves, and acknowledging the heavenly light within them. They begin to understand the divine mission of Jesus; how it is that his coming was and ever is to bless mankind, by turning everyone from his iniquities; that in him, in the great truths which he preached, all nations shall be blessed.

In the exercise of the intellectual powers, in the advancement and discoveries in science, the vague theories of past ages are yielding to fact and demonstration, so as to require no dry argument to prove their truth to the hearer. So also in religion, the highest concern of man. Theories long held in darkness, are now brought to a strict examination; the people are exercising their rational powers, and bringing that which is offered them, to the light of truth in themselves. In this there is much to hope. The intelligent mind receiving truth in the obedience of a little child, comes to be quick in its perception and understanding, of all that belongs to the soul's salvation. This is no mere Quaker doctrine. Certain also of your own writers [*William Ellery Channing*] bear this testimony: "All mysteries of science and theology fade away, before the grandeur of the simple perception of duty, which dawns on the mind of the little child. He becomes subject from that moment to a law which no power in the universe can abrogate. He hears a voice which, if faithfully followed, will lead him to happiness, and, in neglecting which, he brings upon himself inevitable misery." This is the faith that we preach. It commends itself to the understanding and heart of the hearer, bringing him to a close examination of his daily life and practice. Another writer has observed: "The divine principle in man is given, not for the gratification of our curiosity, but for the government of our lives." Were this kept in view, the tone of the preaching on this day of the week would be changed. Abstract theories, as well as the attempted descriptions of a future world, would give place to the enforcing of the great practical duties of life. For while any verbal or ceremonial standard shall obtain, as the essential of Christianity, the standard of pure morality and practical righteousness is proportionally lowered. Especially so, if the theory shall teach, that good works are of no avail, making a wide separation between faith and practice. We have not so learned Christ.

I would then urge upon your consideration how far you are faithful to that in your hearts, which you have felt to be near you, in your solitary moments, when your prayer has ascended, as I doubt not it has at seasons, from the altar of every heart now present. When the quick response of the Father's love has shewn you in what your duty consists, how far, I would appeal to your best feelings, does your conscience acquit you, that you have been obedient to the heavenly vision, that you have confessed this divinity before men? Are ye willing to acknowledge to your companions, oh ye young men, that you cannot conscientiously do this, or are conscientiously bound to do that? Believe me, this confession of the Savior is of far more consequence to you, than a belief in a mysterious divinity. The divinity of Christ was not in mystery or miracle. It was in doing the will of his Father. He was "the Son of God with power according to the spirit of holiness."

Cultivate this ennobling view; be obedient to the truth; so will you make advancement in your several neighborhoods and become wiser than your teachers. You will exalt the standard of justice and mercy above that around which your Fathers have rallied. One object in inviting you here this evening was, to speak plainly, as regards the prevailing errors and sins of the time. This is a most important day—a notable age in which we live. Great principles of truth, noble views of humanity are being advocated. Faith in human nature is increasing, and many are coming, from every department of society, and investigating great questions of human concernment. The former dependence on the monopoly of the pulpit is broken, the people are thinking and acting for themselves and their fellow beings, in their various relations in society. And what is the result? Look at the great temperance movement. Is not this reformation one of the greatest moral miracles of our age? Many are the families in this city, as well as elsewhere, in this and other lands, many the mothers, daughters, and sons, who are hailing the temperance reform; who behold the rescue of their husbands and fathers, and are offering praises unto Him, who has put it into the hearts of the people to plead on their behalf, and to restore such as have fallen. Are you willing, my young friends, who are just coming upon the stage of action, in your various relations in society, to aid in carrying forward this great movement? Will you be faithful, in this great work, by example and precept, and "walk worthy the vocation unto which ye are called"? By practicing total abstinence from that which intoxicates, by ceasing to hand the wine as an act of hospitality to a friend, and by going forward to rescue those who have sunk to the lowest degradation, you may be instrumental in setting the feet of many upon the rock of Temperance, and putting the song of total abstinence into their mouths.

Your growing knowledge of the system of man impresses the importance of observing every law of his physical being, in order to be preserved a perfect whole. The light of truth has revealed to you your noble powers, and the responsibility of exercising them in the purity with which they have been bestowed. If then by your studies you are made intelligently acquainted with these things, and if superadded, you have a quick sense of the divinity in the soul, responding to and according with this knowledge, how increasingly incumbent is it upon you to carry out your principles among your associates, so that you be not found in the background in the great reformation that is taking place in human society.

This is a part of my religion—a part of true Christianity, and you must bear with me, my friends, if I press upon you duties, having reference to your different relations in society, to your intercourse with men, wherever you are placed. It has been my privilege and pleasure to meet with some of you in our Anti Slavery Rooms. When these have been disposed to come there, though perhaps from mere curiosity, to see what the despised abolitionist was doing, I have been glad to meet them, and to offer such considerations as would induce a reflection upon the relation which they bear to our fellow beings in their own country and neighborhood. This, in the view of many, is a subject of delicacy—lightly to be touched. Still it is an essential part of Christianity; and one object in asking your audience this evening, was to offer for your consideration some views connected with it, in the hope that you would at least patiently hear, and "suffer the word of exhortation."

There are many now looking at the subject of slavery in all its bearings, who are sympathizing with the condition of the poor and oppressed in our land. Although many of you may be more immediately connected with this system, yet it is coming to be regarded as not a mere sectional question, but a national and an individual one. It is interwoven throughout our country, into so much with which we have to do, that we may well acknowledge we are all, all "verily guilty concerning our brother." There is, therefore, the greater responsibility that we first examine ourselves and ascertain what there is for us to do in order that we may speedily rid ourselves of the great evil that is clinging to us. *Evil?*—this mighty *sin* which so easily besets us. There are those here who have had their hearts touched, who have been led to feel and have entered into sympathy with the bondman, and have known where the evil lies. I believe there is a work for you to do, when you return home, if you will be faithful to yourselves. You will be brought more deeply to enter into feeling with the poor and oppressed slave; you will find that the mission of the gospel is "to bind up the broken hearted, to preach deliverance to the captive." It would be a reflection upon the intelligence and the conscience of those who are here, to suppose that they would always resist the wisdom and power with which truth is speaking to their hearts upon this subject. There are many disposed to examine, to cultivate their minds and hearts in relation to their duties in this respect. May you be faithful, and enter into a consideration as to how far you are partakers in this evil, even in other men's sins. How far, by permission, by apology, or otherwise you are found lending your sanction to a system which degrades and brutalizes three millions of our fellow beings; which denies to them the rights of intelligent education, rights essential to them, and which we acknowledge to be dear to us.

Is this an evil that cannot be remedied? A remedy is nigh at hand, even at the door. The voice has been heard saying, "Proclaim liberty to the captive, the opening of the prison to them that are bound." "Proclaim ye liberty throughout all the land unto all the inhabitants thereof." To this land peculiarly is this language applicable. In this land especially are we called to be faithful in this subject. Be true to your convictions of duty then, oh my brethren, and you will have the blessing of beholding your own country purged of this iniquity, and be brought to acknowledge that the divine hand of mercy and love has been stretched over our land.

[Here a few persons, irritated by this reference to the question of slavery, left the meeting.][4]

It is not strange that the allusion to this subject should create some little agitation among you; and while I can but regret it, I stand here on behalf of the suffering and the dumb, and must express the desire, that there may be a disposition to hear and reflect, and then judge. I speak unto those who have ears to hear, who have hearts to feel. May their understandings not be closed! May they be willing to receive that which conflicts with their education, their prejudices and preconceived opinions. The subject of slavery you must know, is now agitating the country from one end to the other. The Church and the Legislative Hall are occupied with its discussion. It will be presented to you in all its various bearings, and let me urge such faithfulness to the light which you have, as shall prepare you to become able advocates for the oppressed. So shall the blessing descend upon you as well as upon those for whom the appeal is made. I should not be true to myself did I not thus urge this subject upon your consideration. When you have opportunities for meditation and reflection, when your feelings are soothed by the circumstances around you, may you be led to reflect upon your duties, and the responsibility of your position in society.

I long for you my friends, that you may be so true to your best feelings as to be preserved from the temptations with which you are surrounded, that your hearts may be preserved in unsullied purity. And in so far as any of you have swerved from the right, and have gone down to the chambers of dissipation, or been found in any indulgence from which your better nature would revolt, oh, be persuaded to make a stand in your course, to return, repent, and live. The God with whom we have to do, our tender Father "who is plenteous in redemption, and abundant in mercy," requireth only that those who have departed from the right shall return, shall give up their practices and walk uprightly. "As I live, saith the Lord, if the wicked shall depart from his wickedness and do that which is right in my sight, his wickedness shall no more be remembered. In the righteousness which he doeth he shall live." Are any of you, then approaching the state of the poor prodigal, in your indulgences, in giving unbridled license to your propensities? Remember, that the Father's love is ever near, that he will meet you as you may be disposed to turn from your course and return to his love. He will meet you, as the parable beautifully illustrates, and conduct you to his heavenly mansion, where his banner over you will ever be love.

When we read the numerous revelations unto the faithful of the present day, the advancement in truth and knowledge, in moral duty and obligation, we may well hail the age in which we live, the generation coming on the platform of humanity. Even now behold the nations, beginning to discuss the great question of peace. It has recently been brought before the British Parliament, as well as our own National Legislature, by the statesmen of the age, whether there is not a more rational mode of settling national disputes, than a resort to arms. The labors of an Elihu Burritt, and others not a few, to enlighten the people on both sides of the Atlantic, on the blessings of peace,[5] the glorious principle of the Messiah's reign—the readiness on the part of many, who have been heretofore wedded to their forms and religious services, now to regard war in its just light, as belonging to a barbarous age, unfit for the intelligence and spiritual growth of this time—the increasing faith that true principles are capable of being applied *now*, and that it is no visionary idea that the "sword may be beaten into the ploughshare and the spear into the pruning hook," that "nation shall not lift up sword against nation, neither shall they learn war anymore"—these all give evidence that "the kingdom of God is at hand," when "violence shall no more be heard in the land, wasting and destruction within her borders."

Not only is this hope filling the minds of many of the faithful, but they behold the spirit of mercy spreading over the country.—The prisons are visited; insane hospitals are erected for meliorating the condition of suffering humanity; efforts are made to remove the gallows and other barbarous inflictions from our midst; and an increasing regard for the poor and the lowly, leading many to give countenance to systems which shall raise these, and tend to equalize the condition of the human family. If that equality which is our nation's boast were recognized, we should not see large classes, crushed by existing monopolies, laboring for their scanty pittance. True christian democracy and republicanism would lead us not to "look upon our own things merely, but also upon the things of others." The practical precept of the Son of God requires, "whatsoever we would that men should do unto us, even so should we do unto them."

This then is the religion that is offered to your acceptance. I would not weary you with words, fully believing that each has a Teacher within himself; and obeying this, we need not that any man should teach us. It will be found superior to any other revelation, to everything external. Come then, to this principle, this Word of God in the soul, and you will be led into all righteousness and truth, though you may now shrink from their presentation here.

We have the revelation of God as much in this age as in any that has gone before us, and if we have faith, we shall do the things done in former times and greater—that which has been spoken in the ear in closets, shall be heard upon the house-top.

May all the difficulties that have hindered the progress of true religion be removed. May it be stripped of the gloomy appendages of the sects, and presented to view in its pristine purity and beauty, bearing the impress of the Divinity. Nothing of gloominess, nothing of dullness connected with it: nothing that debars from innocent cheerfulness, or conflicts with any of the rational powers with which we are gifted. The noble intelligence of man has not been allowed its proper place. There is ever a blessed harmony between every revelation of truth and reason, when not corrupted by the false dictates of appetite, or clouded by tradition and superstition.

Let us then be true to our calling, preserving the holy union of faith and righteousness, religion and humanity; so shall all the mists and clouds of ignorance and prejudice be dispelled. "The light of the moon shall be as the light of the sun, and the light of the sun as the light of seven days."

These great and glorious principles filling our hearts, liberty, like day, would break upon the soul, and fill all the faculties with glorious joy. A voice would be heard that mortal ears hear not till Thou, Oh God, hast touched them.

"But oh, Thou bounteous giver of all good,
Thou art of all thy gifts thyself the crown;
Give what thou canst, without thee we are poor,
And with thee rich, take what thou wilt away."[6]

And in acknowledging, O God, that every good and perfect gift is from above and cometh from thee, the Father of lights, we are bound to prostrate ourselves before thee and to bless thy holy name, and in remembrance of thy many mercies, to ask of thee a renewed clothing of that spirit which breathes glory to thee in the highest, on earth peace and good will to men; even thine own spirit which resisteth not evil, nor revengeth wrong, but which through thy power, is enabled to bless them that curse and to pray for them that persecute. We are sensible that this cannot be attained by our finite comprehension, that thou has veiled it from human understanding; for thou continuest to hide these things from the wise and simple and reveal them unto babes.

Grant, then, O Father, that we may be brought unto such a child-like state as to receive all the mysteries that belong to thy kingdom. We would ask to be kept so humble by thy mighty power that we vaunt not ourselves, saying that by our own hand we have gained any victory. But we would acknowledge, that thou only hast the power, and that to thee alone belongs all the glory.

PD "A Sermon to The Medical Students, Delivered by Lucretia Mott," Revised Phonographic Report (Philadelphia: Merrihew & Thompson, 1849).

1. In an undated letter (ca. December 1848) to her sister Martha Wright (1806–75), LM wrote, "The medical students, some of them, have asked me to have a meeting for them" (Hallowell, 309). Her audience was composed of students from the Thomas Jefferson Medical College and the University of Pennsylvania Medical School (Faulkner, 1–2).

2. William Cowper (1731–1800), "The Task" (1785).

3. Alexander Pope (1688–1744), "Messiah: A Sacred Eclogue, in Imitation of Virgil's Pollio" (1712).

4. LM wrote that "some 20 or 30 rose to go out, while the subject of slavery was pressed upon their attention—Part of this number halted at the door & remained to the close —" (to Joseph and Ruth Dugdale, March 28, 1849, in Palmer, 181).

5. In March 1847 the Society for the Promotion of Permanent and Universal Peace petitioned Parliament to set an example to the world by abandoning the "war system" and adopting arbitration in order to make war "all but impossible." American peace activist Elihu Burritt (1810–79) had helped sponsor a peace congress in Brussels in September 1848 (*London Times*, March 10, 1847; *Liberator*, January 26, 1849).

6. Cowper, "The Task."

American Anti-Slavery Society, Minerva Rooms, New York City, May 8, 1849

Lucretia Mott, of Philadelphia, hoped we should not rely for the interest of these meetings, upon our agents and our habitual speakers, but that every one present, like our friend who has just sat down,[1] would speak "as the spirit gave him utterance." We need, she continued, that our confidence in the might of

Truth should be enlarged and strengthened. Much had been said to-day of the tremendous power of the Church and the Government in obstructing anti-slavery work;[2] and yet, as was said of old, "wine is strong and woman is strong, but truth is stronger than all," so would she now say. The Constitution is strong, and the Church is strong, but the Truth is stronger than both, it is omnipotent, and it will triumph yet.

Many now are glorying in the Church, and exulting in her strength, her majesty, and her fair proportions, and they proudly say of her, as some did to Jesus of the temple, Master, see what goodly stones and what buildings are here! But there is a Jesus now, there is a well beloved Son of God in the present, who says to the self-deluded admirers, "I tell you there shall not be left one stone upon another, that shall not be thrown down!" Mrs. M. went on to enumerate the successive points gained in the anti-slavery contest, emancipation at home in numerous cases, full emancipation in the British West India islands, prejudices vanquished, the eyes of so many morally blind opened, so extensive an interest awakened in behalf of the slave, so many colored men now to be found among our most eloquent and welcome speakers, and as editors, colored men admitted to the bar and to the medical profession, and to posts which no *woman* as yet was allowed to fill. She spoke with much respect and interest of the *Louisville Examiner*, and several other journals in the slaveholding States, of the hope she felt of the coming Convention in Kentucky, &c., &c.[3]

PD "Fifteenth Annual Meeting of the American Anti-Slavery Society," *Liberator*, May 18, 1849

1. Mr. Haydock of Hudson, who identified himself as an "ex-wood sawyer," stated he had voted for slaveholders before but now had come to consider "every man . . . whatever his condition or his color, as my brother, and I will vote no more for his oppressor" (*Liberator*, May 18, 1849).
2. Abolitionists Parker Pillsbury (1809–98), Wendell Phillips (1811–84), and Frederick Douglass had all condemned the church's toleration of slavery; Phillips and Douglass also criticized U.S. politicians and laws (*Liberator*, May 18, 1849).
3. The abolitionist paper *Examiner* was published between 1847 and 1849. At its convention to amend its constitution in October 1849, Kentucky voted resoundingly to retain slavery (James A. Ramage and Andrea S. Watkins, *Kentucky Rising: Democracy, Slavery, and Culture from the Early Republic to the Civil War* [Lexington: University Press of Kentucky, 2011], 296).

Cherry Street Meeting, Philadelphia, November 4, 1849

What are the abuses and what are the proper uses of the Bible, and of this day of the week? This question is of some importance for us to seek to answer aright lest we should fall into the popular error that prevails upon this subject. Mingling as we do in religious Society generally, adopting some of its forms, and some of its theories, we have need to be upon our guard lest we fall into the superstition and error and before we are aware, become bigoted in our opinions and denunciatory in our conduct. We know well that in Christendom generally it is assumed

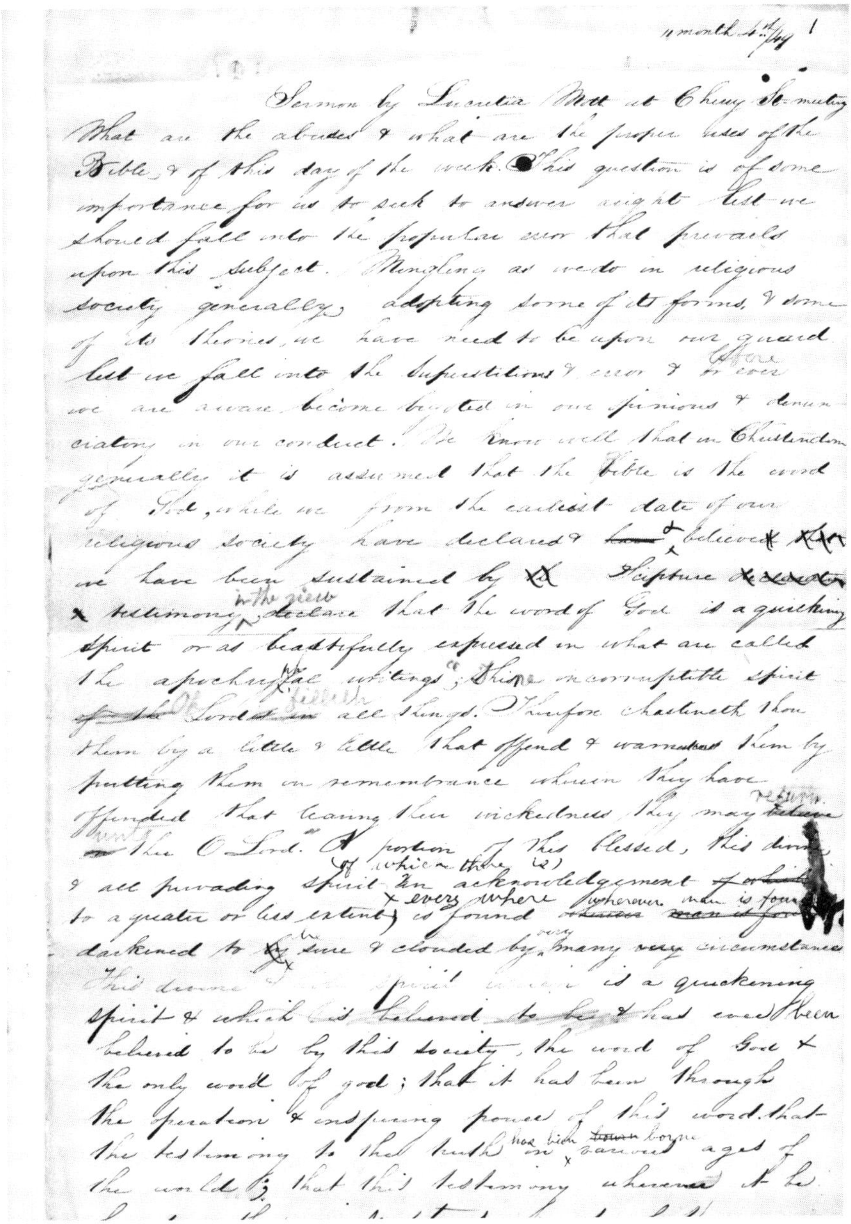

Figure 4. Stenographic report of Mott's November 4, 1849, sermon. (Courtesy of the Friends Historical Library, Swarthmore College)

that the Bible is the word of God, while we from the earliest date of our religious Society have declared and believe we have been sustained by Scripture testimony in the view that the word of God is a quickening spirit or as beautifully expressed in what are called the apocryphal writings, "Thine incorruptible spirit Oh Lord filleth all things. Therefore chasteneth thou them by a little and little that offend, and warnest them by putting them in remembrance wherein they have offended that leaving their wickedness, they may return unto thee O Lord." A portion of this blessed, this divine and all pervading spirit of which there is an acknowledgment to a greater or less extent, every where is found wherever man is found, darkened to be sure and clouded by very many circumstances. This divine and holy spirit which is a quickening spirit and has ever been believed to be by this Society the word of God and the only word of God; that it has been through the operation and inspiring power of this word that the testimony to the truth has been borne in various ages of the world; that this testimony, wherever it be found either in Scriptures or out of them, is but a corroboration of the word and not the word itself; and that word of God, which is quick and powerful which showeth the thoughts and intent of the heart, that engrafted word which is able to save the soul, we find spoken in the Scriptures, but we no where find the Scriptures called the word of God by themselves. We read of one of the ancient Hebrew writers who after being converted to a purer faith, commended the Scriptures as being able to give knowledge of that which is to come, being able to make wise into salvation; giving knowledge of a purer way, but only through the faith of Jesus Christ. What is this faith of Jesus Christ; not as theologians define it, faith in the Trinity and a vicarious atonement, not faith in a system, a mere scheme of salvation, a plan of redemption. Faith of Jesus Christ is faith in the truth, faith in God and in man. The life that I now live in the flesh, said the Apostle, I live by the faith of the son of God, who loved me and gave himself for me. Well what is this other than a faith similar to that which Jesus held, the faith of the Son of God? How many chosen sons of God who have not loved their lives unto death, who have given themselves for their brethren even as the Apostle recommended, that as he Jesus laid down his life for the brethren so do we also lay down our lives one for another? This then perhaps is the more intelligent reading of these Scriptures and of what is spoken of as the word of God and as the saving faith of the Christian. The great error in Christendom is that the Bible is called the word, that it is taken as a whole, as a volume of plenary inspiration and in this way it has proved one of the strongest pillars to uphold ecclesiastical power and hireling priesthood. What has been the power of this book? Is it not uniformly taken among all the professors to establish their peculiar creeds, their dogmas of faith and their forms of worship, be they ever so superstitious? Is not the Bible sought from beginning to end for its isolated passages wherewith to prove the most absurd dogmas that ever were palmed off upon a credulous people; dogmas doing violence to the divine gift of reason with which man is so beautifully endowed; doing violence to all his feelings, his sense of justice and mercy with which the Most High has seen fit to clothe him? The Bible has been taken to make man from his very birth a poor corrupt sinful creature, and to make his salvation depend upon the sacrifice of Jesus in order that he should be saved. When his understanding has been imposed on by a Trinity and atonement in the manner that it has, well may we say that the abuse of the Bible has been a means of strengthening priestcraft, and to give sanction to sectarian ordinances and establishments. We find the religionists, especially those whose greater interest it is to build up sect than to establish truth and righteousness in the earth, and probably many of these in the vain idea that by this means they shall do the other more effectually, ready to flee to the Bible for authority for all their mysteries, their nonsensical dogmas, that have been imposed as articles of belief, as essential doctrines of Christianity. But also my friends has there not been an unworthy resort to this volume to prove the rightfulness of war and Slavery, and of crushing woman's powers, the assumption of authority over her, and indeed of all the evils under which the earth, humanity has groaned from age to age? You know as well as I do how prone the sectarian has been to flee to the Bible to find authority for war, and indeed in the very existence of war, and there is a disposition because of the undue veneration of these records, to regard our God even now as a God of battles. We do not duly discriminate between that comparatively dark age, when they set up their shouts of victory for their successes in their wars whether aggressive or defensive, and the present. There is not sufficient allowance for the state that they were in at that time. Because of the veneration paid to the Bible, we find, even down to the present time, the overruling providence of God is claimed as giving countenance to the most barbarous and horrid wars, that are even in this day, cursing and disgracing the nations of the earth. Slavery, you know how ready the apologists for Slavery and these apologists, to the shame of the church be it spoken, have been abundantly found in the pulpit, have screened themselves behind their imagined patriarchal institution and what sanction has been given to this greatest of all oppressions, this most wicked system which the English language furnishes no words where with rightly to depict the enormity of its cruelty. And this is done even to the present time by these priests of sect, these monopolizers of the pulpit. These ecclesiastics of our day have sought authority from the Bible, and made it the plea for the Sabbath, by quotations there from, that it was of God's sanction, that it was a patriarchal institution. You know as regards sensual indulgency the great obstacles that were thrown in the way of the temperance reformation by the use that was made of the Bible, by authority sought, for indulging in the intoxicating cup. We may rejoice that truth has been found stronger than all these, that thus the great efforts that have been made in our day for peace, for human freedom, for temperance, for moral purity, for the removal of all oppressions and monopolies that are afflicting mankind, have been to a considerable extent successful notwithstanding such obstacles as a popular priesthood, a popular clergy, and a popular belief and the use of the Bible, have placed in the way of these great reformations.

See now the resort to the Bible to prove the superstitious observances of a day. The manner in which this day is observed is one of the strongholds of priestcraft. It forms one of the pillars which must be broken down and which will be broken down, before an enlightened Christian faith. But then it needs that there should [be] boldness to declare this faith. It needs there should be faith to act in accordance with this and to declare the abuse that is now made of the Bible, in seeking to establish forms of worship which long since should have passed away. Superstitions, baptisms, communion tables, and devotions of various kinds and orders, have there found their sanction by improper reference to this volume. Thus by taking the examples of the ancients, even though they may have been comparatively modern, though they may have been disciples of Jesus in his day, yet I believe there is no rightful authority, no Scripture authority, for taking their example as sufficient authority for the continuance of the practice in the present day. We are not thus to use the example or practice of the ancients. It may have been well for them, coming from under the cloud of superstition formerly. They may still have needed their outward school masters to bring them to a higher position, a higher sphere, a higher understanding, a higher dispensation, but are we, because we find that they continued their type under the law, or their baptism which was of John because they continued in their Sabbath observances, are we to do these things? I tell you nay. This divine word which we believe to be our sufficient teacher, draws us away from a dependence upon books, or everything that is outward, and leads us onward and upward in the work of progress, towards perfection. Were we to come to the light we should have less need of the ordinances, for it would lead us away from the customs of the religious world. If we have come as a babe, like stated in the language of the Apostle what need he says, have we any more of these ordained; touch not, taste not, handle not for all are designed to punish with the using but the substance is of Christ. And if ye come to this then let no man judge you as regards meats and drinks or new moons, or Sabbath days.

Remember the Sabbaths are but a shadow of things to come but the substance is of Christ. Those whose dependence is upon apostolic authority cannot find it, but there is notwithstanding a superstitious veneration put in the clerical explanation of that authority which has led many most mournfully to pin their faith upon ministers' sleeves. Therefore we see the religious world gone on satisfying itself with its mysteries, with its mere theories of religion. These they regard as useful but which are really anything but true religion. We see them going on satisfied with their forms and devotions, taking comparatively little interest in the great subject of truth and humanity.

But are those all or the only uses that are made of the Bible and of the first day of the week, for the day has been consecrated to the expounding of these dogmas and the enforcing of useless forms? Are there not also other uses of these, has there not been another reading of the Scriptures? The proper use of them I can verily believe has been understood and is increasingly understood by very many and that the day is a day also for strengthening good feelings, for exciting religious veneration in a profitable way. We can freely admit that the Bible, in the intelligent reading and growing intelligence with which it is perused with proper discrimination, without taking it as a volume of inspiration but only acknowledging that which is inspired, the truth which is eternal and divine being of value to the soul, has [*uses?*] not a few and with a proper appreciation of the day, it also has its uses. How many have found consolation in Scripture testimonials suited to their almost every state? When they were in the low dungeon, then the Lord delivered his angels, and those who are now in a similar state can understand these testimonies and they too sing their song on the banks of deliverance. These find true consolation in these corroborating testimonies for they have passed through similar scenes with those who are now suffering and who are now rejoicing. These are feelings leading to praises and acclamations unto the highest. How many are the testimonies of these Scriptures which suit the state of those who are desirous for truth and righteousness to prevail on the earth, how beautiful is the testimony from the beginning to the end of the Scriptures to the discriminating servant of the highest that is born to righteousness, truth, uprightness, justice and mercy, peace, and universal love. The law of the Lord is declared to be perfect, to be pure, upright and clean, and to abide forever and those who obey the word, are made clear sighted. This truth when heard and suffered to be as a law is as a candle, as a light leading and enlightening the path that leads into the right way. How satisfactory then are the corroborating testimonies of Scripture, but not more so than the testimonies of many other servants of God? Why not regard all the testimonies of the good, as Scripture, recorded in every age and in every condition of life? These Scriptures are valuable because they bring together the testimonies of so many ages of the world, but are there not equal testimonies born to the truth that are not bound in this volume? Certainly there are and we do err not knowing the Scriptures, nor the power of God when we limit the Scriptures, when we limit the truth or indeed when we set so high a value on these Scriptures as to suffer our veneration to lead us to receive truth more from this source than from any other. There is one source which is higher than this, and when we come to it we are drawn away, to some extent from all external dependences, from all outward authorities. And further as regards these Scriptures, if we read them intelligently we shall not fasten upon ourselves any form of worship or conversion, because those in ancient time were in the practice of them. We shall look at these and make all allowance for the state that they were in and suffer them to pass by. As regards days, we shall not be venerators of days because the ancients were, and indeed I have often thought that the veneration which professing Christians paid to this day far exceeds that which was enjoined upon the Jews, among whom the observances were instituted. Well has a modern writer said, that the consecration of the Sabbath or one day in seven, indicates the desecration of the other six, that the consecration of our Churches indicates the desecration of our homes, the consecration of a class leads to the desecration of the great mass of the people, the consecration of this leads to the desecration of others, rather than the dedication of them to holiness and sacredness.[1] I knew a woman some years ago who would spend every day in the week in reading all the novels that were issued from the press and on the first day she would take her Bible and read a chapter and one of Blair's sermons,[2] then close up the books, and state what she had done, and look with a kind of religious horror upon those who would be engaged pursuing some innocent occupation, and whose every time was consecrated to truth and duty, God and humanity. This latter class find a portion of every day for religious devotion and instructive reading. Oh my Friends, the abuse that there is in this day, leading people to regard with a kind of pious horror anything which is innocent in itself. This is a superstition which we at least ought to be rid of. Our fathers suffered enough in bearing their testimonies to the equality of days for us not to be found going back to the beggarly elements. Let us hail, in the present state of Society, the existence of this day as set apart as a day of rest and it may be too of innocent recreation to the toil worn labourer, while there is a disposition to exact so much of him through the week, leaving little time for rest and innocent recreation, and for religious improvement, on other days. Let us hail this as a season that shall give such time though it may not be so used. Let us also hail it as a day furnishing opportunity for exciting the religious veneration of those who still require this for their better nature, be that either in psalmody, in melody [or] in prayer or in some other way suited to their views of what belongs to the day.

I also enjoy while I am coming down to my chosen place of gathering, the liberty, the freedom that is manifested in our fellow citizens, going each to his chosen places of worship. I also enjoy the cleanliness of our courts and alleys, and the little children who one day in a week have on what they call their Sunday clothes and go forth in a feeling of cleanliness and innocent enjoyment. While we feel that there may be these advantages, let us earnestly protest against the superstition which had led to penal enactments to enforce the observance of this day. Let us protest against this spirit for it is a spirit of priestcraft. It is the clerical and ecclesiastical power that's gaining the ascendency in this country so far as it is allowed by the public opinion of the country. It's gaining upon the people and it will make inroads upon us until our liberties are sapped, until we are brought under a yoke which neither we nor our fathers were able to bear. Let us then my friends cherish a religion which shall be rational and which shall be reasonable in its observance and in its requirements. Let us keep hold of the faith that is in accordance with reason and with the intelligent dictates of the pure spirit of God. Let us ever hold up the supremacy of this spirit of this divine guidance as far above all the leadings of men and the teaching of books or the veneration that is imposed by the observance of these, or by worship in meeting houses. We need to understand the worship that is more in our everyday life, that is manifested more by efforts of love and of devotion to truth and righteousness. We need to consecrate ourselves more to God and to humanity and less to forms and ceremonies and to verbal faith. With the proper uses of the day and of the Bible and with the proper use of the Church and of our religious institutions we may then be greatly benefited and improved. But there will be divisions and subdivisions until we come so fully to understand that truth which leadeth into the liberty; that he that upholds truth designs that there should be no usurpation, no power delegated upon one portion of the people over another. Until we come to this, until there is an intelligent testimony born against ecclesiastical usurpations, against hierarchical institutions, against the favored few in the congregation, there must be divisions and subdivisions among us. These things must needs be; therefore when we hear of wars and armors of wars in our midst, let us not be troubled but know full well that the end is not yet, but that we must trust in the growing light and intelligence which is spreading over the human family and which is marking those who are desirous to obtain the right, who are hungering and thirsting after greater righteousness. That in this growing intelligence, these evils which still cling to sect, will be removed, and one great means of removing these, is the diffusion of knowledge among both male and female. The usurpations of the Church and clergy, by which woman has been so debased, so crushed, her powers of mind, her very being brought low, and a low estimate set upon these, are coming to be seen in their true light, but woman must avail herself of the increasing means of intelligence, education and knowledge, she must rise also in a higher sphere of spiritual existence, and suffer her moral nature to be developed, her mind to be made right in the sight of God and then will the time speedily come when the influence of the clergy shall be taken off of woman, when the monopoly of the pulpit shall no more oppress her, when marriage shall not be a means of rendering her noble nature subsidiatory to man, when there shall be no assumed authority on the one part nor admitted inferiority or subjection on the other. One of the abuses of the Bible, for apostolic opinion has been taken, and no doubt false opinion, for there have been abundant quotations and some mistranslations in order to make the Apostle say what the priests declare he did say, has been to bind silence upon woman in the Churches, fasten upon her that kind of degrading obedience in the marriage relation which has led to countless evils in Society and indeed has enervated, and produced for us a feeble race. Oh my friends these subjects are subjects of religious interest and of vast importance. I would that there were successors coming forth in this great field of reform. The Almighty is calling upon both man and woman to open their mouths and judge righteously, to plead the cause of the poor and needy and many there are thus emphatically called to lift-up the voice and declare the truth of God and these will give evidence of the divinity of their mission, just as Jesus did. The spirit of the highest is upon me, the spirit of the Lord is upon me, because he hath anointed me to preach the gospel, because he hath anointed me to bind up the broken-hearted, to preach deliverance to the captive, the opening of the prison doors to them that are bound, and to preach the acceptable ear of the Lord. May these then not be afraid, may they not be ashamed to lift up their voices for the right, to let the sound be heard far and wide and let it go forth to the ends of the earth, that the spirit of the Lord is come upon these and they are called to go forth on this mission. A blessing will be to them for they will acknowledge that the highest has been their mouth and wisdom, their tongue and utterance have been of the Lord that whereas they were a few and feeble but that they have been made strong and mighty in him who is ever with his children, who ever giveth them mouth and wisdom, tongue, and utterance to speak that which he commandeth, strength and perseverance in accordance with right; preaching and doing that which is right by a blessed example, by a pure life, for this is the most effectual preaching of righteousness.

Stenographic Report, Sermons, Mott Manuscripts, FHL

    1. Ralph Waldo Emerson (1803–82), "Domestic Life" (1840).
    2. Most likely the five-volume *Sermons* (1777–1800) by Hugh Blair (1718–1801), a Scottish Presbyterian minister.

Cherry Street Meeting, Philadelphia, November 6, 1849

    Rachel in her sermon stated that if we kept our eyes singly directed to the light we should not be concerned about the existing evils in society.[1]
    I view these Quarterly Meetings as no ordinary occasions. They are opportunities for us to compare ourselves and our progress with our predecessors, with our fathers, and with the great principles upon which they were established, and which we also profess to act upon. They are occasions when we may confer together and seek to provoke one another to love and good works, when we may endeavour to stir up the pure mind one in another by way of remembrance. I have believed that if this Society continues with any degree of prosperity, if it be marked as any living thing, as having any life in it, it must be by the evidence furnished in these examinations of ourselves, in our Quarterly and other meetings, and other opportunities. If we have any evidence furnished of its progress, it is by our progress and advancement in the truth. There is in all religious associations a constant tendency to retrogression. Having begun in the spirit there is a disposition too manifest to seek to be made perfect by the flesh, to go back again to the weak and beggarly elements and to desire, and be willing, to be brought into bondage again. The only way in which we can be preserved from this downward step, from this backsliding, is that we go forward, that we advance, that we follow the light, not that we sit down in listless indolence. The great heresy that is proclaimed in our Society, sometimes is of waiting in a kind of indifference for the light to come to us. This has been one of the most fatal heresies, the most fatal, to the progress of this religious body, of any that has ever been proclaimed. That we may be serving him, whoever seeketh fruits at the hands of his children, by doing nothing, by as has been expressed, waiting and failing to enter into the great harvest field, the great vineyard of the Lord with the paltry plea that no man hath hired us, that we have not been called to this or that work. In every principle, in every testimony that the fathers of this people held, there is progress, there is advancement, and in none more than in the great fundamental one of the guidance of the divine light to the souls of the children of men; that in obedience to this, as our fathers were led out of the traditions that specially marked their age, they had to bear their emphatic and loud testimony against the great theological errors that were existing among the people, preventing their progress, as well as against the great

practical sins of their day. They were going actively against these, having their hearts in the work, being troubled because of these great evils that were afflicting society. Many went forth endeavouring to enlighten the people, being concerned to strengthen their brethren, and we if we continue to make progress and advance and become established, strengthened, and settled on this immutable foundation of God, this inspeaking word in the soul, will manifest it by our works.

There is no more certain law of God of his providence, no more certain evidence of the invariable nature of his law, than the stamp that he has set upon a people, upon religious society as well as upon nations, and individuals, showing just what they are by their fruits. If this Society through the means of its Quarterly and other meetings wherein to take cognizance of the state of its progress, shall not give evidence of progress of advancement, as the light is increasingly opened unto us, surely then in the eternal providence of God, Ichabod will be written upon thy walls, the glory will be departed from thee. And vain will it be for us to cling to the outward habiliments of sect, to say, master behold what a beautiful building is ours, verily it may be said not one stone shall be left upon another of all these systems of all these outward buildings glorious though they may have been in their day, which shall not be thrown down. Then in the advance of society, as has been declared here, that people, that society, that individuals cannot advance while they have the clogs of superstitions and tradition around them holding them back, it is incumbent upon us my friends if we be made sensible of this superstition that we be faithful to the light which we have entering our [*dissent?*] and it may be our earnest protest against them. There are many in this Society who have as much occasion to protest against the traditional views of the Scripture, of the Sabbath, or of the first day of the week, of the Church ordinances therein performed as ever any had in any age of the world. I would that there were not in any a disposition to please men rather than to please God. I would that there were a disposition in us to be willing to be made of no religious reputation among the Orthodox people of our day but to declare openly uncompromising and without reserve and without clothing our sentiments in mystical forms of expression. Our faith in simplicity, the truth as it is in Jesus, as we comprehend it in Jesus. That we may not be bound to Bible traditions, to Sabbath traditions, by imagined divinity of Christ's tradition, by the absurd doctrine of atonement, but that we may stand by the truth as simply and clearly manifested and be willing to take the consequences of all charges that may be made of infidelity or unsoundness of doctrine even though it lead us to be cast out of the synagogue and our names cast out as evil for truth's sake.

Shall we not be able to drink of the cup which Jesus drank, shall we not be able to bear the Baptisms with which he was baptized? I believe we shall and also be kept in the very spirit that would say, father forgive them for they know not what they do, forever blessed eternally blessed be the name of our father, and we should feel the invaluable nature of this treasure. There is a spirit as one said formerly, that I feel, that resisteth not evil nor revengeth wrong but which enables us to bear all things. Paul spoke of a spirit in the outward, which is of a contrary nature. The former spirit may be attained, is attainable. Then let us not fear of any consequences to ourselves. Let us not hesitate to declare openly the whole counsel of God, as we may be called upon to do it.

We behold society holding back. We see that it is not keeping pace with the great advances in the Church of Christ. Remember that the Church of Christ is not our little petty Society, nor any other sectarian organization. That Church is composed of living members and these living members are sent forth even as Jesus was sent forth, with the glorious gospel of peace to proclaim in the earth. The highest evidence that these give of the divinity of their mission, even as Jesus gave of his mission, is that the spirit of the highest is upon them, because they are thus anointed, because they thus go forth to bind up the broken hearted, to preach deliverance to the captive, the opening of the prison doors to them that are bound. Well then we know that in this Church of Christ there are living members now going abroad in the earth, spreading the benign doctrines of the blessed principles of peace, seeking to put an end to the wars that are ravaging the earth and despoiling nations, that are bringing lamentation and woe unto the families of men. The harvest truly is great, pray ye therefore to the Lord of the harvest that he will send forth labourers into this field. We should all be filled with this spirit which shall desire the universal spread of peace on earth and goodwill among men. Let it be regarded as a zeal without knowledge, though you may be accused of being over zealously affected. I tell you nay, it is good to be zealously affected in a good cause, and I rejoice in the great efforts that are being made for the spread of true principles and the carrying of them out in our intercourse with our fellow beings. We should all advance beyond what our fathers saw, and hence it was that Elias Hicks hesitated to put his own sentiments upon paper, because he believed that the generations following him would see truth more clearly than he and his contemporaries saw it. It is the beauty and the glory of truth that there is this progress in it. It is beautiful to behold this. We see many giving up their undue attachment to political parties and to governments, giving up their constitutional veneration, and refusing to have any lot or part in a government and constitution which are based upon the sword, the ultimate resort of which is the destroying weapon. We see this progress in the divine principle of nonresistance, and we hail the day when there shall be greater advances upon this subject. If any sect, be it our own self styled favoured Society or any other society or organization, shall set its face against this progress, if any minister in society shall be found endeavouring to give check to any such progress, mark it my friends, derision will come upon these, Ichabod will be written upon its walls, the glory has departed will be stamped upon any such society. It is well for us then in these Quarterly Meetings, in our examinations, to query now whether those who are chosen messengers, officers and high seat occupants of this Society, are those who are keeping up to the advance guard of progress in the peace reformation; whether they are full of the political periodicals of the day; whether they are going to the polls and voting for warriors and slaveholders; whether they are showing they have the true allegiance to peace principles which their profession would lead us to look for.² So also as regards the great testimony against slavery. We are called, as I believe every living member of the [*ms torn Chur*]ch of Christ is called, to bear a testimony [*ms torn again*]st all oppression, all wrong and all unright[*eousness ms torn*]. There are many such living members [*ms torn Chur*]ch of Christ, up and down in society [*ms torn*], who are indeed earnestly protesting, who are indeed going against this vast iniquity and seeking to enlighten the public mind upon this subject. If this Society or any of its accredited ministers, its members, its officers or high seat occupants, shall be giving their influence against this great progress, and this great and mighty reformation that there is in the earth; more than this if they shall be found enriching themselves with the gain of oppression and reveling in the sweets of unrequited labour that comes through such a polluted channel; if they shall be found engaging in building their houses by unrighteousness and chambers by wrong, living upon their neighbours' service without hire, giving him not for his work, it is certain that declension will follow, and we will be scattered and divided. On the other hand if there be any consistent testimony upon this subject, it will lead to practices far in advance of any practices of our fathers, for they were involved in it to a greater or less extent than we now are. However a profession may be made that a testimony against slavery belongs to this Society, there will be a declension, among us, we will be marked as a declining people, that can never make progress unless we do something. Our fathers never made progress but by holding up righteousness and uprightness, high above all speculations, even the speculation that we may be faithful to the light and do nothing. Beware of this heresy. Beware of the heresy that will lead us into the belief, that we should do nothing to remove the great evils that are in the earth. I rejoice that the Church of Christ is manifested, is marked, is stamped by the inviolable seal of the highest, in that its members are found arrayed against all unrighteousness and wrong, against all iniquity in high and in secret places, against all monopolies that exist in society. I rejoice that Christian democracy is spreading in society at large. Both in other countries and in this, there is beginning to be, at least, a better appreciation of the rights of man. We hail then this true Christian understanding of the equal brotherhood of man. If we as a society continue to uphold aristocracy and give countenance to monopolies which furnish facilities to the rich to become richer, and cause the poor to become poorer, our society can never prosper. It must go down, it will go down, let us cling ever so tightly to its forms, to its outward dress or address, to its arrangements and disciplinary expedients, however these may have been, and are useful. There is nothing that will preserve the life and growth of this people, but by living in its principles, and being faithful in working them out. Herein will my heavenly father, the heavenly father of Jesus, be glorified that his children bring forth much fruits. Mark if there are among the parables one more than another impressing active duties upon the people and the necessity of being fruit bearing branches; it is in this, which Jesus held up to view, showing the importance of actively pursuing and fulfilling the great duties of life, by bearing fruits. How is it in the temperance reformation? Are we by our own practice, and occasionally by our accredited preaching in our Meetings, giving a check to this noble reformation? Are we showing by the stamp upon our countenances that we are still indulging in the intoxicating wine, beer, and cider while this great reformation has reached almost to the uttermost ends of the earth? Depend upon it if this be the case, our testimony against intemperance will be but as a show, as a form, and we shall not have evidence that we are advancing in this also. I hope better things my friends. I trust that this great testimony has found its place among the younger members, at least of our Society, influencing the fathers and mothers so far as to banish the decanters, and bringing us down to the pure water, by which our minds are kept clearer to discriminate, our morals purer, our hearts cleaner for the reception of the blessed light of Christ. May then these Quarterly Meetings be seasons of self examination, and for holding up great principles wherein there is progress one unto another. I could not let this opportunity pass without holding up these things before us, so that we may be profited. If we are really profited by these, it must be by coming home and bringing these principles to bear upon our every day conduct in life. Blessed shall he be who is ready to say, here am I O Lord, send me into the great harvest field of reform where there shall be labour and this labour shall be done

A few words towards the close of this sermon were not heard distinctly. S[medley]. D[arlington], reporter

---

Stenographic Report, Sermons, Mott Manuscripts, FHL

1. Rachel C. Rogers (ca. 1803–82), Philadelphia Hicksite minister (Palmer, 482).
2. At their Quarterly and Yearly Meetings, Friends responded to a series of queries to determine their faithfulness to the principles of the Society. LM refers to a debate that divided the Society of Friends during the 1840s. While some ministers and elders criticized LM and other Quakers for participating in the interfaith antislavery movement, LM asked whether or not the elders' reading and voting habits conformed to the Society's testimony against slavery and war. In 1848 Genesee Yearly Meeting, which had agreed that voting violated Quaker values, split over the issue of worldly activism, and LM's allies formed the Congregational Friends (see Faulkner, 84–85, 132–33).

"Discourse on Woman," Assembly Buildings, Philadelphia, December 17, 1849

There is nothing of greater importance to the well-being of society at large—of man as well as woman—than the true and proper position of woman. Much has been said, from time to time, upon this subject. It has been a theme for ridicule, for satire and sarcasm. We might look for this from the ignorant and vulgar; but from the intelligent and refined we have a right to expect that such weapons shall not be resorted to,—that gross comparisons and vulgar epithets shall not be applied, so as to place woman, in a point of view, ridiculous to say the least.

This subject has claimed my earnest interest for many years. I have long wished to see woman occupying a more elevated position than that which custom for ages has allotted to her. It was with great regret, therefore, that I listened a few days ago to a lecture upon this subject, which, though replete with intellectual beauty, and containing much that was true and excellent, was yet fraught with sentiments calculated to retard the progress of woman to the high elevation destined by her Creator.[1] I regretted the more that these sentiments should be presented with such intellectual vigor and beauty, because they would be likely to ensnare the young.

The minds of young people generally, are open to the reception of more exalted views upon this subject. The kind of homage that has been paid to woman, the flattering appeals which have too long satisfied her—appeals to her mere fancy and imagination, are giving place to a more extended recognition of her rights, her important duties and responsibilities in life. Woman is claiming for herself stronger and more profitable food. Various are the indications leading to this conclusion. The increasing attention to female education, the improvement in the literature of the age, especially in what is called the "Ladies' Department," in the periodicals of the day, are among the proofs of a higher estimate of women in society at large. Therefore we may hope that the intellectual and intelligent are being prepared for the discussion of this question, in a manner which shall tend to enoble woman and dignify man.

Free discussion upon this, as upon all other subjects, is never to be feared; nor will be, except by such as prefer darkness to light. "Those only who are in the wrong dread discussion. The light alarms those only who feel the need of darkness." It was sound philosophy, uttered by Jesus, "He that doeth truth cometh to the light, that his deeds may be made manifest, that they are wrought in God."

I have not come here with a view of answering any particular parts of the lecture alluded to, in order to point out the fallacy of its reasoning. The speaker, however, did not profess to offer anything like argument on that occasion, but rather a *sentiment*. I have no prepared address to deliver to you, being unaccustomed to speak in that way; but I felt a wish to offer some views for your consideration, though in a desultory manner, which may lead to such reflection and discussion as will present the subject in a true light.

In the beginning, man and woman were created equal. "Male and female created he them, and blessed them, and called their name Adam." He gave dominion to both over the animals, but not to one over the other.

> "Man o'er woman
> He made not lord, such title to himself
> Reserving, human left from human free."[2]

The cause of the subjection of woman to man, was early ascribed to disobedience to the command of God. This would seem to show that she was then regarded as not occupying her true and rightful position in society.

The laws given on Mount Sinai for the government of man and woman were equal, the precepts of Jesus make no distinction. Those who read the Scriptures, and judge for themselves, not resting satisfied with the perverted application of the text, do not find the distinction, that theology and ecclesiastical authorities have made, in the condition of the sexes. In the early ages, Miriam and Deborah, conjointly with Aaron and Barak, enlisted themselves on the side which they regarded the right, unitedly going up to their battles, and singing their songs of victory. We regard these with veneration. Deborah judged Israel many years—she went up with Barak against their enemies, with an army of 10,000, assuring him that the honor of the battle should not be to him, but to a woman. Revolting as were the circumstances of their success, the acts of a semi-barbarous people, yet we read with reverence the song of Deborah: "Blessed above woman shall Jael, the wife of Heeber, the Kenite be; blessed shall she be above women in the tent. ****[3] She put her hand to the nail, and her right hand to the workman's hammer; she smote Sisera through his temples. At her feet he bowed, he fell, he lay down dead." This circumstance, revolting to Christianity, is recognized as an act befitting woman in that day. Deborah, Huldah, and other honorable women, were looked up to and consulted in times of exigency, and their counsel was received. In that eastern country, with all the customs tending to degrade woman, some were called to fill great and important stations in society. There were also false prophetesses as well as true. The denunciations of Ezekiel were upon those women who would "prophesy out of their own heart, and sew pillows to all armholes," &c.

Coming down to later times, we find Anna, a prophetess of four-score years, in the temple day and night, speaking of Christ to all them who looked for redemption in Jerusalem. Numbers of women were the companions of Jesus—one going to the men of the city, saying, "Come, see a man who told me all things that ever I did; is not this the Christ?" Another, "Whatsoever he saith unto you, do it." Philip had four daughters who did prophesy. Tryphena and Tryphosa were co-workers with the apostles in their mission, to whom they sent special messages of regard and acknowledgement of their labors in the gospel. A learned Jew, mighty in the Scriptures, was by Priscilla instructed in the way of the Lord more perfectly. Phebe is mentioned as a *servant* of Christ, and commended as such to the brethren. It is worthy of note, that the word *servant*, when applied to Tychicus, is rendered *minister*. Women *professing* godliness, should be translated *preaching*.

The first announcement, on the day of Pentecost, was the fulfillment of ancient prophecy, that God's spirit should be poured out upon *daughters* as well as sons, and they should prophesy. It is important that we be familiar with these facts, because woman has been so long circumscribed in her influence by the perverted application of the text, rendering it improper for her to speak in the assemblies of the people, "to edification, to exhortation, and to comfort."

If these scriptures were read intelligently, we should not so learn Christ, as to exclude any from a position, where they might exert an influence for good to their fellow-beings. The epistle to the Corinthian church, where the supposed apostolic prohibition of woman's preaching is found, contains express directions how woman shall appear, when she prayeth or prophesyeth. Judge then whether this admonition, relative to *speaking* and asking questions, in the excited state of that church, should be regarded as a standing injunction on woman's *preaching*, when that word was not used by the apostle. Where is the Scripture authority for the advice given to the early church, under peculiar circumstances, being binding on the church of the present day? Ecclesiastical history informs us, that for two or three hundred years, female ministers suffered martyrdom, in company with their brethren.

These things are too much lost sight of. They should be known, in order that we may be prepared to meet the assertion, so often made, that woman is stepping out of her appropriate sphere, when she shall attempt to instruct public assemblies. The present time particularly demands such investigation. It requires also, that "of yourselves ye should judge what is right," that you should know the ground whereon you stand. This age is notable for its works of mercy and benevolence—for the efforts that are made to reform the inebriate and the degraded, to relieve the oppressed and the suffering. Women as well as men are interested in these works of justice and mercy. They are efficient co-workers, their talents are called into profitable exercise, their labors are effective in each department of reform. The blessing to the merciful, to the peacemaker, is equal to man and to woman. It is greatly to be deplored, now that she is increasingly qualified for usefulness, that any view should be presented, calculated to retard her labors of love.

Why should not woman seek to be a reformer? If she is to shrink from being such an iconoclast as shall "break the image of man's lower worship," as so long held up to view; if she is to fear to exercise her reason, and her noblest powers, lest she should be thought to "attempt to act the man," and not "acknowledge his supremacy"; if she is to be satisfied with the narrow sphere assigned her by man, nor aspire to a higher, lest she should transcend the bounds of female delicacy; truly it is a mournful prospect for woman. We would admit all the difference, that our great and beneficent Creator has made, in the relation of man and woman, nor would we seek to disturb this relation; but we deny that the present position of woman, is her true sphere of usefulness: nor will she attain to this sphere, until the disabilities and disadvantages, religious, civil, and social, which impede her progress, are removed out of her way. These restrictions have enervated her mind and paralysed her powers. While man assumes, that the present is the original state designed for woman, that the *existing* "differences are not arbitrary nor the result of accident," but grounded in nature;[4] she will not make the necessary effort to obtain her just rights, lest it should subject her to the kind of scorn and contemptuous manner in which she has been spoken of.

So far from her "ambition leading her to attempt to act the man," she needs all the encouragement she can receive, by the removal of obstacles from her path, in order that she may become a "true woman." As it is desirable that man should act a manly and generous part, not "mannish," so let woman be urged to exercise a dignified and womanly bearing, not womanish. Let her cultivate all the graces and proper accomplishments of her sex, but let not these degenerate into a kind of effeminacy, in which she is satisfied to be the mere plaything or toy of society, content with her outward adornings, and with the tone of flattery and fulsome adulation too often addressed to her. True, nature has made a difference in her configuration, her physical strength, her voice, &c.—and we ask no change, we are satisfied with nature. But how has neglect and mismanagement increased this difference! It is our duty to develop these natural powers by suitable exercise, so that they be strengthened "by reason of use." In the ruder state of society, woman is made to bear heavy burdens, while her "lord and master" walks idly by her side. In the civilization to which we have attained, if cultivated and refined woman would bring all her powers into use, she might engage in pursuits which she now shrinks from as beneath her proper vocation. The energies of men need not then be wholly devoted to the counting house and common business of life, in order that women in fashionable society, may be supported in their daily promenades and nightly visits to the theatre and ball room.

The appeal of Catharine Beecher to woman some years ago, leading her to aim at higher pursuits, was greatly encouraging. It gave earnest of an improved condition of woman. She says, "The time is coming, when woman will be taught to understand the construction of the human frame, the philosophical results from restricted exercise, unhealthy modes of dress, improper diet, and other causes, which are continually operating to destroy the health and life of the young. **** Woman has been but little aware of the high incitements which should stimulate to the cultivation of her noblest powers. The world is no longer to be governed by physical force, but by the influence which mind exerts over mind. **** Woman has never wakened to her highest destinies and holiest hopes. The time is coming when educated females will not be satisfied with the present objects of their low ambition. When a woman now leaves the immediate business of her own education, how often, how generally do we find her, sinking down into almost useless inactivity. To enjoy the social circle, to accomplish a little sewing, a *little* reading, a little domestic duty, to while away her hours in self-indulgence, or to enjoy the pleasures of domestic life,—these are the highest objects at which many a woman of elevated mind, and accomplished education aims. And what does she find of sufficient interest to call forth her cultivated energies, and warm affections? But when the cultivation and development of the immortal mind shall be presented to woman, as her especial and delightful duty, and that, too, whatever be her relations in life; when by example and experience she shall have learned her power over the intellect and the affections, **** then we shall not find woman, returning from the precincts of learning and wisdom, to pass lightly away the bright hours of her maturing youth. We shall not so often see her, seeking the light device to embroider on muslin and lace" (and I would add, the fashionable crochet work of the present day); "but we shall see her, with the delighted glow of benevolence, seeking for immortal minds, whereon she may fasten durable and holy impressions, that shall never be effaced or wear away."[5]

A new generation of women is now upon the stage, improving the increased opportunities furnished for the acquirement of knowledge. Public education is coming to be regarded the right of the children of a republic. The hill of science is not so difficult of ascent as formerly represented by poets and painters; but by fact and demonstration, smoothed down, so as to be accessible to the assumed weak capacity of woman. She is rising in the scale of being through this, as well as other means, and finding heightened pleasure and profit on the right hand and on the left. The study of Physiology, now introduced into our common schools, is engaging her attention, impressing the necessity of the observance of the laws of health. The intellectual Lyceum and instructive lecture room are becoming, to many, more attractive than the theatre and the ball room. The sickly and sentimental novel and pernicious romance are giving place to works, calculated to call forth the benevolent affections and higher nature. It is only by comparison that I would speak commendatory of these works of imagination. The frequent issue of them from the press is to be regretted. Their exciting contents, like stimulating drinks, when long indulged in, enervate the mind, unfitting it for the sober duties of life.

These duties are not to be limited by man. Nor will woman fulfill less her domestic relations, as the faithful companion of her chosen husband, and the fitting mother of her children, because she has a right estimate of her position and her responsibilities. Her self-respect will be increased; preserving the dignity of her being, she will not suffer herself to be degraded into a mere dependent. Nor will her feminine character be impaired. Instances are not few of woman throwing off the encumbrances which bind her, and going forth in a manner worthy of herself, her creation, and her dignified calling. Did Elizabeth Fry lose any of her feminine qualities by the public walk into which she was called? Having performed the duties of a mother to a large family, feeling that she owed a labor of love to the poor prisoner, she was empowered by Him who sent her forth, to go to kings and crowned heads of the earth, and ask audience of these; and it was granted her. Did she lose the delicacy of woman by her acts? No. Her retiring modesty was characteristic of her to the latest period of her life. It was my privilege to enjoy her society some years ago, and I found all that belonged to the feminine in woman—to true nobility, in a refined and purified moral nature. Is Dorothea Dix throwing off her womanly nature and appearance in the course she is pursuing? In finding duties abroad has any "refined man felt that something of beauty has gone forth from her"? To use the contemptuous word applied in the lecture alluded to, is she becoming "*mannish*"? Is she compromising her womanly dignity in going forth to seek to better the condition of the insane and afflicted? Is not a beautiful mind and a retiring modesty still conspicuous in her?[6]

Indeed, I would ask if this modesty is not attractive also, when manifested in the other sex? It was strikingly marked in Horace Mann when presiding over the late National Educational Convention in this city.[7] The retiring modesty of William Ellery Channing was beautiful, as well as of many others, who have filled dignified stations in society. These virtues, differing as they may in degree in man and woman, are of the same nature and call forth our admiration wherever manifested.

The noble courage of Grace Darling is justly honored, leading her to present herself on the coast of England, during the raging storm, in order to rescue the poor, suffering, shipwrecked mariner.[8] Woman was not wanting in courage, in the early ages. In war and bloodshed this trait was often displayed. Grecian and Roman history have lauded and honored her in this character. English history records her courageous women too, for unhappily we have little but the records of war handed down to us. The courage of Joan of Arc was made the subject of a popular lecture not long ago, by one of our intelligent citizens. But more noble, moral daring is marking the female character at the present time, and better worthy of imitation. As these characteristics come to be appreciated in man too, his warlike acts, with all the miseries and horrors of the battle-ground, will sink into their merited oblivion, or be remembered only to be condemned. The heroism displayed in the tented field, must yield to the moral and Christian heroism which is shadowed in the signs of our times.

The lecturer regarded the announcement of woman's achievements, and the offering of appropriate praise through the press, as a gross innovation upon the obscurity of female life—he complained that the exhibition of the attainments of girls, in schools, was now equal to that of boys, and the newspapers announce that "Miss Brown received the first prize for English grammar," &c. If he objected to so much excitement of emulation in schools, it would be well; for the most enlightened teachers discountenance these appeals to love of approbation and self-esteem. But, while prizes continue to be awarded, can any good reason be given, why the name of the girl should not be published as well as that of the boy? He spoke with scorn, that "we hear of Mrs. President so and so; and committees and secretaries of the same sex." But if women can conduct their own business by means of Presidents and Secretaries of their own sex, can he tell us why they should not?[9] They will never make much progress in any moral movement, while they depend upon men to act for them. Do we shrink from reading the announcement that Mrs. Somerville is made an honorary member of a scientific association? That Miss Herschel has made some discoveries, and is prepared to take her equal part in science? Or that Miss MITCHELL of Nantucket has lately discovered a planet, long looked for?[10] I cannot conceive why "honor to whom honor is due" should not be rendered to woman as well as man; nor will it necessarily exalt her, or foster feminine pride. This propensity is found alike in male and female, and it should not be ministered to too improperly, in either sex.

In treating upon the affections, the lecturer held out the idea, that as manifested in the sexes, they were opposite, if not somewhat antagonistic; and required a union, as in chemistry, to form a perfect whole.[11] The simile appeared to me far from a correct illustration of the true union. Minds that can assimilate, spirits that are congenial, attach themselves to each other. It is the union of similar, not opposite, affections, which are necessary for the perfection of the marriage bond. There seemed a want of proper delicacy in his representing man as being bold in the demonstration of the pure affection of love. In persons of refinement, true love seeks concealment in man, as well as in woman. I will not enlarge upon the subject, although it formed so great a part of his lecture. The contrast drawn seemed a fallacy, as has much, very much that has been presented, in the sickly sentimental strains of the poet, from age to age.

The question is often asked, "What does woman want, more than she enjoys? What is she seeking to obtain? Of what rights is she deprived? What privileges are withheld from her?" I answer, she asks nothing as favor, but as right, she wants to be acknowledged a moral, responsible being. She is seeking not to be governed by laws, in the making of which she has no voice. She is deprived of almost every right in civil society, and is a cypher in the nation, except in the right of presenting a petition. In religious society her disabilities, as already pointed out, have greatly retarded her progress. Her exclusion from the pulpit or ministry—her duties marked out for her by her equal brother man, subject to creeds, rules, and disciplines made for her by him—this is unworthy her true dignity. In marriage, there is assumed superiority, on the part of the husband, and admitted inferiority, with a promise of obedience, on the part of the wife. This subject calls loudly for examination, in order that the wrong may be redressed. Customs suited to darker ages in Eastern countries, are not binding upon enlightened society. The solemn covenant of marriage may be entered into without these lordly assumptions, and humiliating concessions and promises.

There are large Christian denominations who do not recognize such degrading relations of husband and wife. They ask no magisterial or ministerial aid to legalize or to sanctify this union. But acknowledging themselves in the presence of the Highest, and invoking his assistance, they come under reciprocal obligations of fidelity and affection, before suitable witnesses. Experience and observation go to prove, that there may be as much harmony, to say the least, in such a union and as great purity and permanency of affection, as can exist where the more common custom or form is observed. The distinctive relations of husband and wife, of father and mother of a family are sacredly preserved, without the assumption of authority on the one part, or the promise of obedience on the other. There is nothing in such a marriage degrading to woman. She does not compromise her dignity or self-respect; but enters married life upon equal ground, by the side of her husband. By proper education, she understands her duties, physical, intellectual and moral; and fulfilling these, she is a help meet, in the true sense of the word.

I tread upon delicate ground in alluding to the institutions of religious associations; but the subject is of so much importance, that all which relates to the position of woman, should be examined, apart from the undue veneration which ancient usage receives.

> "Such dupes are men to custom, and so prone
> To reverence what is ancient, and can plead
> A course of long observance for its use,
> That even servitude, the worst of ills,
> Because delivered down from sire to son,
> Is kept and guarded as a sacred thing."

So with woman. She has so long been subject to the disabilities and restrictions, with which her progress has been embarrassed, that she has become enervated, her mind to some extent paralyzed; and, like those still more degraded by personal bondage, she hugs her chains. Liberty is often presented in its true light, but it is liberty for man.

> "Whose freedom is by suffrance, and at will
> Of a superior—he is never free.
> Who lives, and is not weary of a life
> Exposed to manacles, deserves them well."[12]

I would not, however, go so far, either as regards the abject slave or woman; for in both cases they may be so degraded by the crushing influences around them, that they may not be sensible of the blessing of Freedom. Liberty is not less a blessing, because oppression has so long darkened the mind that it cannot appreciate it. I would therefore urge, that woman be placed in such a situation in society, by the yielding of her rights, and have such opportunities for growth and development, as shall raise her from this low, enervated and paralyzed condition, to a full appreciation of the blessing of entire freedom of mind.

It is with reluctance that I make the demand for the political rights of woman, because this claim is so distasteful to the age. Woman shrinks, in the present state of society, from taking any interest in politics. The events of the French Revolution, and the claim for woman's rights are held up to her as a warning.[13] But let us not look at the excesses of women alone, at that period; but remember that the age was marked with extravagances and wickedness in men as well as women. Indeed, political life abounds with these excesses, and with shameful outrage. Who knows, but that if woman acted her part in governmental affairs, there might be an entire change in the turmoil of political life. It becomes man to speak modestly of his ability to act without her. If woman's judgment were exercised, why might she not aid in making the laws by which she is governed? Lord Brougham remarked that the works of Harriet Martineau upon Political Economy were not excelled by those of any political writer of the present time. The first few chapters of her 'Society in America,' her views of a Republic, and of Government generally, furnish evidence of woman's capacity to embrace subjects of universal interest.[14]

Far be it from me to encourage woman to vote, or to take an active part in politics, in the present state of our government. Her right to the elective franchise, however, is the same, and should be yielded to her, whether she exercise that right or not. Would that man too, would have no participation in a government based upon the life-taking principle—upon retaliation and the sword. It is unworthy a Christian nation. But when, in the diffusion of light and intelligence, a convention shall be called to make regulations for self-government on Christian, non-resistant principles, I can see no good reason, why woman should not participate in such an assemblage, taking part equally with man.

Walker, of Cincinnati, in his Introduction to American Law, says: "With regard to political rights, females form a positive exception to the general doctrine of equality. They have no part or lot in the formation or administration of government. They cannot vote or hold office. We require them to contribute their share in the way of taxes, to the support of government, but allow them no voice in its direction. We hold them amenable to the laws when made, but allow them no share in making them. This language, applied to males, would be the exact definition of political slavery; applied to females, custom does not teach us so to regard it." Woman, however, is beginning so to regard it.

"The law of husband and wife, as you gather it from the books, is a disgrace to any civilized nation. The theory of the law degrades the wife almost to the level of slaves. When a woman marries, we call her condition coverture, and speak of her as a *femme covert*. The old writers call the husband baron, and sometimes, in plain English, lord."[15] **** The merging of her name in that of her husband is emblematic of the fate of all her legal rights. The torch of Hymen serves but to light the pile, on which these rights are offered up. The legal theory is, that marriage makes the husband and wife one person, and that person is the *husband*. On this subject, reform is loudly called for. There is no foundation in reason or expediency, for the absolute and slavish subjection of the wife to the husband, which forms the foundation of the present legal relations. Were woman, in point of fact, the abject thing which the law, in theory, considers her to be when married, she would not be worthy the companionship of man.

I would ask if such a code of laws does not require change? If such a condition of the wife in society does not claim redress? On no good ground can reform be delayed. Blackstone says, "The very being and legal existence of woman is suspended during marriage,—incorporated or consolidated into that of her husband, under whose protection and cover she performs every thing." Hurlbut, in his Essays upon Human Rights, says: "The laws touching the rights of woman are at variance with the laws of the Creator. Rights are human rights, and pertain to human beings, without distinction of sex. Laws should not be made for man or for woman, but for mankind. Man was not born to command, nor woman to obey.**** The law of France, Spain, and Holland and one of our own States, Louisiana, recognizes the wife's right to property, more than the common law of England.**** The laws depriving woman of the right of property are handed down to us from dark and feudal times, and not consistent with the wiser, better, purer spirit of the age. The wife is a mere pensioner on the bounty of her husband. Her lost rights are appropriated to himself. But justice and benevolence are abroad in our land, awakening the spirit of inquiry and innovation; and the Gothic fabric of the British law will fall before it, save where it is based upon the foundation of truth and justice."[16]

May these statements lead you to reflect upon this subject, that you may know what woman's condition is in society—what her restrictions are, and seek to remove them. In how many cases in our country, the husband and wife begin life together, and by equal industry and united effort accumulate to themselves a comfortable home. In the event of the death of the wife, the household remains undisturbed, his farm or his workshop is not broken up, or in any way molested. But when the husband dies, he either gives his wife a *portion* of their joint accumulation, or the law apportions to her a *share*; the homestead is broken up, and she is dispossessed of that which she earned equally with him; for what she lacked in physical strength, she made up in constancy of labor and toil, day and evening. The sons then coming into possession of the property, as has been the custom until of latter time, speak of having to *keep* their mother, when she in reality is aiding to keep them. Where is the justice of this state of things? The changes in the law of this State and of New York, in relation to the property of the wife, go to a limited extent, toward the redress of these wrongs; but they are far more extensive, and involved much more, than I have time this evening to point out.[17]

On no good ground can the legal existence of the wife be suspended during marriage, and her property surrendered to her husband. In the intelligent ranks of society, the wife may not, in point of fact, be so degraded as the law would degrade her; because public sentiment is above the law. Still, while the law stands, she is liable to the disabilities which it imposes. Among the ignorant classes of society, woman is made to bear heavy burdens, and is degraded almost to the level of the slave.

There are many instances now in our city, where the wife suffers much from the power of the husband to claim all that she can earn with her own hands. In my intercourse with the poorer class of people, I have known cases of extreme cruelty, from the hard earnings of the wife being thus robbed by the husband, and no redress at law.

An article in one of the daily papers lately, presented the condition of needle women in England. There might be a presentation of this class in our own country, which would make the heart bleed. Public attention should be turned to this subject, in order that avenues of more profitable employment may be opened to women. There are many kinds of business which women, equally with men, may follow with respectability and success. Their talents and energies should be called forth, and their powers brought into the highest exercise. The efforts of women in France are sometimes pointed to in ridicule and sarcasm, but depend upon it, the opening of profitable employment to women in that country, is doing much for the enfranchisement of the sex.[18] In England also, it is not an uncommon thing for a wife to take up the business of her deceased husband and carry it on with success.

Our respected British Consul[19] stated to me a circumstance which occurred some years ago, of an editor of a political paper having died in England; it was proposed to his wife, an able writer, to take the editorial chair. She accepted. The patronage of the paper was greatly increased, and she, a short time since, retired from her labors with a handsome fortune. In that country however, the opportunities are by no means general for Woman's elevation.

In visiting the public school in London, a few years since, I noticed that the boys were employed in linear drawing, and instructed upon the black board, in the higher branches of arithmetic and mathematics; while the girls, after a short exercise in the mere elements of arithmetic, were seated, during the bright hours of the morning, *stitching wristbands*. I asked, why there should be this difference made; why they too should not have the black board? The answer was, that they would not probably fill any station in society requiring such knowledge.

But the demand for a more extended education will not cease, until girls and boys have equal instruction, in all the departments of useful knowledge. We have as yet no high school for girls in this state. The normal school may be a preparation for such an establishment. In the late convention for general education, it was cheering to hear the testimony borne to woman's capabilities for head teachers of the public schools. A resolution there offered for equal salaries to male and female teachers, when equally qualified, as practiced in Louisiana, I regret to say was checked in its passage, by Bishop Potter; by him who has done so much for the encouragement of education, and who gave his countenance and influence to that convention.[20] Still the fact of such a resolution being offered, augurs a time coming for woman which she may well hail. At the last examination of the public schools in this city, one of the alumni delivered an address on Woman, not as is too common, in eulogistic strains, but directing the attention to the injustice done to woman in her position in society, in a variety of ways. The unequal wages she receives for her constant toil, &c., present facts calculated to arouse attention to the subject.

Women's property has been taxed, equally with that of men's, to sustain colleges endowed by the states; but they have not been permitted to enter those high seminaries of learning. Within a few years, however, some colleges have been instituted, where young women are admitted, nearly upon equal terms with young men; and numbers are availing themselves of their long denied rights. This is among the signs of the times, indicative of an advance for women. The book of knowledge is not opened to her in vain. Already is she aiming to occupy important posts of honor and profit in our country. We have three female editors in our state—some in other states of the Union. Numbers are entering the medical profession—one received a diploma last year;[21] others are preparing for a like result.

Let woman then go on—not asking a favor, but claiming as right, the removal of all the hindrances to her elevation in the scale of being—let her receive encouragement for the proper cultivation of all her powers, so that she may enter profitably into the active business of life; employing her own hands, in ministering to her necessities, strengthening her physical being by proper exercise, and observance of the laws of health. Let her not be ambitious to display a fair hand, and to promenade the fashionable streets of our city, but rather, coveting earnestly the best gifts, let her strive to occupy such walks in society, as will befit her true dignity in all the relations of life. No fear that she will then transcend the proper limits of female delicacy. True modesty will be as fully preserved, in acting out those important vocations to which she may be called, as in the nursery or at the fireside, ministering to man's self-indulgence.

Then in the marriage union, the independence of the husband and wife will be equal, their dependence mutual, and their obligations reciprocal.

In conclusion, let me say, "Credit not the old fashioned absurdity, that woman's is a secondary lot, ministering to the necessities of her lord and master! It is a higher destiny I would award you. If your immortality is as complete, and your gift of mind as capable as ours, of increase and elevation, I would put no wisdom of mind against God's evident allotment. I would charge you to water the undying bud, and give it healthy culture, and open its beauty to the sun—and then you may hope, that when your life is bound up with another, you will go on equally, and in a fellowship that shall pervade every earthly interest."[22]

PD "Discourse on Woman by Lucretia Mott Delivered at the Assembly Buildings, December 17, 1849. Being a Full Phonographic Report, Revised by the Author" (Philadelphia: T. B. Peterson, 1850).

1. On December 4, 1849, poet and critic Richard Henry Dana Sr. (1787–1879) delivered a lecture entitled "Woman and Her Influence on Society" in Philadelphia in which he upheld men's supremacy and criticized the women's rights movement (*Pennsylvania Freeman*, December 13, 1849; "Woman," Box 36, Dana Family Papers, Massachusetts Historical Society).

2. John Milton, *Paradise Lost*, Book 12.

3. These asterisks, appearing in the printed version here and below, indicate omissions from the texts LM quotes.

4. Dana closed his lecture urging that a woman "not turn iconoclast, and with sacrilegious, self-destroying hand, break in pieces the image of man's lower worship." He stated that "In her ambition to act the Man, she only ceases to be the Woman." Earlier he stressed the "essential difference between man and woman, and the importance to both that this difference should be regarded as a law grounded in their several natures" ("Woman," 45, 10, 1).

5. LM quotes from *Suggestions Respecting Improvements in Education* (1829), 8, 53, 54–55 by Catharine Beecher (1800–1878). LM's own words appear in parentheses.

6. LM had met British Quaker minister and prison reformer Elizabeth Fry (1780–1845) when traveling in England in 1840 (Palmer, 237). Dorothea Dix (1802–84) was a prison and hospital reformer. Dana worried that "when woman grows dissatisfied with what is distinctively womanly, and begins to talk of privileges and rights in common with man, she has already quitted the better part of womanhood and gained, let it be repeated, not what is manly, but what is mannish instead" ("Woman," 42).

7. At the National School Convention, held October 17–18, with educator Horace Mann (1796–1859) presiding, a resolution to equalize the salaries of women and men was introduced but did not pass (Palmer, 190–91).

8. Grace Darling (1815–42), a British lighthouse keeper's daughter, had rescued shipwrecked seamen in 1838.

9. Dana spoke of girls like Miss Euphronia Brown excelling in school along with women lawyers and doctors, resulting in "too much of publicity for the well-being of woman." Woman cannot "possess notoriety" and retain "untinged her feminine nature" ("Woman," 34).

10. Astronomers Mary Fairfax Somerville (1780–1872), from Great Britain, Caroline Herschel (1750–1848) from Germany, and the American Maria Mitchell (1818–89), a relative of LM.

11. Dana said, "Examine each of these, and you will find in each . . . that which indicates a something to be supplied, & in excess, also in the one to meet a want in the other . . . till both are completed through a process of mutual imparting & receiving" ("Woman," 13–14).

12. William Cowper, "The Task" (1785).

13. For some Americans and Europeans, the violence of the Terror served as an example that equality must have limits. In his lecture, Dana stated that the French Revolution had produced "political rights for women in common with men . . . an infidel spirit . . . [*that*] is alive again" ("Woman," 3).

14. Henry Peter Brougham, Baron Brougham and Vaux (1778–1868), British reformer. LM had first met the British author Harriet Martineau (1802–76) in 1836, when Martineau toured the United States. Martineau's *Society in America* was published in 1837.

15. LM quotes from *Introduction to American Law* by Judge Timothy Walker (1806–56), published in 1837 (235, 236, 244, 245).

16. Elisha Powell Hurlbut (1807–89), *Essays on Human Rights and Their Political Guaranties* with additions from George Combe (1845, 1848, 1853). William Blackstone's compilation of the English common law held that husband and wife were "one person in law" and that person was the husband. Hurlbut was elected a judge of New York's Supreme Court in 1847. He rejected English common law in favor of inalienable individual rights. His radical reading of legal history, influenced by phrenology, significantly influenced the arguments of woman's rights advocates. See Gordon, 1:86.

17. The 1848 Married Woman's Property Act in New York allowed married women to retain any real and personal property that they owned before marriage and to keep any gifts to them thereafter. Pennsylvania followed in April 1848, with a similar law (Gordon, 1:68; Palmer, 239).

18. In England women often worked sixteen hours a day for only a few shillings per week. In France, the socialist Robert Dale Owen wrote approvingly that women worked in offices, omnibuses, dry goods stores, and post offices ("The Needle Women of London," *The World We Live In*, August 3, 1844, 116; "Situation of Women in France," *The Beacon*, February 25, 1843, 113).

19. William Peter (1788–1853) was the husband of Sarah Worthington Peter, who was active in women's education in Philadelphia (Palmer, 226).

20. Episcopal bishop Alonzo Potter of Philadelphia (1800–1865). See note 7, above, regarding the October convention.

21. In January Elizabeth Blackwell (1821–1910) had received her M.D. from Geneva Medical College in New York.

22. Quoted verbatim from Nathaniel Parker Willis, "Minute Philosophies," in *Inklings of Adventure* (1836), 2:236.

Cherry Street Meeting, Philadelphia, March 31, 1850

Whene'er I take my walks abroad
How many poor I see,
What shall I render to my God
For all his gifts to me.

Not more than others I deserve,
Yet God has given me more;
For I have food while others starve
Or beg from door to door.

How many children in the street
Half naked I behold,
While I am clothed from head to feet,
And covered from the cold.

Figure 5. Cherry Street Meetinghouse, built 1828. (Courtesy of the Friends Historical Library, Swarthmore College)

> While some poor creatures scarce can tell,
> Where they may lay their head,
> I have a home wherein to dwell,
> And rest upon my bed.
>
> While others early learn to swear
> And curse, and lie, and steal,
> Lord I am taught thy name to fear,
> And do thy holy will.
>
> Are these thy favours day by day
> To me above the rest.
> Then let me love thee more than they
> And try to serve thee best.

This poetic hymn composed by Watts and committed to memory by many a child contains but the idea that is inculcated in the religious training of most of the children of the age.[1] It is the kind of praise and thanksgiving which are offered from most of the pulpits not only in Christendom but we may safely presume in the world. How far such thanksgiving and such language is befitting us, how far it is in accordance with the more enlightened revelations of truth and justice it is for us to consider. This morning as I took my seat at our breakfast table with only my husband present, I remarked that I did not know that we need pause long for the spirit of thanksgiving, that my heart and soul were poured out in daily continued thanksgiving and praise for blessings and enjoyments; but that I could not feel that it would be right to return thanks for anything like peculiar blessings or special favors; for indeed my heart at times smote me with the feelings that there belonged to us at least our share of the reproach and condemnation that things are *as* they are. That there is a broad distinction in Society as so truly blessed portrayed by this simple yet sublime poet that "we have food while others starve or beg from door to door." I often feel it to be a profitable reflection to dwell on this subject, because it may lead to the laying of the axe at the root of this corrupt tree, rather than leading to a blind dependence upon an imagined providence to bring about a different state of things without man's agency. I have been instructed sometimes, in reading the early language of John the Baptist, the fore-runner of the [blessed?] Jesus as well perhaps as his own language "behold now the axe is laid at the root of the tree; and every tree that bringeth not forth good fruit must be hewn down and burned in consuming fire."

There is a great deal of true philosophy conveyed in this assertion; for however we may rejoice at the alleviations which are so generously and benevolently imparted to suffering humanity, and which to some extent are applied to existing evils, yet we must see as we look at the subject correctly that it is not until right shall take place, until the axe shall be laid at the very root of these evils, that they can be destroyed. I often rejoice and am made glad that there is so much of humanity in man, so much benevolence in his nature, that it has led and still leads to a great deal being done for the erring and vicious in the name of benevolence and charity, which belongs to them in the name of justice. I rejoice that we are so constituted by our nature that we *can*, and do accommodate ourselves to the circumstances in which we are placed; and while we may be far from viewing those who are living in self-indulgence, luxury and excess as peculiarly blest of God, or even as desirable to emulate, at the same time we must admit that God, in his wisdom, in his unbounded and illimitable benevolence, has abundantly crowned the earth with blessings, and given unto man of his abundance, richly to enjoy; and that it is desirable that all classes of Society partake of these rich blessings. While all this may be admitted, there is a fatal want of faith and confidence, in the power with which God has gifted the creatures he has made, to bring about such a state of Society as we acknowledge to be desirable, but which, in the erroneous teachings and views which are instilled in our religious Education, we are so prone to put off to some millennium day—some too frequently far distant future, when by some miraculous providence the kingdom of this world shall become the kingdom of our Lord and of his Christ.

The fact is mournful that nearly all the preaching and praying, and the religious observances or beliefs of the world, go to strengthen this idea rather than impress upon men their individual and co-operative duty to do justice to their fellow-beings, to exercise mercy to all classes of Society. We may remember the complaint uttered against Jesus was, that he mingled with the lowest classes of that age, the publicans and sinners of his time. It was in vain that he assured them that men might have different walks in life, one being called to one work of reformation and another to another; that while John came neither eating nor drinking, the son of man might come both eating and drinking; yet both were liable to have their motives called in question, and to be judged by the zealous of their day—the accusers of the brethren of their time. Of John they said "he hath a devil," of Jesus they said "behold a glutton and a wine bibber; he suppeth with publicans and sinners." How beautifully Jesus closed this with the language "wisdom is justified of all her children." If we could so believe, and hail the virtuous efforts for the renovation of Society, and the improvement of man's condition in life—if we could bid God speed to every effort having for its object the redemption of the race, then do I believe we should cease to indulge the arrogant language, that "we are blest, while others starve or beg from door to door." We should be led to look how far, in the free agency which so peculiarly marks the character of man, we have abused it, and by means of unjust or improper distinction in Society—by Hierarchies, by Aristocracies, and kingly nobilities, by the setting of man above his fellow man and making him his ruler,—how far we have been instrumental in bringing about these manifold evils, which now require all the wisdom with which man is gifted, both by his nature, his divine reason, and his still diviner revelation, to discover the right means of effecting so speedy a change, that year after year shall not consign its thousands of starving people to an untimely grave.

True religion, the religion of Jesus, if we understood it aright, would lead us into the true philosophical spirit of political economy, not in the partisan sense of the word, by any means; but into such a true consideration of the causes of these great evils as would lead into laying the axe at the root of the corrupt tree of arbitrary power which has been produced by the assumption of false claims of man over his fellow-man. This cause has produced this most deplorable state of things. Let our text then be, all things whatsoever ye would that men should do unto you do ye even so unto them. Likewise let the true principles of justice be ever exalted in our midst; and let us be desirous to be armed with such a power—and this power is ever present to give us the ability, if we seek it—as will enable us to do our individual part in the work [of] human improvement and thereby be instruments in bringing about a better state of things. This will never impair in us the spirit of heart-felt thanksgiving and praise, for the blessings that abound in life, even while we see that perhaps our own superior power of acquiring, or the more favorable circumstances in which we have been placed, have secured to us a greater share of these enjoyments. While we may be ready to say with the Psalmist "thou has cast my lines in pleasant places"; we have a goodly heritage; we shall at the same time feel a great responsibility resting upon us to better the *outward condition* of our fellow beings. Thus whether it shall be confined to the limited circles in which some are accustomed to move—for there is all this diversity of gifts even in acting out these common duties of life—or whether it shall extend to some embracing extensive ideas, yet it still will be recognized as one of the first duties to mark us as Christians and brethren, as children of God.

If there is any one thing more strongly inculcated and enjoined in the testimony of the ancients, both sacred and profane as they are called, than another, it is the duty of administering to the necessities of the suffering, of giving aid to the weak and perishing. Righteous conduct, right doing, good works, practical righteousness, or whatever name we may apply to it, has been inculcated by the good—the truly pious in all ages of the world. And this goes to show the universality of God's love to man; it goes to show that when we come to essential duties—when we leave mere creeds, even the ceremonial observances of the sectarian—there is then no difference found among the children of men as to what belongs to the attributes of God. Justice and right have ever been his fundamental principles, mercy, and love, his darling attributes. These have been stamped high above all sacrifices in every age.

[A short quotation not heard].

This Jesus applied to himself when he went about doing good. Was it not the body to which he ministered? And was this because he was sent to minister to the body only? By no means. While he relieved the sufferings of his fellow beings, he at the same time infused his blessed gospel of glad tidings of great joy unto all people, by directing them to that fount within themselves, whence the pure water which springeth up into everlasting life—that heavenly manna which all might partake of—that which cometh down from heaven, from a source higher than earth, and nourishes the immortal soul. He then, never separated his spiritual from his outward duties; and when the Apostle following him would give the highest evidence of love to God, he said "if thou seest a brother or sister naked, destitute of daily food, give them not the things needful to the body only"—mark the body.

Let not our religion be directed into a strain which shall lead us into less sympathy for suffering and erring humanity, and let mercy, which must ever be coupled with justice and love, influence us, and we shall be instrumental in relieving the afflicted mourners in Zion. We shall experience a reward, for true it is, that those who go forth, thus ministering to the wants and necessities of their fellow beings, experience a rich return—their souls being as a watered garden, as a spring that faileth not. They are then prepared, and then only, to administer the true spiritual food, and they go to the lowly mourners in Zion to cheer them up. And while they know that they too have their dark and cloudy days (for who of us has not, and it is needful for the soul that there should be days of overcast as it is in outward nature) when they come into the true philosophy, they will attempt to account physically, for that which many a poor sufferer imagines to be the withdrawal of spiritual sustenance and consolation. I believe it to be our duty to lead the mourners to seek the spiritual manna; and oh! do I believe, that it has been from the neglect or non-observances of the laws of our being that great depression is felt, and many have gone mourning on their way believing it to be a special judgment or at least, an immediate withdrawal of their beloved from their souls, for the sake of trying their faith. Oh! how is it that we bring the highest down to our limited human understanding. Let us understand cause and effect so far as we can, by the study of ourselves, spiritually and physically, and we will never be abridged of anything that is truly spiritual or divine. We may, with the mourning Prophet Jeremiah, have a right to say "mine eyes are running down with water because the comforter that should relieve my soul is far from me." Again may we adopt his language, and return multiplied blessings and thanksgivings because "that when I was in the low dungeon thou heardest me."

In quoting the language which dwelt with me from the time of my taking my seat in this meeting, I thought there might be many present ready to make profitable reflections not in accordance with this language, but in dissent. I quoted scarcely a word of it with approval for I believe it to be based on long taught error. I thought by bringing out these few lines, so familiar to most of us, we might perhaps be led to religious contemplations as much as by quoting a text from the Bible.

I am aware that very much is being done around us for the benefit of the suffering and erring: and we may well rejoice in these efforts, the more as they seem to be now directed to the early training, to the moral and intellectual culture of those, who have been so long neglected and suffered to grow up as circumstances around them favored or otherwise; who have been permitted to live in our midst the living subjects of vice, crime, temptations, and consequently sorrow. Feeling hearts have gone forth even to the outskirts of our cities, and mingled with those who seek to place them in a position where their better nature and powers would be called forth, and this fact is worthy of all praise.

It is greatly gratifying to behold this spirit in man, and I would that every pulpit of this city were used this day to commend these efforts, this extension of favor to those without the pale of their Church. It is a mournful fact that most of the preaching and praying, is addressed to those who are within the pale of the Church. We need a church for humanity, a religion that shall reach the suffering and downtrodden; we need a Christianity, that is, we need to learn the true Christianity that will lead us to put our souls in the souls' stead of the oppressed.

There is now going the rounds of the papers an address which will produce a most baneful influence upon society, on the great subject of humanity, slavery, tending to direct the mind to it as a kind of providential thing, and scarcely admitting it to be an evil.[2] O! I would that there were religion enough, Christianity enough, humanity enough, in the circumstances in which we are placed—surrounded by three millions of suffering and dumb—to use such means as are in our power to insure the downfall of this foul and most iniquitous system. Oh! that there were hearts to so feel for these suffering and dumb, as to lead us to cry aloud and spare not, showing unto this nation its transgression, and the high professors of Christianity their short comings. If this were the case we should not see and hear and read of the efforts that are made to sustain this giant, monstrous evil. We should rather be led to look at our own garments, to see how far they were cleansed from participation in its iniquities; to feel that we must not build our house by unrighteousness, nor our chambers by wrong, we must not use our neighbor's services without wages and give him not for his work. Here we should be brought to feel that the true fast which the most high has chosen is to undo the bonds of wickedness, and let these oppressed go free and to break every yoke.

Let us rejoice and be glad that there is so much of this spirit still moving about in society, that this reformation is taught with a zeal and earnestness, with a Christian spirit—which is a spirit of true and earnest protest—that will never cease until Ethiopia shall lift up her hands and the last day approaches when all shall rise, liberty be proclaimed throughout the land to all the inhabitants thereof. We may hope, and while there is the spirit of true liberty in the heart, it is impossible to reject it, that while there is suffering, slavery and wrong—not only these but the oppressions which we behold around us more remotely allied to this iniquitous system of slavery, such as the relations of those who are called the employers and laborers—there will be a continual struggle to attain a better state of things. We all ought to be laborers for it is not God's design that some of us should live in luxury and unbounded indulgence, while others are toiling morning, noon, and night for bread. This ought never to be a subject of thanksgiving or of praise, but blushing and confusion of face, that such is the state of things around us that we are ignorantly partaking to such an extent as tends to perpetuate evil rather than good. These are the subjects of reflection with which my mind has been filled this day, and I offer them to you under a sense of imperative duty, believing that there might be others, intelligent minds not a few present, with whom they may be so received as to lead them to other reflections which shall show the duties that belong to us as individuals, and the awful responsibilities that attach to us to fulfill these duties; and in the fulfillment of them we shall experience that blessed reward, that blessed return (for I would not use the word in the sense in which it has so often been used) of that peace and tranquility which knows no alloy and which flows as the waves of the sea.

To J. McKim

This sermon completes the series. I have not been as particular as regards rhetoric, grammar etc as I sometimes am, feeling pretty confident that the author would not let them go out without every thing being right.

Smedley Darlington [Esq?] Reporter

Stenographic Report, Sermons, Mott Manuscripts, FHL

1. Isaac Watts (1674–1748), *Divine Songs* (1715), Song 4.
2. John C. Calhoun's speech "On the Slavery Question," delivered to the Senate on March 4, was reprinted in the *Liberator*, March 15 and 22, 1850.

Women's Rights Convention, Brinley Hall, Worcester, Massachusetts, October 23–24, 1850[1]

[*October 23, Morning Session*]

MRS. LUCRETIA MOTT suggested whether it would not be well to make some arrangement for the publication of the address of the President. She did not propose to review the sentiments advanced; they would be responded to generally by the friends of reform. There were two or three expressions in the address and in the call for the Convention which she did not fully approve.[2] She thought THEY might be construed as a profession of too great gentleness in discussing this subject. She thought they should find it necessary to take an antagonistic position, and to meet the prejudices and opposition of the world with directness and an earnest expression of the truth. They must attach blame to those who had persisted so long in depriving woman of her rights, in passing laws which deny her the control of her property and place her beyond the pale and protection of equal laws. She said they must mourn over the admitted inferiority of woman; over her slavish subjection to the evil customs and prejudices of society. It was not strange, after so long a period of degradation, she should be enervated and contented with her inferior position. She desired that we might speak with the earnestness and severity of the truth—with an earnestness and severity that should make the ears of man tingle for the degraded position in which he has kept woman during so many ages, and especially under the influences of the religion and teachings of the Son of God.

[*October 23, Evening Session*]

MRS. LUCRETIA MOTT said: The language of those who favor our cause implies a degree of kindness when they speak of *giving* us our rights, *permitting* us to receive them; but she was not disposed to receive them in this way; she was in favor of *demanding* them, in the name of our common humanity. She wanted a resolution framed that should express this demand. She wanted Woman's freedom and independence acknowledged as a right; that they should be secured to her, yielded, not given; that those restrictions which have prevented her from rising to her true position should be removed, leaving her a fair opportunity to rise in the scale of being, and make herself what God designed she should be. That she sometimes does this despite the obstacles that surround her, is evidence of her capacity. There are some signs of progress and encouragement to cheer us onward. A Medical School is instituted in Philadelphia for the education of female physicians, and a large number have already entered their names as students. An Academy of Design is also established, where Women may learn a knowledge of drawing and design, which shall enable them to find useful employments.[3] Journeymen, tailors and tailoresses are forming associations so as to do business for themselves, and the value and dignity of labor is rising and will command its proper reward to the Woman as well as to the Man. Woman's labor has not been appreciated, but it is coming to be appreciated. And many Women, by sufferance, to some extent, are raising their voices in the name of religion and humanity. In the Society to which she belonged, and among one or two other Societies she named, Women stand on an equality with Men, and have the same rights of speech. But this was not generally the case.

She regretted that so much time had been wasted in applying the Bible argument to these reforms. All we have to do is to step forward in the right, and the theologians will have to do this work, of reconciling the Bible with these principles of everlasting truth and right. She alluded to the writings of George and Andrew

Combe as having at first encountered this objection, that the truths they taught of Phrenology and Philosophy were opposed to the Bible.[4] A work was written to refute them on this ground. But while the works of these men had reached many editions, it had fallen into oblivion, and now an appendix is written by an American Divine to show the harmony between them. Mr. Combe, probably, had no objection to this, but it was not his work. He left that to the ecclesiastics. And so it had been with the other sciences and in the Anti-Slavery reform. She was not understood to want reverence or respect for the Bible, but the work of reconciling any apparent or imaginary conflicts was not their appropriate work. They should stand forth on the great principles of justice and humanity; and she alluded to the fact that there were "honorable women, not a few," who had dared to prophesy in the name of Christ.

She alluded to the application of Women to be admitted to the World's Convention a few years ago. It was a great era in the progress of Reform. The signs of the times all show that Woman is alive and awaking to a sense of her degraded and inferior position, and is beginning to demand her rights—not begging for a privilege, but demanding a full recognition of that to which she is entitled by virtue of her humanity.

She made reference to the language of Mrs. Foster, who she feared would be construed to favor the use of violence and bloodshed as one of the means of obtaining these rights.[5] She thought she might not be understood. What she said on that subject was based upon the supposition that certain other things were right. She wished that her friend had given her own views of the subject. Mrs. Mott then went on in a few eloquent and powerful remarks, to urge that the weapons of their warfare were not carnal, but spiritual, and mighty through God, to the pulling down of strongholds.[6] That they must fight with the sword of the spirit, even the word of God; they must appeal to the pure sentiments of the mind, and the justice of their cause. She was opposed to any twaddle on that subject, as well as her friend. We want to speak earnestly and truly the words of honest and sober conviction. We want to speak in tones of reproof to those on whom the guilt of these wrongs rests. We want to say as Jesus did "Ye fools and blind," "Ye hypocrites," and to our Sisters, who are still indifferent and contented with their position "O, thou slothful and slow of heart, rise up in the strength of thy Womanhood and Christ shall give thee light." There is no greater mistake than to suppose that what is called non-resistance is a timid and inefficient method of meeting those evils. It is the strongest kind of resistance—the resistance of moral sentiment, of justice and truth. It will not permit us to injure our fellow beings, to take their lives, but it leaves to us that higher resistance which comes from God.

* * * *

Mrs. LUCRETIA MOTT, made another impressive speech, in which she fixed the blame of these wrongs of Woman on the wrong doer. She did not believe in *abstract* wrong. Where there is oppression there is an oppressor. She thought the wrong in this case rested on man, and he should be held responsible for it. She marveled that her friend Wendell Phillips should take the view he did.[7] He did not reason thus when he spoke of the wrongs of the Slave.

* * * *

Mrs. MOTT made some further remarks, touching the promise of the Woman, in the marriage ceremony, to love, honor, and obey. She said these words were put in the Woman's mouth by the priest, or rather, repeated by the priest and not the Woman, though she reluctantly answers "Yes." In the religious society of which she was a member it was not so; there was a perfect reciprocity of obligation as they stood in the presence of heaven, without priest or magistrate, and invoked the Father's blessing. And she believed there were as happy and harmonious unions formed in that society as in any other religious association.

[*October 24, Afternoon Session*]

LUCRETIA MOTT said she was glad their young friend from Oberlin had stated so clearly a part of the scriptural argument on the subject.[8] These expositions had been familiar to her for years, and she had come to the conclusion that it would not be profitable to consume too much time with the Bible argument. Let those who are interested in that branch of the subject take a favorable opportunity to investigate it. She thought the true ground to take is to address themselves to the justice, the humanity and the common sense of those who hear. She would, however, say that it was very plain, from the Bible, that Women did preach the gospel. They had the gift of prophecy. She quoted the passage, "I will pour out my spirit upon all flesh, and your sons and daughters shall prophesy." To be a prophet or a prophetess was to be a teacher. She quoted several other passages, showing the equality of woman's privileges from the Bible, and said she had many more at her fingers' ends. But she did [*not*] think the argument necessary. Yet she would not have had the young friend, who had spoken on this subject, say one word less than she did.

[*October 24, Evening Session*]

LUCRETIA MOTT then made the closing address to the Convention. She alluded to the Bible argument, and said that many of those injunctions of Paul were applicable only to the circumstances of the Christians in that age; and suggested whether Paul and the other Apostles might not have imbibed some of the spirit and ignorance of their age on the subject; whether they were not influenced somewhat by the prevailing view that obtained at the time respecting Woman; and whether Paul, never having lived in the marriage relation, was fully competent as an authority on this subject. There could be no doubt that the general tenor, the spirit and the teachings of Christianity were all on the side of Woman's Rights.

She then delivered a most affectionate valedictory, dwelling for a moment on the simple and truthful words of Sojourner Truth, the poor woman who had grown up under the curse of Slavery, "that goodness was from everlasting and would never die, while evil had a beginning and must come to an end."[9] She portrayed the mountains of difficulty that stood in the way of this reform, and said, "Are ye able to bear all this?" Then she uttered words of encouragement and hope. She pictured Jesus Christ, the Messiah, encountering the same difficulties; but the common people heard him gladly and many there are who shall rise up in behalf of our cause, and call it blessed. Mark, said she, the words of Jesus: "Lift up your eyes and behold the harvest, white for the reaper. Pray ye that laborers may be sent into the harvest." We must be living agents of this work. If ever there was an age, since the Messiah, when the people should do those "greater works" which he said they should do who obey his word, this is that age. She alluded to the success of the Temperance and the Anti-Slavery reforms. Look at all these movements, and be not discourage[d]—persevere unto the end. Quoting from the sainted [*William Ellery*] Channing, she said, "Mighty powers are at work, and who shall stay them?" She said the *sainted* Channing, because of the good works he had done. It seemed to her, after his death, as she sat alone in her room, thinking of him, his presence was with her, and the halo of his divinity round about her. In regard to this movement she said—he or she who is least in the kingdom, is greater than these. She alluded to the writings of Jane Eyre, Harriet Martineau, Mary Howitt, in terms of approbation,[10] and as a sign of promise; to Catharine Beecher's appeal twenty years ago on behalf of woman. Then she passed to her closing remarks. Are we not now separating from each other with grateful hearts? The day spring from on high hath visited us. We have met around this altar of humanity, and though no vocal prayers have been offered, she trusted an oblation had arisen from our hearts. "And how, Lord, let thy servants depart in peace; for our eyes have seen thy salvation."

PD J. G. Forman, "Woman's Rights Convention," *New York Tribune*, October 25 and 26, 1850, WASM

1. This convention is considered the founding of a national women's rights movement (Faulkner, 149). Multiple versions of the convention were printed, and the official published *Proceedings* did not include LM's remarks. See John McClymer, "How do Contemporary Newspaper Accounts of the 1850 Worcester Woman's Rights Convention Enhance our Understanding of the Issues Debated at that Meeting?," WASM.
2. In her presidential address, Paulina Wright Davis (1813–76), physiologist and abolitionist, stated, "we must be gentle with the ignorance and patient under the injustice which the old evils induce . . . neither rebellion nor revolution, neither defiance nor resistance . . . is either possible, expedient, or proper." Included in the call to the convention, which LM had signed, was the statement that "The sexes should not, for any reason or by any chance, take hostile attitudes toward each other . . . but they should harmonize in opinion and co-operate in effort" (*Proceedings of the Woman's Rights Convention, Held at Worcester, October 23d & 24th, 1850* [Boston: Prentiss & Sawyer, 1851], 10, 4, WASM).
3. The Philadelphia School of Design for Women had been established in 1848; the Female Medical College of Pennsylvania in 1850 (Faulkner, 152).
4. LM's interest in phrenology had been stimulated by her friendship with George Combe, who advocated the study of the skull's shape as a means of understanding social problems and as a guide to human nature (see Palmer, 63, 148, for example). With his brother Andrew Combe (1797–1847), George had established the *Phrenological Journal* in 1823. Opposition stemmed from phrenology's emphasis on nature's pre-eminence, not God's.
5. According to McClymer, only the *New York Herald* published the controversial remarks of Abigail Kelley Foster (1810–87). The *New York Herald* quoted Foster as claiming, "We have our rights, and the right to revolt, as did our fathers against King George the Third—the right to rise up and cut the tyrants' throats. On this subject I scorn to talk like a woman. We must give them the truth, and not twaddle" ("Woman's Rights Convention, Awful Combination of Socialism, Abolitionism, and Infidelity," October 25, 1850, WASM).

6. LM paraphrases the AASS's 1833 Declaration of Sentiments, which rejected "the use of all carnal weapons for deliverance from bondage; relying solely upon those which are spiritual" (*Liberator*, January 4, 1834).

7. Wendell Phillips said that "He did not think all the guilt of these wrongs to which women are subjected rested on Man. He thought Woman must share equally the guilt with him" (*New York Tribune*, October 25, 1850, WASM).

8. In addressing the Apostle Paul's statement that women should refrain from speaking in churches, the Congregational and later Unitarian minister Antoinette Brown, later Blackwell (1825–1921), quoted biblical passages to show that Paul meant that women were not prevented from speaking everywhere, but only from interrupting "the good order and demeanor of churches" (*New York Tribune*, October 26, 1850, WASM).

9. Sojourner Truth (ca. 1799–1883), abolitionist and women's rights activist, had emancipated herself from slavery in Ulster County, New York.

10. Charlotte Bronte (1816–55) published *Jane Eyre* in 1847; Mary Howitt (1799–1888), Quaker poet.

Isaac T. Hopper Memorial Service, Broadway Tabernacle, New York City, May 12, 1852

LUCRETIA MOTT, an elderly Quaker lady, then laid aside her bonnet, and advancing to the pulpit or altar, delivered a funeral address in a steady, clear and audible voice, and collected manner. I cannot say—she commenced—that we come here on this sad occasion, because I do not think that, in the termination of a life thus spent, and having attained to a full age, there is any cause of sadness; but I think we ought rather to rejoice in the goodness and benevolence of the Highest, that, when the time is come when we must expect the faculties bestowed on us by God, to wane and to fade; it is the act of God's benevolence that we should be removed. When this event comes upon us all, it needs not that we call it a sad occasion if we have lived as did our brother. It needs not that we mourn for him. It is true that the tender ties of nature and of affection cannot be severed without a present pang. It has long since seemed to me not a fitting occasion to enlarge in eulogy of the deceased. Enough has been said.[1] The discriminating public of all denominations uniting in the one testimony as to his worth, have done so much to supersede on this occasion the expression of many words. I would only refer to the early days of his life, which he dedicated to God, to goodness, to do his duty and to labor in his vocation. In that early day his strongest conviction, perhaps, was, that the spirit of the Highest was resting upon him, calling on him and anointing him "to preach deliverance to the captive, to open the prison to those who are bound, and to set at liberty those who are bruised." That he was faithful to this conviction through good and evil report, many of the poor fugitives of our land, and many a heartbroken slave, can abundantly testify, and resolutions passed by the Anti-Slavery Society also bear testimony to his fidelity.[2] Mrs. Mott's address was plain, forcible and affecting, and drew tears from a portion of her auditory.

PD "The Late Isaac T. Hopper," *Pennsylvania Freeman*, May 27, 1852

1. R. N. Havens, vice-president of the Prison Association, acknowledged Hopper's "simple but firm character... and of the practical benefit he had conferred on discharged convicts" (*Pennsylvania Freeman*, May 27, 1852).

2. Hopper had died on May 7, 1852. His antislavery activities had begun in the 1790s, and he had been disowned by the New York Monthly Meeting in 1841 for publishing antislavery articles critical of fellow Quakers, particularly George F. White, in the *National Anti-Slavery Standard* (Faulkner, 120; Palmer, 94, 104).

Women's Rights Convention, Horticultural Hall, West Chester, Pennsylvania, June 2–3, 1852

[*June 2, Morning Session*]
LUCRETIA MOTT addressed the Convention, briefly referring to the importance of the movement and expressing her gratification on seeing the response given to the call, by the great number of persons assembled. She saw before her not only a large delegation from the immediate vicinity, but a goodly number from other and distant States.

The movement for the enfranchisement of Woman was indeed making rapid progress. Since the first Convention held at Seneca Falls, in 1848, where a few women assembled, and notwithstanding their ignorance of Parliamentary modes of conducting business, promulgated these principles, which took deep root, and are already producing important results, other large Conventions have been held in different places, which have done much towards disseminating the great principles of equality between the sexes; and a spirit of earnest inquiry has been aroused.

She referred to the fact that the agitation commenced in those States most distinguished for intellectual and moral culture—that we in Pennsylvania were ready to embrace their views on this subject, and she trusted that the Convention now assembled would be neither less interesting nor less efficient than those which have been already held.

[*June 2, Afternoon Session*]
MRS. MOTT spoke of the great change in public opinion, within her recollection, in regard to the so-called sphere of woman. There had been progress. Twenty-five years ago people wondered how a modest girl could attend lectures on botany; but modest girls did attend them, and other places, in former times, frequented only by men; and the result was not a loss of delicacy, but a higher and nobler development,—a truer modesty. She took a hopeful view of the cause, and closed with words of encouragement.

[*June 3, Morning Session*]
LUCRETIA MOTT (see 7th Resolution,) thought it important that we should not disclaim the antagonism that woman's present position rendered it necessary she should assume.[1] Too long had wrongs and oppressions existed without an acknowledged wrong-doer and oppressor. It was not until the slaveholder was told, "thou art the man," that a healthful agitation was brought about. Woman is

told that the fault is in herself, in too willingly submitting to her inferior condition; but, like the slave, she is pressed down by laws in the making of which she has had no voice, and crushed by customs that have grown out of such laws. She cannot rise, therefore, while thus trampled in the dust. The oppressor does not see himself in that light until the oppressed cry for deliverance.

The extract from Luther's will which has been read, while it gives evidence of the appreciation of the *services* of his wife, to a certain extent, and manifests a *generous* disposition to reward her as a faithful wife, still only proves the degrading relation she bore to her husband.[2] There is no recognition of her equal right to their joint earnings. While the wife is obliged to accept as a gift that which in justice belongs to her, however generous the boon, she is but an inferior dependent.

The law of our State and of New York, has within a few years been so amended that the wife has *some* control over a part of her property. Much yet remains to be done; and if woman "contend earnestly" for the right, man will co-operate with her in adjusting all her claims.

We have only to look back a few years, to satisfy ourselves that the demands already made are met in a disposition to redress the grievances. When a delegation of women to the World's Anti-Slavery Convention in 1840, could find no favor in London, what were the reasons assigned for the exclusion? Not that the *right* of representation was not as much woman's as man's, but that "they would be ridiculed in the morning papers."

Daniel O'Connell felt the injustice done to those delegates, and in a letter on the subject expressed himself:[3]

Dr. Bowring advocated the admission of the delegates at that time; and afterward in a letter to this country,[4] said: "How often have I regretted that the woman's question, to me of singular interest, was launched with so little preparation, so little knowledge of the manner in which it had been entangled, by the fears of some, and the follies of others! But, bear up! *for the coming of those women will form an era in the future history of philanthropic daring.* They made a *deep*, if not a wide impression; and have created apostles, if as yet they have not multitudes of followers. The experiment was well worth making. It honored America—it will instruct England. If in some matters of high civilization you are *behind* us, in this matter of courageous benevolence how far are you before us!"

Since that time women have fairly entered the field, as students of Medicine and as Physicians, as Editors and Lecturers, engaged in schools of design, and in the taking of Daguerres, as well as in some other works of art, and in holding Conventions in several of the States of our Union for the advocacy of our entire claims.

A National Society has been formed; and the proceedings of these Conventions and Society Meetings have been fairly reported and have received favorable notices in many of the papers of this country, as well as in the Westminster Review in England.[5]

PD *The Proceedings of the Woman's Rights Convention Held at West Chester, PA, June 2d and 3d, 1852* (Philadelphia: Merrihew and Thompson, 1852), 4, 19, 28–30, WASM

1. LM here addressed the seventh resolution, which stated that in "demanding" equality with men, women did not seek "separate advantages, or in any apprehension of conflicting interests between the sexes" (*Proceedings*, 31).

2. Quaker minister Joseph Dugdale (1810–96) urged husbands to write wills leaving all property to the surviving wives, and as an example quoted the will of Martin Luther (1483–1546). Luther wrote that he was leaving his estate to Katharina von Bora Luther (1499–1552) because "'she has always conducted herself towards me, lovingly, worthily and beautifully, like a pious, faithful and noble wife'" (*Proceedings,* 27).

3. Writing LM on June 20, 1840, Irish Member of Parliament (Whig) Daniel O'Connell (1775–1847) stated that the convention's fear of ridicule "was an unworthy, and indeed, a cowardly motive" and praised the prominent role of American women in the antislavery movement (Palmer, 77–78).

4. The letter of British reformer John Bowring (1792–1872) to WLG had been published in the December 25, 1840, *Liberator* (Palmer, 237).

5. LM served as vice-president of the women's rights convention in Worcester in October 1851. "The Enfranchisement of Women" by the British writer Harriet Taylor Mill (1807–58) praised the work of the 1850 Worcester convention and stated that women were indeed the intellectual equals of men (*Westminster Review*, July 1851, reprinted in *New York Tribune*, July 18, 1851; see Palmer, 209). The convention adopted, along with others, the seventh resolution (*Proceedings*, 31).

Women's Rights Convention, City Hall, Syracuse, New York, September 8–10, 1852

[*September 8, Morning Session*]

As the question on the adoption of the report was about being put, Mrs. MOTT arose and stated, that as there might be objections to her appointment, she desired that the vote on each officer might be taken separately. The Chairman (Mrs. [*Paulina Wright*] DAVIS) put the question accordingly, and the entire audience, with the exception of her husband [*JM*], voted that Mrs. MOTT should preside.

The President and other officers, who also were unanimously elected, having taken their seats, the President remarked, that she was unpractised in parliamentary proceedings, shrinking ever from such positions, and was therefore quite unprepared for anything like a suitable speech. She invoked, however, great and heartfelt attention to the business before them, dispensing with all egotism or self-display. She referred also to the success that had attended this movement in the past—to the respect with which the press had spoken of our proceedings—and the favor of the public generally. She suggested some things, relative to the proprieties of the present meeting—its business, &c. She said, let it not be supposed, because certain preliminaries had been entered into, that therefore the entire responsibility rested upon a few—but enjoined upon all to take their liberty, and each to feel free to act as moved by his, or her, present convictions.

* * * *

Mrs. MOTT thought differently from Mrs. N., that woman's moral feelings were more elevated than man's.[1] She thought that with the same opportunities for development, there would probably be about an equal manifestation of virtue.

[*September 8, Afternoon Session*]

E. OAKES SMITH[2] presented the following Resolution, offered by LUCRETIA MOTT: *Resolved,* That as the imbruted slave, who is content with his own lot, and would not be free if he could, if any such there be, only gives evidence of the depth of his degradation—so the woman who is satisfied with her inferior condition, averring that she has all the rights that she wants, does but exhibit the enervating effects of the wrongs to which she is subjected.

The above was laid on the table, for further consideration.

[*September 8, Evening Session*]

LUCRETIA MOTT took the stand, and spoke at considerable length. She cited several examples to prove that women were equal in strength to men and superior in industry.

It was impossible, she said, for one man to have arbitrary power over another, without becoming despotic. She did not expect our friend to see how woman is robbed. Women were to feel it. Slave-owners did not perceive themselves oppressors, but slaves did. GERRIT SMITH alluded to one woman, whom our friend would call out of her sphere.[3] If he believes in the Bible, he must acknowledge that Deborah, a mother in Israel, arose by divine command and led the armies of Israel. She also referred to the wife of Heber, the Kenite, who drove the nail into the head of the Canaanite General, and was celebrated therefor in the songs of Israel. She thought female preaching in harmony with the doctrine of Paul. She referred to Paul's directions to women how to preach, and his exhortations to them to qualify themselves for [this] function, and not to pin their faith on ministers' sleeves.

She cited Willis' Unwritten Philosophy,[4] and advised Mr. BRIGHAM not to stake his wisdom against the allotment of the Almighty.

Our schools were opened at last to women, and they had now sent out teachers. Colleges were now opened and LUCY STONE and ANTOINETTE BROWN[5] had entered, had obtained their diplomas, and now went out and pleaded the cause of the slave, and of their own sex, with an eloquence almost equal to that of our young friend, here.

The medical world was now open to woman; and noble examples had been set by talented females. Woman's sphere had been enlarging and widening, till it is now filling, not only the whole earth, but also heaven.

* * * *

Mrs. MOTT asked whether her young friend had sent a protest to old England against Victoria's proroguing Parliament.[6] In the yearly meetings of the Friends, documents read by the men, had been read by the woman's clerk, that they might be better understood.

She closed by saying, that LUCY STONE and ANTOINETTE BROWN wanted to treat this subject more at length, to-morrow, and she hoped her young friend, BRIGHAM, would be present and discuss the question farther.

[*September 9, Morning Session*]

The President said, this was not, as yet, a permanent organization, but only a Convention for the time being. Perhaps it would be deemed advisable to form an organization, and then standing Committees could be appointed, and all the usual machinery. She thought it would be premature to send the funds to WENDELL PHILLIPS, the Treasurer of the last Convention, unless no other Treasurer were appointed.[7]

* * * *

PRESIDENT—Woman's Rights women do not like to be called by their husbands' names, but their own.

* * * *

The PRESIDENT—The Church and public opinion are stronger than law.

* * * *

The PRESIDENT thought this Convention as orderly, regular and parliamentary, as those of men.

[*September 9, Afternoon Session*]

E. O. SMITH, one of the Vice Presidents, took the Chair, while LUCRETIA MOTT addressed the Convention in favor of agitation.

She said, allusion had been made by the last speaker to the condition of France. A petition was presented, during the Provisional Government, before the last uprising of the people in that country, for the rights of woman.[8] Some of the greatest philosophers there present, saw that women were right in their claim; they saw in it a new future for woman. The reason of the failure of the Revolution of 1789, was that they failed to be represented by one half of the intelligence of France—intelligence different but not inferior, and for that very difference essential to form a complete Republic. Woman had long suffered under a nightmare of oppression, without the power to state the cause of her suffering. Those only shunned or hated discussion, who, being in the wrong, feared the light. The common remark in the social circle is, "what do you want?" *Women* would not ask that question, if they were not stupefied with the gilded pill of flattery, in place of rights.

It was said this morning, that woman could take her rights in a quiet way, without making so much talk about it;[9] this is not the case, as is shown in the efforts already made. In all reforms we have the assertion that agitation is not best; that God in his own good time will bring about the desired end; it had often been said, in the meetings of which she was a member, that if Friends would keep still, and not mix in the excitements of the day, Providence would bring about all reforms. She was a believer in agitation—in the wisdom of not keeping still. Jesus was an agitator; he told the Scribes and Pharisees they made the law of God of no effect, by their traditions; and urged the practical carrying out of the law of righteousness. She added, that the wife was degraded in the marriage relation, in the false vow of obedience to her husband. [*William*] Blackstone defines the law of marriage to be that the husband and wife are one person, and that person, the husband. Thus women are degraded by law, by the monopoly of the Church, and all the circumstances with which she is surrounded. She must therefore boldly affirm her rights. Lucy Stone, whom they all delighted to honor, had to do battle for her rights, even in that college (Oberlin) which was the first to open its portals for the equal education of women with men. Antoinette Brown, also a student in that seminary, had to meet the prejudices against women's preaching, and to show that no Apostolic or other Scriptural prohibition could be found. Women must go on, in the exercise of their talents and powers. The first efforts were feeble, but they would gain strength. Some women had resolved to study Law. We had already successful practitioners of Medicine. The salaries of female Teachers are now from five hundred to one thousand dollars per year. The teacher of Grammar in the Girard College,[10] a woman, is acknowledged superior to most men. The number of female Editors is constantly increasing. Schools of Design, and other branches of the Fine Arts, are offering employment to women. The U.S. Mint employs three to four hundred women. Persevere then, until no woman shall confess her own degradation, by saying she has all the rights she wants.

Mrs. MOTT's resolution was then adopted. Adjourned.

[*September 10, Morning Session*]

LUCRETIA MOTT said, she knew that prayer was customary on such occasions, at the opening of meetings, but that she could not conscientiously call for it; it was due, however, that opportunity should be given when asked.

* * * *

PRESIDENT—That question is not before the Convention.[11] We come to affirm great fundamental truths, and all we find in the Book to corroborate these truths, we gladly receive. We have as good a right to use our ability in bringing Jesus and the Apostles to confirm our opinions, as the several Divines have to use their ingenuity to bring the Bible to bear on their peculiar views.

Rev. MR. HATCH—That is not the question. What I wanted to know is, whether this Convention recognizes the Bible, or not?

PRESIDENT—This question has not been considered, and, therefore, is not decided.

[*September 10, Afternoon Session*]

The PRESIDENT reminded the Convention that they should not compromise their dignity, because the speaker [*Hatch*] did his.

* * * *

The PRESIDENT hoped he would keep in order,[12] and not retail the vulgar conversation of his associates.

He went on further, in a similar strain, until the indignation of the audience became universal. The President said, he had so outraged the feelings of the Convention that he could not be permitted to go on.

* * * *

The PRESIDENT vacated the Chair, and spoke briefly in opposition to the resolution.[13] In the early days of Anti-Slavery, great pains were taken to show that the Bible was against Slavery: opponents coming forward, the time of Conventions was too much occupied by the bandying of Scripture texts. Other occasions than those, were therefore judged best for such discussions. The advocates of Emancipation found their business was to affirm the inherent right of man to himself and to his earnings—that none had a right to imbrute him—that it was essentially sinful, and that slaveholders were men-stealers. These being self-evident truths, no argument or outward authority was needed to prove it. We already see the disadvantage of such discussions here. It is not to be supposed that all the advice given by the Apostles, to the women of their day, is applicable to our more intelligent age; nor is there any passage in Scripture, making those texts binding on us.

A gentleman then quoted: "All Scripture is given by inspiration of God, and is profitable, etc." Does this not apply to the latest period?

LUCRETIA MOTT said, in reply: If the speaker will turn to the passage, he will find that the word "*is*," being in italics, was inserted by the translators. She accepted it, as in the original, "All Scripture *given* by inspiration of God, is profitable, etc." She claimed some familiarity with the Scriptures, and should have no objection, at a suitable time, to discuss this question. She concluded by moving that the resolution be laid on the table. Unanimously carried.

[*September 10, Evening Session*]

P. W. DAVIS said, if a stock company of two thousand dollars was formed, the paper could go on.[14]

The PRESIDENT said, this ought to be done, and not leave the other undone. She was in favor of a newspaper devoted to this reform, and alluded to the value of the Anti-Slavery papers.

* * * *

The PRESIDENT had a word to say; she had no liking for these votes of thanks. We no doubt all felt thankful that the Convention had passed off so satisfactorily; and she was thankful that she had been able to perform her part better than she expected. Let that suffice.

PD *Proceedings of the Woman's Rights Convention, Held at Syracuse* (Syracuse, N.Y.: J. E. Masters, 1852), 13, 15, 23, 35, 38, 46, 50, 64–65, 76, 88–89, 90–92, 95, 97, WASM

1. Clarina H. Nichols (1810–85), editor of the *Windham County Democrat* in Brattleboro, Vermont, stated that women possessed the "moral field" and women should thus seek a "more elevated position, because her moral susceptibilities are greater than those of man" (*Proceedings*, 14).
2. Elizabeth Oakes Smith (1806–93), women's rights lecturer from New York City.
3. J. B. Brigham, referred to as "a school teacher," stated that men's and women's "spheres were not the same, and that woman was only truly lovely and happy, when in her own sphere and her own element." Women should be "keepers at home, and mind domestic concerns." To this the abolitionist Gerrit Smith (1797–1874) replied that LM could make Brigham "feel the power of a woman." Smith recounted the biblical story (Judges 9:53–54) of King Abimelech who, when threatened by an unnamed woman, ordered his aide to kill him, "that he might not be slain by a woman" (*Proceedings*, 35).
4. In Nathaniel Willis's short story "Unwritten Philosophy," the narrator inculcates in a friend's daughter a love of "high attainment and wonderful discovery" in serious reading (N. P. Willis, ed., *The Legendary, Consisting of Original Pieces*, vol. 2 [Boston: Samuel Goodrich, 1828], 229).
5. Although Antoinette Brown and Lucy Stone (1818–93) were among the first female students enrolled at Oberlin College, Brown was refused a student's license to preach in 1850. When Stone was not permitted to read her commencement essay to a mixed audience, she refused to write one.

6. Brigham stated that "woman had less voice than men" (*Proceedings*, 36). Queen Victoria (1819–1901) had ascended to the throne in 1837.

7. The convention formed a central committee with representation from each state, including Wendell Phillips and LM, to plan another national convention. Phillips continued as treasurer (*Proceedings*, 92).

8. Ernestine Sismondi Potowski Rose (1810–92), a Polish-born women's rights lecturer, condemned the unscrupulous tactics of Louis Napoleon in securing his re-election in 1852 (*Proceedings*, 72). Following the February 1848 revolution in France, which created the Second Republic, two organizations, the Society for the Emancipation of Women and the Committee for the Rights of Women, demanded women's political and social equality, arguing, "There cannot be two liberties, two equalities, two fraternities" (quoted in Bonnie Anderson, *Joyous Greetings: The First International Women's Movement, 1830–1860* [New York: Oxford University Press, 2000], 157–58).

9. Jane Elizabeth Jones (1813–96), former editor of the *Anti-Slavery Bugle* in Salem, Ohio, stated that "she was one of those who, instead of talking about rights, took them, without saying anything about it" (*Proceedings*, 46).

10. Founded in Philadelphia in 1848, Girard College offered free education to white male orphans. From the beginning, the college employed a matron and female teachers ("Opening of the Girard College," *Friends' Review*, January 8, 1848; "Girard College," *Family Visitor*, April 17, 1851).

11. Junius L. Hatch, a Congregational minister from Massachusetts, inquired if the present convention considered the Bible as "paramount authority" (*Proceedings*, 88).

12. Hatch then described "female loveliness" as consisting of " that shrinking delicacy which, like the modest violet, hid itself until sought" (*Proceedings*, 90).

13. On September 9 Antoinette Brown had introduced the resolution: "*Resolved*, That the Bible recognizes the rights, duties and privileges of Woman as a public teacher, as every way equal with those of man" (*Proceedings*, 66).

14. In 1853 Davis founded the *Una*, the first newspaper dedicated to women's rights. On the convention, see Faulkner, 153; Palmer, 219–21; Gordon, 1:212–14.

Pennsylvania Anti-Slavery Society, Horticultural Hall, West Chester, Pennsylvania, October 25–26, 1852[1]

[*October 25 Session*]

Lucretia Mott remarked, that, on coming together after a year's separation, it is natural that our religious feelings should be excited. While objections are felt to a formal service of prayer at the opening of our meeting, it is well that we all cultivate a prayerful spirit. Last year some of us came to our anniversary with saddened and anxious hearts, almost desponding in view of the persecutions we were witnessing and enduring for righteousness' sake.[2] But our resolutions were as unyielding in principle, and as bold in spirit as ever, a fact remarked by spectators. Now, those who have observed the fulfillment of our hopes and predictions, come together rejoicing, and with songs of melody and thanksgiving in our hearts. It is meet that this feeling should awaken devotional aspirations, and find expression. She therefore proposed a brief period of silence.

* * * *

Lucretia Mott wished that we should not come together to glorify each other. Our platform is free for all, but let us call no one upon it to show himself merely as a spectacle to the meeting. Theodore Weld[3] once replied to a proposal of a vote of honor to himself, "Let us strike a level above which no abolitionist shall raise his head; let us drop a curtain behind which every abolitionist shall work, and there dig his grave."

* * * *

Lucretia Mott did not like the sentiment in the Report under discussion, and regretted its introduction.[4] We should attribute all good to the Infinite Source of good. The evils of the Fugitive Slave Law are infinite. Ask the colored people, whom it has scattered like sheep upon the mountains, what can compensate them for their sufferings and terrors and losses. See how it has corrupted the Northern people, and how easily men, at first shocked at it, have become reconciled to it. This speculation is incapable of demonstration. It opens a controversy without end. Is it not better to speak evil as evil, not deducing from it any consequences which do not strictly belong to it? Does it not tend to weaken our abhorrence of wrong? There is nothing easier than to quote texts of Scripture in favor of any theory, as every sect supports its faith by such texts. I am not willing to admit that Harriet Beecher Stowe was moved to write Uncle Tom's Cabin by that law; if she says so, I think she mistakes the influences which have moved her. I believe, rather that it has been the moral sentiments and truths promulgated by the Liberator, the National Era, and the public discussion of the subject, upon her pure mind, exciting it to feel for the oppressed.[5] If you point to the progress of our cause, through persecution, as evidence that the efforts of its enemies have helped it on, I have as good a right to say that, but for these impediments, slavery would have been abolished before now. I hope the Society will instruct the striking out of these passages of the Report.[6]

[*October 26 Session*]

Mrs. Mott believed the Society had never pursued the measure of voting.[7] Our measures, as described in the Declaration of Sentiments adopted at the formation of the American Anti-Slavery Society, were to organize Anti-Slavery Societies, to send forth agents; to circulate books, tracts and periodicals; to seek to enlist the pulpit and the press in the cause of the suffering and the dumb; to aim at the purification of the churches from the guilt of slavery; and to encourage the labor of freemen instead of slaves. Nothing was said of voting, and probably nothing was thought of it. Whatever acts upon the parties and politics of the country is thus for *political action*. Our exhibition of the political and economical evils of Slavery and advantages of Freedom, our exposure of the aggressions of the slave power in and through the government, are such.

* * * *

Mrs. Mott recommended the Anti-Slavery Fair to the patronage and assistance of all friends of the cause, stating that the Female Anti-Slavery Society in the city, and our friends in Europe were actively engaged in preparations for it.[8] In conclusion, she offered the following resolution in behalf of the Fair, which passed unanimously.

Resolved, That we earnestly request the active co-operation of the abolitionists of Pennsylvania in the Annual Anti-Slavery Fair of this State, believing it to be an important department of anti-slavery labor, whether regarded in its pecuniary or its moral aspect.

PD C. M. Burleigh, "Pennsylvania Anti-Slavery Society," *Pennsylvania Freeman*, November 6, 1852

1. The PASS had been founded in 1837 (Palmer, 91).
2. Passed in 1850, the Fugitive Slave Law permitted southern slaveholders to seize fugitives in free states and, in effect, assumed that all African Americans were slaves unless they could prove otherwise. At the October 7, 1851, PASS meeting, LM had expressed determination to pursue even more antislavery efforts because of the Christiana Riot of September 11, 1851, and other incidents involving free blacks as well as fugitive slaves (*Pennsylvania Freeman*, October 16, 1851).
3. Before a throat ailment ended his lecturing career in 1836, Theodore Weld (1803–95) was one of the most successful agents of the AASS.
4. The Fifteenth Annual Report of the PASS declared that the "wicked devices of our enemies had been overruled by an all-wise Providence" (*Pennsylvania Freeman*, November 6, 1852).
5. An article in the *Liberator* (April 30, 1852) stated that the "legislative act of 1850" had caused Harriet Beecher Stowe (1811–96) to depict slavery's evils "in a *living dramatic reality.*" *The National Era*, a newspaper based in Washington, D.C., had serialized *Uncle Tom's Cabin* from June 1851 to April 1852.
6. On October 26 the PASS unanimously agreed to publish its annual report (*Pennsylvania Freeman*, November 6, 1852).
7. In a debate on the first resolution reaffirming the Society's measures to end slavery, several members raised the prospect of taking "political action" and what that action entailed (*Pennsylvania Freeman*, November 6, 1852).
8. PFASS, founded in 1833, sponsored antislavery fairs from 1836 to 1861, often in conjunction with the PASS meetings, to raise money for the cause (Faulkner, 197).

Pennsylvania Anti-Slavery Society, Assembly Buildings, Philadelphia, December 15–16, 1852

[December 15 Session]

Mrs. Mott agreed with the cheering views presented, but would not have the darker side of the picture forgotten, or overlooked.[1] We have much to do yet. Indeed, we have but begun our work. Though we have almost reached the second decade since the formation of the American Anti-Slavery Society, the number of slaves is still increasing, and the alarmed slaveholders are laboring with unabated zeal to secure new power and fresh markets for their slaves. This should not discourage us, but should prompt us to renewed activity and earnestness. When we "remember those in bonds as bound with them," this fact would make us sad, but that we find a daily reward and encouragement in our work, cheering and strengthening our hearts. This is, as Cyrus Burleigh[2] has said, "God's benediction upon the faithful worker." Such occasions as this make me cheerful. I love these Fairs, and am never weary with them, and never ready for the lights to be put out. To those whose hearts are in this work of Anti-Slavery truth it is never tiresome or old. It is well for the slave that it is so, and also that his friends shall cherish a hopeful spirit. At the same time, we should, in no respect relax our own labors in the trust that the cause can do without us. Let us not leave it to Congress, but continue to urge its members up to duty, and continue to make the public sentiment which will sustain them, reproving those even whom we delight to honor, when they compromise principle. This fidelity I admire in [*William Lloyd*] Garrison.

Mrs. Mott, in conclusion alluded to some of the hopeful events which have recently transpired, among them the late meeting of women at the house of the Duchess of Sutherland, to adopt an Address to their sisters in America, concerning American Slavery.[3]

* * * *

Mrs. Mott remarked that it was in connection with this new Anti-Slavery movement in England that our friend and co-laborer Sarah Pugh,[4] was detained abroad, instead of being with us as usual, exercising an active oversight of our Fair. The importance of her presence was scarcely known until we learned it from her absence. This has taught us how true it is that "Blessings brighten as they take their flight."[5] But much as we need her presence, we are reconciled to her absence, by the knowledge that she is doing an important work for our cause in England. Her visit there was peculiarly opportune, and has already done much to remove prejudice and false impressions from many honest minds, misled by the sectarian calumnies, and malicious representations against prominent American Abolitionists, so busily circulated by the British and Foreign Committee, with the aid of Anna Richardson.[6] Some, who by these influences had been made to regard Garrison and his associates as "infidels," have been already enlightened and won over as co-workers with us in this holy cause. Based as it is on eternal truth, they thus became co-workers with justice, co-workers with Christ and God. We rejoice to see that, even in our own country, many who had, for a time been alienated from us, are again returning and uniting with us.

[*December 16 Session*]

It was argued by Mrs. Mott that we might let our works speak for us, adopting the sentiments of Jesus to the disciples of John, "Go tell John the works that ye do see and hear." George Combe, when asked by certain ministers how he reconciled the teachings of his science with the Bible, answered them: "I leave that to you." So we, as Abolitionists, may calmly pursue our work, leaving it to others to see its resemblance to Christianity. To claim the name, seemed like an attempt to conciliate the narrow sectarian bigotry which has called us infidels. Then there are those who do not take the name of Christian who hate slavery. Let us make our platform broad enough to receive all who wish to come.

* * * *

Mrs. Mott introduced a resolution against the purchase of slaves, which after a slight verbal amendment was unanimously adopted as follows:

9. *Resolved*, That the increasing application for means to purchase slaves from their claimants should receive no countenance or aid from Abolitionists, nor from the community generally; such purchase being—if not an indirect

acknowledgment of the right of property in man,—an unwise appropriation of funds, which are so much needed to accomplish our great work—the overthrow of the slave system and the emancipation of every slave.[7]

PD C. M. Burleigh, "Anti-Slavery Convention," *Pennsylvania Freeman*, December 23, 1852

1. Among the resolutions offered were two acclaiming the "steady and irresistible progress" in the antislavery movement and the "increase of Anti-Slavery influence and talent in Congress" (*Pennsylvania Freeman*, December 23, 1852).
2. Cyrus M. Burleigh (1810–55), temperance and antislavery lecturer.
3. On November 26, 1852, Harriet Leveson-Gower (1806–68), duchess of Sutherland, had organized a message on abolishing slavery from British women to the women of America.
4. Sarah Pugh (1800–1884), a member of the PASS and PFASS, had been a delegate to the June 1840 World's Anti-Slavery Convention. Pugh traveled in Europe from fall 1851 to October 1853, and at a meeting of the Bristol Ladies' Anti-Slavery Society, she offered "explanations on points which had embarrassed their movements," trying to ameliorate the prejudice against Garrisonians (*Memorial of Sarah Pugh. A Tribute of Respect from her Cousins* [Philadelphia: J. B. Lippincott Company, 1888], 61).
5. Edward Young (1683–1765), *Night Thoughts* (1742–45), II, line 600.
6. Mott's phrasing is unclear. The British and Foreign Anti-Slavery Society had sided with the American and Foreign Anti-Slavery Society in 1840 when it separated from the AASS, and had also opposed the participation of women delegates at the World's Anti-Slavery Convention. Anna Richardson (1806–92) of Newcastle, England, an abolitionist and free produce advocate, allied with Garrison and the AASS (see Faulkner, 107; Palmer, 78, 81, 95, 147, 188).
7. Many abolitionists disagreed with the PASS resolution, and supported purchasing fugitive slaves. For this debate, see Faulkner, 115–16.

Women's Rights Convention, Broadway Tabernacle, New York City, September 6–7, 1853

[September 6, Morning Session, LM presiding]
It may be well, at the outset, to declare distinctly the objects of the present Convention. Its purpose is to declare principles, not to descend into the consideration of details: the principles, namely, of the co-equality of woman with man, and her right to practice those arts of life for which she is fitted by nature. Those are our great principles, and the assertion of them is our only present purpose. When they shall have been well recognized, then it will be quite time enough to speak of the proper mode of carrying them into universal practice. Already, some of the rights of woman have been conceded to her; but many yet remain, from the enjoyment of which she is most unjustly restrained. But let us take courage; although we are met by ridicule, through the newspaper press, magazines, and periodicals, let us rely on the inherent justice of our cause and our own exertions. The community are already beginning to see that there are many occupations which woman can fill with efficiency and propriety, that

were, until lately, closed against her. A generous feeling has befriended woman to this extent; but now, when it is perceived that she, and those who aid her, for the sake of justice of her cause, claim for her the full exercise of her faculties in the various walks of life to which men alone are now admitted; when her high and just aim is perceived—naturally, perhaps, there is a great deal of opposition to her, perhaps the more in proportion as she the more completely fits herself for pursuing those heretofore forbidden paths. We are prepared for a great deal of religious prejudice and even hostility; that is, prejudice and hostility claiming the name of religious. No wonder, for it is something new for woman to aim at the highest office—that which places her in the pulpit. But already has her voice been heard there, and to her credit.[1]

We have obstacles to encounter, but let them not dismay us, for they are not insurmountable. In the Temperance Reform, as well as in many others, it has been seen what difficulties can be overcome by vigorous and systematic efforts, based on inherent truth and justice. We came here full of hope, and prepared to prove that our cause is just. Woman has long been the mere slave of social custom, the unreasoning victim of conventional cruelty. Her voice has been suppressed, or fixed down to the slenderness of her cambric needle. But I was pleased to hear her, on some late occasions, use it in all the harmonious fullness with which the Creator has endowed it; and here, I trust, she will make it heard in the furthest corners of this hall.

I have not come prepared to open this convention with an address worthy of the principles we advocate, and I could wish that the Chair were filled by some other. To one thing I particularly request notice, namely, that the Convention shall give its undivided attention to whatever subject shall at the time be before it. Otherwise we shall be led into devious paths, and the time that should be devoted to a definite aim will be wasted on irregular and useless subjects. We are now organized and prepared for business. I introduce to the Convention Lucy Stone.

* * * *

I must ask leave to make a correction. The president of the meeting adverted to, was not Mrs. Mott, but Mrs. Mott's husband:[2] our first meeting was not prepared—had not yet acquired sufficient moral courage—to place a woman in the chair.

* * * *

I think it well here to ask speakers to bear in mind, as much as possible, the Resolutions that have been read, so as, as far as possible, to make the remarks they shall offer bear on these Resolutions.[3] This is called a "Woman's Rights Convention," but, I apprehend, the phrase, "Human Rights" would more appropriately express its principles and its aims, as I am glad to find they have been set forth by the speakers here this morning. However, let us not be misunderstood. This Convention does not arrogate to itself the power of settling the propriety of a woman's choosing any particular profession. The idea of the leaders of this movement is not that women should be *obliged* to accept the privileges which we demand should be open to her. There are, no doubt, many women who have no inclination to mingle in the busy walks of life; and many would, in all probability, feel conscientious scruples against voting, or taking any office under the present constitution of this country, considering some of its provisions. That, however, supplies no objection to the coequality which we assert. This we mean to attain and keep. The unwillingness of some to vote (assuming such to exist), does not destroy the right of a class. Elizabeth Jones, in a convention at Waterloo, when asked what women wanted, replied, "I want to vote, and be voted for."[4] In such circumstances, it is not beyond the reach of possibility, that the law might be purged of its inconsistencies and its hardness to be understood: and perhaps thus come within the assumed feeble intellect of woman. So in theology. Even the liberal Dr. [*William Ellery*] Channing maintained that its mysteries were too intricate, its difficulties too numerous and formidable, for the female mind to overcome them. Perhaps this science too might be simplified until it came within our reach. I concur fully in the wish that those who are against, as well as those who are for us, will come here and speak their sentiments. I hope and believe they will be courteously received, and earnestly desire that they may give themselves up to the guidance of the truth which may be here elicited, no matter how much it may jar with their preconceived opinions. In conclusion, I hope there will be no long speeches, but that all that may be said shall be terse, and directed plainly to the subjects before the Convention.

[*September 6, Afternoon Session*]

It may, perhaps, be as well to say no more, in the way of anticipation, as to how the newspapers will act in reporting these proceedings. The better way will, probably, be to hope for the best. When the sitting of the Convention shall have ended, then all will be able to judge how the journals have acted, whether fairly or otherwise.

I feel much regret that the debate of the present session took so wide a range.[5] Our time is limited, and it is earnestly requested that all speakers will strictly confine themselves to the matter under discussion. There has been, perhaps, too much time given to debating the subject of hissing, and such other disturbances. These matters would, most probably, be better left in the back ground on the present occasion. We expect to hear some speakers of note at the session of this evening; we shall probably be favored with addresses from Antoinette L. Brown, Rev. Wm. H. Channing,[6] and Mrs. E. L. Rose, among others.

[*September 6, Evening Session*]

I will again request the speakers to adhere strictly to the subjects presented in our Resolutions, and to the questions under discussion, and not to allow themselves to be diverted by any demonstration either of approval or disapproval, made among the audience. I would request of them not to reply to, or take any notice of, any such demonstration. I will now introduce to the Convention the Rev. Antoinette L. Brown.

[*September 7, Morning Session*]

The uproar and confusion which attended the close of our proceedings of last night, although, much to be regretted, as indicating an unreasonable and unreasoning disposition on the part of some, to close their ears against the truth, or rather, to drown its voice by vulgar clamor, yet, when viewed aright, and, in some phases, present to us matter of congratulation.[7] I do suppose, that never, at any meeting, was public propriety more outraged, than at ours of last evening.

I suppose, no transactions of a body assembled to deliberate, were ever more outrageously invaded by an attempt to turn them into a mere tumult; yet, though voices were loud and angry, and the evil passions exhibited themselves with much of that quality to affright, which usually, if not always, attends their exhibition—not a scream was heard from any woman, nor did any of the "weaker sex" exhibit the slightest terror, or even alarm, at the violent manifestations which invaded the peace of our assemblage.

I felicitate the women on this exhibition of fortitude; of calm moral courage. Should not our opponents, if they have any reason among them, reflect, that these exhibitions are, in reality, some of the strongest arguments that can be offered to support the claims which we stand here to advocate? Do they not show, on the one hand, that men, by whom such an overpowering superiority is arrogated, can betimes demean themselves in such a way as to show that they are wholly unfit for the lofty functions which they demand as their exclusive right? And, on the other hand, do they not conclusively show, that women are possessed of, at least, some of those qualities which assist in calmness of deliberation, during times of excitement and even danger! I think it was really a beautiful sight to see how calm the women remained during last evening's excitement; their self-possession, I consider something truly admirable. I know that, in the tumult and noise, it would have been vain for any woman to raise her voice in an attempt to check it. Indeed, I am satisfied, the outrage was predetermined, and I regret that the aid of the police had to be called in to quell it. Had there been here a company of women who were taught to rely upon others, they would, doubtless, have felt bound to scream for "*their protectors*"; but the self-reliance displayed, which must have its basis in a consciousness of the truth and justice of our cause, and which kept the members of the convention unmoved, amid all the prevailing confusion, gives us matter of real congratulation. Let us rejoice in this, my friends; and let us remember, that, when we have a true cause—while our cause rests on the basis of right—we have nothing to fear, but may go on unmoved by all these petty circumstances, by which we may be surrounded.

A request was made last night by some person, I don't know who, or rather a challenge was offered, that three good reasons should be given why women should vote.[8] Perhaps, had the person making this demand had this question put to him, namely, "What reasons are there why men should vote?" he would have considered the reasons so self-evident as to make any answer superfluous. Yet it would be found difficult, I apprehend, to assign any reason, why men should vote, which would not be found to be an equally good reason for extending the elective franchise to women. He asked, however, why women should be allowed to take a part in the civil government of the country. This question will, I doubt not, be answered today by some one more able than myself; and if the person who asked it be present, and open to conviction, he will hear reasons sufficient to convince him that women have the right to vote. I only repeat the question now, as one of the subjects claiming consideration today.

As to woman's occupying a high position in the social state, the very scriptures, to which our antagonists point in ill-founded triumph, as determining the matter against us, supply instances in abundance of the high estimation in which women were held. Nor is there any need of citing instances (so well are they known) of the part which woman took in the propagation of the true faith, and the *ministration*, too. In that passage wherein mention is made of the wives of deacons, (as the vernacular version gives it), a reference to the original text, and a true rendering of it will show that the real expression is, *the female deacons*. This single fact is a sufficient commentary on the fairness of some of the means employed to conceal the rights which really belong to women.

A good deal of stress is laid on the command given to women (as it is said) to be silent in the Church. The text is to be found in 1st Corinthians, ch. xiv., v. 34 and 35. But has this text the force and application which is demanded for it by our opponents? A calm and thorough investigation will show that it has not. It was one of those ordinances, or recommendations, the character of which was merely local, or confined to a certain place, and appropriate to a certain time. The same apostle who spoke thus, gave directions as to women prophesying, preaching or praying, and attiring themselves. But all these injunctions are as binding, and have as wide an application, as that relating to woman's being silent. Are these now observed? Manifestly not; and thus, is the admission made, that such commands referred to and were meant to have cogency in, only a certain place and at a certain time. They are to be taken in a modified sense, and to be referred only to the customs of a time that has long passed away. What were the real circumstances under which the words, "*it is not permitted to them to speak*," were applied to women? Circumstances of disagreement and tumult in the Church, where many men spoke together, and loudly, so that scarcely any voice could be distinctly heard. In such circumstances it was but a reasonable counsel to women to hold their peace for the time. It is added that "*if they will learn anything, let them ask their husbands at home*," which was also the reasonable proceeding as matters stood, and showed this, that women were enjoined to have an interest in the affairs of the Church, and also to take counsel on the same.

All such commands, (like that relating to attire, which so plainly contemplates an oriental and ancient mode of dress), must, to be reasonably taken, be received only as local, and suited to a particular time; and when these conditions of locality and time are withdrawn, the command ceases to have any cogency.

[*September 7, Afternoon Session*]

The time for adjournment having now arrived, I must interfere to announce the fact. If the gentleman choose, he can have the rest of his half hour, or twenty minutes, at the evening session. I am sorry we cannot satisfy the gentleman by answering his objections as intelligently (to his mind) as he seems to think he has stated them.[9] However, perhaps, even our dullness may be turned into an argument to give us the liberty we demand; because, if we received that liberty, it is possible we might use it in such a way as, after due time, to be able to answer so learned an opponent as he is. He must remember it is hard for weak woman to answer such solid arguments, and he must pity us if we do not come up to his standard of excellence. If he lay stress on his Scripture argument, that the wife must obey the husband, it may in some cases come to cut the other way; as in mine, for example, because *my* husband wishes me to vote, and therefore, according to the Scripture, the gentleman must, even in his own reasoning, allow me the right to vote. In one place, the gentleman said that woman had already turned the world over; and that man must be cautious not to allow her to do so again. Perhaps, if he reconsidered these statements, he might be willing to retract the latter; because, if she turned the world over once, and put the wrong side up, he ought now to allow her to turn it back, that she may bring the right side up again.[10]

PD *Proceedings of the Woman's Rights Convention, Held at the Broadway Tabernacle, in the City of New York, on Tuesday and Wednesday, Sept. 6th and 7th 1853* (New York: Fowler and Wells, Publishers, 1853), 4–5, 17, 19–20, 33, 35, 40, 54–57, 85–86, WASM

1. Antoinette Brown would be ordained as a Congregational minister in Wayne County, New York, on September 15, 1853.

2. Lucy Stone had just referred to LM as having presided over the Seneca Falls Convention (*Proceedings*, 17).

3. Among the eight resolutions read by Lucy Stone were assertions that men's political "monopoly" was a "monstrous usurpation"; that women's political participation would cause no "domestic dissension"; and that the nation's "moral laxity . . . and the ignorance, wretchedness and enforced profligacy of the poor . . . are the necessary results of [*women's*] exclusion from those diversified employments which would otherwise furnish them with useful occupation" (*Proceedings*, 6).

4. At the September 1852 Syracuse Convention, Jones had stated, "women had a natural right to vote, which no human laws could abrogate" (*Proceedings of the Woman's Rights Convention, Held at Syracuse* [Syracuse, N.Y.: J. E. Masters, 1852], 46). The reference to Waterloo likely refers to the Yearly Meeting of Congregational Friends there in June 1853.

5. WLG and Cyrus Burleigh had decried the recent unfavorable press coverage of women's rights conventions, WLG especially, in a lengthy speech, singling out the *New York Times* and the *New York Herald*. After a few remarks by others on woman's rights, Lucy Stone objected to a statement from Paulina Wright Davis, who asked men to "'give us the opportunity.'" Stone declared, "I would say to them, '*Take, take*'" (*Proceedings*, 22–35).

6. William Henry Channing (1810–84), Unitarian clergyman and nephew of William Ellery Channing.

7. Ernestine Rose's speech was interrupted several times by "indecorous conduct, and impertinent voices"; however she continued with the "utmost calmness" (*Proceedings*, 46–47). According to the *New York Times* (September 7, 1853), Rose's speech was "greeted with hisses, but she finally got a hearing." As she tried to continue to speak, "the audience would not listen to her inducements." Rose managed to conclude her speech amid "hisses, groans and cheers." Lucy Stone then spoke, after which the uproar still continued with "Confusion and a babel of tongues" until LM stated, "My Friends! the Convention is adjourned till 9 o'clock tomorrow morning!"

8. At the close of the September 6 session, Mr. Elliott asked for three reasons why women should vote (*Proceedings*, 54).

9. Dr. J. K. Root had stated that the Bible clearly expressed men's superiority to women, and that men are "naturally empowered with superiority as dictator, adviser, and ruler. Therefore, if he declares woman should not vote, and enter the competing walks of life, it is sufficient reason why she should not do so" (*Proceedings*, 85).

10. At the Akron Woman's Rights Convention, May 29, 1851, Sojourner Truth had expressed the same sentiment ("Ar'nt I a Woman?," *Anti-Slavery Bugle*, June 21, 1851). The New York meeting's evening session met with so many hostile interruptions that Vice-President Rose called the police and finally moved the convention adjourned. Prior to adjourning, the group approved a resolution commending LM for the "grace, firmness, ability and courtesy with which she has discharged her important and often arduous duties" (*Proceedings*, 89, 94–96; see also Faulkner, 154–55).

Women's Rights Convention, Melodeon Hall, Cleveland, October 5 and 7, 1853

[October 5, Evening Session]

I would yield the floor to anyone who has anything to say at this time, and would gladly do it. I approve of the suggestion which has been made, that we should be limited as to time, for we are such imitators of men and customs around us, that perhaps we may forget that we are not upon the floor of Congress, and so may inflict long speeches upon the people.

I am glad you have had presented before you, in the address you have just heard, a synopsis of the laws in relation to women, and the sentiments of some of the commentators upon those laws;[1] and I want you to observe, (for it stands in proof of what our brother said this afternoon), that there is a constant advance in truth, a constant uprising and appreciation of that which in the earlier days of an enterprise was not anticipated. So in this movement; [*William*] Blackstone stated what was then regarded Law, (for it did not then appear to be understood, although he too defined it), as a "means of sustaining justice and the right"—but in giving a statement of what was Law, it was received by the people as tantamount to Gospel; for Law and Gospel, Church and State, have been thus united. But it is to be broken up as regards woman, just as the religionists of our country have attempted to break it up, and have succeeded in the Church, as applicable to men. Our more modern expounders of the Law, in many cases, present to the public the degraded position of women in society, because of such enactments, claiming to be, *Law*. Of these are a [*Elisha*] Hulburt, in an essay on Human Rights; and a [*Timothy*] Walker, I think, who first presented the fact to the public—or in the reader, not so public as I wish it was—that the Law has made the man and wife one person, and that one person the husband! and Mr. Hulburt has presented the condition of woman in a light which cannot fail to be striking to those who will read his essays.

Look also at the Philosophers of the present time, and the Revolutionists of the last upheaving in Europe. Why, when woman went forth at the last effort to establish a republic through the provisional government in France, and claimed to have equal representation with man, some of the greatest statesmen acknowledged the justice of her request, and responded to it, that she had sat in darkness long, that this claim of women would have to be respected; that woman had too long been suffering under a night-mare of oppression.[2] It was to me a striking comparison at the time I read it. The only cause of the failure of the revolution of 1789, was that it was represented by only one half of the intelligence, of the race—an intelligence differing it is true, in some of its peculiarities, but from that very difference calculated to form a truer republic. Victor Hugo in alluding to this effort on the part of woman for the redress of the wrongs and grievances under which she had suffered, says, that as the last age was notable for the effort to gain Men's Rights, so the present generation would aim to create a revolution in public sentiment which should gain the independence of woman.[3]

Now these steps are beginning to be followed out everywhere. The Westminster Review, one of the cleverest journals in England, gave a very fair and interesting notice of the first National Women's Convention in Worcester, and that article has been republished in this country in pamphlet form. There have been repeated notices also in the best of our own periodicals, encouraging women to go on and advocate their claims.

But, we are told sometimes that we are satisfied; that it is not woman who is urging this movement, and that she really does not wish any change in society. Has the slave been oppressed so long that he cannot appreciate the blessings of Liberty? and has woman been so long crushed, enervated, paralyzed, prostrated by the influences by which she has been surrounded, that she too is ready to say she would not have any more rights if she could? Why she does not know her position, and whereof she affirms. A clergyman in Auburn, N.Y., soon after the Syracuse Convention, delivered a sermon pronouncing it an infidel convention,—for you know that is the usual weapon of defense against whatever appears to conflict with accepted creeds. He said the ladies of *his* congregation, "he was happy to state, were not sensible of any chains binding them, not sensible of any liberties taken from them." Now this is the common boast—there are persons in your own city who stated on being invited to come to this convention, that they had other engagements, they had to sew at the Home Missionary Society; and if they had not other engagements, they had all the rights they wanted, and did not care to come.

I heard not long since of some one who had several hundred acres of land left him by his father; a friend was speaking to him about the profitableness of his estate; he replied, the profits were not so great as might be supposed; the expenses of the family were large, for he had to *keep his mother* a good many years, and she lived to be ninety years old! He was asked if she were an active, industrious woman in her early days. O yes! in those days she was a very industrious woman. His father and she commenced life poor, but gathered together this great estate by their united industry. How is it then that you can say that your expenses have been increased by having to keep your mother? He felt rebuke much afterwards, and such was the impression it produced, and so great was the change in his views that in his will he recognized no difference between his sons and daughters. He saw the injustice of his past position, and was disposed to make some redress for the wrong done his own mother in making her, in her old age, dependent upon him.

Now, in this particular, there has been a great change in our country. The doing away [with] the laws of primogeniture has opened the eyes of the people, to much evil on all sides, for we cannot begin to look at and redress any one of the wrongs done to mankind in the past, without being carried farther than we imagine, in our first attempt. It was a true philosophy that Jesus uttered, when he said "He that has been faithful over a little, shall be ruler over more."

It is for the following generation to go on and make yet other advance steps. Such advances are beautiful when we come to look at them. Those of the past have given some Theologians noble ideas; they have come to have more expanded views and to rejoice in the belief of the continued advance of humanity. How much better the Theology which has resulted from these great movements. They have led us to read our Bibles better. Many cannot so read Christ, that progress is going to break up the foundations of society. Why, our own society which has been supposed to make greater strides than others, especially for the rights of man—and they have upon the questions of the ministry and the marriage covenant—has been affected by these advances. As regards the ministry, they did not see so clearly, that it must embrace women also. They took only the ground that ordination must not take the form of a human ceremony; that it was God alone who could appoint to the ministry. Well, they found that this God ordination was manifest in their women also. They began to look at their Bibles, and found there that women were sent forth to minister to the people, as in ancient time. When Deborah was Judge in Israel, when the Captain would not lead the army, and a woman had the glory of the conquest made. Again, when they were in exigency, they went to Huldah, and she counseled them.

It is not Christianity but priestcraft that has subjected woman as we find her. The Church and State have been united, and it is well for us to see it so. We have had to bear the denunciations of these revered (irreverend) clergymen, as in New York, of late. But if we look to their authority to see how they expound the text, quite likely we shall find a new reading. Why, when John Chambers returned to Philadelphia, from the World's Temperance Convention at New York, he gave notice that he would give an address, and state the rights of woman as defined by the Bible. Great allowance has been made by some of the speakers in this Convention, on account of his ignorance, and certainly this was charitable.[4] But I heard this discourse. I heard him bring up what is called the Apostolic prohibition, and the old Eastern idea of the subjection of wives; but he kept out of view some of the best ideas in the scriptures.

Blame is often attached to the position in which woman is found. I blame her not so much as I pity her. So circumscribed have been her limits, that she does not realize the misery of her condition. Such dupes are men to custom, that even servitude, the worst of ills comes to be thought a good, till down from sire to son it is kept and guarded as a sacred thing.[5] Woman's existence is maintained by sufferance. The veneration of man has been misdirected, the pulpit has been prostituted, the Bible has been ill-used. It has been turned over and over as in every reform. The temperance people have had to feel its supposed denunciations. Then the antislavery, and now this reform has met, and still continues to meet, passage after passage of the Bible, never intended to be so used. Instead of taking the truths of the Bible in corroboration of the right, the practice has been, to turn over its pages to find example and authority for the wrong, for the existing abuses of society. For the usage of drinking wine, the example of the sensualist Solomon is always appealed to. In reference to our reform, even admitting that Paul did mean preach, when he used that term, he did not say that the recommendation of that time, was to be applicable to the churches of all after time. We have here, I had liked to have said, the *Reverend* [*Antoinette*] Brown. She is familiar enough with these passages to present some of them to you; for it is important when the Bible is thus appealed to, and thus perverted, that it should be read with another pair of spectacles. We have been so long pinning our faith on other people's sleeves that we ought to begin examining these things daily, ourselves, to see whether they *are* so; and we should find on comparing text with text, that a very different construction might be put upon them. Some of our early Quakers, not seeing how far they were to be carried, became Greek and Hebrew scholars, and they found that the text would bear other translations as well as other constructions. All Bible commentators agree that the Church of Corinth, when the Apostle wrote, was in a state of great confusion. They fell into discussion and controversy; and in order to quiet this state of things, and bring the Church to greater propriety, the command was given out that women should keep silence, and it was not permitted them to speak, except by asking questions at home. In the same epistle to the same Church, Paul gave express directions how women shall prophesy, which he defines to be preaching, "speaking to men" for "exhortation and comfort." He recognized them in prophesying and praying. The word translated *servant*, is applied to a man in one part of the scripture, and in another it is translated minister. Now that same word you will find might be applied to Phebe, a Deaconess. That text was quoted in the sermon of John Chambers, and he interlarded it with a good deal of his ideas, that woman should not be goers abroad, and read among other things "that their wives were to be teachers." But the "wives" properly translated would be "Deaconesses." It is not so Apostolic to make the wife subject to the husband as many have supposed. It has been done by Law, and public opinion since that time. There has been a great deal said about sending Missionaries over to the East to convert women who are immolating themselves on the funeral pile of their husbands. I know this may [*be*] a very good work, but I would ask you to look at it. How many women are there now immolated upon the shrine of superstition and priestcraft, in our very midst, in the assumption that man only has a right to the pulpit, and that if a woman enters it she disobeys God; making woman believe in the misdirection of her vocation, and that it is of Divine authority that she should be thus bound. Believe it not, my sisters.—In this same epistle the word "prophesying" should be "preaching"—"preaching Godliness, &c." On the occasion of the very first miracle which it is said Christ wrought, a woman went before him and said, "whatsoever he biddeth you do, that do." The woman of Samaria said, "come and see the man who told me all the things that ever I did."

These things are worthy of note. I do not want to dwell too much upon scripture authority. We too often bind ourselves by authorities rather than by the truth, we are infidel to truth, in seeking examples to overthrow it.[6] The very first act of note that is mentioned when the disciples and apostles went forth after Jesus was removed from them, was the bringing up of an ancient prophecy, to prove that they were right in the position they then assumed. On the occasion when men and women were gathered together on the holy day of Pentecost, when every man heard and saw those wonderful works which are recorded, then Peter stood forth—some one has said that Peter made a great mistake in quoting the prophet Joel—but, he stated that "the time is come, this day is fulfilled the prophecy, when it is said I will pour out my spirit upon all flesh, and your sons and your daughters shall prophesy." &c.—the language of the Bible is beautiful in its repetition—"upon my servants and my hand-maidens I will pour out my spirit and they shall prophesy." Now can any thing be clearer than that?

It has sometimes been said that if women were associated with men in their efforts, there would not be as much immorality as now exists, in Congress, for instance, and other places. But we ought, I think, to claim no more for woman than for man; we ought to put woman on a par with man, not invest her with power, or claim for her superiority over her brother. If we do, she is just as likely to become a tyrant as man is; as with Catherine the Second.[7] It is always unsafe to invest man with power over his fellow being. "Call no man master"—that is the true doctrine. But, be sure there would then be better rule than now; the elements which belong to woman as such and to man as such, would be beautifully and harmoniously blended. It is to be hoped there would be less of war, injustice and intolerance in the world than now. Things are tending fast that way, and I hope we shall all be prepared to act. These Conventions ought to give encouragement to the steps of advancement. Now that women are capable of reading, and beginning to be their own painters and historians, you see how much is brought out from history. I heard a lecture last year which astonished me with its number of remarkable women, not only in medicine, but in the Law and jurisprudence, farther back than the twelfth century—all this is encouraging women to go forward in this movement. Why only lately a woman stood forth in England, or France, and pled her own cause and gained it.

And the more her powers are cultivated, the more woman will see the light in which she has been regarded, and when she comes to unite herself in that most holy marriage relation, she will not submit to the authority the church now binds upon her. Women are bound by the church on one hand, and acknowledge subjection to the laws and to the husband under the church and the law, on the other part. I cannot bear to hear woman blamed. She is taught that she must promise that she will be obedient to her husband. I know some ministers now who make a little change in this respect. A minister said to me the other day, that he did not make the parties promise to obey. He used the word "dutiful," for the wife; "well then," I said, "you will make it apply to the husband also, will you not?" He replied perhaps he would hereafter.

I alluded to my own society making no difference between man and woman in the ministry and the duties of the marriage covenant. It seemed to be a great step for those early reformers, William Penn and George Fox,[8] moving as they did in fashionable society, amid the universal veneration for power in that country. It was a great step for them to take—making the marriage relation entirely reciprocal—asking no priest to legalize their union, but declaring their own marriage, and themselves invoking the Divine aid.

When woman shall be properly trained, and her spiritual powers developed, she will find in entering the marriage union nothing necessarily degrading to her. The independence of the husband and wife should be equal, and the dependence reciprocal. But Oh! how different now! The so-called church, and the state together, have made her a perfect slave. Talk of the barbarous ages! Why the barbarous ages are now! Even now, she may be yoked with the beasts of burden in the field. In France, she loads herself most heavily with the baggage of passengers. The Irishwoman now goes about barefoot, the husband with shoes and stockings;—she with her child in her arms, he carrying nothing. I have seen these cases again and again in a little travel of a few months in the old world; and what might those see who go throughout the continent. Woman is not considered there as out of her sphere in pitching hay upon the stack; when the coach stops for relays of horses, the coachman does not leave the box, but a woman comes out and takes the four horses, leads them away, and returns with the other four from the stable. Talk of the barbarous ages! They are now!

Notwithstanding all these things, women in this country will not come to our conventions to hear Women's Rights. They may be the mere toys and playthings of society, and do not therefore feel these things. They can amuse their husbands, and brothers, and fathers by beautiful notes of music or by the dance, and I do not say that these things are not very well when practiced at home instead of in public places, and not continued till late hours of the nights. When we consider the character of the romance, the sickly sentimental yellow-covered literature that she reads, we cannot expect that she will be much. Then in other cases, she has too much to do to be a fine show. These are the extremes. We want woman to come forth and walk in a higher sphere than either of these. Let her come forth and fill it, and she will certainly show forth the beauty of higher aims in life. Why, today, a woman at one of your most respectable hotels, dressed in a fashionable manner, saw one of our women in the street dressed in a Bloomer costume.[9] She thought it "an insult to decency," and expressed herself very indignantly. But how was she dressed herself? Why, laced so tight that she could scarcely breathe, and her clothes so long that when she went out into the dusty streets her garments formed a kind of broom to gather up the dust. *This* is beautiful! *This* is fashionable!

But blessed be the advance of the age, for it is teaching woman in principles of physiology. Many are going forth teaching this science to ears anointed to hear, and finding eyes skillful to see, and souls wise to so observe the laws of health, that they may not be subject to disease, or require so much of miserable medical treatment. Then again many are availing themselves of the profitable occupations of society, in the way of mercantile business. In Philadelphia it is no uncommon thing to see women behind the counter. To be sure if they are only employed the merchant can rob them of half their wages. But they are becoming capitalists, and setting up their own stores. In some of the works of the Artizan, in Jewelry, in Daguerreotyping, and in many other departments, women are coming forward and showing themselves apt scholars; that they can do something besides stitching wristbands and making samplers. In early days, how many hours were employed in making emery strawberries, in foolish fancy work, and in overworked samplers. Women are now beginning to learn that men can do without so much stitching. Indeed, so greatly is Discovery progressing, that machines are already doing a large portion of this work. A woman in the Crystal Palace[10] sits by a sewing machine to show the visitors how one woman, in a day, can perform the work of thirty or forty women in the same time! On the Island of Nantucket—for I was born on that Island—I can remember how our mothers were employed, while our fathers were at sea. The mothers with their children round them—'twas not customary to have nurses then—kept small groceries and sold provisions, that they might make something in the absence of their husbands. At that time it required some money and more courage to get to Boston.—They were obliged to go to that city, make their trades, exchange their oils and candles for dry goods, and all the varieties of a country store, set their own price, keep their own accounts; and with all this, have very little help in the family, to which they must discharge their duties. Look at the heads of those women; they can mingle with men; they are not triflers; they have intelligent subjects [of] conversation.

This then is what we ask for woman, that she may be so prepared for life's duties, that [she] can fill her walk in life respectably, and show that she can be something more than a slave, on the one hand, or a toy, or an effeminate being on the other. She is giving the proof of this. She is doing this today. Go on then and encourage her, O! my brothers. I have no idea that there is on the part of man, or the race, such a disposition to love the wrong, as many suppose. We have been so much accustomed to false Theology, that we might think the whole race were really fallen, if we did not *know* better. Why, this very afternoon, I heard quoted in the Temperance Convention—but there is no such passage in the Bible, "The heart of man is prone to evil, and that continually."

Now we know that man is prone to good, and that continually. Job stated that "man was prone to *trouble*, as the sparks to fly upwards." But how has Theology perverted it! Man is prone to *evil*! Why the very evils there are in society around us, are greatly mitigated by the goodness of heart, that is natural in man. His *inherent* love of justice, right, mercy, and goodness, are ever operating upon him, and leading him to act aright. Why is it that good works have such great success all over the world? Translate that sermon on the Mount into all languages, and the response to it, is world wide. Why is it that Harriet Beecher Stowe has had such success throughout the wide world? Because her work reaches the sense of right in the universal human heart.

Did Elizabeth Fry, of England, neglect her family? No! After rearing her eight or ten children, she went forth and did the things that Howard did,[11] and greater. See Dorothea Dix, and what a ministering angel she has been! Look at the licentiousness of our own city of Penn, and see how Myra Townsend went forth and established a reformatory house for her sisters;[12] see how she gathered them there and improved their situations, and awakened in them a desire for a better life. The other day I had a letter from a young married woman,[13] who told me she had heard a woman say when she had eleven children, she had less trouble with them, than when she had but four, for as the older ones grew older, they were a help to her in caring for the younger. She wrote to me putting five or six questions to me on the subject of woman's rights. She was going to deliver a lecture in Pennsylvania. She had had advantages that we did not have in our day. She had been a little accustomed to in public, and though she had the care of her little children, and with her own hands had to make the bread for family of twenty, yet she was ready to do what she could. She had hard work to do where she lectured, for many of her auditors were ignorant Dutch women. Mrs. Mott apologized for having occupied so much time and gave way to Mrs. Emma R. Coe, of Buffalo.[14]

[*October 7, Morning Session*]

Mrs. Mott (*Addressing Mr. Keeler*) I would ask, whether thee knows that Gen. Carey was the writer of that editorial offered here last evening?[15]

Mr. Keeler.—He is the editor of that paper.

Mrs. Mott.—Is thee impressed that he is *not the* author of that editorial?

Mr. Keeler.—I should judge from his course at the convention of New York, that he *was* the author of that article.

Mrs. Mott.—I would only wish to say, that if he is the author of that article, as we have had reason to believe he is, it stands before us, and should be a reason for our disapproval far above the excited state of that New York Convention. We could make allowance for that, because we know how strong party and sectarian zeal became, and how apt people are to act for the time, in a manner which their cooler judgment condemns; but, if after due consideration, he wrote that article, it seems to me, that so far from endorsing him in other respects, we ought to pass a resolution charging him with the most outrageous falsehoods, with falsehoods tending to dishonor and insult woman in the highest degree, as far as with the pen he could do it. I have no doubt of Gen. Carey's interest in the Temperance cause, and fear his late conduct may injure him in that cause, as the conduct of John Chambers may injure him. If he did not stand up in the church—in his coward's castle, the pulpit—and thrust his missiles at woman, which are calculated to lessen woman's influence, in the Temperance cause, as well as against many evils, he would have much greater power to do good. He cannot harm us, but every wrong act, is an obstruction to good acts; and we have all the more difficulties to surmount. I do not believe that good comes out of evil. I believe that evil, works evil, and evil only, and that continually; and thus, evil things must and do stand in the way of the progress of truth. And such an article as that, believed to be from the pen of Gen. Carey,—from the high regard in which he is held, and worthy therefore of double honor in the Temperance cause,—is calculated to do any amount of harm, to the cause of Temperance, too; for just as fast as he thrusts his weapons in the way of woman he retards the cause of Temperance. Now, let us look at it dispassionately, and see if we can pass a resolution to endorse every other act of Gen. Carey's, except that one in New York. I like the spirit which prompted the seconding of that resolution, by Antoinette Brown, but I do think it an error of judgment.[16]

[*October 7, Afternoon Session*]

Mrs. Mott—I said it was *John Chambers* coward's castle; and I do say, that *such* ministers *make* it castle of cowards; but I did not wish to make the remark general, or apply to all pulpits.[17]

* * * *

We ought to thank Dr. Nevin for his kindly fears, lest we women should be brought out into rough conflicts of life, and overwhelmed by infidelity. I thank him, but at the same time, I must say, that if we have been able this afternoon to sit uninjured by the hard conflict in which he has been engaged, if we can maintain our patience at seeing him so laboriously build a man of straw, and then throw it down and destroy it,[18] I think we may be suffered to go into the world and bear many others unharmed.

Again, I would ask in all seriousness, by what right does Orthodoxy give the invidious name of Infidel, affix the stigma of infidelity, to those who dissent from its cherished opinions? What right have the advocates of moral reform, the Woman's Rights movement, the Abolitionists, the Temperance advocates, or others, to call in question any man's religious opinions? It is the assumption of bigots. I do not want now to speak invidiously, and say sectarian bigots, but I mean the same kind of bigotry which Jesus rebuked so sharply, when he called certain men "blind leaders of the blind."

Now we hold Jesus up as an example, when we perceive the assumption of clergymen, that all who venture to dissent from a given interpretation, must necessarily be infidels; and thus denounce them as infidel; for it was only by inference that one clergyman this afternoon, made Joseph Barker deny the Son of God.[19] By inference in the same way, he might be made to deny everything that is good, and praiseworthy, and true.

I want that we should consider these things upon this platform. I am not troubled with difficulties about the Bible. My education has been such, that I look to that Source whence all the inspiration of the Bible comes. I love the truths of the Bible. I love the Bible because it contains so many truths; but I never was educated to love the errors of the Bible; therefore it does not startle me to hear Joseph Barker point to some of those errors. And I can listen to the ingenious interpretation of the Bible, given by Antoinette Brown[20] and am glad to hear those who are so skilled in the outward, when I perceive that they are beginning to turn the Bible to so good an account. It gives evidence that the cause is making very good progress. Why, my friend Nevin has had to hear the Temperance cause denounced as infidel, and proved so by Solomon; and he has, no doubt, seen the minister in the pulpit, turning over the pages of the Bible to find examples for the wrong. But the Bible will never sustain him in making this use of its pages, instead of using it rationally, and selecting such portions of it as would tend to corroborate the right; and these are plentiful; for notwithstanding the teaching of Theology, and men's arts in the religious world, men have ever responded to righteousness and truth, when it has been advocated by the servants of God, so that we need not fear to bring truth to an intelligent examination of the Bible. It is a far less dangerous assertion to say, that God is unchangeable, than that man is infallible.

PD *Proceedings of the National Women's Rights Convention, Held at Cleveland, Ohio*, phonographically reported by T. C. Leland (Cleveland, Ohio: Gray, Beardsley, Spear and Co., 1854), 56–67, 148–50, 166–68 WASM

1. In lieu of a speech, WLG submitted seven resolutions, stressing that the rights of man extended to woman, including that of the franchise. Amelia Jenks Bloomer (1818–94), a women's rights activist from Seneca Falls, had requested that her address not be published (*Proceedings*, 55–56).

2. LM possibly refers to Victor Considerant (1808–93), a member of the French Assembly who had proposed granting suffrage to French women (Paula Doress-Worters, ed., *Mistress of Herself: Speeches and Letters of Ernestine L. Rose* [New York: Feminist Press, 2008], 87).

3. French novelist Victor Hugo (1802–85).

4. At the World Temperance Convention in New York City, September 6, the Reverend John Chambers (1797–1875), pastor of the (Presbyterian) Ninth Associate Reformed Church in Philadelphia, joined others in preventing Antoinette Brown from speaking, even though Brown had been admitted as a delegate. When Brown tried to persevere, Chambers shouted, "shame on the woman," and asked Pennsylvania delegates to withdraw in protest (*New York Tribune*, September 7, 1853, reprinted in *Liberator*, September 16, 1853; Mark E. Lender, *Dictionary of American Temperance Biography* [Westport, Conn.: Greenwood Press, 1984], 91–92). See also Faulkner, 154–55.

5. William Cowper, "The Task" (1785).

6. LM often signed autographs "Truth for Authority, not Authority for Truth." See also "Race Street Meeting," March 14, 1869, below.

7. Catherine the Great (1729–96) ruled Russia from 1762 to 1796.

8. William Penn (1644–1718), British Quaker and founder of the Pennsylvania colony; George Fox (1624–91), founder of the Society of Friends.

9. The Bloomer costume, consisting of a short skirt over trousers, was named for Amelia Bloomer, although it was initially created by Elizabeth Smith Miller based on a Turkish design.

10. Constructed in New York City in 1853, the Crystal Palace was modeled after the 1851 London exhibition of that name.

11. John Howard (1726–90), also a British prison reformer.

12. Mira Sharpless Townsend (d. 1859), a Philadelphia Hicksite Quaker who founded the anti-prostitution Rosine Society (Palmer, 279; Nancy Isenberg, *Sex and Citizenship in Antebellum America* [Chapel Hill: University of North Carolina Press, 1998], 130).

13. Unfortunately, LM kept few of her incoming letters (Palmer, xxxi).

14. Emma Robinson Coe (1815–1902), women's rights lecturer in Michigan and Ohio (Gordon, 1:234; 6:190).

15. Keeler, secretary of the Ohio State Temperance Alliance, offered a resolution disapproving the conduct at the World's Temperance Convention of Samuel Fenton Cary (1814–1900), a leader of the Ohio temperance movement, and known as "General" for his service as paymaster general of Ohio. Keeler's resolution also expressed gratitude for Cary's "self-sacrificing devotion to the cause of Temperance." At the September Temperance Convention, Cary had offered a resolution that the platform was "not the appropriate sphere of woman." At the Cleveland convention, Antoinette Brown recounted the refusal of the Temperance Convention to allow her to speak. She read several paragraphs from an Ohio temperance publication written by Cary implying that she had "made an unwomanly entrance into the convention, and upon the platform itself." Brown further stated, "measures [were] taken to browbeat the convention into receiving Miss Brown" (Lender, *Dictionary*, 84–86; *New York Times*, September 7, 1853; *Proceedings*, 115–16, 146).

16. The convention "almost unanimously" resolved to table Keeler's resolution, not wishing to "characterize, or endorse, Gen. Cary's conduct, or that of any other man" (*Proceedings*, 149).

17. When Edwin H. Nevin (1814–89), Presbyterian clergyman from Cleveland, asked permission to refute assertions from British clergyman Joseph Barker, he encountered several objections, but LM moved that he be allowed to speak. In the ensuing exchange Nevin said, "Only one word has fallen from *Woman* in this convention, to which I can take exceptions, and that fell from the lips of a lady whom I have venerated from my childhood—it was, that the pulpit was the castle of cowards" (WLG *Letters*, 4:170–71; *Proceedings*, 165–66).

18. British clergyman Joseph Barker (1806–75), who had recently moved to the United States, had complained about the "priesthood's" criticisms of the women's rights movement. He said these clergymen claimed that the Scriptures were "against the Woman's Rights Movement," and further characterized the movement as based on "infidel principles." Barker concluded that he had "come to regard the term Infidel, as the most honorable that can be given to a man" and that all he had spoken was meant "to subserve the cause of freedom and the elevation of woman." With "Bible in hand," Nevins "launched out into an irrelevant eulogium upon 'his Christ'" and then characterized Barker as "an Infidel from foreign shores, who had come to teach Americans Christianity!" As he concluded his remarks (which were not fully reported), Nevins met with objections both from Barker and WLG (*Proceedings*, 135–36, 145–46, 165–66; WLG *Letters*, 4:170–71).

19. When Nevin expressed doubts "as [to] the belief of Mr. Barker, in the doctrines of Christ... Mr. Barker repeatedly corrected him, but Dr. Nevin very ingeniously continued to re-affirm them in another shape" (*Proceedings*, 165–66).

20. In her final address to the convention, Brown stated that she believed that the Bible was God's "revelation of his will to man," as opposed to Barker's opinion that the Bible was not "the special word of God." She declared that each member had to decide "for himself and herself. *The convention is committed to neither*" (*Proceedings*, 150).

Rose Street Meeting, New York City, November 11, 1855

Denouncing the still prevailing King and Priestcraft, Mrs. MOTT had the courage to express what many repress, and declare that Protestantism was only a modification, not a thorough reform of a degrading superstition. In glowing terms she claimed to plant her platform where Christ and St. John had erected it for Humanity, but she said she should separate herself from the Priests and their tools who have degraded that platform into worldly ecclesiastical business establishments. Gathering hope from all the bright features of the progressive symptoms of practical Christianity around us, Mrs. MOTT proved that all the leading reforms of the age—Anti-Slavery, Temperance, and all the benevolent and philanthropic movements of the day—have sprung, not by the dogmas propounded by either the Church of Rome, or England, or any other material organization, but from the individual soul of man, from the Divinity rising within man—from the Divinity of which Christ was the most celestial exemplar.

In the course of her address, which, begun in somewhat impassive and monotonous strain, increased in fervor and eloquence as, in advancing, she was carried away by the holiness of her theme, Mrs. MOTT spoke in terms of the most enthusiastic regard of all those noble laborers in the cause of humanity—preachers, teachers, lecturers, and, above all, editors—who in defiance of a corrupt public opinion, battle with the combined hosts of the Slave Oligarchy, ready to sacrifice their popularity, their fortunes, everything, to the attainment of the great object in view. But how have these world-redeeming impulses made their way in the heart of so many noble men and gentle women? By dogmas? by creeds? By the degrading faith in the God-decreed depravity of men? No! exclaimed Mrs. MOTT. No, no! By sympathy for fellow-men—by love of God—by faith in the perfectibility of the human mind—by faith in the Divinity residing within man, residing within woman. All honor, all praise, all hail to the great Messiah who founded Christianity; but did he not say himself, that other Messiahs will come after him? Did he not point out in every word, to the fact that every age will yield other Messiahs, called forth by its requirements? Was His whole life not a constant protest against Priestcraft, whether palpable as in the Vatican, or less palpable as in some Protestant Churches? Did He not do good by the wayside, as he went along, without reference to clime, locality, form, creed, cast, race, condition, and thus call upon humanity to follow the example, and upon the human soul to awaken to its intrinsic Divinity, and to cast off forever and ever the tyranny of churches, and the thought-killing despotism of the Priesthood?

All the progressive features of our age were summed up by Mrs. MOTT with wondrous compactness; and while their existence was traced by her to the growing anxiety of the human mind to emancipate itself from the influence of Priestcraft, "*every one to do his own and her own thinking*," to pass from the childhood of civilization into the riper sphere of manhood, Mrs. MOTT opines that the development of those various contemplated reforms would only be retarded by a relapse into the old enslavement of thought, and could only be accelerated by a daily-increasing appreciation of the capabilities of the human soul, *by the world with recognition of the god in man.*[1]

PD "Lucretia Mott in New York," *New York Times*, November 12, 1855

1. The article described the "vehement orthodoxy of two persons" who reacted to Mott's "bold asseveration" that Christ is not a "finality, but that God ever sends Christ to his children." In an unpublished letter to Martha Coffin Wright, November 16, 1855,

LM briefly described this reaction, saying her sister may have seen the *New York Times* account "a column describg. that miserable opponent Richd. Cromwell . . . The other was not a Quaker—one who has spoken before, & been set down—such a rush as there was to thank & express satisfactn" (*New York Times*, November 12, 1855; Mott Manuscripts, FHL).

Women's Rights Convention, Broadway Tabernacle, New York City, November 25–26, 1856

[*November 25 Session*]

Mrs. LUCRETIA MOTT suggested that the speakers should make their remarks brief, and keep as much as possible to the point, in order that there might be an intelligent consideration of the resolutions submitted to the convention. However gratifying it might be to listen to eloquent words, it was needful, in a convention like this, that they should come together for business purposes, and that they should go forth from it prepared to do something. They should resolve to be aggressive reformers. A great deal had been said about woman's peaceable and passive nature; this reform was one which needed all the combativeness of the spirit of Jesus; it needed that they should go forth armed with panoply divine. They should go forth into society as nonconformists, even as Jesus was. There was a duty for woman to perform in overthrowing and overcoming all those obstacles that had been placed in her way. The strong power of custom had closed the avenues of scientific preferment, and legislative enactments had deprived her of her just rights. She must not be kept back by the sneers and scorn that attend a movement of this kind.

The statement made by the President of the convention, of what had already been achieved in the course of the last few years, in consequence of this movement in behalf of woman's rights, and with comparatively little labor, was enough to repay them for coming together.[1] The little progress, in this respect, that Pennsylvania had made, had been overlooked by the speaker. The laws of Pennsylvania were in a state of modification. There was a speaker present who would tell them about the efforts making in France.[2] Some present might be familiar with the fact that immediately after the attempted Revolution in that country, when a delegation of women waited upon the Provisional Government and asked for an equal representation, numbers of that Provisional Government entertained their appeal respectfully, some of them declaring that the only reason why the former Revolution had failed was, that France was only represented by one half of her people. Woman was suffering under the nightmare of oppression, and it was for her to raise her voice and make her plea before the people; for oppressors rarely saw themselves in their true light until the oppressed cried for deliverance. There was a native goodness in the heart of man that was ready for the reception of an appeal on every subject of moral reform; but at present so ignorant were the wisest of men on this subject of woman's legal disabilities that they had scarcely begun to imagine the extent of those wrongs. Some years ago the speaker heard an intelligent advocate of the law in London say, that although it had been his business and his profession, for years, to settle marriage estates and other business in behalf of women, yet he never imagined the extent of the oppression that she endured, until he read the report of the proceedings of the first Woman's Convention in Worcester. He then examined the whole subject, and such was his conviction of the truthfulness of the statements made at that convention, and the necessity of spreading the facts before the people, that he sent a sum of money to this country to aid in the publication of documents, and requested copies of all such publications to be sent to each of his daughters in England. And not only that gentleman, but the able editors of the *Westminster Review*[3] had taken up the subject, and published an able article from the pen of a woman [*Harriet Taylor Mill*], called out by the proceedings of the first convention at Worcester. So this reform had now made a good beginning, and if they continued faithful and active their labors would not be in vain.

[*November 26 Session*]

At this late hour it will not be proper for me to add many words, even were it necessary. You have heard all, it seems to me, that can be said upon the subject, and if I would add anything it would be rather to offer an encouraging view as to what has already been effected, and to inspire the hope that the time is not far distant when those wrongs and evils, under which woman is suffering—so clearly depicted at this and at former Conventions—will be so obvious to the thinking men of the American People, that they will be ready to redress them. And although woman may not yet be so awakened to the consideration of the subject as to be sensible of the blessing of entire freedom, she will, I doubt not, as she comes to reflect on the subject more and more, see herself in her true light. It only needs that we should look back a few years to see the progress that has been made. Even in England, in 1840, when a few women went over as delegates to the World's Anti-Slavery Convention, although the call had been made so universal, yet they were afraid to welcome women to a seat in that Convention, lest they should be ridiculed in the morning papers. Daniel O'Connell, Dr. [*John*] Bowring, William Howitt, and some able and strong men of that time, it is true, came forth and approved the claim of women to a seat; and O'Connell showed that, even then, women exercised the right to vote as holders of bank stock, and as members of the East India Company, and some other institutions of that country.[4] Their youthful queen [*Victoria*], too, had just then ascended the throne, thus showing how very inconsistent it was to make objections to the claim of equal rights for women. Dr. Bowring at that time, or soon after, wrote a letter to the friends in this country, saying that he had feared that the woman question was launched among them without sufficient preparation; but the coming of these women would form an era in the history of philanthropic bravery; that they had left a deep if not a wide impression; that they had created apostles, if as yet they had not many followers. Well, the result, as shown from the facts presented to you this evening, the petitions to Parliament, for the redress of the wrongs of women, the willingness to receive, to so great an extent, such a memorial, all go to show a change that has taken place in the minds of many there.[5] Some of you must know that among the English authors, when Maria Edgeworth wrote, within the day and generation of some of the older ones of us, she was not willing to let her own name appear as an author, but her first works, and those of her sister, were put forth in the name of her father, because it was not considered decorous then for a woman to appear as an author.[6] It was supposed to be without the sphere of woman. And you know how since that time woman has advanced in the literary field. You know that when the work entitled "Jane Eyre" appeared, with a fictitious name, it was said to be a work of too great power for any woman—that it must have been written by a man. It proved, however, to have been written by a woman.

So we have seen already, in the few years' efforts that have been made in this Woman's Rights Reform, how colleges for women, schools of design, and other institutions, heretofore unknown, have sprung up, opening to woman new fields, and extending and elevating her sphere.

I was glad this morning when that young man came forth with his objections against our claim, based upon the Bible;[7] and although it would not be proper to go into a theological discussion of the question, it is of the greatest importance that religiously-minded women, those who have been accustomed to regard this volume as their rule of faith and practice, should be led to examine these Scriptures, and see whether these things are as our opponents claim. And if they will read that book intelligently, not with the eye of the theologian, nor with a blind faith in what their ministers have taught them; but with a reliance upon their own judgment, they will discover that the Scriptures cannot be wielded against us. They will find that from the earliest days of which the Scriptures give account, honorable women have risen, notwithstanding the obstacles of the times in which they lived, to a high degree of eminence. There were the Deborahs, the Huldahs, the Annas, and others, in olden times, who filled conspicuous places, and to whom the honorable men of the age resorted for counsel in times of exigency. Deborah assured one of the captains of the host that he was not to succeed, for the honor of the battle was to be given to a woman. She was a prophetess; and if you will read you will find that prophetesses were recognized as well as prophets from the earliest days. And in later times, Anna and the woman of Samaria, and others were employed to speak to the men of the city, to all those who looked for redemption in Jerusalem. And women were recognized in the very first noble act that was brought to view after the disciples came together, which was a realization of the old prophecy, that the time should come when women as well as men should prophesy. And even Paul, though he is quoted so much as an authority for bringing women under subjection, even he gave special directions to woman how she should attire herself when she did publically pray or prophesy; and in the seeming prohibition of woman's speaking in church, there is no mention of preaching, of praying, or of prophesying. There is something said, to be sure, about the subjection to the husband, but it was also said that it was spoken in a mystery, in reference to the Church, evidently not intending thereby to apply it literally. In the metaphors of that age you know there is great liberty taken on other subjects; why not on that? Even though Paul should approve of many things, being himself under the influence of the Jewish customs of that age, with regard to woman, I would ask of those who most religiously bind themselves to the authority of Scripture, whether they find any Scripture text from the beginning to the end of the Bible that makes it incumbent upon them to receive any recommendation given by Paul to the women of the Church of that day, as necessarily applicable to the women of the Church of this day, unless it be in the great principles of virtue, of justice and of love, which are unvarying in all ages of the world? NO; when theologians quote Paul as against us, they should be careful lest they prove too much; for, if the recommendations of Paul were to be applied now, no woman would be allowed to enter into a second marriage after having lost her first husband. Paul says he thinks they should not marry again, and at the same time says, he thinks he has the Spirit of the Lord. But this prohibition of Paul is not applied now, and hence theologians do not bring it up against us, as they do some other prohibitions in regard to women.

And I would ask that young theologian, who quoted the Bible against us, what he thinks of the direction concerning holding his peace when he is in his pulpit, when anything is revealed to him that sitteth by, allowing that person to utter his thoughts, so that all may speak, and all be edified? With the exception of the Quakers, and perhaps the Methodists, there is always one singled out as the "oracle of God" to the congregation; and this recommendation of Paul is entirely ignored. So also with the direction to wash one another's feet, and many other things.

It would be well for people to remember that this readiness to bring up the Bible against this reform has been equally manifested in regard to every other reform. I would not undervalue the efficacy of these Scriptures to any that may profit thereby, but I would ask that all should read them so intelligently as to discriminate between that which belonged to the age exclusively in which it was written, and that which is applicable to the time in which we live. Very great changes occur in history, very great advances are made, and we must make this discrimination in everything.

The young man [*Leftwich*] who spoke here this morning asked whether it was not a new idea, this claim of equality for women, this claim in her behalf of the inalienable right to life, liberty and the pursuit of happiness. Strange as it may appear, the great statesmen and politicians of the age do not seem to be aware of the application of the principles they are constantly upholding. The very men who signed the Declaration of Independence, many of them educated under English aristocratic institutions, did not seem to know how far those principles would carry them. Some of them at that time were very much opposed to educating the working-classes, for fear it would raise them above their proper level. And more recently, many who professed so great a reverence for these republican principles, were strongly opposed to a universal popular education, in place of the charity schools that disgraced the age.

There has been a great advance as regards the education of women. Many of our grandmothers did not know how to write their own names, it being then regarded as unnecessary for woman to learn to write. Now she has so far come up to the level of the intelligence of society as to rise above the mere drudgery of life, and demand something more.

Catharine Beecher in her first public work expressed the belief that the time was coming when woman would not be satisfied with her present low aims; and when she returned from the precincts of education she would no longer be satisfied with seeking a little reading, and working devices on muslin and lace, but, her powers being called out, she would be seeking immortal minds, wherever she could fasten impressions that should never be effaced. She did not anticipate the fastening of impressions on immortal minds in public conventions. No; she revolted at such an idea, because she had been educated by her father to believe that the pulpit and the public platform was no place for woman.[8] But a few months ago, I received a note from her, inviting me to attend at a large public school, where she was going to deliver an address to men and women; showing that her own mind has undergone a change upon the subject, in the general advancement of public opinion.

The religious veneration of woman has been so misdirected by her religious training, that she needs to be taught to judge for herself. She will find, when she does so, that the Scriptures have been perverted, and that the customs of society are not always founded in truth and justice. Nor will her veneration for the good, the true, and the divine, be lessened when she learns to respect the divinity of her own nature; nor will she be ashamed of this new Gospel of truth, or afraid to declare it before the people. She will behold a vision of a new heaven and a new earth, wherein dwelleth righteousness; and entering in, she will find all that will supply the wants of her spiritual nature. She will find the inspiration that was in Paul, and in all the servants of the Most High, in olden times, is not withheld now, even from woman, but that she will be prepared to go forth upon the mission whereunto she may be called.

Believe me, my sisters, the time is come for you to avail yourselves of all the avenues that are opened to you. I would that woman would wake up to a sense of the long-continued degradation and wrong that has been heaped upon her! Like the poor slave at the South, too many of our sex are insensible of their wrongs, and incapable of fully appreciating the blessings of freedom. I therefore submit, in reference to this subject, the following resolution:

Resolved, That as the poor slave's alleged contentment with his servile and cruel bondage, only proves the depth of his degradation; so the assertion of woman that she has all the rights she wants, only proves how far the restrictions and disabilities to which she has been subjected have rendered her insensible to the blessings of true liberty.[9]

PD *The Seventh National Woman's Rights Convention* (New York: Edward O. Jenkins, 1856), 7–9, 79–84, WASM

1. Lucy Stone considered the event as a "day of congratulations." She recounted the advances in women's property rights in the New England states, New York, and the Midwestern states in such a short time (*Proceedings*, 4–5).

2. Ernestine Rose later spoke on this topic (*Proceedings*, 35).

3. Along with John Stuart Mill (1806–73), the novelist George Eliot (1819–80) served as assistant editor of the *Review*.

4. In a letter to LM of June 20, 1840, O'Connell had stated these privileges (*Pennsylvania Freeman*, September 17, 1840). William Howitt (1792–1879), a British Quaker, had written to WLG that the exclusion of women at the 1840 London Convention because they were considered "heretics" contradicted Quaker doctrine (Palmer, 236–37).

5. Stone stated that Lord Henry Brougham had presented a petition to Parliament signed by Elizabeth and Robert Browning, Elizabeth Gaskell, and Harriet Martineau, among others. The date was March 1856 (*Proceedings*, 6; Gordon, 1:371).

6. LM may have meant the works by Richard Edgeworth (1744–1817), which his daughter, the British novelist Maria Edgeworth (1767–1849), had helped write: *Practical Education* (1798) and *Professional Education* (1809). Maria Edgeworth's *Castle Rackrent* was published anonymously in 1800, but she soon acknowledged authorship (Elizabeth Harden, *Maria Edgeworth* [Boston: Twayne, 1984], 24, 95).

7. A young man identified as Mr. Leftwich, a theological student from Virginia, queried whether the women's rights claimed in this convention "were founded on Nature or Revelation." He stated that the "test" of a claim must be "its universality" and women's rights did not pass this test. "Woman was not fitted for the pulpit, the rostrum, or the law court," he contended. "God gave her a mild, sweet voice, fitted for the parlor . . . let her be content with the holy and beautiful position assigned to her by her Maker" (*Proceedings*, 36–39).

8. Catharine Beecher's father was the Presbyterian minister Lyman Beecher (1775–1863).

9. The convention passed the resolution unanimously (*Proceedings*, 84; see also Faulkner, 157; Palmer, 254–55).

Yardleyville, Pennsylvania, September 26, 1858[1]

'The kingdom of God is within us,' and Christianity will not have performed its office in the earth until its professors have learned to respect the rights and privileges of conscience, by a toleration without limit, a faith without contention. This is the testimony of one of the modern writers.[2] And have we not evidence, both from our own religious records, and those of all the worshippers of all ages, that there has been this divine teaching acknowledged, in some way or another—that there is a religious instinct in the constitution of man, and that, according to the circumstances of his birth, of his education, of his exercise of his free agency, has this religious essence grown, and brought forth similar fruits, in every age of the world, among all peoples? This has been likened, by various figures, emblems, parables, to things without us and around us. It has been variously interpreted, variously explained; for no nation has a spiritual language, exclusively such. We must therefore speak of our spiritual experiences in language having reference to spiritual things. And we find this has been the case, especially in the records of the Jews, the scriptures of Israel, and what are called 'Christian scriptures.' They abound in emblems and parables.

This divine illumination is called 'the spirit.' It is said that 'God breathed into man life,' a spirit, his 'own image,' which is spiritual, and he became a *living* soul. The after writers acknowledge this divine spirit —'Thou gavest also thy good spirit to instruct us.'

An idea has prevailed that the immortality of this spirit was not understood till about eighteen hundred years ago; but if we read the old scriptures intelligently, we shall find the acknowledgment of its eternity, as well as its divine nature. 'Then shall the dust return to the earth as it was, and the spirit shall return to God who gave it.' And these same writers, even though they were very much clouded, and the clearness of their views obscured by traditions, so that when Jesus came among them, he said, 'they made the word of God of none effect by their traditions'; yet, the far-seeing among them acknowledged that these obscurities must pass away, and that the time should come when the divine light should be more clearly understood, 'when thou shalt hear a voice behind thee saying, This is the way, walk ye in it.' And it is spoken of sometimes as the 'still small voice.' It is spoken of again as a new covenant that should be made: 'I will write my law in their hearts,' the law of justice, mercy, forgiveness, that they should have no more need of the old proverb, 'The fathers have eaten sour grapes, and the children's teeth are set on edge.' 'But if a man be just, and do that which is lawful and right,' 'in his righteousness that he hath done he shall live.' On the other hand, 'when the righteous turneth away from his righteousness and committeth iniquity, in the wickedness that he doeth shall he die.'

So we see that the teachings of this divine spirit have been the same in all ages. It has led to truth, to goodness, to justice, to love. Love was as much held up among these old writers, these old religious teachers, and as clearly set forth, as in the later day. Their testimony fell upon ears that heard not, upon eyes that saw not, because they had closed their eyes, shut their ears, and hardened their hearts. They had substituted something else for this divine light; this word, which, in a still earlier day, Moses declared to his people was 'nigh unto them, in the mouth, and in the heart.' The truths of inspiration are the way of life, and he that walketh in the right shall grow stronger and stronger. These were the teachings of the light to walk uprightly; to act righteously; to be just; to be faithful. 'With the merciful, thou wilt show thyself merciful; with an upright man thou wilt show thyself upright; with the pure, thou wilt show thyself pure.' Believe not, then, that all these great principles were only known in the day of the advent of the Messiah to the Jews—these beautiful effects of doing right.

We should come to understand the divinity of this spirit, and its teachings to us now. I believe there is a growing understanding of it. It has been likened unto leaven, which was hid in the meal, 'till the whole was leavened'; and also to the little seed that was sowed in the field, which became 'the greatest among herbs.' The word of God is life-giving, fruitful; and as it is received, it produces its own generation, sometimes called re-generation. Another beautiful figure is sometimes employed, the change in the physical being. We have first the little child; then the young man; then the strong man in the Lord. All these things we must read and accept intelligently, rationally. Too long has the religious element been upheld to the veneration of man through some mystery whereby he could understand the growth of his own divine nature. Why, it needs no miracles. They belong to darker times than ours. It is when we are wide awake, and capable of reading, reflecting, and receiving this ingrafted word, that we come to know the anointing that teacheth all things. And we shall not need that any man teach us. We shall come away from these false dependencies. We shall come to the source—the immediate access which we have made to the source of all truth, to the source of all good. I know this is merely regarded as the Quaker doctrine, the ignis fatuus of the Quakers, and it is every where spoken against. We know how it was treated in the early days of the Quakers. We know how the Son of God was received when he preached; and it was because his teachings led him to non-conformity with the rituals of the day. He was led to bear his testimony against the doctrines of the Scribes and Pharisees of his time.

All ecclesiastical history goes to assure us, that when there has been a sectarian standard raised, and a mere verbal theology and ceremonial performances instituted, good works have invariably been lowered. We all know how bitter the sectarian spirit has become—how hatred and antipathy have grown up among the people, and among people making the highest profession of the name of Jesus, who become horrified, shocked, if any shall deny what they are pleased to consider his divinity; and yet, if any speak of the fruits of obedience to the law of justice and of goodness in the soul, they brand it as mere morality, mere human benevolence, and the religion by which salvation is wrought. This is the tendency of sects, and it needeth a prophet to come forth declaring your circumcisions, your false lights, to be of no avail. This has been the uniform condition of acceptance, the working of righteousness—doing justly, loving mercy, and walking humbly before God—and not in oblations and sacrifices.

And so, down to the present time, we see the same tendency and the same results. We need prophets among us, bold non-conformists, to come forth and say, Verily, your baptisms are not the right tests; your communions are not the proper evidence of your intimate union with the Father and with the Son. What are your Sabbath-day observances but conventional rites? Verily, your silent meetings, your plain attire, your peculiar language—are they the rightful tests of your sound faith, your pure worship?' No more than that of any other denomination. We may take every denomination, and where we find them setting up their forms as an evidence of worship, above the pure acts of devotion to God, manifested by love to the people—to the common children of God, the world over—wherever this is to be found, there is need of the right testimony to be borne; there is need that we should say, he is not a true Christian who is one outwardly. We need higher evidences, therefore, than now exist. Christianity will not have performed its work in the earth, until its followers have learned to respect the rights and privileges of conscience, by a toleration without limit, a faith without contention.

What have we to do with granting to another a point, a belief, a doctrine? It is assumption. It leads to despotism. It has led to crucifixion; and it leads in the same direction now, as far as the customs of the times will admit. The *name* is cast out now, just as much as ever. And why is it? Because there is a verbal creed set up. Because there are doctrines fixed upon as being the essential requirements of believers. They assume that the scriptures are the word of God instead of taking them and ascertaining the uniform testimonies to righteousness and truth, as found in the various pages, and discriminating between these and the practices of those ancients, many of whom were semi-civilized, many of whom regarded their God as the God of war. The scriptures should be read intelligently, so that we should not be going back to the example of those ancients as our authority for the present day. They do not justify that. I would not shock the religious feelings of any, but I would ask them to read their scriptures again, and see if they can find any authority for sustaining their actions, and especially such as have done injury to their fellow-beings and themselves. Especially are they appealed to for sanctioning the use of wines and strong drinks, as our authority for the far-extending influence of these for evil among the children of men. So has it been the practice to cite the example of olden times in approval of the *abomination* of American slavery, as being a patriarchal institution. It is time that we should no longer err. We do err, not knowing the scriptures nor the power of God, when we resort to this Bible to find authority for any thing that is wrong. We have a divine teaching to which we should adhere. The great principles of justice, love and truth are divinely implanted in the hearts of men. If we pay proper heed unto these, we shall have no occasion to go to the ancient practices to find authority for our actions in the present day.

We cannot help our opinions in these matters; this is impossible. They grow up with us, and depend on circumstances, on our education, and immediate influences. We are justified in our skepticisms. It is our religious duty to be skeptical of the plans of salvation. The veneration of believers has been held to them by not allowing them to think. They have been afraid to exercise the test of enlightened reason which God has given them lest they should be called infidels—should be branded with infidelity. It is time the theology of the day had passed away. And it has, to a great extent. It is modified. As an instance, we might refer to the New School Presbyterians, arraying themselves against the old Calvinistic doctrines.[3] Others might be enumerated. The people now are ceasing to believe what their verbal creed teaches them. If there was a freedom and independence among them, such as the truth would give, they would be less trammelled. 'If the truth shall make you free, ye shall be free indeed.' How few are made free by the truth! They are hampered by their undue adherence to the gloomy appendages of the church. I would not set a high opinion on the Catholic Church, the Episcopalian, Presbyterian, Methodist, Quaker, or any other. They all have their elements of goodness, and they all have their elements of bondage; and if we yield obedience to them, we become subject to them, and are brought under bondage. If we acknowledge this truth, and bow to it, we shall dare to show our dissent. We will let them alone, treating them with a toleration without limit, a faith without contention, with regard to their opinions.

The doctrines of Christianity are perverted in order to sustain the doctrine of total depravity. We take not to ourselves that which belongs to ourselves. The proper sense of the divine nature of man, in all its relations, first the animal, next the intellectual, and then the spiritual, is not properly understood. This is a beautiful trinity in the human being. We shall find 'the glory of the natural to be one, and the glory of the spiritual another.' While the general faith of Christians is to denounce the animal, and to build up a kind of new birth on this degradation, we are erring, we are not acknowledging the divinity of all man's instincts as we ought; and hence it is I deem it necessary to speak forth, and be branded with heresy. And believing this, and asserting it before the people, I cannot feel that I am advocating a mere Quaker dogma. It is not a mere Quaker doctrine. In this latter day, we find it being regarded more and more by every sect, and by those who attach themselves to no religious denomination. They acknowledge this when it can be regarded free from the gloom of sect.

When we thus appeal to the teachings of the divine spirit, we shall find it to exist in every human breast. This is *the* revealed religion, and it is time that it was claimed as such. It is time that that which is regarded as mere morality should be preached as the everlasting, divine truth of God; and as it is shining in the hearts and minds of the children of men, and they come to receive it, they will behold its glory, and it will be the glory of the only spiritually begotten of the Father, dwelling in them as full of grace and of truth. They overlook it because of its simplicity.

There is an acknowledgment of the regenerating power of the eternal, so far as we may call it regeneration by application to natural things, without basing it on the assumption that the first birth is evil. Jesus said, 'Except a man be born again, he cannot see the kingdom of God.' But he spoke to those dark Jews, who did, no doubt, need to be born again, to die out of their old forms and ceremonies. Well did he answer Nicodemus, who thought this such a miracle, 'That which is born of the flesh is flesh; and that which is born of the spirit is spirit. Marvel not that I said unto thee, "Ye must be born again."'

We may all admit, that if we receive the divine spirit, in its operations in our soul, there will be no mistake; it will be found a reprover of evil; and if we obey it, it will be regenerating in its nature. It will make us understand that which is spiritual, and to discriminate between that which is spiritual, without underrating the natural. If we suffer the propensities to have the mastery over us, we must reap the consequences. Look at slavery in our country; look at war. Whence come wars? 'Come they not hence, even of your lusts that war in your members?' If we attempt to govern ourselves and our feelings by these low principles, they, of course, will lead to evil, to wrong, to wickedness. The apostle says, 'the natural man receiveth not the things of the Spirit of God; neither can he know them, because they are spiritually discerned.' The natural man hath natural powers and abilities; the intellectual man hath powers differing from these; and the spiritual man knoweth not the propensities of the natural.

We are not to be regarded as denying the Scriptures, because we have not so read them, and so learned Christianity, as have many of the authors of the theological opinions of the day. Men are too much wedded to these opinions. Women in particular have pinned their faith to ministers' sleeves. They dare not rely on their own God-given powers of discernment. It is time that ye had looked to these scriptures, and studied them rationally for yourselves, and not follow the teaching which interprets them in support of the wrong, instead of the right. Women in the earliest days associated with men in carrying forward the great principles of truth, as advocated by that remarkable son of God. A Deborah arose, and Huldah, a prophetess. It was a woman who announced to the people of Samaria the advent of Christ: 'Come see a man which told me all things whatsoever I did.' And this induced the men to go forth 'out of the city, unto him.' And they said unto the woman, now 'we have heard him ourselves, and know that this is indeed the Christ.' And the very first act of the day of Pentecost was to declare that the time would come when the spirit should be poured out upon women. Phoebe was a minister of Christ. Priestcraft has rendered the word so as to apply to man instead of woman. The degradation of the women of that day had its effect.

People should judge more intelligently than to take the practices of former times, and make them a test for practical Christianity of this day. 'The kingdom of God is within us'; the 'word is nigh, in the heart, and in the mouth.' If any are so faithless as still to need outward corroborative testimony, they will find it in all ages, and from the earliest times, as recorded in the Bible. And this is the value of the scriptures among us. We have no right to go to them now to establish a creed or form. We cannot control our opinions; we cannot believe as we will: therefore belief is no virtue. We have not the power to control our being; it is by the circumstances around us, by our power of receiving, that we come to see, and to know, and believe; therefore we must make a different use of the Bible, in order to make it to us a book that is invaluable.

Goodness has been goodness in all ages of the world, justice, justice, and uprightness, uprightness. 'I will make all my goodness pass before thee.' This was a beautiful answer to Moses. This is the way that God manifests himself to his children. It has been so in every age. It is emphatically the case in the present day, which is marked by the advances that have been made in this generation. It is this which should be held up as an evidence that Christianity is being better understood; that the veneration of the people is being drawn away from undue observances of Sabbath days, of the worship of churches; that they are coming to judge in themselves what is right, when they are disposed to do this. How plentifully are the testimonies of the scriptures found to be in favor of the right, in all ages!

The fact, then, that God has chosen is easily recognized: 'To loose the bonds of wickedness, to undo the heavy burdens, and to let the oppressed go free, and that ye break every yoke.' Jesus did not say, Blessed is the believer in the trinity: blessed is the believer in the popular scheme of salvation; blessed the believer in a mysterious divinity attached to himself. He said nothing of the kind. He called them to judge of himself by his works: 'If I do the right works, believe me, and the Father also, for I come from the Father.' 'Blessed,' he said, 'are the merciful; blessed the pure in heart; blessed the meek,'—not the 'meek' that bow before sect. We must know a meekness that will make us 'as bold as a lion,' that we may proclaim righteousness, and reclaim this generation from its sins, and denounce this meekness before sect. Jesus declared this by his life of goodness, of active righteousness, of pure morality, of sympathy for the poor. It is for the love of his principles that we should place him on the high pedestal that those who delight to worship him ceremonially want to do.

It is not strange that there should be atheism in the world, while such false ideas of God are inculcated in the hearts of the people. We cannot in any way come to the worship of God, by any of these fancied attributes, without humanizing him. Therefore, we must come to know him by our merciful acts, our pure, our upright conduct, our every-day righteousness, our goodness. We must come to be with him by declaring 'woe unto the transgressor.' We must not make compromises with injustice. If the mission of Jesus was so emphatically to bring 'peace on earth and good will to men,' we must endeavor to carry it out, and not place it away in the distance, in the 'millennium.' Why, the millennium is here; the kingdom of God has come. This is what we want to preach. Oh that the fruits of this divine spirit should appear, which are love, peace, joy, goodness, truth; the spirit that is first gentle, pure, full of mercy, full of good fruits. Here is no disparagement of good works.

We forget the practical parts of the Bible, in our zeal for preaching up a religion that is to do nothing. And so we must let war go on 'until the millennium comes.' In the olden time, they knew that war was wrong, and hence the far-seeing proclaimed the day when 'they shall beat their swords into ploughshares, and their spears into pruning-hooks; nation shall not lift up sword against nation, neither shall they learn war any more.' They looked forward and prophetically proclaimed the day when the 'King cometh, who is just, and having salvation.' 'And I will cut off the chariot from Ephraim, and the horse from Jerusalem, and the battle-bow shall be cut off; and he shall speak peace unto the heathen; and his domination shall be from sea even to sea, and from the river even to the ends of the earth.' If we are believers in this, and believe in the Messiah that came with such a beautiful announcement, it is time that we should love the name of Christ; should part with war, and leave nations to settle their disputes in some way that will put an end to the barbarism of war. It is abominable that we should retain it—that we should still have recourse to arms.

But the efforts for the dominion of peace are greater now than ever before. The very first message transmitted to us across the Atlantic, by means of that mightiest instrument of men, the offspring of the divine, intellectual intelligence of man, wrought in our day, was a prophetic view of greater peace on earth.[4] There is something so beautiful in this universal instinct of men for the right, that I am pained to know that people of intelligence, professing Christianity, should vouchsafe their assent to the duration of any of the relics of the dark ages. Let us do away with these things. We need the faith that works by love, and purifies the heart. And sorrowful is it that the hearts of men should be turned from the right by the temptations that so easily beset them, and lead them to do injustice to their fellow-man, binding him down to slavery. Ah! The chains of human bondage! They should make everyone to blush and hang his head. Mournful is it that they should countenance the Sabbath day, and then, to-morrow, recognize a system by which their fellow-men are sold at the auction-block to the highest bidder. We should bear our testimony against the nefarious claim of the right to property in man: and the worst of this is, that we should hear this institution claimed as sanctioned by the Bible. It is the grossest perversion of the Bible, and many ministers have thus turned over its pages so unworthily, to find testimonies in favor of slavery. 'Woe unto him that useth his neighbor's service without wages, and giveth him not for his work.' This is what we want to quote. And we are all guilty of the blood of our brother. The crime is national. We are all involved in it; and how can we go forth and profess to believe the faith of the Son of God, with all these great wrongs and evils clinging to us, and we upholding them? Have we nothing to do with it? Everyone has a responsibility in it. We are called to bear our testimony against sin, of whatever form, in whatever way presented. And how are we doing it? By partaking of the fruits of the slave's toil? Our garments are all stained with the blood of the slave. Let us, then, be clean-handed. Seek to be so; and if we find the monstrous evil so interwoven with what we have to do, politically, commercially, by manufacturing interests, by our domestic relations, then so much the more need is there for our laboring. Every church in the earth should be roused; every people, every profession, and interest. We find democratic, republican America clinging to slavery; and it will be found the last stronghold of the sin in the civilized world. 'He that doeth truth cometh to the light'; but we have rejected the light of Christ. We are told that the Lord, in his own time, is going to put an end to this thing. How, except in some way or other to defend the right? 'Break ye the bands of wickedness'; 'Proclaim liberty throughout all the land, unto all the inhabitants thereof.' And because ye have not done so, ye shall fall victims to the plagues that are around you. Here is where we need faith, to know that we must reap the reward of our doings.

I have nothing to do with preaching to you about what we shall be hereafter. We even now, by our obedience, come unto that kingdom which is righteousness, peace, and joy in the Holy Spirit. We know something of an inheritance into that higher life where there is that communion with the Father, so that we can understand, as far as is given us to understand, that we may elevate ourselves above that which is mortal to that which is immortal.

We need, therefore, this faith, which will make us believe and know, that if we do the wrong, we must receive for the wrong that we are doing; for there is no respect of persons with God. He 'rewardeth every man according to his works'; and according to the fruits of his doings. God's laws are eternal, and I wish there were more conscientious believers in the immutable laws of God. When such a man as George Combe comes forth, teaching the everlasting laws of truth to the children of men, he is called a mere materialist. I would not exchange the true test for all the theology that ever existed. All the theological assemblies and gatherings united could not give such benefit to the world as the truths and writings of George Combe, and others who have a profound veneration for the laws of God.

It is impossible to hold any nation in slavery, when their minds shall be enlightened sufficiently to appreciate the blessings of liberty. When the sacred principles of truth come to be evolved to the understandings of the children of men, how will all your theologists sink before them! The rightful test, then, of the Christian character will be peace, and love, and justice, and a claim of greater equality among men. There will no longer be the lordly heel of a government trampling upon the children of men—no longer a high-bred aristocracy, exercising their exclusiveness—no longer an aspiring priesthood, bringing all under its spiritual domination. It is time these things were understood: time that we should show how simple the religion of Jesus is. This was the highest theology uttered by Jesus: 'By their fruits ye shall know them.' The good man, out of the good treasure of his heart, bringeth forth that which is good; and the evil bringeth forth that which is evil. The soil must be good, and the seed received must be cared for, so that it may produce its own. And what will it produce? Ah, what will it not produce, my young friends? Overlook not the truth of God. There is nothing that requires that ye should underrate your natural powers. Let them grow with your growth and become strengthened, and you will be made advocates of the right.

This is really a notable age, and we have to hail it that we have not to wait for a far-distant day for the kingdom of God to come. There is an advancement, and its influence is felt so much that the minister begins to be ashamed to turn over the leaves of the Bible to prove the wrong, rather than to find therein advocacy of the right. The young people ever hear truth gladly; in their hearts, there is an instinctive revolting from wrong. Did not the love of power abide to such an extent among us, there would be an instinctive revolt against slavery and wrong doing. And see how the reformer can stand before the Bible and say, Ye tell us that ye treat the slave kindly; but I say unto you, hold no slaves at all. Do justice to the colored man. Do away with your infernal prejudices; they *are* infernal. This impure spirit, this wrong that ye indulge in, is not from above; it is earthly, sensual, devilish. A grave charge rests upon ye who countenance the wickedness of American slavery.

Public sentiment is changing. What though the political horizon may lower, believe me, the time is near,—the kingdom of God, of justice and mercy, is entering, that will be for the salvation of the slave. Believe me, that the labors of a Beecher, a Chapin,[5] a [*William Henry*] Furness, a [*William Lloyd*] Garrison, and many other advocates of the right and true of our day, preceded by those of a [*Elias*] Hicks, a [*Thomas*] Clarkson, a [*William*] Wilberforce, and their confederates of former days, have not been in vain. God ever blesses the rightful laborer. 'In the morning sow thy seed, and in the evening withhold not thy hand; for thou knowest not whether shall prosper, either this or that, or whether they shall both be alike good.' So, having thus gone forth, we see now how it is renovating, how it is purifying the church from its corruptions.

The temperance movement is likewise prospering. It has given evidence of great advancement in this day. War, too, is falling from its original foothold in the earth. There is greater delight manifested in right doing. The power of moral-suasion is becoming better understood. These are good indications, and, with many others, they point to a happier and better state of things, the fruits of the ushering in of the great and glorious gospel, that which was to level distinctions, cause the highways to be straightened, and institute equality among men. Let that so be brought about that the reformer shall say to the poor, 'Come up hither! come up higher!' thus awarding justice to these, and recognizing their rights, and their equality with themselves. The day is coming, it has come; 'the kingdom of God is at hand.'

The people flock more to hear moral discourses than to hear the preaching from the pulpit. This would not be the case were the preaching of the pulpit like that of Jesus. There is a quick understanding in the fear of the Lord among the people, and I will trust the people. I have confidence in their intuitive sense of the right, of the good. It is this great heart of the people we are to preach unto, to proclaim liberty and truth, justice and right unto; and let it be done.

The immediate teaching of God's holy spirit, inspiring love for the brethren, inspiring a desire for the promotion of good, is your mission. Oh, it is your heavenly call; obey it, and look not for any thing marvellous. Obey it, my young friends! Come ye unto the harvest, and labor truly. There is need to labor in a world lying in evil. There is need of preachers against the excesses of the age. There is need of preachers against the existing monopolies and banking institutions, by which the rich are made richer, and the poor poorer. Thou, oh man of God, flee these things and follow that which is right! It is contrary to the spirit of this Republic that any should be so rich. Let this blessed Christian equality prevail. Let us have a Republic that shall be marked by its Christian principles; and by its *Christian*, I mean its universally *right* principles. These are eternal; divine in their origin, and eternal in their nature. Let us have faith in these, and then let us believe that the 'kingdom of God is within us,' and that Christianity will not have performed its office in the earth, until the believers have learned to respect its rights and privileges, by a toleration without limit, a faith without contention. That faith will fill the heart with holy joy. Thanksgiving will come up from such a heart, and there will be an entering into the joy of the Lord, acknowledging that he is good; that his mercy is everlasting; and that his truth endureth through all ages.

PD "A Sermon Delivered at Yardleyville, Bucks Co., Pa., Sept. 26, by Lucretia Mott, Reported Phonographically," *Liberator*, October 29, 1858

1. LM had been listed as one of the speakers at antislavery meetings September 25 and 26 in Bucks County (*National Anti-Slavery Standard*, September 18, 1858). While there she most likely spoke at one of the Quaker meetings nearby.

2. Frederick Joseph Foxton, *Popular Christianity: Its Transition, State and Popular Development* (1849), 5.

3. In 1836 the Presbyterian General Assembly split, with the less conservative "New School" group supporting revivals and moving away from Calvinism. The New School Presbyterians split further in 1857 over slavery.

4. Although it did not prove ultimately successful, on August 5 a transatlantic cable had been laid. On August 16 the message from England read, "Europe and America are united by telegraphic communication. Glory to God in the highest, on earth peace, good will toward men."

5. Henry Ward Beecher (1813–87), Congregational minister in Brooklyn; Edwin H. Chapin (1814–80), Universalist minister in New York City.

American Anti-Slavery Society, Assembly Rooms, New York City, May 11, 1859

Mrs. LUCRETIA MOTT, of Philadelphia, who was received with loud applause, then addressed the audience. She was glad to hear such an encouraging view presented as that given by the last speaker, while yet she admitted the necessity for such watchful and critical censors as Parker Pillsbury and others.[1] It was needful that they should be watched over and watch even themselves, so that they should not be so elated with what had been done as to lead them into any compromise or unfaithfulness in regard to what remained to be done. There was still a great deal to do, for the number of slaves in our country had greatly increased since the labors of the Abolitionists began, and they must toil on, toil ever; they must find new paths to walk in, and they would see these continually opening before them. It was not necessary now that they should go over the old ground, and reiterate that which was so needful at the beginning, because the public sentiment had been elevated, and the popular periodicals and newspapers advocate anti-slavery, to a certain extent; but there was always something new to be said; every good Abolitionist, out of the treasures of his heart, could bring forth "things new and old," and thus their meetings were made very interesting.

Mrs. M. said she had just left a large company of women, gathered together to consider the great principles and testimonies of the Quaker Society.[2] Anti-Slavery had occupied their attention a part of the time. This Society although it did not come strictly into the category of those who were in communion with slaveholders, had yet, owing to the various causes which had operated upon the whole country, been slow to speak out and act out, honestly and faithfully, their anti-slavery principles and sentiments. They had needed laborers among them, as in other Societies, and their labors had not been without their effect. The efforts which had been made in the land had produced a result at which they all rejoiced, giving, as it did, evidence of great gain to the cause.

Mrs. Mott then referred to the importance of adhering to the principle of moral suasion as the most effectual means for the accomplishment of this great work. She hoped they would not lose their faith on this point. They should all remember that they set out on the ground of moral resistance—not merely passive resistance, but resolved to go forth with weapons that were not carnal, but spiritual, and which had proved mighty, through God, as far as they had been wielded, to the pulling down of this stronghold. She believed, if they continued to wield these weapons, they would go on, conquering and to conquer.

* * * *

LUCRETIA MOTT took the platform, and spoke at some length, urging the importance of faithfulness to the great work in which they were engaged which is not merely to protect the fugitive, but to enlighten the public on the great sin of American slavery, and so to hasten the time when the chains of every slave in the land shall be broken.

PD "Twenty-Sixth Annual Meeting of the American Anti-Slavery Society," *National Anti-Slavery Standard*, May 21, 1859

1. LM's long-time friend and PASS activist James M. McKim (1810–74) stated that the antislavery movement was already "improving our politics, meliorating our religion, and raising the standard of public and social morals." On May 10 Parker Pillsbury had stated that the AASS had been too tolerant of institutions such as the Republican Party and the *New York Independent*, who make "specious and strong anti-slavery pretensions and professions" but who are "still in governmental or ecclesiastical union and fellowship with slavery and slaveholders" (*National Anti-Slavery Standard*, May 21, 1859).

2. The *New York Times* (May 13, 1859) stated that LM had left a Quaker meeting of one thousand women "who were determined to make Anti-Slavery one of the great points for which they would hereafter contend." This meeting was probably the Philadelphia Yearly Meeting of Women Friends, which LM attended on May 10. Slavery was discussed then, only in milder language than the *New York Times* reports (*Friends Intelligencer*, vol. 16, no. 16 [July 2, 1859], 244–46).

Anti–Slavery Sympathy Meeting, Assembly Buildings, Philadelphia, December 16, 1859

Mrs. Lucretia Mott explained the circumstances of the expulsion from the Hall, characterizing it as the proceeding of a pro-slavery mob, and commenting very severely upon the indignities offered.[1] The same thing had happened before. Pennsylvania Hall was burned, and the next year the Mayor requested that no Anti-Slavery meeting should be held, and that prominent Abolitionists should not be seen walking the streets in the company of colored persons.[2] Now they are asked to get redress by law, which they spurn contemptuously. The goods are stored in the upper saloon of the Assembly Buildings, and Mrs. Mott hoped that their partial mutilation would only increase the anxiety to purchase them. The meals prepared for yesterday will be there in readiness after this meeting, and although, perhaps, they will not taste quite so well as then, their spoiling should also be cheerfully accepted.

* * * *

Mrs. Mott replied to a voice from the audience that had the goods on exhibition at the Fair not been removed yesterday, they would have been held in the Hall until to-morrow noon, when the leases of the premises would expire, and then thrown out or disposed of in any way that seemed best to the authorities.

Mrs. Mott proceeded to compliment the press (or a large portion of it) for its co-operation with the cause of justice. Since the trial of Daniel Dangerfield[3] the Abolitionists have had great confidence in the reporters of most of the papers.[4]

PD "Anti-Slavery Sympathy Meeting This Morning," *Anti-Slavery Bugle*, December 31, 1859, from the *Philadelphia Evening Bulletin*, December 16, 1859

1. Before this meeting, tension was already high in Philadelphia over the execution of John Brown (b. 1800) on December 2. Some Philadelphians had held a mass "Union" rally on December 13 to condemn Brown and other abolitionists, including LM, for their "disunion doctrines." On December 12 the annual PFASS Anti-Slavery Fair had opened at the Concert Hall, but on December 15 officers served a "writ of ejectment" because proslavery factions had objected to the fair's flag extending over Chestnut Street. The fair thus moved to the Assembly Buildings nearby. According to the *Anti-Slavery Bugle*, "One sentiment prevailed—that of deep indignation at the intervention of the civil authorities in the progress of the Fair at Concert Hall, and at the demonstrations in front of, and outside National Hall, last evening" (*Anti-Slavery Bugle*, December 31, 1859; *Liberator*, December 30, 1859; *National Anti-Slavery Standard*, December 24, 1859; Palmer, 292–93; report by Mary Grew in Hallowell, 392; see also Bacon, 195).

2. The mayor of Philadelphia in 1839 was Isaac Roach (1786–1848).

3. Dangerfield had been arrested in Harrisburg as a fugitive slave and was taken to Philadelphia. Confronted with evidence of Dangerfield's lengthy residence in Harrisburg, the commissioner freed him (*New York Times*, April 5, 7, 1859; see also Hallowell, 387–90, for LM's role at the trial).

4. The fair continued until Saturday. It was unclear whether sales had been affected by the disruption but it was considered "a complete success" (*National Anti-Slavery Standard*, December 24, 1859).

Pennsylvania Anti-Slavery Society, Town-Hall, Kennett Square, October 25–26, 1860

[October 25, Morning Session]

LUCRETIA MOTT expressed her pleasure at the happy auspices under which the meeting assembled. These meetings were refreshing occasions. It was pleasant to greet old friends and see the faces of associates with whom we have so long labored in this most holy cause. If it was right to weep with them that weep, it was also meet that we should rejoice with them that do rejoice; and I am sure you are all rejoicing over the evidences of our progress and the proofs of what has already been accomplished. We have no religious observance with which we mark the beginning of these meetings, but our hearts well up nevertheless with grateful joy at the signs of the times, and the evidences of approaching triumph to the cause in which we are engaged.

[October 26, Morning Session]

Mrs. MOTT would add her testimony to the value of THE STANDARD and the importance of its circulation. She had a letter on the subject from Mrs. [*Maria Weston*] Chapman, parts of which, at her request, Miss Mary Grew read.[1] The letter speaks of the high value of the paper, and possibility and duty of raising it still higher. Mrs. Mott spoke of the importance of preserving and distributing an

Figure 6. Executive Committee, Pennsylvania Anti-Slavery Society, ca. 1851. *Back row, left to right*, Mary Grew, Edward M. Davis, Haworth Wetherald, Abby Kimber, James M. McKim, Sarah Pugh; *front row, left to right*, Cyrus Burleigh, Margaret J. Burleigh, Benjamin Bacon, Robert Purvis, LM, JM. (Courtesy of the Friends Historical Library, Swarthmore College)

anti-slavery paper. It had been a principle with her not to destroy any of these precious leaves of the Tree of Truth. She had a new bundle of *Liberators*, and *Bugles*, and STANDARDS with her for distribution, and also hoped people would come forward and help themselves. Mrs. Mott was glad to hear that Dr. Cheever and his friends were willing to come on our platform.[2] She was glad of the cooperation of all new helpers, and especially of one so able as Dr. Cheever. But she did not think that his cooperation with us was going to exonerate us in future from the charge of being "Infidels"; and she was not concerned whether it did or not. We could afford to be called by that name or any other our enemies might devise, so long as we in our lives and action, as individuals and as a Society, we brought forth the peaceable fruits of righteousness. Dr. Cheever would be called "Infidel" too; and we are infidel to the religion of a formal, pro-slavery, time-serving Church.

[*October 26, Afternoon Session*]

LUCRETIA MOTT was glad that the resolution does not sanction the measures resorted to by John Brown, as in contradistinction to those approved by this Society, and by the American organization of which it is a part.[3] Mrs. Mott read from the Declaration of Sentiments what she said were her views, and what were at the same time the authorized doctrines of this Society. "Our principles lead us to reject and to entreat the oppressed to reject all carnal weapons, relying solely on those which are mighty through God to the pulling down of strongholds." We did not countenance force, and it did not become those—Friends and others—who go to the polls to elect a commander-in-chief of the army and navy, whose business it would be to use that army and navy, if needed, to keep the slaves of the South in their chains, and secure to the masters the undisturbed enjoyment of their system—it did not become such to find fault with us because we praise John Brown for his heroism. For it is not John Brown the soldier that we praise; it is John Brown the moral hero; John Brown the noble confessor and patient martyr whom we honor, and whom we think it proper to honor in this day when men are carried away by the corrupt and pro-slavery clamor against him. Our weapons were drawn only from the armory of Truth; they were those of faith and hope and love. They were those of moral indignation strongly expressed against wrong. Robert Purvis has said that I was "the most belligerent Non-Resistant he ever saw."[4] I accept the character he gives me; and I glory in it. I have no idea, because I am a Non-Resistant, of submitting tamely to injustice inflicted either on me or on the slave. I will oppose it with all the moral powers with which I am endowed. I am no advocate of passivity. Quakerism, as I understand it, does not mean quietism. The early Friends were agitators; disturbers of the peace; and were more obnoxious in their day to charges which are now so freely made than we are. Mrs. Mott concluded by expressing her pleasure that the resolution committed the Society to nothing inconsistent with the high moral grounds it had ever occupied. O'Connell had said that no revolution was worth the cost of a single drop of human blood.[5] John Brown had well illustrated in his own case the superiority of moral power to physical power; of the sword of the spirit to the sword of the flesh.

* * * *

Mrs. MOTT, while fully appreciating the generous and maidenly feeling of the last speaker, regretted to hear from one so young even a hypothetical approval of resort to violence.[6] She never liked to hear people say what they would do or what they would not do in certain cases. None of us can tell what we would do. Principles are not to be settled by imagining extreme and improbable cases. "He that taketh the sword shall fall by the sword"; and none are so safe from violence as those who use no violence.

[*October 26, Evening Session*]

LUCRETIA MOTT said that Dr. Stebbins was mistaken about the character of the Anti-Slavery Convention of 1833.[7] There were comparatively few clergymen in that body, and there was deep earnestness, but no cant. She then went into an argument, drawn from facts, as to the usefulness of the Anti-Slavery Society, first having followed Dr. Stebbins in his review, showing that the facts that he stated were susceptible of a different explanation. She referred to the good work done in putting down the Colonization Society, in elevating the condition of the colored people, in promoting better views generally of human rights and duties, etc., etc.

* * * *

The following resolution, offered by Mrs. Mott, was then brought up for consideration:

Resolved, That while we see the penalty for the sin of slavery in the impoverished soil and the depraved morals of the South, we of the North cannot claim exemption from the consequences of our part in this great sin while we continue our commercial intercourse with the slave holder, and freely partake of the produce of the unrequited toil of the poor slave.

* * * *

Mrs. MOTT held that we should have no union with slaveholders, politically, religiously, or commercially. We ought not to use the products of slave's unrequited toil. In purchasing slave-grown productions we furnished the slaveholder with the motive and the means for continuing his system.[8]

PD "Twenty-Fourth Annual Meeting of the Pennsylvania Anti-Slavery Society," *National Anti-Slavery Standard*, November 3, 1860

1. First published in 1840, the *National Anti-Slavery Standard* was the official newspaper of the American Anti-Slavery Society. Mary Grew (1813–98), Philadelphia abolitionist and women's rights activist, was the corresponding secretary of PFASS.
2. George Cheever (1807–90), pastor of the Church of the Puritans (Congregational) in Manhattan, had spent most of his career as an antislavery moderate, but became a prominent critic of slavery in the late 1850s.
3. Resolution 4 expressed sympathy for abolitionist John Brown, and concluded "there lives and burns in the Northern heart a genuine admiration of heroism" (*National Anti-Slavery Standard*, November 3, 1860). On October 16, 1859, Brown led an attack on a federal arsenal in Harper's Ferry, Virginia, as part of larger plan to overthrow slavery. Three days later, he was captured by the U.S. military.
4. Robert Purvis (1810–98), one of LM's close friends and allies, was a founder of the American Anti-Slavery Society and a member of Philadelphia's African American elite.
5. Daniel O'Connell was an outspoken opponent of violence, and a similar quote may be found in John Mitchel, *The Last Conquest of Ireland (Perhaps)* (Glasgow: R. & T. Washbourne, 1876), 12.
6. The previous speaker was Anna Dickinson (1842–1932), a Philadelphia abolitionist and Republican Party orator, who had "objected to certain non-resistance sentiments which had been expressed" (*National Anti-Slavery Standard*, November 3, 1860).
7. Sumner Stebbins of Chester County, Pennsylvania, a medical doctor and Progressive Friend, claimed that "New England ministers" had dominated the founding meeting of the AASS, and he preferred the Republican Party to the "dead weight" of the AASS (*National Anti-Slavery Standard*, November 3, 1860; "Pennsylvania Yearly Meeting of Progressive Friends," *Liberator*, May 23, 1862; "Chester County Medical Society," *Medical News*, June 1852).
8. J. Miller McKim replied to LM's resolution that he was "glad" to have slaveholders spend their money in Philadelphia, as it could then be applied to "the uses of freedom." The resolution was tabled (*National Anti-Slavery Standard*, November 3, 1860).

Fifteenth Street Meeting, New York City, June 1, 1862[1]

LUCRETIA MOTT, who spoke at length, yesterday, in the Fifteenth-street meeting, holds also to the principle of non-resistance, but unlike some other gifted minds, she condenses her arguments, and puts them forth—here for her compeers a problem solved, there for the younger mind an offering more precious than costliest gems to wear, fadeless and forever; and even to the little child an impressive thought is given, to carry it over the troubled ripples in life's young stream. Her remarks touched with force, but not diffuseness, upon our political crisis. Her opening sentence was, "The Kingdom of Heaven is within man"; and she went on to show that the Kingdom of Heaven was *peace*, therefore *war* was at variance with it, and while we participated in the sentiments of strife and bloodshed, we were without God's kingdom in our hearts. She believed that as Scripture records of a triumphant scheme we might, in this day, have done—have brought our enemy to terms by acts which would have been to him as coals of fire upon his head. Reference was made to the act of emancipation in the District of Columbia,[2] as being no result of the war, but of a concentration of public opinion brought about by petition after petition laid before the authorities in power. She urged the necessity of further effort upon the part of the faithful workers—they should now, while strife and confusion are overwhelming the land, be up and be doing, knowing no rest till the oppressed are free and an end put to the war; not this one alone, but *all* wars and fighting. A tribute was paid to the generous resources of our plan of Government, by which the social position was made no test of worth, but where the way was opened for *all* to advance; and she hoped the day would come when the poor "*contraband*"[3] and *every* American-born child might enjoy the privileges of education and recognition in self-support. New-York, with its wealth of educational institutes and libraries free to all, was spoken of with admiration. Much of the eloquent speaker's address was doctrinal, and referred to the principles of Friends and other denominations, as affected by and affecting the times and the march of civilization. She declared that there was *no such thing as theological science*, and in the course of some logical (but, as she confessed, usually denounced as heretical) remarks, undertook to show how God was *himself* the teacher of his people, and as we accepted the light of His inspiration within our own souls, we should obtain the Kingdom of Heaven. Inspiration, she told her audience, did not cease with the time of the Apostles; it was ever present to those who had the breath of life breathed into their souls, *thus becoming born again*, and the newly-born child has the breath of physical life breathed into his nature, "This," she said, "is *my Trinity*—this the divinity of man, the *spiritual*, the *intellectual*, the *physical*," weak in itself, but strong in the presence of Jesus, and guided ever as we accept of His spirit by our Father in Heaven.

PD "Progress of the Friends' Yearly Meeting," *New York Times*, June 2, 1862

1. Internal evidence suggests that this was delivered on Sunday, May 31, two days after New York Yearly Meeting ended on May 29.
2. The Senate and House passed the District of Columbia Emancipation Act, which freed slaves in the nation's capital, on April 3 and 11, respectively. President Abraham Lincoln signed the law on April 16, 1862.

3. On August 6, 1861, adopting the policy of General Benjamin Butler (1818–93) at Fort Monroe, Virginia, which declared fleeing slaves to be "contraband of war," Congress passed the First Confiscation Act, allowing the Union army to employ fugitives and disregard slave owners' claims. As a result, the word "contraband" became a synonym for "freed people."

30th Anniversary of the American Anti-Slavery Society, Concert Hall, Philadelphia, December 3–4, 1863

[*December 3 Session*]

I deem it but just to state, that although we [*women*] were not recognized as a part of the Convention [*of 1833*] by signing the document, yet every courtesy was shown to us, every encouragement to speak, or to make any suggestions of alterations in the document, or any others.[1] I do not think it occurred to any one of us at that time, that there would be a propriety in our signing the document. In the evening, at our house, I remember a conversation with our friend SAMUEL J. MAY, in the course of which I remarked, that we could not expect that women should be fully recognized in such assemblages as that, while the monopoly of the pulpit existed. It was with diffidence, I acknowledge, that I ventured to express what had been near to my heart for so many years, for I knew that we were there by sufferance. It was after the Convention had gathered on the second day, that the invitation was sent out. THOMAS WHITSON[2] came to our house with an invitation to women to come there as spectators or as listeners. I felt such a desire that others than those assembled at our own house should hear, that I wanted to go here and there, and notify persons to go; but I was asked not to use up the whole morning in notifying others, for we must try and be there ourselves. When I rose to speak, with the knowledge that we were there by sufferance, and it would be only a liberty granted that I should attempt to express myself, such was the readiness with which that freedom was granted, that it inspired me with a little more boldness to speak on other subjects.

When this Declaration, that has been read to us here to-day, and that we have so often delighted to hear, was under consideration, and we were considering our principles and our intended measures of action; when our friends felt that they were planting themselves on the truths of Divine Revelation, and on the Declaration of Independence, as an Everlasting Rock, it seemed to me, as I heard it read, that the climax would be better to transpose the sentence, and place the Declaration of Independence first, and the truths of Divine Revelations last, as the Everlasting Rock; and I proposed it.[3] I remember one of the younger members, DANIEL E. JEWETT,[4] turning to see what woman there was there who knew what the word "transpose" meant. (Laughter.)

It has been honestly confessed that there was not, at that time, a conception of the rights of woman. Indeed, women little knew their influence, or the proper exercise of their own rights. I remember that it was urged upon us, immediately after that Convention, to form a Female Anti-Slavery Society; and at that time, I had no idea of the meaning of preambles and resolutions and votings. Women had never been in any assemblies of the kind. I had only attended one Convention—a Convention of colored people in this State[5]—before that; and that was the first time in my life I had ever heard a vote taken, being accustomed to our Quaker way of getting the prevailing sentiment of the meeting. When, a short time after, we came together to form the [Philadelphia] Female Anti-Slavery Society, which I am rejoiced to say is still extant, still flourishing, there was not a woman capable of taking the chair, and organizing that meeting in due order; and we had to call on JAMES McCRUMMELL, a colored man, to give us aid in the work.[6] You know that at that time, and even to the present day, negroes, idiots and women were in legal documents classed together; so that we were very glad to get one of our own class (laughter) to come and aid us in forming that Society.

[*December 4 Session*]

When I see these young men and strong coming forward with acknowledgments of their indebtedness to the cause, and rejoicing that they have been among its later advocates; and when I look around upon this platform, and see here a LUCY STONE, an ELIZABETH JONES, and a THEODORE TILTON,[7] all laboring so effectively in the field, I feel that we older ones may indeed retire, and thank God that he who has blessed us all our lives long is now blessing the lads; for there is surely no greater joy than to see these children walking in the anti-slavery path.

I feared yesterday that we were dwelling too much upon the past. We were so deeply interested in the earliest movements of this Anti-Slavery Society, that we did not go back, except by mere incidental mention, to BENJAMIN LAY and RALPH SANDIFORD, who dwelt in caves and dens of the earth, of whom the world was not worthy, to ELIAS HICKS, THOMAS CLARKSON, and all those earlier laborers; we did not go back as far as that.[8] I feared, however, that we were not enough leaving the things that were behind, and pressing forward toward those that were before. Although I did not entirely agree with our friend FOSTER, and was glad that he was answered as he was—for I have so large Hope that I always take encouraging views of things when I can—yet I felt that there were duties to be performed in our case in regard to freedmen as well as in regard to those still held as slaves in our land.[9] It is of little consequence to us now what we have suffered in the past, what obloquy, reproach and contumely we have endured in our religious societies, and in other relations in society. We might, as women, dwell somewhat upon our own restrictions, as connected with this Anti-Slavery movement. When persons interested in the cause were invited to send delegates to the London Convention of 1840, and some of those delegates were women, it was found out in time for them to send forth a note declaring that women were not included in the term "persons," but only men; and therefore, when we arrived in London, we were excluded from the platform. Yet, let me say, in justice to the Abolitionists there, that we were treated with all courtesy, and with a good deal of flattery in lieu of our rights. But all those things we may pass by.

Last evening, when we were listening, some of us, to the eloquent and earnest appeals made by HENRY WARD BEECHER,[10] we saw in the assemblage some who, a few years ago, rushed from their seats in the church, because they could not bear to hear WILLIAM FURNESS speak so plainly on the subject of slavery, and who warned friends from abroad that they must not come to our houses because we were Abolitionists. When Madame PULSZKY and her friends came, and were asked to go with me on a visit to the Penitentiary, and the carriage was at the door, word came that they were discouraged from coming, because we were Abolitionists![11] When I see those men coming forward now, and joining in the applause for the thorough anti-slavery sentiments of HENRY WARD BEECHER and others, so far from blaming them, or setting them at naught, I would rather welcome them at this eleventh hour, and I hope they may receive their full penny, if they work diligently to the end. I have felt sometimes almost with the Apostle, willing to be accursed of my brethren for this cause's sake; but willing afterwards, when they come forward and mingle with us, to give them the right hand and invite them upon the platform, and glad to hear them, if they have anything to say on the right side. When I saw these things last evening, I remembered the remark of RAY POTTER,[12] one of the signers of the Declaration, who, in a speech in Rhode Island, said that Abolitionists had the great Temple of Liberty to rear, and must do all the rough and hard work; but when it was near the top, he said, then would come forth people to lay their little fingers upon it, and say, "We have got it up!" I could not but remember this last evening, and also a few weeks ago, when I rejoiced to see the crowds listening to the words that proceeded out of the mouths of PHILLIPS BROOKS and others upon this very platform. When I heard some of the members of the Freedmen's Association, in this meeting,[13] talking about the objections that were met and answered again and again by the Abolitionists years ago, of the duties connected with the liberation of the slave which we must perform, I felt that, after all, we were but unprofitable servants, and had not done as we ought to have done in regard to doing away with that deep-rooted prejudice which is the concomitant of slavery, and which we know can never be removed while slavery exists. Some of us women can perhaps more fully sympathize with the slave, because the prejudice against him is somewhat akin to that against our sex; and we ought to have been more faithful than we have been, so that when we hear the words applied to us, "Come, ye blessed of my Father," we might be ready to ask, "When saw we thee ahungered, or athirst, or in prison, and ministered unto thee?" It seems to me, therefore, as has been recommended here to-day, that we should keep on our armor. It may not be necessary to continue our operations in precisely the same way. But it will be necessary to multiply our periodicals, and scatter them, as we have done heretofore, with good effect. When our friends were talking of what was done, and how we were received in the beginning, and when Church and State were, as our friend GARRISON showed so clearly, arrayed against us, I remembered that then, just as in olden times, the common people heard us gladly.[14] In truth, the original good heart of the people—excuse my theology—cannot resist the wisdom and the power with which Truth speaks to their understanding; and therefore it was that we were gladly received among them. Many have come and made their acknowledgments, that when we were mobbed, when Pennsylvania Hall was burned, they were in the wrong, they were in the mob; but now they say, "Whereas I was blind, now I see, and I am willing now to be faithful to what I see." Let us welcome them, hail them in their coming, and gladly receive them. And with all these coadjutors, the work will go on, emancipation will be proclaimed and we may be just as confident and earnest as we were before our friend FOSTER reproved us. I think we may rejoice and take courage. I like a little addition to the rejoicing of good old Simeon: "Now lettest thou thy servant depart in peace, for mine eyes have seen *of* thy salvation"; for the whole salvation has not come, but we have seen *of* the salvation.

PD *Proceedings of the American Anti-Slavery Society at its Third Decade*, Phonographic Report by Henry M. Parkhurst (New York: American Anti-Slavery Society, 1864), 41–43, 64–67

1. Samuel J. May had mentioned that women had attended the founding convention of the AASS, but did not sign its Declaration (*Proceedings*, 40).

2. Thomas Whitson (1796–1864) was the Quaker founder in 1832 of the mixed-sex Clarkson Anti-Slavery Society of southeastern Pennsylvania.

3. The Declaration of Sentiments stated, "With entire confidence in the over-ruling justice of God, we plant ourselves upon the Declaration of Independence and the truths of the Divine Revelation as upon the EVERLASTING ROCK" (*Liberator*, January 4, 1834).

4. Daniel E. Jewett attended the founding convention of the AASS as a delegate from Massachusetts (*Liberator*, January 4, 1833).

5. LM likely attended one of the annual Conventions of Free People of Color held in Philadelphia from 1830 to 1833 (Howard Holman Bell, ed., *Minutes of the Proceedings of the National Negro Conventions, 1830–1864* [New York: Arno Press, 1969]).

6. A founding member of the AASS, James McCrummell was a barber and dentist (Faulkner, 64, 66).

7. Theodore Tilton (1835–1907) was a New York journalist allied with Henry Ward Beecher.

8. These pioneering abolitionists include Philadelphia Quakers Benjamin Lay (1677–1759) and Ralph Sandiford (1693–1733).

9. Stephen S. Foster warned abolitionists not to be "over-confident" that war would bring the end of slavery, asking, "Are we more deeply penetrated by a sense of the sinfulness of slavery than were our fathers?" A voice from the audience cried, "Yes," and Charles C. Burleigh argued that the most intelligent men in the country were now willing to support immediate emancipation (*Proceedings*, 57, 60).

10. Beecher noted that the last time he spoke in Philadelphia he had a police escort, but he vowed "that if a man will now set his face toward emancipation, I will never look an inch behind him to see what he thought yesterday or the day before" (*Proceedings*, 53, 54).

11. Terezia Walder Pulszky (1819–66) had traveled to the United States with Hungarian revolutionary Louis Kossuth to raise support for their cause (Palmer, 217).

12. Rhode Islander Ray Potter (1795–1858) was a founder of the New England Anti-Slavery Society and the AASS (WLG *Letters*, 5:341).

13. Phillips Brooks (1835–93) was an Episcopal minister in Philadelphia. On November 3 he had given a speech in Concert Hall "in behalf of the free negroes," possibly during the meeting of the American Freedmen's Aid Commission, which united five regional freedmen's aid societies (Alexander Viets Griswold Allen, *Life and Letters of*

Phillips Brooks, 3 vols. [New York: E. P. Dutton, 1901], 1:464; Carol Faulkner, *Women's Radical Reconstruction: The Freedmen's Aid Movement* [Philadelphia: University of Pennsylvania Press, 2004], 33).

14. WLG noted that, years ago, members of the AASS were denounced as "fanatics, madmen and incendiaries." He asked, "Did we not go to our cherished religious denomination, or to our political party, and expect, as soon as our appeals were made, it would give a patriotic or Christian response? How were we disappointed in every direction!" (*Proceedings*, 22, 25).

American Anti-Slavery Society, Church of the Puritans and Cooper Institute, New York City, May 10–11, 1864

[*May 10 Session*]

SPEECH OF LUCRETIA MOTT

I shall detain the meeting but a few moments. I only wish to express the great interest I have taken in the several speeches that have been made, and to say that I wanted one word should be added, before the meeting closed, in behalf of the warfare which has been carried on by this Society from this platform, and which has resulted, as I believe, in the great change of public sentiment which has been alluded to. The evils of this war were very forcibly presented in the early hour of this meeting,[1] but, as was well expressed, they are inevitable, because we know that war, being of evil, must produce evil, and that continually; still, I would say, I had hoped that better things would accompany our salvation, and the salvation of the country, so that another generation, following this, might be born into a Republic far transcending the Republic that grew out of the Revolutionary War; because the war is now carried on by a people differing very much from the people of that time; an intelligent, instructed people, who have had the advantages of a Republic so far; and when peace shall be restored, they will be prepared to come forward and act unitedly to remove the many evils and wrongs that remain, and the mighty debt which has accumulated in the nation. And then the war has not been a warfare of brute force merely, and the materials that will be brought in with which to build up the Republic will be very different from the materials that were at command after the first war of our country. We shall have a free, liberated people, rather than an agreement that a large portion shall still be held as slaves; there will not be, therefore, that great drawback to our nation's prosperity. Let us, then, hope that in spite of the evils of this war, there is a day approaching when the Republic will be better understood, and the principles of a truly Christian Democracy better carried out, than ever before. So help us God!

Then, again, in the warfare, as it has been carried on, the Administration has been not only at Washington. It has been acknowledged here that woman has had something to do with it; that woman has been cooperating in the warfare which has been going on. I am desirous that our Anti-Slavery Society, in its annual meetings, and in all its meetings, should keep the standard of liberty and truth high as in the beginning; and if in thus holding it up, it shall become the duty of men like Wendell Phillips to present the errors and short-comings of the Administration, let them do it;[2] and let us rejoice that we, as a Society, are not part and parcel of the Government, the Administration, or the Cabinet, not even as John Bright was;[3] that we are not responsible; that we have not any load upon our shoulders that shall tend to make us compromise. Let us be careful how we commit ourselves, as a body, as a Society, to one candidate or another. We are in danger of becoming partisans in our feelings, by holding up one man or crying down another, any further than their acts warrant us in doing so. I wish we could hold up Frémont a little more for the act he did, (applause,) but I am glad to hear Abraham Lincoln held up, as we have just now, for the many things that he has done; and where he has fallen short, it is our duty to rebuke him.[4] It is our duty to ourselves to keep the standard high, and to bring the acts of all classes, even of Kings and Governors, to the test of that standard.

I only rose with the desire to express this, and to hold out the hope that we are coming to a great and glorious day, when, I believe, whatever belongs to the great moral warfare of the nation will be commended, not to us, a handful of abolitionists merely, but to the great heart of the people. A proof of this is seen in the willingness, on the part of the people, to sign petitions and send them forth, and to join in the battle armed in the full armor of God; not depending on carnal weapons—knowing, however, that these things must needs be, in a government based, as ours is, and as all nations are, upon the sword—not depending on horses and chariots, but depending on the Lord God; and, going forth with these weapons, we know they will be effective. Let our faith be firm, then, that they will ever be effective; we can never anticipate fearful, deplorable results from such a warfare, because it has its origin in God, in goodness, in love, in plainness of speech, in justice and mercy and truth.

I never had anything more to confirm my faith in the infinite and the eternal than the success of our weapons of warfare, wielded as they have been, morally, in season and out of season, full of fight as we have been, using the severest language that our dictionary could furnish us with, or that our thoughts could bring forth, to describe the monster slavery. I remember that Wm. Lloyd Garrison, in his first work, almost—"Thoughts on Colonization"—remarked that when Wilberforce spoke against the African slave trade, how vituperative his language was considered; "but now," said he, "when the scorn of the whole civilized world is brought against this iniquitous system, how mild and inefficient his speeches do appear."[5] So with us; we were afraid to use the word "man-stealers" in the beginning; we had been accustomed to speak soft words; but we found that the necessity was laid upon us, from the fact that we had to speak of slavery as it was; to hold it up to the utter execration of mankind, and to enlist the pulpit and the press in behalf of the suffering and the dumb. I say it is this great moral warfare that has been carried on, that has produced this wonderful change which we are now rejoicing in; and I only desire that we may be just as true as Wendell Phillips has been to-day, not praising men unduly because they have done something, but demanding that they should do the whole. And do not let us be so distrustful of human nature, of the good heart in man, as to suppose that if men have done wrong, they have done as nearly right as they could. Why, human nature judges what is right. Let us have confidence in the human heart. Even the *Herald* came out in defense of Frémont's proclamation,[6] and the people were ready to say Amen! But we are too much accustomed yet, as our friend said they are in England, to honor people in office. We know them—we know how loyal they are; but we, the people here, we are the administration. Woman is taking her place—here is Susan B. Anthony calling attention to the Women's National League[7]—and the men and women united, the people united, are to become the administration of the country; and then we shall look on these petty servants of ours that are in office, and while we shall give them all the honor they deserve, we shall feel that we must honor most MAN; MAN, wherever he is found; MAN—the Black man and the white man; yes, and WOMAN, too. (Applause.)

[*May 11 Session*]

LUCRETIA MOTT thought there had not been as much attention given to the consideration of our present and future responsibilities of labor as should have been in the course of the discussions. She exhorted all to continued faithfulness and activity in the use of our weapons of moral warfare.

PD Jas. M. W. Yerrinton, "Thirty-First Anniversary of the American Anti-Slavery Society," *Liberator*, May 20, 1864.

1. In his speech criticizing Lincoln's administration, Phillips had commented on the "evils of war" (*Liberator*, May 20, 1864).
2. Phillips proposed a resolution that "while we do not wish to criticize the wishes of the Administration, still, as Abolitionists, we feel bound to declare that we see no evidence of its purpose to put the freedom of the negro on such a basis as will secure it against every peril" (*Liberator*, May 20, 1864). At this meeting, abolitionists were divided: while Garrison supported President Lincoln, Phillips endorsed John C. Frémont (1813–90) as a Republican presidential candidate (WLG *Letters*, 5:213).
3. John Bright (1811–89), a Liberal Member of Parliament, a firm supporter of the Union cause, and a fellow Quaker.
4. As commander of the Department of the West, General Frémont had emancipated slaves of Missouri Confederates in August 1861. Lincoln overturned Frémont's proclamation, and removed him from command that November (Palmer, 316). Lincoln issued his Emancipation Proclamation freeing all slaves in Confederate states on January 1, 1863.
5. Adapted from William Lloyd Garrison, *Thoughts on African Colonization* (Boston: Garrison and Knapp, 1832), 9.
6. Following Frémont's emancipation proclamation, the *New York Herald* (September 1, 1861) stated, "considering the audacities and atrocities of the rebel invasion of Missouri and its local affiliations, General Frémont has been driven to the extremities indicated . . . a general liberation of the slaves belonging to the rebels of our revolted States will unquestionably be the ultimatum of a protracted war."
7. British abolitionist George Thompson (1804–78) had noted that the English "judge[d] them [*politicians*] more leniently" because of their need to do what was politically possible rather than what was ideal (*Liberator*, May 20, 1864). With Seneca Falls Convention organizer Elizabeth Cady Stanton (1815–1902), abolitionist and feminist

Susan B. Anthony (1820–1906) formed the Women's Loyal National League in May 1863 to support the Union "in so far as it makes war for freedom" (quoted in Faulkner, 181).

Women's Rights Convention, Church of the Puritans, New York City, May 10, 1866

MRS. LUCRETIA MOTT expressed a hope that there would be no adjournment,[1] and proceeded to say: I am sorry to come before you with so impaired a voice, and with a face so scarred;[*] but, I rejoice that as we who have long labored in the cause become less able to do the work, the younger ones, the [Theodore] Tiltons and the Harpers, come forward to fill our places.[2] It is no loss, but the proper order of things, that the mothers should depart and give place to the children. It is now more than twenty years since this Woman's Rights movement began in this country. We were allowed to read, if we could not understand much; and could read that Blackstone defined the law, "that the husband and wife were one person, and that person the husband"; and we labored therefore to change the law, so as to recognize the wife as a person with civil rights.

It has been said this morning that every appeal that has been made to the legislatures of the several States, has been favorably received, and answered by changing the laws for the benefit of woman. I can but hope, comparing such an audience as this with the handful who met with Elizabeth Cady Stanton, in the first Convention, in a little Wesleyan church at Seneca Falls, and seeing Henry Ward Beecher for the first time on our platform, and speaking such noble words for woman, I can but hope that it will not be as our friend Frances D. Gage[3] expressed her fear it would, that the degradation which centuries had created among us, would require centuries to remove; but that, as in the great anti-slavery movement, in regard to which the most ardent Abolitionists never anticipated that we should live to see the work accomplished, and yet a great work has been wrought, for which we all feel increased veneration for that power which not by might, but by His Eternal Spirit, will work the change in this equally important enterprise, to free woman from her enslavement; for it is an enslavement, although not equal to the degradation of the poor black slaves, and although I have never liked to use the word "slavery," as applied to the oppression of woman, while we had a legalized slavery in our country. But the oppression of woman has been such, and continues to be such, by law, by custom, by a perverted Christianity, by church influence. This very church is an indication, from the darkness of its appearance as we entered it this morning, that they love darkness here rather than light, I will not say "because their deeds are evil," but because they are ignorant and know not what they do. They profess to follow the apostle Paul; but they understand him not, they know not the Scriptures nor the power of the gospel, which is indeed glad tidings and good news to the human race: glad tidings of great joy unto all people.

---

* Mrs. Mott had a severe cold and hoarseness, and her face was bruised from a fall from a street car.

We are beginning to realize this in regard to the millions who have been slaves in our land. And this is an earnest to us that the good time is not distant, that light and civilization have advanced. As our President said, we have in our army such minds as Spencer, and Mill, and I would add Buckle, and many others; and they are diffusing light, intelligence and civilization, and advocating the right.[4] We have women also. We have Frances P. Cobbe; whose name I speak with pride and rejoicing; and in the literary world we have Charlotte Bronte, and Harriet Beecher Stowe, and many others, who are consecrating their talents to the great cause of womanhood, and freedom, and right.[5] So we find women as artists, in all its branches, everywhere; and even in a Catholic country Rosa Bonheur receives the cross of Honor (or something of that sort, about which you know more than I do);[6] for I am now only one of the fossil remains, asking you in my imperfect way, to sit here a little longer with your work. Remember that the apostles sat all night, in their beginning, and that the Abolitionists, when we were crowded into an upper chamber, were glad to continue hour after hour preparing our resolutions.

Another thought was suggested to me this morning. If it were true, as we were told, as it was not true, that the slave was satisfied with his condition of slavery, it only proved the depth of his degradation, for liberty was no less a blessing to him because he was ignorant of it. So when woman asserts again and again that she has as many rights as she wants it only gives evidence of the depth of her degradation; and when the rights which we demand shall be conceded to her, they will prove no less a blessing than if her ignorance had never led her to deny or to dispute the propriety of asking for the redress of the grievances under which she labored.

When, in 1848, the women of France went to the Provisional government and asked that they might be represented under the new order of society the most intelligent and enlightened statesmen of that country came forward and said that the only reason why France did not succeed in the former Revolution of 1789 was that she represented then only half the republic; that woman was as necessary to form a complete republic as man; that although she differed from man, that very difference was essential to form a complete republic.

Woman has been laboring for years under the present condition of society which, like a great nightmare, crushes her down, so that she is unable to tell the cause of her suffering. When some of us in 1840 were sent forth as delegates to the World's Convention at London, and were denied the right of acceptance because we were women, [Daniel] O'Connell and William Howitt came forth and pled our cause; and a short time after, Sir John Bowring said that the coming of those women to England would form an era in the history of philanthropic doings, and would create a deep if not a wide impression there. I like to allude to these things to show what progress we are making. Education has done much for us. We now have women as physicians, and in various departments of society. A little while ago when the daughters of [Richard] Edgeworth put out their volumes, they were afraid to publish them over their own names, and borrowed the name of their father. And when Lady Morgan wrote her history, in her introduction she mournfully says that "man tells woman that obscurity is her true glory, insignificance her distinction, ignorance her law, and passive obedience the perfection of her nature," and proceeds to state the effect of this erroneous and vicious teaching on the mind and powers of woman.[7]

Young women of America, I want you to make yourselves acquainted with the history of the Woman's Rights movement, from the days of Mary Wollstonecraft.[8] All honor to Mary Wollstonecraft. Her name was cast out as evil, even as that of Jesus was cast out as evil, and as those of the apostles were cast out as evil; but her name shall yet go forth and stand as the pioneer of this movement. I want to note the progress of this cause, and know now that Woman's redemption is at hand, yea, even at the doors. (Applause.)

PD *Proceedings of the Eleventh National Woman's Rights Convention* (New York: Robert J. Johnston, 1866), 49–52, WASM

1. Stephen S. Foster proposed adjourning in order to "perfect an organization, and take such further measures for the prosecution of our cause as may then and there be deemed expedient" (*Proceedings*, 49).
2. Frances Ellen Watkins Harper (1825–1911) was an African American orator and writer active in the antislavery, women's rights, and temperance movements.
3. At the Eleventh National Woman's Rights Convention, Stanton served as president; Frances Dana Gage (1808–84), an activist and author from Ohio, spoke on women's gains in "Civil Rights" at the state level (*Proceedings*, 5, 43–44).
4. In her address, Stanton asked, "With such minds as Herbert Spencer, John Stuart Mill, Garth Wilkinson, Victor Hugo, Ruskin and Mazzini, all writing up the dignity of man and Republican institutions, showing how order and beauty may come out of this confusion, and all alike pointing to woman, shall not woman herself put on a new virtue, dignity and courage, to meet the responsibilities the best minds of the age now press on her conscience?" (*Proceedings*, 13). Herbert Spencer (1820–1903) included a chapter on "The Rights of Women" in his *Social Statics; or, the Conditions Essential to Human Happiness Specified, and the First of Them Developed* (London: John Chapman, 1851). As a Member of Parliament, John Stuart Mill advocated for women's suffrage in 1866 and 1867 (Gordon, 2:70). Historian Henry Buckle (1821–62) delivered "The Influence of Women on the Progress of Knowledge" in 1858 (*Fraser's Magazine for Town and Country* [April 1858], 395–407).
5. Frances Power Cobbe (1822–1904) was an Anglo-Irish writer and reformer.
6. Rosa Bonheur (1822–99) was a French artist.
7. This quote is from *Woman and Her Master* (London: Harry Colburn, 1840), published by Sydney Owenson (1783–1859) under her married name Lady Morgan.
8. Mary Wollstonecraft (1759–97) was the English author of *Vindication of the Rights of Woman* (1792).

Fifteenth Street Meeting, New York City, November 11, 1866

"The Lord is in his holy temple, let all the earth keep silence before him." Those who can thus, in silence, feel after and find Him who is not far from every one of us—for, as saith the apostle, "in Him, we live, and move, and have our being"—those need not make the harmony of sweet sounds to attune the heart to praise, melody, and thanksgiving; but, in this nearness of approach unto Him, they can feel with the psalmist, that they love His law, and it is their meditation both day and night. Now, this is a reality: it is no fancied mount of transfiguration, but it is an experience in which the desire is often felt: "Lord, evermore give us this bread." The worship in spirit and in truth is the worship that is called for at our hands. It is a great privilege we have, it is true, to enter His courts with thanksgiving, and into His gates with praise, to acknowledge that the Lord is good, His mercy everlasting, and His truth enduring to all generations. But the worship which is required of us, is the active use of all our God-given powers, all our faculties, our intellectual as well as our nobler spiritual gifts. All these consecrated to God, to truth, to righteousness, to humanity, and acts in accordance with such consecration, constitute the worship which is needed, and very different from mere Sunday worship paid in oral prayer, in sacred song, or in silent bowing of the head. We are too apt to confound these means to an end, legitimate, acceptable, noble as they are, with the end itself. We are too apt to mistake Sabbath-observances and Sunday worship for that which the Father is seeking from us all—for the obedience which is called for.

We have just heard the inquiry made [*by a preceding speaker*] as to what must be the state of mind "in the trying hour." I asked myself, What is that trying hour? Many put it off, supposing it to be when the head is laid upon the pillow of death, perhaps, or to a fancied day of judgment. But we need to understand, "the trying hour" to be every hour when our consciences are awakened to a sense of our situation—a sense of our unworthiness, it may be needing repentance of sins, or with present duties imposed upon us, when the trying hour is the struggle whether we shall do our duty. Some men's sins, the apostle says, go before-hand to judgment and some they follow after. Many understand this as going before death and after death, but it seems to me that it is before they are committed: when we are tempted, we are brought to judgment, to consideration, to reflection, as to how far we shall yield or give up, or come to a right decision as to our course of life.

We need to bring our experience, our religious faith, duties, and worship more down (or *up*, I would say) to our every-day life, more to our real existence. We need to pray for strength; for, the great efficacy of prayer is not to pray for partial favors, which would be, perhaps, in violation of the very laws we have transgressed, and which bring upon us their proper penalty, not to pray for special favors which we have no right to ask, but to pray that strength may be given us to do what is required of us, to stand fast, to have a conscience void of offense toward God and toward man. We may not have sins to repent of when brought together, if we are every day desirous to be found thus doing our duty and invoking the Divine Power to aid us in this great desire of our hearts. We know we are human, we feel our weaknesses, and we feel the spirit of thanksgiving and praise for all His mercies, which are new every morning. When we are thus brought together, and can sit down, and can feel one with another, and enter into our own hearts' communion, and know His divine presence, notwithstanding our infirmities, our human weaknesses,—these are profitable considerations for us individually. But I often feel that we have need to press on the consideration of the people the great duties of life, which belong to them, *collectively*, and which, as individuals, we are bound to exert ourselves to promote, in order that the Kingdom of God may be, in reality, near at hand, nigh even at the doors. There is great instruction in the records of the past in finding how the great seers, the anointed of God, in every age, were always looking for a higher and better state of things, a kind of millennium, and often prophesying that this state should come, when peace should reign, when the government of the Divine and the Eternal should be extended from sea to sea, and from the rivers unto the ends of the earth; and this we find described in the Scriptures in various ways; and each writer in his turn has called upon the people around to do their part to bring in this kingdom—to hasten the time, when in the figurative language of Scripture, the lion and the lamb shall lie down together, when all violence shall cease, all wars, all injuries one of another, when there shall be regard one for another in every way, when loving our neighbor as ourselves shall be more prevalent in the earth. And this millennium was not completed at the advent of the Messiah to the Jews: it seemed barely begun in the darkness in which he found them, borne down by unmeaning ceremonies, useless forms and sacrifices, which were never called for from on high, but which were only suited or adapted by Moses and others to the weakness and low condition of the people with whom they dwelt and labored. In this dark state the great truths uttered by Jesus often seemed to fall to the ground; and he lamented over them: "Are ye yet without understanding?" "Shall the Son of man, when he cometh, find faith in the earth?" Some of these mournful interrogatories show how he deplored the condition of things which he found among his own people; and yet he was ever hopeful of a better state of things, as was his forerunner: "He that cometh after me is mightier than I; he shall baptize with Spirit and with fire." And so Jesus, using terms of the truth, in his language, said, "The bread that I give you, cometh down from Heaven; if ye eat my flesh (that is, take the truth which I proclaim to you, receive the word which is thus spoken to you) ye shall have everlasting life; for, my flesh and my blood are meat and drink indeed." He found that they were very outward in their reception, their understanding of it, accustomed as they were to hieroglyphs, symbols, figurative language: "Are ye yet without understanding?" "Know ye not that the flesh profiteth nothing?" "The words which I speak unto you, they are spirit and life. Let him that is athirst come unto me and drink." What did it mean? I know that theology makes this all outward, all suited to an outward atonement, to a vicarious sacrifice, the general orthodoxical idea of salvation by Christ.

I think, however, the spiritually-minded, the clear intelligent reader and thinker, may understand this in a far wider sense, and it is time that this theological gospel of despair had passed away. Even the disciples, outward and ignorant as they were, said: "Thus spake he of the spirit which they who believe in him shall receive." And so with the apostles: Jesus called them continually to the freedom which the truth would give—the liberty which was of God, and which was to be bestowed by obedience, by doing right, by doing the will of the Father; and in this way, his gospel was indeed, "glad tidings of great joy unto all people." Gloomy theology makes it not so. The bigoted, the intolerant converts to this theology make it any other than "glad tidings of great joy to all people."

The gloomy ascetic, whether Quaker or Catholic, makes it just so revolting and repulsive to the young. Therefore, if we attempt to preach the religion of Jesus, salvation by Christ, we have need to understand it better, or we shall never know what these "glad tidings of great joy" really mean. We must learn to exhibit by our very countenances that we have attained to this state.

True religion makes not men gloomy. Penances, asceticism, old sacrifices, "daily crosses"—all belong to a more gloomy religion than that of the benign and beautiful spirit of Jesus. (The term "daily cross" occurs only once in the New Testament—in the Bible, I believe). We know well there are sacrifices to make in our life, in the pursuit of our duty, the attempt to uplift the lowly, to spread the gospel of glad tidings of great joy unto all people. We know that the right hand and the right eye (to use again a figure of speech) have to be parted with at times; but always we feel the conviction that we enter into life thereby and its rich experiences.

It was no new doctrine that Jesus preached. When asked what it was he preached, he declared that it was not new. "The peace that passeth understanding" had long before been spoken of. Even the disposition to return good for evil had been recommended long before his day. We make a great mistake and limit the Holy One of Israel, when we date the commencement of true religion eighteen hundred years ago. There have been evidences of it in every age, and even now in all the nations under the sun, in a form more gross or refined, according to the circumstances of the times, of the age, of the nations, we find recognitions of the Divine and the Eternal, the Creator of us all, and in some form, ceremony or worship offered unto Him. The native Indians of our forests have their worship; and having witnessed some of their strawberry festivals and dances, and religious operations,[1] I have thought that there was, perhaps, as much reasonableness and rational worship in it as in passing around the little bread and wine; or, I might name, perhaps, some of the peculiarities of our own people; for all sects, all denominations have their tendency to worship in the letter rather than in the spirit—with an outward rather than an inward salvation.

The apostolic in every age, the-sent-of-the-Father, are ever calling for a higher righteousness, a better development of the human race, a more earnest seeking to equalize the condition of men. And now, when the call is, "Behold the kingdom of God is at hand," it is a disgrace on our profession of Christianity—the present unequal condition in Christendom—these vast distinctions that exist in Europe, even in England, between the rich and the poor. The lordly aristocracy, the kingly government, the aspiring priesthood there, and your own tenement houses here—all these things go to show how little we have really advanced; and yet, with other views of the subject, how much, how great is the progress. I more frequently have cause to rejoice in the evidences of the progress of real Christianity, real truth, righteousness, and goodness, than to be pained by evidences of anything like a retrograde movement. I never look back to the past as the Golden Age, but always forward to it, as coming; and I really believe it to be nigh, even at the door, though not perhaps by man's calculation. And, indeed, one (may I say apostle?) of our own day, our great and good Elias Hicks, dared not to leave much record of his own experience and religious views of things, because he saw the generations to come must be in advance of him, must go on unto perfection, must see and act further than he had done—that difficulties would be overcome, that the trammels of superstition and tradition would be removed; but not entirely, he said, for, wars would never cease among men until the professors of Christianity had learned to read the Bible more intelligently, more as they would other books, and come to a right judgment as regards the acts there required. Something on this wise he has left; and I am glad he has; because there is a tendency, having begun well, and run well for a time, to suffer ourselves to be hindered from obeying the truth, and to go back again to the weak and beggarly elements of theology. Hence I am glad that there is enough left for some of us, the older ones, to recur to as being the faith for which we struggled thirty years ago, and by which we conquered, as I believe. I want that we should hold fast to this inward guidance, this inward teaching, without wavering.

Another of the seers of our age (and I like sometimes to quote those not of our own household) an anointed one, declared: "Mighty powers are at work in the world and who shall stay them? God's word has gone forth, and it shall not return unto him void. A new comprehension of the Christian spirit, a new reverence for humanity, a new feeling of brotherhood and of all men's relation to the common Father. This is among the signs of our times."[2]

This was declared before the late struggle, and the late events for the removal of the bonds of slavery from millions of our fellow-beings. We see that this reverence for humanity has done its work in so far, and we can believe that it is going on if we are faithful; if we can understand the Christian spirit and act it out, we shall be instrumental in hastening the day when the kingdoms of this world shall become the kingdom of our Lord and his Christ. The day may be hastened: it is man's instrumentality that is needed. We acknowledge a mighty power far above all human effort, and indeed independent, as I regard it, of the battle-field, that has brought about the marvelous work and wonder of our day; but it was not without many having to make sacrifices, to suffer their names to be cast out as evil, and having to go forth as with their staff in their hands and passing through this Jordan before we could reach the promised land. How should one have faced a thousand and two, put ten thousand to flight, had not the Lord been on the side of justice, mercy, and truth? This has been manifested, and in so many ways that I now have great hope that the time will not be long, before the great barbarism of war will be placed in its true light before the people, and they will easily learn that where the disposition exists to resort to means for the redress of grievances (either national or individual) other than physical force, the way will be found. The prayer we need is for strength to our feeble human efforts, and it is granted, blessed be His name: "Whatsoever ye ask believing, ye shall receive." Have faith, then. This idea, if we can only receive it aright, not applying it to outward events but to inward confidence in the sufficiency of the mighty power of God, the sufficiency of the attributes with which we are furnished; if we will only carry them to Him and do His work and not look to man for praise, for help; if we will come out of our sectarian inclosure, and bind not ourselves to any theories or speculations, but go on in fullness of faith—the desired end will be truly attained.

The great historian, probably the greatest historian in our day, Buckle, has very erroneously, it seems to me, attributed the advancement of the world so far in civilization, more to the intellectual development of man, than to his spiritual and moral growth and advancement.[3] It seems to me that he mistook the mere sectarian effort of days past (which he said died out in a generation and produced no great effect upon the world) for the moral effort at human progress. Let us see what has really been the progress since the great law of love of right, of regard to man, was proclaimed more clearly and extensively by Jesus of Nazareth. Let us see what has been the progress since that time, despite the checks given, as I deem many of them, by the organization of the sects; that is, by erroneous theories involved in those sects. Notwithstanding all these, there has been such progress in human society that now the writers of the present day may well claim that there is a better understanding of God dwelling with man, the Holy Spirit being with us, and of man's regard to his fellow-being. The efforts that are made for education, for improvement, morality, and the great numbers in all parts of Christendom, in various parts of the world, enlisted in behalf of improving the condition of society—all go to disprove the idea, which I fear, when put forth by such a historian, would have an undue influence, and warp the judgment of many of his readers, and lead to a lighter estimate of moral effort than really belongs to it. He asked, what new law since the days of Jesus of Nazareth? We might as well ask, what new law in science? There is no new law in truth: we want no new law. It is no new doctrine which I preach, said Jesus. But we want a better carrying out of the law, a better life, a better recognition of the Divine, and of the great duties of life springing from the right worship of the Divine, and the Eternal. I allude to this simply, because I know that when a writer becomes popular we are apt to receive his say-so without much criticism or instruction; and I believe we have intelligence, judgment, and capacity to read and understand; and I rejoice that woman is so elevated; and I would not ask more evidence of the great moral advancement in society, than the estimate that is set upon woman in our day; and she can read, and reflect,—and judge understandingly of what she reads. Let us rejoice in these things. I would not disparage—far be it from me—any intellectual advancement:—I regard it all divine. We are as responsible for our intellectual as for the highest gifts of God's holy spirit to the soul: "First that which is natural, afterwards that which is spiritual." It is theology, not the Scriptures, that has degraded the natural; the intelligent reading of the Scriptures will not disparage man. A gloomy theology has done this to the full extent; lowered the estimate of good works; and dethroned reason in so far that it is almost dangerous to hold up reason to its rightful place, lest it should be charged to the French atheists. Why, my friends, we are responsible, divinely so, for our reason and its right cultivation; and I am glad to perceive that the people are not afraid to think, and that skepticism has become a religious duty—skepticism as to the schemes of salvation, the plans of redemption, that are abounding in the religious world; that this kind of doubt, and unbelief are coming to be a real belief; and a better theology will follow—has followed. The old Calvinistic scheme is very much exploded—very much given up. The Thirty-nine Articles are called in question by their own subscribers;[4] and the creeds of many Dissenters are set at naught; and the formula of religion is changing: less and less value is set on ceremonies. We find that which generations ago, was the holy eucharist is now the simple memorial bread and wine: a very simple thing it has become. Even with this idea, many, I believe, if they were faithful, would find that they go to the table unworthily, and would feel bound to withdraw from it. The fear of man proves a snare to many; and we do not make as much progress as we should by reason of this fear of sect, of man, of non-conformity. We need non-conformity in our age, and I believe it will come; as heterodoxy has come, as heresy has come, so I believe there will be non-conformity enough to set a right estimate, and no more than a just estimate, upon days, and times, and places of worship.

These subjects occupied my mind in the few moments that we were sitting together this morning, and I felt too that we were gathered, as our brother expressed it, with an idea and feeling of worship which would perhaps supersede all discourse of such common things of life, would raise the mind up to an elevation where we might be brought together in spirit, and the prayer in spirit individually reach the Father of spirits, who would be found to be very near us—not a God far off, but a God near at hand; and that his holy attributes of love, justice, right, and truth would be manifested in us, and that we should be drawn together as heart to heart, and, with the heart, the language of praise and thanksgiving might ascend. And I trust even now it will be found, that these every-day duties of life presented to us, and this great worship of obedience in common things, in regard to the poor and the lowly, and in all the relations of society, will not make us less prayerful; and that there will be such obedience and faithfulness even among the young that they will also come into this Kingdom, in their very youth, and find it all beautiful within, as one of the old writers has said; "The King's daughter is all glorious within." There are many now rather doubting whether the feelings they have are indeed all that they are to look for—whether it is He that shall come or look we for another. My young friends, you have both seen him, and it is he that talketh with you, and if you receive him in the hour of his coming, in simplicity and lowliness, in the little duties presented to you, perhaps among your young companions, ye shall see greater things than these; ye shall go on until ye can acknowledge that this is indeed He that shall come into the world; and great will be your blessing; great will be your peace; and when that peace which passeth understanding shall be yours, then will the language of praise ascend; and you will be made to rejoice evermore, and, in all things, to give thanks.

PD "Discourse by Lucretia Mott," reported by Andrew J. Graham, *The Friend* (December 1866), 173–75

1. LM had witnessed the dance at her visit to the Cattauragus (Seneca) Reservation in 1848 (Palmer, 166).
2. Adapted from William Ellery Channing, *An Address Delivered at Lenox, on the First of August, 1842, the Anniversary of Emancipation in the British West Indies* (Lenox, Mass.: J. G. Stanly, 1842), 38.
3. Henry T. Buckle's *History of Civilization in England* appeared in multiple volumes from 1857 to 1861 (London: J. W. Parker).
4. The Thirty-Nine Articles defined the doctrinal position of the Anglican Church.

Pennsylvania Anti-Slavery Society, Franklin Institute, Philadelphia, November 22–23, 1866

[November 22 Session]

I hardly feel satisfied with the statement of our friend, Edward M. Davis, of the action of the Executive Committee.[1] We have all been surprised at the marvelous progress which has been made. We have witnessed the growth of the political parties in this country; for I believe both parties have grown and are coming round right as regards according the right to the ballot to the freedman. But on the other hand we have watched the accounts that have been furnished—some in the daily papers, and some in letters and communications directly to us, and in personal visits, of the cruelty that has been practiced at the South; and those accounts have come to us with the expressed desire that we should keep on and not resign our organization. They have told us that the time has not yet come, while the slave in so many instances is only nominally and legally free, while in fact the almost unlimited power of his oppressor continues; and that in many parts of our Southland large numbers of families of slaves are still actually held in bondage, and their labor extorted from them by the lash, as formerly; that while, so far as the law is concerned, they may no longer be publically bought and sold, yet they have been actually sold and transferred from place to place.

All these facts show the necessity of our cause, and the continued existence of the Anti-Slavery Society, not-withstanding the legal abolition of the accursed system. All this has kept us on the watch, and has kept our interest alive in the great cause. Although there has not been much done in the way of public meetings, in sending forth agents and lecturers, we have not been idle. Early in the Summer we circulated some forty or fifty circulars to our friends.[2] There must have been some irregularity in the mails—for we received fewer responses than usual; but there are some of our friends here to whom we sent them, and we hope they will make amends for the shortcoming of the past.

I felt that it was due that we should say something more with regard to what had been done; and I have therefore mentioned these facts to show the mighty work that is still before us, to secure manhood to the long bound and long enslaved. From the time of the proclamation of emancipation up to to-day, what a wonderful change has been wrought in the public mind! The hearts of the benevolent, the good and the pure, not particularly of those who have been associated in our anti-slavery organization heretofore, but all over the country, young men and strong, young women and active, have been reached, and they have felt it their duty to consecrate themselves and their all, for the time being, to the education of those poor, wronged, stricken, needy slaves. They have gone these three or four years, again and again, returning during the unhealthy months, but, with scarcely an exception, returning to the work with willing hearts, with no disposition to relax their efforts. And the results of their labors have been cheering, in the readiness to learn which has been manifested. Last evening we had letters read in our Friends Freedmens Association,[3] from the pupils of those who had labored but a short time there and who had therefore had but a few months' instruction; and it was wonderful to see the progress they had made not only in handwriting, but in their composition.

But this is only one evidence of the great and marvelous uprising of this people. The political progress of the nation is wonderful. Even while we mourn that so much wrong yet exists, we are all astonished and wonder at the advance in our land so far above our most sanguine calculations; for the most sanguine anticipations of the Abolitionists never reached what has been realized within a year or two. I want, therefore, in the beginning of our anti-slavery meeting, that we should be affected in our hearts so much as to offer the silent thanksgiving of praise to Him who is greater than we, whose power is mightier than all, in that so much has been effected through us more than we could hope for.

* * * *

The last speech of our friend[4] reminds me of another part of the duty of the Executive Committee that they have not been altogether unmindful of; that is, in relation to the exclusion of the colored people from the horse cars of our city. That has often been with us the subject of reports and complaints, and individual efforts and appeals have been made to the directors of the companies; and the work is still in progress. There has been scarcely a meeting of the Society when the subject has not been discussed, and one Standing Committee has reported from time to time the result of its labors with the conductors and with the officers, so far as they have had an opportunity to petition and to appeal to them, or rather, to remonstrate—for I think we ought always to remonstrate rather than petition. It is a shame to ask for a right. We ought to demand it. The hour has come to demand it now. In New York, within the past two weeks, I have gone back and forth in the horse cars and scarcely a day that colored persons have not come in entirely upon an equality with the whites. There is as much crowding and pushing to make room for them as for the whites. But here, to our shame be it spoken, our respectable colored citizens are forbidden to take seats in the cars, while drunken white men may ride and roll over against us in those same cars. Only a few weeks ago, in one of our cars, a filthy, drunken man sat beside me, and leaned against me so as to produce considerable discomfort. When I left the car I said to the conductor that if he had been a black man, I suppose he would not have been allowed to ride. It is a shame that we should still be obliged to bring up this subject in Philadelphia.

* * * *

As our friend, Miss [*Susan B.*] Anthony, has just attended the glorious Convention at Albany,[5] it seems to me particularly fitting that we should hear from her, not only on account of the success of that Convention, but whatever other remarks she may have to make, particularly upon the subject of suffrage for the freedmen.

[*November 23 Session*]

I will make a few remarks at the opening of our meeting upon the subject of our free platform. It has always been our rejoicing that we have preserved our platform free, and have welcomed the voice of an opponent. At the same time I want to say that we do not hold ourselves as a debating society, but a gathering of those who are as of one mind and one heart in the great cause for which we are associated. Considering that the time is ours, and that the time is very precious, I want to suggest that the good sense of any speakers who may be in opposition to us, must be depended upon to limit them in their opposition. Their good sense will teach them that they ought not to consume much time, and draw forth opposition and rejoinder, and so use up our time to disadvantage rather than to the benefit of the great cause for which we are associated. I should be sorry to have to limit the time of each speaker. It is very cramping to the speaker to be thus limited. I wish all to remember that there are many who wish to say something to us here. We have also a number of strangers here, and common courtesy demands that we should give an opportunity to them. Our friend Frances D. Gage has traveled somewhat, and knows somewhat, from her association with the people, of the Radicalism that there is abroad. I presume she will say something to us to-day. Then our friend Aaron M. Powell[6] has had no opportunity, and our friend Susan B. Anthony has said very little; and I might name others. I make these remarks only to suggest that it is our duty to be brief, and for any opponent not to consume too much time in the expression of opposition.

PD "Twenty-Ninth Annual Meeting of the Pennsylvania Anti-Slavery Society," *National Anti-Slavery Standard*, December 1, 1866, 1–3.

1. Edward M. Davis (1811–87), abolitionist, women's rights activist, and LM's son-in-law, stated that the executive committee had not planned an evening session so members could attend the meeting of the Freedmen's Society. After LM's remarks, Davis apologized "on behalf of the Executive Committee for having done so little," but stated he disagreed with abolitionists who had withdrawn from PASS in favor of "Freedmen's Associations" (*National Anti-Slavery Standard*, December 1, 1866).

2. LM probably refers to circulars announcing the PASS annual meeting (Palmer, 378). At a meeting on December 5, the PASS executive committee announced that circulars and collections at the meeting had raised $90.43 (PASS Executive Committee, Minute Book 1856–1870, Pennsylvania Abolition Society Papers Series 5.48, Historical Society of Pennsylvania).

3. The Friends Association for the Aid and Elevation of the Freedmen, founded in 1864, sent teachers to southern states through 1870 (Palmer, 338, 341, 443–44).

4. Alfred Love (1830–1913), a pacifist, had spoken in favor of expanded voting rights and greater democracy (*National Anti-Slavery Standard*, December 1, 1866).

5. On November 21–22 the American Equal Rights Association, which had been formed on May 10, gathered in Albany to demand an amendment to the New York State Constitution granting equal suffrage regardless of race or sex (*Independent*, November 15, 1866).

6. Aaron M. Powell (1832–99) was the editor of the *National Anti-Slavery Standard*.

American Equal Rights Association,[1] Church of the Puritans, New York City, May 9–10, 1867

[*May 9 Session*]

The PRESIDENT (Mrs. MOTT) said: The report which we have had, although not written, is most interesting.[2] A great deal of it is new to me. My age and feeble health have precluded my engaging actively in this cause, other than in a very limited way. There are so many actively engaged in the cause, that it is fitting that some of us older ones should give place to them. That is the natural order, and every natural order is divine and beautiful. Therefore, I feel glad of the privilege—although my filling the office of President has been a mere nominal thing—to withdraw from the chair, and to yield the place to our friend ROBERT PURVIS, one of our Vice-Presidents. The cause is dear to my heart, and has been from my earliest days. Being a native of the island of Nantucket, where women were thought something of, and had some connection with the business arrangements of life, as well as with their domestic homes, I grew up so thoroughly imbued with woman's rights that it was the most important question of my life from a very early day. I hail this more public movement for its advocacy, and have been glad that I had strength enough to co-operate to some extent. I have attended most of the regular meetings, and I now feel almost ashamed, old as I am, to be so ignorant of what has happened during the last year. We need a paper—an organ that shall keep those who cannot mingle actively in our public labors better informed. THE STANDARD has done much; and I find in many other papers a disposition to do justice, to a great extent, to our cause. It is not ridiculed as it was in the beginning. We do not have the difficulties, the opposition and the contumely to confront that we had at an early day. I am very glad to find such an audience here today; and far be it from me to occupy the time so as to prevent Mr. [*Samuel J.*] MAY, Mr. [*Charles C.*] BURLEIGH, and others, from having their proper place.

* * * *

The argument that has been made that women do not want to vote is like that which we had to meet in the early days of the Anti-Slavery enterprise that the slaves did not want to be free. I remember that in one of our earliest Woman's Rights Conventions, in Syracuse, the reply was made to this argument, that woman was not much to be blamed, because the power of the government and of the church, that was vested in man by the laws, made it impossible for woman to rise,³ just as it was impossible for the slave to rise while the chains were around him, and while the slaveholder's foot was upon his neck. The common and civil law of England made woman a cypher, and blotted out her civil existence upon her marriage. Blackstone, in his commentaries, says that the law made the husband and wife one person, and that person the husband. This being the power of the husband over the wife, as established by law, that despotism followed which must ever be exercised, when power is vested in one over another, be it man or woman, to the great injury of the victim. The law had crushed woman; and the Church, supporting the law, had assumed that the Bible forbade women from using her rights. And if she asked to be a religious teacher, the perversion of the words of Paul was presented to keep her back. When she became a wife, the Church stepped in, and asserted the authority of the husband, and made the wife acknowledge her inferiority and promise obedience to him. That extends down to the present time. That is the law of marriage now among the great body of religious professors in the land; and it is well for woman to know it. Until she can be brought to a sense of her natural and inalienable rights, to go forth and defend herself against these chains of society, she will be kept in this low state.

The resolution which was offered in Syracuse, as nearly as I remember it, was that as the assertion that the slave did not want his freedom, and would not take it if offered to him, only proved the depth of his degradation, so the assertion that woman had all the rights she wanted only gave evidence how far the influences of the law and customs, and the perverted application of the Scriptures, had encircled and crushed her.⁴ This was fifteen or twenty years ago. Times are altered since. In the Temperance reformation, and in the great reformatory movements of our age, woman's powers have been called into action. They are beginning to see that another state of things is possible for them, and they are beginning to demand their rights. Why should this church be granted for such a meeting as this, but for the progress of the cause? Why are so many women present, ready to respond to the most ultra and most radical sentiments here, but that woman has grown, and is able to assume her rights?

In regard to the remark of Mrs. [*Frances Dana*] Gage that by the want of the consecration of marriages by the Church, the sacred and holy ordinance of marriage is prostituted, I wish to say that it does not follow that marriages unattended by religious ceremonies are therefore not true marriages.⁵ It is now two hundred years since George Fox took the ground, far in advance of the age in which he lived, that the parties themselves were sufficient for the marriage union; that marriage did not necessarily require either to be sanctified by the minister or legalized by the magistrate; but that the parties themselves, acknowledging the religious obligation of so sacred a union, were sufficient. And in that Society, the parties were at liberty to appoint their own time and place, and to invite such of their friends and neighbors as they wished to be present; then, in acknowledgment of the divine presence, their obligations to each other were announced, entirely reciprocal, with no assumption of authority on the one hand or promise of obedience on the other; but entire reciprocity, and a pledge of fidelity and affection until death should separate them. For two hundred years, the marriages in the Society of Friends thus conducted, have been held as sacred, the union has been as harmonious, and the management of the children as free from complaint, as any other marriages in the community. The Parliament of England, after a time, saw fit to legalize such marriages; and so in our own country do the laws of the several States.[6]

In many of the States the laws have been so modified that the wife now stands in a very different position as regards the right of property and other rights, from that which she occupied fifteen or twenty years ago. You see the same advance in the literary world. I remember when Maria Edgeworth and her sister first published their works, that they were afraid to publish their own name, and borrowed the name of their father. So Frances Power Cobbe was not able to write under her own name, and she issued her "Intuitive Morals" without a name; and her father was so much pleased with the work, without knowing it was his daughter's, that it led to an acknowledgement after a while.[7]

The objection has been made to me—"Here you assume equality and independence. Now, I feel dependent on my husband for everything." Women in our Society do not feel dependent for anything. They are independent themselves; and in the true relation of marriage the husband and wife will be equal. Let woman be properly educated: let her physically, intellectually and morally be properly developed; and then, in the marriage relation, in spite of law and custom and religious errors, the independence of the husband and wife will be equal.

I was delighted with the remarks made in our Anti-Slavery meeting by our friend Durant, that the conscience, and the sense of right in man, was the basis of law.[8] The idea seemed rather new; but it occurred to me that our friend Burleigh told us that twenty years ago. We were told, too, that when the work of the Anti-Slavery Society should be finished, there would still be work to do. And although Wendell Phillips is sensitive with regard to the introduction of this question upon the Anti-Slavery platform, adhering so strictly to the Constitution of that Society that he does not want anything attached to it of other great reforms of the day which do not legitimately belong to it, I think we shall find that he will continue to be as able an advocate for woman as he has been, and that he really does not lower our standard in any respect.[9]

[*May 10 Session*

Debate on resolution pledging continued action until "equal suffrage and citizenship are acknowledged throughout our entire country irrespective of color."]

The PRESIDENT (Mrs. Mott) said that woman had a right to be a little jealous of the addition of so large a number of men to the voting class, for the colored men would naturally throw all their strength upon the side of those opposed to woman's enfranchisement.

PD *Proceedings of the First Anniversary Meeting of the American Equal Rights Association* (New York: Robert J. Johnston, Printer, 1867), 5, 28–30, 53, WASM

1. The purpose of the American Equal Rights Association (AERA) was to secure "Equal Rights to all American Citizens, especially the Right of Suffrage, irrespective of race, color, or sex" (Palmer, 372, 381).

2. Susan B. Anthony, secretary of the AERA, explained that she had been too busy to write a report of their activities: "With but half a dozen live men and women, to canvass the State of New York, to besiege the Legislature and the delegates to the Constitutional Convention with tracts and petitions, to write letters and send documents to every State Legislature . . . to urge Congress to its highest duty in the reconstruction . . . has been a work that has taxed every energy and dollar at our command" (*Proceedings*, 5–6; Gordon, 2:60–61).

3. At the Syracuse meeting, Ernestine Rose had stated, "If woman is insensible to her wrongs, it proves the depths of her degradation" (*Proceedings of the Woman's Rights Convention, Held at Syracuse* [Syracuse, N.Y.: J. E. Masters, 1852], 64, WASM).

4. See Women's Rights Convention, September 8, 1852, Afternoon Session.

5. In her speech, Gage argued in favor of voting rights for freedwomen because without this protection they refused to get married in church: "Are you to leave her there yet, and desecrate marriage, by making it such a bond of slavery that the woman shall say, 'I do not want to be married, to suffer oppression!'" (*Proceedings*, 27).

6. Although under the Marriage Act of 1753, England and Wales required a formal ceremony in the Church of England for a marriage to be recognized as legal, Quakers and Jews were exempted. In the United States, marriage was a civil matter, and states recognized a variety of ceremonies as well as common law marriages (Michael Grossberg, *Governing the Hearth: Law and Family in Nineteenth-Century America* [Chapel Hill: University of North Carolina Press, 1985], 75–76).

7. Cobbe first published her anonymous *An Essay on Intuitive Morals* in 1855. Her father was Charles Cobbe (1781–1857).

8. Thomas J. Durant (1817–82), a northern-born Louisiana politician and lawyer, who, during the Civil War, rejected slavery and advocated black suffrage, made an "able address" at the 34th Annual Meeting of the AASS in New York City ("The Anniversary," *Independent*, May 16, 1867).

9. Phillips prioritized suffrage for black men, arguing that it was the "Negro's Hour," but he joined the American Equal Rights Association in their campaign for universal suffrage in New York State (Faye Dudden, *A Fighting Chance: The Struggle over Woman Suffrage and Black Suffrage in Reconstruction America* [New York: Oxford University Press, 2011], 73, 89–90; Palmer, 372).

Free Religious Association, Horticultural Hall, Boston, May 30, 1867

OUR PRESIDENT[1] announced me as a representative of the Quaker Sect, or the Society of Friends. I must do our friends at home the justice to say that I am not here as a representative of any sect. I am not delegated by any portion, or by any conference or consultation of Friends in any way. I am here, as some say, "on my own hook." And if I can be heard, in my feebleness, it will not be to present to your view, as our first speaker has done for Universalism, the various phases of the Society of Friends—the Orthodox portion, the Hicksite portion, the Progressive Friends,[2] or any of these,—because I think people generally are more interested in these divisions of their own denominations than outsiders, or than the other sects are. And I do not know whether it is so profitable a use of the time to enter into the little differences which have caused divisions among religious denominations, as to take a more general view of the advantages and disadvantages of religious organizations.

I had not understood, in coming here, the precise nature of the meeting; I did not know how Radical the Convention was expected to be. One speaker, who has just sat down, has deprecated the idea of dissent from all congregational association; but it seems to me that a convention on so broad a basis as I had understood this to be, should learn better than to deprecate any religious dissent or "come-outer-ism" from organization, and that there should be understood among us the charity, the toleration (if I may use that "proud, self-sufficient word," as some one has called it),[3] to bear all things, and to recognize the march of the religious sentiment in all ages. And I have regretted, since I sat here, that our friend, known to so many, and probably to all of you here,—William Lloyd Garrison,—who is not in the country, is not able to be here. He is the representative of no religious (as such) or sectarian organization, although the Anti-Slavery Society, by its advancement of right and justice, has found itself eminently a religious organization, I think.

The movements of the present age are striking and deeply interesting. The fact of a Jew being called to a Unitarian pulpit in Cincinnati recently, and the fact of a Jewish sermon being published in one of the papers in Philadelphia,[4] and being commented upon with favor since that time,—these facts, as well as other evidences, go to show the enlarged ideas and enlarged spirit of the religious world,—or at least of Christendom,—in this country, and in England. Look at the divisions and subdivisions, and the free inquiries now in the Church of England. First a few individuals here and there came out, and then there came others, and great scholars among them. And this was also noticeable among the Unitarians; and these were so liberal that for years, I believe, no Unitarian association in this country has ventured to reprint their Radical works. Following these, there were the seven essays, with their products startling the church, and an examination was made on a charge of excommunication.[5] Following these, was Bishop Colenso, going still further, and making the others almost admitted to be Orthodox, since he went so much further than they.[6] Thus I see in the English church great confusion, from the dissenting spirit. The various dissenting churches in England and in this country (I will not take the time to enumerate them), have been coming forward in recognition of religious ideas that are implanted in all human hearts, the universal religious elements of our constitution. As culture, and education, and civilization advance, these associations are gradually coming out of the old superstitious, traditional ideas in which they have been educated; and although the articles of faith remain the same; although the articles of the church, or the various creeds, in their verbal standing, may remain untouched, and it would appear that were indeed the same; some of them Orthodox, as they are termed (we all claim to be Orthodox, I suppose), and some of them old and very strange notions, yet if you hear them explained now,—though people admit that they believe the creed really says,—they put very different interpretations upon it. Still although these persons do shorten the creeds every time, each still remains Orthodox just as much after the shortening as before. And we have now had movements through the Unitarians and Universalists, and, more especially perhaps, through the Spiritualists;[7] for although I have never attended their meetings, and know but little of them, except what other persons have told, yet I understand they have effected more against the dogmas of the time, than other congregational organizations have as yet done. I know our Friends are very jealous of any association with Unitarians or Universalists, or even with the Progressive Friends. And therefore I say that I am here representing myself, and not the Friends, although I am much attached to the organizations to which I belong. And I shall hope that in the discussion which may follow, there may be the broadest recognition of existing sects and denominations; that there shall not be a con-sociation and continuance with existing denominations; but on the other hand that there shall be such a recognition of the come-outer element, if I may so call it (I do not know what to call it),—a dissent from organization.

I believe, as fully as that the command was given to Abraham, that the command is now to many, "Leave now the kindred of thy father's house, and go into the land that I shall show thee." As George Fox was drawn away from all organizations of his time, and had to retire alone, and there be instructed from a higher power than himself, from the divine word; and claim that as the highest authority for action; no Bibles, no human authorities, no ministers, no pulpits, no anything that should take the place of this divine, inward, everyday teacher, so simple in its instruction,—as he, I say, was thus called out from all his kindred, and from his father's house, and brought unto the land that was therefore shown unto him; so I say there is an increased number now of this description. I remember especially one whose book I have read with very great interest, who even from Spain, came out in advance of the friends of progress and of the most liberal Unitarians in England and in this country—Blanco White.[8] I regret that those who were called to the reformation in the land were not satisfied with being destructives. Immediately they went to again constructing. Our friend, I think, before me, deprecated the idea of the destruction of religious organization. I do not know that it is to be deprecated. I know that there can not be any movement, any fellowship of anybody together without some form or some rules of government. But in a republic like this, if I understand self-government aright (I wish there was some better nomenclature; we have the term self-government, and we have the same term to represent self-government in a republic), we have yet to learn something that shall recognize independence of the mind, and the truth that maketh free, and that by which if we are made free we are free indeed. I have as full faith in the religious experience and devotion of those who have withdrawn from all religious association, going occasionally to hear the liberal preaching around them. Now I cannot say that these are not just as religious in their devotion as the most sectarian observer of forms. Many of these believe it to be better to come out openly in the matter of prayer. They believe it a very wise recommendation of Jesus Christ of Nazareth, that divine

Son of God, "When thou prayest, enter into thy closet, and when thou hast shut the door, there pray in secret, and thy Father, which seeth in secret, shall reward thee openly."

I say I represent myself. I am a kind of outlaw in my own society. It is a universal custom for us to rise in time of prayer. It is considered out of order for any to keep their seats. I have not felt free to do this for many years, and have been subjected to reproach and contumely by those with whom I have been associated. It is very difficult for us to be non-conformists with those with whom we associate. It seems to me that we show this infidelity (if I may so speak), this denial, in our indisposition to follow in some of the acts of conformity more than in any other way. It is of little matter to me what the creed shall be as regards trinity and unity, as regards what has been explained here as Universalism, or in a more limited way. We know so very little of the after life, that I am glad that the intelligence of the age is leading us to apply our religion more to this life, and to every-day practice and every-day necessity, and uprightness and goodness, and to enter into our heaven here.

I was interested a few weeks ago, at the opening of a Unitarian house of worship in Germantown. One of the speakers said that they had got a "regular built church."[9] It had a font, and table, and pulpit, &c., and he did not like the idea that churches should be converted into lecture rooms. Now it seems to me that it is a great progress, that a church may be used sometimes for lectures. I want our friends to be liberal enough; and I should be glad to see a more general disposition to have a church or place of worship a freer place of gathering. And when our friend speaking in Germantown, a large portion of the people present were Friends, and large numbers that had been admitted into that society were unaccustomed to the baptismal font; and it seemed to me that he was behind the age in speaking in the way he did. But I notice that the father of the young Mr. Neal who was to be ordained,[10] in turning over the pages of his Bible, chanced to open to the passage in the last of John the divine, that had always been rather a favorite one, where it speaks of the new Jerusalem that cometh down from God out of heaven, and he read that in that new Jerusalem there was no temple found. Now if that be the case, why may we not suppose that some of these regular radical supporters have entered this new Jerusalem? But how are we to judge of them, and how are we to judge these persons who love their baptismal font and communion table, love the Lord Jesus Christ? How are we to judge whether they do or do not, except by their every day practice and good works? We must hold these up, and with this view.

I do not wish, as a single individual, to commit the society to which I belong, in any wise. But I would desire that the convention may result in so enlarged a charity and so enlarged an idea of religion, and of the proper cultivation of the religious nature and element in man, as to be able to bear all things, and to be able to have that extended charity that is not offended, and does not deprecate going on before, and to have charity for those who are behind, and also for those who go on before.

May we then in thus coming together learn charity; and if we want an organization, let us not suppose that it must necessarily be an organization similar to any in existence, that are recognized as churches. I do not mean the Quakers; but we can have an organization, and have it understood there shall not be a regular minister who shall be obliged every appointed day to have a sermon prepared, and a prayer, perhaps, whether in the spirit or not. I often pity your ministers who have to come forth with their prepared sermons every Sunday. Why not carry out the precept that when anything shall be revealed to him that standeth by, let the first hold his peace?

I remember some thirty years ago, that on being introduced to Dr. Burleigh[11] (we do not like to say "Reverend" among Quakers), by Dr. [*William Ellery*] Channing, I asked him why there should be a monopoly in excluding woman from the pulpit. He said, "It is something that never entered my mind." I believe a large portion of the people never thought of the thing. But believe me, my friends, when I tell you that this monopoly will have to be broken up, and that there will be a ministry among us of a freer character than that which has been known heretofore.

Now, I do not know how far I have presented what was required by the platform this morning, but these are the thoughts which were in my mind, and which I have attempted to give forth, without any preparation.[12]

PD *Free Religion: Report of Addresses at a Meeting Held in Boston, May 30, 1867* (Boston: Adams and Co., 1867), 11–15

1. Octavius B. Frothingham (1822–95), a Unitarian minister, chaired the meeting, which had been called to consider the "conditions, wants, and prospects of Free Religion in America" (*Report*, 3).

2. Henry Blanchard (1833–1918), a Universalist minister from Brooklyn, New York, preceded LM. Blanchard described the current trend in Universalism "to become a thoroughly organized body," with schools, colleges, and a hierarchy, "modified somewhat by the tendency to become liberalized by degrees." Blanchard considered a Free Religious Association impractical, and proposed that "all Liberal Christians" join "in one body" (*Report*, 8, 10, 11). In the late 1840s and early 1850s activist Hicksite Quakers left their meetings to form the "Congregational" or "Progressive Friends," which welcomed all those who shared a commitment to radical reform (Palmer, 177–78).

3. LM quotes a letter from abolitionist Lydia Maria Child (1802–80), March 5, 1838 (Mott Manuscripts, FHL).

4. Rabbi Max Lilienthal (1814?–82) of Congregation Bene Israel, a proponent of Reform Judaism, preached in churches in Cincinnati, one of the first rabbis in the country to do so. LM may refer to this positive report: "Mr. Morais delivered an eloquent address on the commemoration of the Passover in the synagogue on Seventh street, near Cherry" (*Philadelphia Inquirer*, April 7, 1866).

5. The controversial *Essays and Reviews* (London: John W. Parker, 1860) featured articles by seven liberal Anglican ministers, embracing rational and critical approaches to reading the Bible.

6. Bishop John William Colenso (1814–83) of Natal subjected the Scriptures to historical analysis in his book *The Pentateuch and Book of Joshua Critically Examined* (New York: D. Appleton, 1862) (Palmer, 327).

7. Blanchard had described the larger trend toward liberal Christianity and its impact on Universalism, as a tension between traditional Universalists, who believed in the Bible, and those liberal Universalists who rejected "old interpretations of the text." After LM, Robert Dale Owen spoke of the diffuse religious movement known as Spiritualism, which believed in the possibility of individual spiritual development and knowledge of the afterlife, as "invigorating" a variety of denominations (*Report*, 9, 27).

8. One of LM's favorite examples of liberalism, Joseph Blanco White (1775–1841), a Spanish priest, converted first to the Church of England, and then to Unitarianism (John Hamilton Thom, ed., *The Life of Joseph Blanco White* [London: J. Chapman, 1845]; Palmer, 152).

9. The building was located at Chelten Avenue and Greene Street.

10. Possibly Mr. Newall of the Unitarian Society of Germantown ("Unitarian Society of Germantown, PA," *Christian Inquirer*, July 19, 1866; Palmer, 378).

11. Possibly Charles C. Burleigh's father, Rinaldo Burleigh (1774–1863), a graduate of Yale College and the head of Plainfield (Conn.) Academy.

12. At the meeting, delegates formed the Free Religious Association to "promote the interests of pure religion, to encourage the scientific study of theology, and to increase fellowship in the spirit" (*Report*, 54–55).

Second Unitarian Church, Brooklyn, New York, November 24, 1867

WHEN the heart is attuned to prayer, by the melody of sweet sounds, or, it may be, by silent introversion, it seems sometimes almost as if words were a desecration. Still, we have need to stir up the pure mind, one in another, by way of remembrance, to endeavor to provoke one another to love and to good works. And in yielding to the invitation to gather with you here this morning, it was in accordance with a desire previously felt that I might have such an opportunity to gather with those accustomed to gather here; not supposing, however, that there would be the general notice or invitation extended which I found in the papers.[1] And in coming now and mingling with you I have felt somewhat of the desire of the condition that existed in the first coming together of the disciples after their Beloved had left them; when they were so moved by the Divinity of His presence and the inspiration of His faith, and of their faith, of His God and their God, that—the record states—they spake one to another so that each man heard in his own tongue in which he was born, whether Parthian or Mede—and so on. It is not needful that I should go on.

Now I can suppose this. I can believe it to have been done without mystery or without miracle—and, therefore, I seek no supernatural aid, but the Divine aid, which is natural, which is the Divine gift of God to man equally with his intellectual powers; seeking only this aid I feel that we may now speak one to another so that every man may hear in his own tongue in which he is born. To us, coming together here this morning, with all our variety of sentiments and of use, as to worship, there is, after all, notwithstanding this diversity—there is a language through which we can address one another that is universal in its application. And we find this to be the case from the hearty response that is returned to truth when read—to righteousness, to justice and mercy, and all the attributes of the Deity with which we have any right to see the acquaintance. We find that there is this appreciation of the right. Why, to these same beatitudes which have just been read, who is there that would not respond? Into what language can they be translated, free of the encumbrances of theology, in which there would not be a recognition of their divinity?

I believe that there would be none. And knowing that it is customary, in presenting what is called "a sermon" to the people, that there should be a text taken from the Scriptures, and, not being accustomed to bind myself to such a form or such an arrangement in preaching, I had not selected any particular passage of the Bible; but, after sitting down with you here a text arose from the Apocrypha, the truths of which there found are to me just as canonical as any other part of the Scriptures. Indeed, coming down to a later time in the full faith that the revelation of God is as clear, as plain, and his inspiration as universal now as in any former time, I can, with as much veneration for the truth, cite occasionally the good words of more modern inspiration—of that which proceedeth from those who have been enlightened in our generation and day, equally so with those who have been enlightened in any other time. And this does not lessen our regard for the Scriptures, but increases, rather, an intelligent appreciation of Scripture; though not for it to be made the idol of Christendom, as it seems to me it is, to some extent. Indeed, long before that time, long before the advent of Christendom, we find from the researches that have been made elsewhere, that they disclose a divinity as pure, a revelation of God as sacred as the revelations found here. And this research is most valuable to us in that it furnishes corroborative testimony to the eternal inspiration of God, to the Divine teaching of His Holy Spirit, which is coming to be, I rejoice to believe, more the acknowledged faith of Christendom. Beginning, it may be, with the despised name of Unitarian and of Quaker (but 'Quaker,' I must say first, as George Fox and his co-workers preceded what is called the Unitarian beginning), I rejoice to believe that this universal gift of God is now presented not only by those in a clearer light, as the advance has gone on, but a Bishop [*John William*] Colenso comes forward; the learned and distinguished ones of the dissenting denominations are beginning to assert this as transcending all other authorities, including the Church arrangement of the Thirty-nine Articles—that the authority of this truth is beginning to be declared as paramount, however all those may be aids to piety, to devotion, and a confirmation of our faith.

Well, the passage is this—"For thine incorruptible Spirit searcheth all things" (or proveth all things); "therefore chastenest thou them, by little and little, that offend, and warnest them by putting them in remembrance wherein they have offended, that leaving their wickedness they may return to thee, O Lord." This I consider to be the prevailing language of the Divine Spirit, this the voice of the Word of Truth which we may so speak of and declare that every man may hear in his own tongue wherein he is born, whether Presbyterian, Unitarian, Methodist, or Episcopalian—Catholic or Protestant,—Dissenters, or what are called Infidels—though I would rather not use any term that might not seem sufficiently respectful to the free-thinker, for I believe free-thinking to be a religious duty; and a skepticism of the religious plans that prevail—however those may be in religious veneration,—I believe that such proving all things, such trying all things, and holding fast only to that which is good, is the great religious duty of our age. The superstitions of the past must give way to this incorruptible spirit which searcheth all things. Our own conscience and the Divine Spirit's teaching are always harmonious; and this divine illumination is as freely given to man as his reason, or as are many of his natural powers. Let us believe this, my friends! Why, it is a Trinity of a great deal more consequence to us than any theological trinity that may be taught; and far nearer, because it may become self-evident; while a trinity that is contrary to reason can never become self-evident to the natural man, or to the component parts of his nature. And this faith is in accordance with this Divine teaching, this supreme teaching of the apostle. First, that which is natural, or animal, and after, that which is spiritual. "The natural man receiveth not things of the Spirit of God, for they are foolishness unto him; neither can he know them"—Why? Not because the Natural man is weak, but "because they are spiritually discerned." Let us believe this, and then we shall find God's ways to be explicable and not inexplicable. God's ways are not "past finding out." The more we apply this to the revelation of God's truth, the more we shall discover the invariable nature of this law; and it will modify the prayers that are put to Him, which are often an abomination. The apostle said, Ye asked and received not, because ye asked amiss. Let us bring our kingdom of heaven here—down, if you call it down, for it has been placed up so high that even your ministers cannot speak of God without the uplifted eye. But the Quaker cannot do that, because that which is known of Him is revealed within: and so of the "engrafted word which is able to save the soul." Why, the young are setting up or imagining some wonderful operation because the persecuting Saul needed a light above the brightness of the sun to see that it was indeed Jesus whom he persecuted. Believe me, my younger friends, when you would ask, Where is he? and, Who is he? Thou hast both seen him and it is he that talketh with thee. It is so simple, so beautiful, and I think so plainly in accordance with his teaching—if they would not overlook this Spirit dwelling in them.

And this, it seems to me, is my mission to you. It was my mission in Boston last spring, where I mingled with a large company who imagined in some measure that they had outgrown religious organization.[2] How my heart yearned for them. The congregation came together and heard with patience the simple words that I uttered, and though feeling as on the brink of the grave, I, on arriving here, with this feeling in my heart, the more readily come to you and mingle with you. (But with reluctance, knowing that at this hour of the day there is in Philadelphia such an objection to have women come into the pulpit.) And not only on this account, but from the education I have received and which by conviction has become an adoption, and as a testimony in favor of a free gospel ministry, a testimony in favor of an acknowledgment of the Divine Spirit teaching women and men equally to declare that which God hath done for their souls, and to incite their brethren to say, "The Lord, He is God"; and believing that George Fox and his contemporaries in their day did a mighty work towards breaking down the monopoly of the pulpit, until I am glad to see there are no longer in your churches the high enclosures for single persons, as in the churches in England, but that all is widening and spreading, until encouragement is given that the time is coming when the ministry will be more extended, and when there will be a different understanding to that by which one person ministers year after year to the same people. I am glad to see an effort made to this end in your radical journals. I know that this is very different to the learned and beautiful discourses that are delivered from this place, yet I think if men and women practised more to give utterance to their thoughts they might learn to do it with more effect. All this, however, may be merely educational with me.

The special mission which brought me to you, which took me to Boston, was to call upon those who seemed to see beyond the dry theology of the day—why, even one of your own writers [*Ralph Waldo Emerson*] has said that the consecration of the Sabbath intimates the desecration of the other days of the week[3]—and seeing all this and the more enlightened views, as I think, which are presented from time to time by a certain class of thinkers, views that are well worth receiving, though they may be slow to find entrance into the minds and hearts of the orthodox, because a liberal faith is always everywhere spoken against by the more thoughtless among them—seeing all this my mission is to call upon you. Why not judge ye for yourselves what is right? Yet after all, the fear of man is so strong that too often the believer suffers himself to believe in the truth. I know the stigma cast upon the Quakers because they could not receive the peculiar theology of the day, as the English Quakers have received it, and now, that generation having passed, and a people having been raised up who know not Joseph, they are now beginning to go back again to the weak and beggarly elements of theology. This is painful to see because I believe Truth to be ever progressive. As Jesus used to say so frequently: "If the truth make ye free, then are ye free indeed." This is no new doctrine, as he affirmed: and so let us believe it, my friends. I have been accustomed from early life to receive these truths as I found them, the reading of the Bible often being more to me than my daily food, and yet never read as a religious ceremony, but in asking for the truth and finding it. "Blessed are the poor in spirit, for"—though I dwell in the high and holy place—"theirs is the kingdom of heaven. Blessed are the pure in heart, for they shall see God. Blessed are the merciful for they shall obtain mercy." To the pure, thou wilt show thyself pure. To the merciful, thou wilt show thyself merciful. To the upright, thou wilt show thyself upright. By many it has been said that peace has its origin with Jesus. By no means. Why the apostle had to quote the old testament itself. "If thine enemy hunger, feed him; if he thirst, give him drink, for in so doing thou shalt heap coals of fire on his head."

My friends, let us see how universal this truth is, how universal its requirements, how the entering of sacred temples is as nothing compared with walking uprightly and speaking the truth in the heart. "I am weary of your Sabbaths, of your solemn assemblies, because ye grind the face of the poor, saith the Lord." The requirements of truth have ever been similar in all ages, and as nations have been prepared by circumstances to receive it, they have ever found it requiring "righteousness and true holiness." I want this age to be more zealous of good fruits, of every-day righteousness and true holiness, in business, in all the transactions of life. Hearing last night some of your politicians talking together about the corruption in this State[4] and in Pennsylvania, I said, Why is it that your religion is not brought into politics? Why is it that your religious worship has regard to Sabbath day devotion rather than an everyday truth? Why is it that you are not uplifting the poor and the lowly? In the paper yesterday I saw that call to give to the Lord the best hour of to-day. Ought you not to give it to him every day? Man's instincts are all favorable to this. Talk of the native wickedness of man! Why there would not be half the wickedness in Albany or in Harrisburg that there is, if theology had not taught people there, that human nature was more prone to wickedness than to goodness. We are expected to be pure because God is pure; to give up our lives for the brethren even as Christ gave up his life for the brethren. This doctrine leads us to content with a lower state of morals than we desire to be. We need that the standard of religion should be lowered and give place to a standard of "righteousness and true holiness." Jesus said, "Except your righteousness exceed the righteousness of the scribes and Pharisees ye cannot enter the Divine government." Herein is the Father glorified.

Now we need, specially in this day, to be bringing forth good works, and to have our faith firm. We need a faith that shall remove mountains, far more than we need a faith in mysteries and in miracles. And this we have seen brought about in our day. Is it not a marvelous work that, by crying aloud and sparing not, God who has seen the afflictions of his people has come down to deliver them, letting them see that they were verily guilty concerning their brother? Apart from the battle field which, lamentable to be said, is still the ultimate appeal of nations, we have seen how this Northern people demanded the abolition of slavery. And your servant in Washington issued his [*Emancipation*] proclamation—a wonderful proclamation it was. And what has been the result? Did the most sanguine Abolitionist anticipate such a result? Nay, it was by the almighty power of God, and yet it is marvelous in our eyes. The instrumentality seemed so simple—yet such was the influence of the power of truth over error, of justice over injustice and cruelty! Here is the great law—the power of justice and mercy and truth over injustice and cruelty and falsehood. It is mighty through God. One does chase a thousand and two put ten thousand to flight. We have seen it in our day, and we are called upon to rejoice at the condition of our country in that we are now better prepared to carry out true Republican—true Republican-Democratic principles.

Have the oldest among you ever seen the time when the heart and the hand have been so wonderfully opened to the degraded and the poor as it is to-day, where there are thousands who are gathered every year to educate, to lift up this large class of our emancipated fellow-beings? When again the attempt which is being made to give them equality before the law, in every sense—to put the ballot in their hands—why, it is among the most wonderful works of our day! What next? What other reformation is needed? Why, I ask you, are you going to permit barbarism of war to go on generation after generation, when you all acknowledge it to be greatest of evils that afflict mankind? "He that taketh the sword shall perish by the sword." War being evil, its results are evil. They must be evil and that continually. Well, now, this is no isolated Quaker doctrine against war, because for two hundred years we have settled our differences peacefully, without even going to law one with another, by reference, by arbitration. And thus we have interested the serious, thinking public to advocate peace; and it is beginning now to be advocated beyond the pale of our religious society or of any other. Why, my friends, you ought to be ashamed that you did not honor Worcester[5] more when he devoted himself to enlightening his fellow-beings by circulating statements for peace and against war. [*William Ellery*] Channing followed. How beautifully he wrote in favor of peace and against war! And yet not taking the ground that war was inconsistent in self-defense. Still, as far as he did go, how valuable are his writings.[6] They were printed in England and reprinted in 1840. (Are they out of print now?) I love Dr. Channing. I love his prophetic words, and believe they are equal to and more easily understood than the prophecies of Daniel. I never read in any Quaker book a clearer testimony in their works than in your own Dr. Channing to this principle in the human mind: I refer to the inward principle, to the power of discerning and doing right, to the voice of God to man. This is the greatest gift of God to man. "All the mysteries of science and of theology fade away before the simple perception of duty which dawns upon the mind of a little child. From that moment he stands before a tribunal on the decision of which his whole happiness rests. He hears a voice which if faithfully followed will lead him to happiness, and refusing to attend to which will lead him to inevitable misery."[7]

I love to think of such words as these, so that when they are asking, Show us the way of truth and of life—you let them know that it is He who is thus reasoning with them. Believe me, that as you bow to it, as you yield to it; as you faithfully follow the intimation of duty (and each must find his own mission), as you believe that it is He—His Divine Spirit, His Words, His Power that shall come up from thee, His holiness that dwelleth in thee, then shalt thou know the commandment of the Lord to be pure, enlightening the eye, the statutes of the Lord to be right, rejoicing the heart. Then shall we see that while we are satisfying ourselves with the enjoyments of this life, apart from His Divine teaching, that we are strangers to "the peace of God which passeth all understanding." Believe, then, my friends, that God giveth us richly all things to enjoy. But it is a day of extravagance, and retrenchment is needed. There needs that you should look to your adornings, and see whether the meek and quiet spirit, the "pearl of great price," is not of far more value than that in which you may be decked for a time and enjoy "the pleasures of sin for a season." I pray to God, the apostle said, that ye do no evil. Not that ye should appear as prudes, but that ye should do that which is honest. This is what is wanted: that you should do that which is honest in society. The gospel understood, is "glad tidings of great joy" to all people. Are you making it so? Are you doing your part to make it so? Here is the eight-hour labor demand.[8] Do you consider that these eight-hour laborers have as good right to make that demand, and to reap the fruits of their labor, as your school teachers would have, as your minister has? I know that we have splendid gifts in these days, far better than a mere devotion to the building of almshouses. We have the munificence of a Peabody, and of your own Stewart, if it may be; and of Vassar, who has founded a college for the education of women.[9]

Oh, that I had another hour to speak to the young women! But I want these great subjects to be taken hold of and acted out. I am glad that there is a stir about these tenement houses. Let this be a country, as it ought to be, the tendency in which is to equalize society—but no great agrarian movement, no infringement upon the rights of individuals. And then, Free Trade. Why, there is a principle in that far more than in the protective system. Women, to be sure, have no right to meddle with political economy. The law has made the husband and wife one person, and that person the husband—Blackstone says. But while woman is thus bridged over in every way—if this is the case—if we are not expected to enter into the difficult questions of finance and of political economy, believe me—and I speak as to wise men!—believe me, if you are worthy the name you bear, you will take up some of these great questions; you will bring your religion right into your politics, right into your commerce. And why should you not? Why should we be satisfied to let the State be corrupt in its doings? Why should we be satisfied to let your votes go for the wrong rather than for the right? Believe me, if your works are pleasing to God, they will after all be acceptable to man; for, after all, everybody loves truth better than error, everybody loves goodness better than wrong-doing.

I want you to think of these things; and if we know them, happy are we if we do them. I feel that an apology is necessary for the time I have spent. I feel grateful for the kind and attentive audience you have given me, and I wish to thank you, and in separating from you, to add, in a spirit of gratitude to the Lord who has put it into the hearts of so many to love the right better than the wrong—that the Lord is good: His mercy is everlasting, and His truth endureth to all generations.

PD "Discourse by Lucretia Mott," *The Friend*, vol. 3, no. 25 (January 1868), 12–18

1. On November 23 the *Brooklyn Daily Eagle* announced that LM would preach at the Second Unitarian Church, on the corner of Clinton and Congress Streets, at 10:30 a.m.
2. LM refers to the founding meeting of the Free Religious Association on May 30.
3. Emerson, "Domestic Life."
4. LM may refer to the ongoing New York state constitutional convention. On November 23 Representative [Solomon?] Graves of Herkimer presented a resolution to address allegations of "bribery and corruption imputed to the Legislature" (*New York Tribune*, November 25, 1868).
5. Noah Worcester edited the pacifist *Friend of Peace* and founded the Massachusetts Peace Society.
6. Channing's peace sermons are collected in *Discourses on War* (Boston: Ginn & Co., 1903).
7. From Channing, "Honour Due to All Men."

8. On November 19 Workingmen's Associations and Eight-Hour Leagues had staged a procession in Washington, D.C. (*New York Times*, November 20, 1868).

9. George Peabody (1795–1869) became wealthy as a Boston dry goods merchant and financier; Alexander Turney Stewart (1803–76), who owned one of the earliest department stores in New York City, developed an interest in tenement houses (*Brooklyn Daily Eagle*, November 23, 1868); and Matthew Vassar (1792–1868), founder of Vassar College in Poughkeepsie, made his fortune as a brewer.

Pennsylvania Peace Society,[1] Assembly Buildings, Philadelphia, November 17–18, 1868

I think it is very important that we should have just such speeches as we have listened to.[2] While we have the Government based upon war, and the paraphernalia of war is so attractive, it must be that there are some among us who shall go great lengths and speak as we have heard this evening, and present the crime in its true light, and it is well that there is daring enough among us to speak the whole truth on this subject. Everything depends upon going to the root of the matter and speaking of radical principles. Long enough have we been accustomed to apologize for the slave-holder, to be reconciled to the system because it was connected with the government, because iniquity was protected by law. The fact that there were those who came forward and held up this great crime in its true light, roused the people, and they did not love to have it so.

I regard the abolition of slavery as being much more the result of this moral warfare which was waged against the great crime of our nation, than as coming from the battle field, and I always look upon it as the result of the great moral warfare. It is true that Government had not risen to the high moral point which was required to accomplish this great object, and it must use the weapons it was accustomed to employ, and in its extremity it was compelled to do this great work. So in regard to war, it must be held in its true light and the enormity of the crime be laid where it belongs.

Such arguments as we have heard this evening, and others that can be presented should be given and I doubt not that there will be persons who will go forth imbued with peace principles who will be able to go on farther and farther.

The progress that has already been made is encouraging.

I remember when Joshua Blanchard[3] and other friends entered upon the subject some were afraid to go too far and too fast, they thought that war in self-defense must be permitted, and they were looking forward for some millennial day when peace would take the place of war.

We know there has been progress since that time, and from that time the peace principles have spread considerably, and as far as we have gone we have become more nearly sound in the principles of peace, and now we look at war in its true light, and it is well to do all we can to enlighten people on this great subject, so that they shall come to look at the possibilities of peace.

We have to look for a change in public sentiment in the government before we shall have attained to the state that the advocates of peace desire.

We must be able to speak of things which we have known, what our hands have handled of this good word of life.

When we thus present to the people the sound policy of the peaceful state, the reasonableness of arbitration and reference among nations for the settlement of International difficulties as we have been accustomed to settle individual difficulties.

When all the troubles that are connected with man's relations, that are now made the causes of war, have been presented to the people in the light which they can readily perceive to be true, they will readily accept them for there is a love of peace in the heart of every one. They will come to see that there is a reasonable principle that will lead us to abandon the barbarism of war.

It will not be long before the whole nation may be brought to see that peace is possible and desirable in a christian state.

Another result, that we may look forward to with hope, is the removal of the death penalty and when this is the case we can present this to the people as something that can be carried out now.

It will be just as it was with Slavery, just as the rights of man are coming to be considered all over the world in a far better light than they ever have been before.

These things may be brought about long before all mankind have come to acknowledge the great principles of right, the love of liberty and the hatred of oppression, so will it be with the barbarism of war, it will be so presented to the people that they will be aroused to a sense of its enormity. Thus placing the crime where it belongs, and then showing that Governments can be maintained without resort to deadly force. I believe the governments can be brought to be like kingdom of our Lord and his Christ, without waiting till all shall be converted to the principles of peace. This is my idea of this work, that it is much nearer at hand than many suppose, and I am sure our faith should be firm now, that prayers were manifestly answered in regard to the great crime of Slavery.

So it seems to me that war should be presented to the people in a way that shall lead them to examine it carefully. Why we know how it was with the practice of duelling only a short time ago and this has been held up to view in such a light that it is no longer considered admissible—so we have had the barbarism of Slavery presented, and we must do the same on the question of war and we may hope to influence the public mind, and present the great principles of christianity, of right, of justice, of peace and love.

We may hope to influence the public mind and also the nations, that they may be led to appeal less to the force of arms, and look for the reasonable mode—of arbitration. We have long been accustomed to settle our individual differences in this way. We should look at human beings as accessible to the truth, as easily prevailed upon to accept the truth if we only go to work in the right way.

We see that all the societies for moral reform have marked our age so emphatically, are doing great good among the people, and the churches are moving in these directions, and the people can bear to hear of these things and by speaking of these evils in their true light and at the same time being hopeful, we shall find our efforts blessed.

Notwithstanding all the apparent love of war and fighting, there is an innate love of peace, an innate love of justice, the hearts of the people are right. Let us therefore respect these and keep on in our work, do that which hands find to do, and though our meetings may be small, not many of us, not many learned, not many great ones, we must be satisfied to work on. We can do much better than we did in the early days of the women's Anti-slavery Society, we did not know how to take a vote—we had to call in a colored man [*James McCrummell*] and ask him.

But in this Peace movement we understand better what to do, there will be stronger men and stronger women and they will all aid us and I doubt not the time is far nearer than many of us anticipate, when this barbarous custom will be abandoned, and I always mean to have hope that the good will ever prevail.

PD *Bond of Peace*, vol. 2, no. 1 (January 1869), 13–14

1. LM, JM, and Alfred Love had founded the Pennsylvania Peace Society in 1866, with the first convention to be held in January 1867 (Palmer, 381).
2. Speakers included Levi K. Joslin, who argued that war is murder in the first degree and "that Church and Government are the chief criminals" (*Bond of Peace*, 1).
3. Joshua Blanchard (1782–1868), a Boston merchant, was a long-time member of the American Peace Society, but objected to its refusal to condemn the Civil War. In 1866 he was one of the founders of the Universal Peace Union (Valarie H. Ziegler, *The Advocates of Peace in Antebellum America* (Macon, Ga.: Mercer University Press, 1992, 2001), 149–52.

Race Street Meeting, Philadelphia, March 14, 1869

There is a principle in the human mind which renders all men essentially equal. I refer to the *inward* principle, to the power of discerning and doing right, to the moral and religious principle. This is the great gift of God to man; I can conceive no greater. This sentiment of one of the apostles of our times [*William Ellery Channing*] is worthy of all acceptation.[1] But as the veneration of the believer and worshiper among us generally is directed more to the outward authority of the Scriptures, I would quote: "This is the true light which lighteth every man that cometh into the world."

This principle, or doctrine, or great tenet of the Quakers, so called, of the Religious Society of Friends from its origin, is becoming more and more the accepted creed of many of the enlightened of other professions. Many attached to other religious organizations, and who have a right to that attachment, have still an increasing interest and faith in this divine inward principle.

It matters less as to the various beliefs with regard to the doctrine of the Trinity or Unity, of Predestination or Fore Ordination of any kind. As regards many of these religious tenets of the professors, they are held in faith or they are not, according to the circumstances of education and the daring, the increasing daring of men, to do their own thinking, to reason and judge for themselves, to "try all things, prove all things, and only hold fast to that which is good."

Figure 7. Race Street Meetinghouse, built 1856. (Courtesy of the Friends Historical Library, Swarthmore College)

After the Apostle Paul had enlarged on the catholicity, if I may so speak, of the religion which he would advocate and spread, he returned to his Jewish education, and said the question might be asked: "What advantage then hath the Jew? or what profit is there of circumcision?" And his answer was "Much every way." So it seemed to me reflecting on this great interrogatory and its answer, since I took my seat here; so it seemed to me might be said of the Quaker, or Friend, with the general belief—the belief in the universal salvation of all sects or denominations, and equally those of no particular sect or denomination with the universality of the light which they preach: what advantage then hath the Quaker? or what benefit in these peculiar and specific teachings?

May we not answer: much every way. And why? Because from the early days of this Society of the faith in this *inward* principle and its teachings as the great monitor, directing aright, turning to the right hand or to the left, saying: this is the way; walk in it. The attention of the people has been directed to this, and to its immediate teachings, in every little concernment of life. The great duty has been constantly urged of faithfulness in little things, of obedience to every manifested duty, clearly discriminating and judging intelligently whether this manifested duty arises from mere sectarian education, from the circumstances of ignorance in which we have been placed, or the clear undisputed teachings of this Divinity within. So judging, so concluding, then results the great duty of yielding to its manifestations, of making such sacrifices as truth may require, or in other words this inward light as truth may require. And then the philosophy of it is apparent to us that whoever has faith in the light, shall be made ruler over more, "If thine eye be single, thine whole body shall be full of light." And the converse by experience is found to be equally true, he who is unjust or unfaithful in the light, will be also unfaithful or unjust in that which is greater.

Then, again, is the righteous judgment which all may be free, one of another, of the acts of men to judge: "By their fruits ye shall know them. For of thorns men do not gather figs, nor of the bramble bush gather they grapes." Knowing and learning by experience this philosophy that they learned, we have been taught to manifest our faith by our works, by our fruits, by our everyday life, and that made to appear in comparative trifles, letting the skill and power of conscience direct in matters of business and trade, in our intercourse every way in society, leading us to look at the laborer and his wages, the producer and the capitalist, as he is called. I would there were fewer capitalists. I desire this religion of the fruits, this all pervading religion of God and of Christ and of humanity, the tendency of which is conclusively to level, to bring all into oneness and into equality before God and before men. "All the highways and banks of long continuance shall be cast down and the valleys filled up, that Israel may go safely in the fear of the Lord." This was a beautiful prophecy so many years ago. And then we might pray the Forerunner of Jesus: Make straight, smooth, level; make all plain. Prepare ye the way of the Lord. The Kingdom of God is at hand.

It has always been the call of the reformer: The Kingdom of God is at hand. Because the entrance into this Kingdom is made so plain, so easy: "Thou shalt not see a fierce people, a people of deeper speech than thou canst perceive; of a stammering tongue that thou canst not understand." The way shall be plain. "The wayfaring men though fools shall not err therein."

I know it is often gloomily pointed out, with all the gloomy asceticism of Romanism. I would that we remembered that wisdom's ways were always ways of pleasantness, and all her paths were paths of peace. Sacrifice though there may be and must be, "taking up the cross," to use that symbolical phrase, and the being brought to a willingness to part as with the right hand or the right eye, so as to enter this Kingdom pure; yet clearly being brought to a willingness to make this sacrifice, to bear this cross, then comes the peace that is without understanding, the peace that flows as a river, the cheerfulness that comes of a pure conscience, the good hope that cometh of a cheerful countenance. All this emphatically belongs to a religious life in order that religion may be rightly understood. In order that it may be, we have much to do in clearing away these gloomy appendages of the sects. The idea that religion, that devotion to truth and to humanity should lead us to go mourning on our way, making our path through life gloomy, and despondent, and full of trouble: why it is all an error of education. It is all an error of religious training. It comes not of the pure principle of life and light. When Jesus invited those who were weary and heavy laden, whether it was with tradition, or it may be with the vices and other sins of whatever character, by whatever means they were borne down, weary and heavy-laden. His call was to them to come unto the Truth; for "Me" is but a synonym for the truth. "Come unto Me, and ye shall find rest unto your souls." "Take My yoke on you." What yoke? The simple plain yoke of obedience to His Father, our Father, to His God and our God. "Take My yoke upon you, and learn of Me; for I am meek and lowly in heart, and ye shall find rest unto your souls. My yoke is easy." Mark this, my friends! Look not at religion as some cold achievement, or attainment, or profession, but believe it belongs at once to simplicity of youth as well as to older age. "You will find My yoke easy, and My burden light."

Now, we need to be made sensible of this; we need to bear with the gloomy ideas connected with piety and devotion. I am glad this day is coming to be better understood, and that in the various teachings of the little children in the Sunday Schools there is a greater opportunity to interest them in the little common things and the little everyday duties of life without making the teachings of the characters of old catechisms, of old theories and worn-out systems.[2] As far as I can understand—and I am interested in hearing what facts I can, and in noticing the results of this Sunday School teaching—I believe that there is a great advance in society, and we see it too in the life around us, with regard to the observance of this day of the week. I was glad today, and it was a great accommodation to me, to find the passenger cars running on this day of the week.

All these things come not from a greater disinclination to religious training, not from the desire for an opportunity that shall lead into licentiousness, but from a better understanding of what truth requires, of what this inward light requires, this inward principle in man's soul, to make life at liberty for just such religious entertainment as this day of the week affords: For the Jew, for the Catholic and the Protestant, as well as those who are unconnected with the religious associations, and who find their enjoyment and their religious devotions out of and aside from any sectarian union, who are equally good and pure and religious in taking their pleasure and their means of piety in the broad woods and forests of our country, or in the retirement of their chamber and closet, in their reading and all the various ways in which they may be employed in the day of the week. I say, with all these we do see there is a better understanding of the requirements of truth, of religion, of devotion and of worship. We are coming to understand that the quiet, retired prayer which Jesus recommended, in the closet with the door shut, directed to the great Source of all good, to the Father of all Spirits—that these prayers in secret are answered openly, and are as rich in the fruition as any of the vocal, oral utterances in the assemblies of the people. We are learning this also, and other denominations are beginning to have their solemn pauses in the assemblies of the people, their silent prayers arising with their invocations.

All these things encourage me in the belief that there is an advance, especially when I see the influence of the early teaching of George Fox, William Penn, and their associates. When we go further back, we see throughout the teachings of Jesus this inward Divinity, this inward light likened to a seed, to a little leaven, to all these simple comparisons, spreading its influence in His life and character, and showing the good fruits of the God-dwelling life in its results. In His benevolence continually occupied in action, in His mercy, His charity ever abounding, in His pity for the afflicted, in every aspect of His character we see the bearing of this same inward principle, this God dwelling in man. Then when George Fox and his contemporaries came out in the midst of a perverse and corrupt generation, in the midst of the darkness of a benighted age, and declared this principle and showed by their life and conversation what it would lead unto, their good acts, their testimonies against oppression and wrong, their testimony as in the progress of things it came forth against iniquity, intemperance and every wrong. How bold a stand they made with regard to the ministry equalizing it in its operations, in its advocacy with men and women, enlarging the pulpit, and holding their religious meetings in such a way that everyone present feeling bound to give utterance to the convictions of his soul, to tell what had been done for his soul or her soul, should be at liberty to do it. All this, I say, has had its influence, not only immediately around them at the time but, through their descendants, others enter into this labor, which has come down to us unto this day.

Then there is their testimony against the extravagance and luxurious indulgence of the age. Their testimony to simplicity of life and character, even though, by being carried out from generation to generation, it has manifested itself with too much peculiarity, perhaps, for it could not have been borne as it has been without evidencing, to some extent, its defect, peculiarity. Peculiarity in their garb, their language, their address one to another. All having been of good reason in the origin of the testimony, may now be borne more traditionally; and the time may come that some of these things will pass away, and a more intelligent appreciation of the principle will leave out some of these peculiarities. A non-conformity in some of these may be required of some of us, who would be only faithful to our convictions of non-conformity. I wish that in all denominations those enlightened among us were true to their highest convictions. Here, still, we need faith. Faith! Faith in theological systems? Faith in divinities and atonements? Faith in the divinity of elections and reprobations? Faith in baptisms and communions? Faith in worship, obtaining salvation by merit? In all these things, I ask: What is it? I overlook the question. What we need of faith is in the teachings of this inward principle, letting it bear upon our life, our conduct, and our highest conditions being brought out, now.

If there were more of non-conformity in the various denominations, there would not be a solitary Bishop [*John William*] Colenso here, and another radical there. There would be more rising up and protesting against all articles and creeds and confessions of the past; there would be more acknowledging that they came to the table unworthily, that they could no longer submit their minds to the control of others, nor their bodies to water baptism. I mourn when our young friends, imperfectly educated as they may be in our principles, are ready to go back "to the weak and beggarly elements" from which our fathers were withdrawn, feeling that the time was past, that they were now called with a baptism that was not with water, with a baptism that was "the answer of a good conscience towards God," a baptism that pardoned all their old lives as well as the sins which may most easily beset them. This baptism was union with the Highest, not dependent on the bread and on the wine, not dependent on any of the forms of the Church, but a union in the Spirit. A Sabbath of rest of which the outward Sabbath never could do more than typify; a rest wherein we feel we have come to that rest which is of God; "a rest that was good, and a land that was pleasant, and he bowed his shoulder to bear."

Let us, then, try to understand better what these great figures mean; what these "schoolmasters to bring to Christ," as the Apostle said, are. Then let there be honesty enough, faith enough in the principles we profess to come out of it and say: We can no longer worship in this, that, or the other way: we can no longer give credence to the Thirty-Nine Articles, or accept the provisions of the Discipline. Our own Discipline, in advance, as we may regard it, of all the other systems or principles of government that we know of, may yet contain peculiar passages and obligations which ought to be removed. We are not to found our veneration upon anything outward, upon any confession of the times, or upon any arrangements, or systems of our fathers. We are to take truth for our authority, and not authority for truth.

Then, again, in the influence of the teaching, the practical teaching of the Society of Friends—I came not here with any feeling of vain glory for the Society of Friends. Far be it from me! If I look with any peculiar interest, now, on any one religious movement over another, attached as I am to the Society in which I was educated and wherein I have been for many years, still I look with interest beyond anything else to a great movement now in New England, and in some other parts of our country; and judging from a German document[3] offered to me a day or two ago, spreading among this large class of people of this country, for a free religious organization, like that which has had its existence for a year or two in New England, the basis which is this same inward divine light that I love to honor, that I would have the veneration of all of every denomination in the community. This being the basis as I believe, of this religious movement, it has my heartiest sympathy. The leading journals of the day are also going into the advocacy of this principle and its teachings, as the essential and all sufficient for salvation, as beyond all authority, as not requiring authority acting with it to sanctify it, or to sustain it.

The divine principle is "the light that lighteth every man that cometh into the world." This, I say, as it is now manifesting itself on our eastern coast and in some parts of these middle states, has my interest, my desire for its progress and that it may be carried out in such a practical way as to have its direct bearing on its adherents in all their relations in society. I look to it; I look to our friends, if they will only be true to their principles, and be the reformers they ought to be.

I look to this class for such changes in the commercial world, in the monetary system of the country, in all the relations of capital and labor, in all the influences around us—I look to these to do away with, to remove the terrible oppression, the terrible wrongs which so large a part of our fellow-beings in this and other lands are groaning under, and which can only be removed by the Divine power opening and putting it into the hearts of the people to plead on their behalf. I say the only means I know of appointed by God in any age of the world, is the faithfulness of His children, the obedience of those who are sent, the Sons of Him in every age, the Messiahs of their age, who have gone forth proclaiming greater liberty, greater truths to mankind, greater duty for that entire community. Yes, though they may be few in number comparatively, though they may be weak in force comparatively, yet it has been said, and it may be again: "I have chosen the weak things to confound the strong and the wise."

And this is a remarkable truth. We see it in regard to the early movements of our Friends, in the ignorance of many of them, in their want of early culture, in their going about in all the simplicity of truth to proclaim the principles of the divine nature and the duties of life. Yet see their influence, and how their labors were blessed. We have seen this remarkably in our day in the great anti-slavery proclamation, so much more effectual than the most ardent abolitionist could have anticipated in his time. We see it now operating throughout the country in the increased respect for the freedman of the land. Why, it is marvelous in our eyes! There was nothing so enlarged my spirit, my devotional feeling if I may so speak, as the wonderful success attendant on the comparatively small labors of those who have been engaged in the reformatory movements in the several generations past. It is wonderfully designed that "one shall chase a thousand, and two put ten thousand to flight," when these are under the right guidance and have the right principles of action, and move as directed by that wisdom which is ever profitable to truth.

I know that a large part of this audience have no affinity particularly with the Quakers, with the Friends, so called. Some of us are very tenacious of our words. I believe if the words be enumerated, then the phenomena to which they refer will be comprehended. If it be better understood to use the term "Quaker," let it be used, although the term "Friend" is better, is our choice, and shows our nature precisely. We take a Catholic ground and acknowledge this universal light to be in all. And I wish all held out faithfully to the testimony; acknowledging as I do how limited may our practice compare with this inward light, I still feel there is great advantage in our Friends' principles, much to be gained from it in every way. I therefore desire greatly that our young people may so acquaint themselves with our distinctive principles, and with the details wherein they differ from those held by other denominations, and with those practices which are indulged in in the world. I desire that you all should so make yourselves well acquainted with these testimonies and principles, as to be ready to come out and acknowledge yourselves on the side of the right. I desire that no one should be any longer inquiring: "Who is the Lord, that I may believe Him?" But "if any man shall say to you, Lo, here is Christ; or: Lo He is there; believe him not."

In the multiplicity of these calls, I wonder not that many of the young should be saying: "Who shall show us the Lord?" I wonder not that many theories and opinions are expressed after the meeting as to what this, that, or the other means. And I want the young to understand the answer: "Thou hast both seen Him, and it is He that talketh with thee." Yes, this is the light which we preach, and this the great truth which brings salvation. No outward atonement there, no outward divinity there, but the pure divinity of Christ within; if I may use that term which is so often misunderstood that I would rather use its synonym Truth, its synonym,

Light, its synonym, Light Divine "which lighteth every man that cometh into the world."

Then though we have not seen Him, let us believe in Him. Very soon, in very early life this truth has been claiming access into the heart. Has it not been thy reprover for wrong doing, and thy approver for doing right, filling the soul with love of Christ Jesus and allegiance to God? Has not this been the cause of every divine prompting? Well then, "believe in this and thou shalt see greater things than these." "To those who received Him, power was given to become the sons of God." Then to thy advantage believe in this Name, in this principle, in this power.

Believe it then, and follow. Let not the mere pleasures of life, allowable as these may be with the proper limitation, allow not these pleasures so to take this place and to fill the heart that there shall be no room for this Beloved of the souls who stands at the heart waiting for entrance until, to use the figurative expression, His "head is filled with dew, and His locks with the drops of the night." I know how truly the religious people love the Scriptures, and I love to quote them. I have been accustomed from very early life to examine and test the tenets endeavored to be forced upon us by such esteemed ones as these earnest friends. I have never been accustomed to look at the Bible as a plenary inspiration, but I love these Scriptures, and love to find their testimonies to the truth in every age of which they treat. I love to find also among other ages and other people the same testimonies to the truth and to righteousness. They all tend to strengthen, to give force, to prove that they claimed and observed these teachings in every condition and operation of the mind as able to act, to convert, to adjust to the level of all these attributes of the Deity. For these instinctive principles of our higher nature are all by which we can claim to touch the Almighty. We cannot find them out other than as He reveals Himself by His Spirit and by His goodness manifested towards us or in the corroborative testimony of the ancients, either in or out of the Bible, to the great truths of all humanity.

Let, then, the belief and faith in this principle lead us more and more to humanity, to the divinity of humanity, to the divinity of Christ. Is it his divinity to place a halo of glory over him and regard him as the second person of the Deity? Is it not rather to recognize that divine humanity which we may find in all God's creatures everywhere, if we will look aright? Let this divinity be acknowledged. We shall not receive less the divinity of Christ in the rational understanding of it, in the unsectarian understanding of it. We shall not less admire the beautiful life and character that we have unfolded in these Gospels, as they are called. We shall come to understand the power of the Gospel, that power of God unto salvation, if we come to receive it in the simple way I have described, carrying our religion out into society, in all the duties of life; leading us to look not merely on the influenced will but also on the influence diffused; leading the rich to rejoice in being brought low so that the poor may be exalted.

These are the proofs of this divinity, and it is this I would endeavor to urge upon the consideration of my hearers. I speak as to the wise; judge ye what I say.

I am not afraid of any of these words that may be appropriated to those who do not hold the faith in what is regarded as soundness of orthodoxy. I am willing even, as the Apostle said "to be of no reputation among men" if I can hold forth the truth, so that any may be brought to accept the truth. This divine power is in every human being to lead forth into correct principles, into correct actions, out of all impurity, out of the excessive indulgence of the propensities, to lead to a regard of life and our great duties in the spiritual, true, inward light.

Believe me, if this was the case there would be fewer deaths in childhood, in youth, in early manhood, than we now find them to be. We are not born, as one said the other day, to live, to suffer, to die; but to live, to enjoy, and to die when our time shall be fulfilled. I believe as the laws of physiology and of life come to be better understood—and I rejoice in their introduction into the early education of youth—when these come to be better understood, there will be a responsibility attached to us to preserve that life and keep it in its proper state, so that we may live to old age. It will then become almost a sin to be sick. It is wrong. There are more suicides than generally appear. There is more lying at our door, now, of wrongs bringing on premature death than many are aware of. We are invited to learn this.

I would that the great principle of war was so held up—that first principle that we are so apt to neglect—that we might look with the same eye of faith towards the horizon of that time when the people shall indeed learn war no more. I lament more than I can express that a military education and training is being introduced into our public schools.[4] It has no business there. With such a profession as we are making, a Christian profession, we have no right to be instructing children in the art of war, in the art of murdering their fellow beings.

My friends, this is a subject in which our faith is so wanting, that it seems entirely utopian to many to speak of the days when war and a recourse to arms for settling national grievances shall be brought to a close. But believe me, as in the other great revolutions of the times so is this doomed to come to an end. War to come to an end! War no longer to have advantages and success attached to it with glories and honors thrown around it! War no longer to continue! There is coming to be an understanding of a better means of settling wrongs and difficulties than a resort to arms.

I came here today purposely to attend a little meeting,—I know it will be a small one—in the northern part of our City, in Spring Garden Street; to consider, with a little handful there, how we may best advocate and support the principle of hostility to a war, and to urge upon nations to hold a Congress of Nations to argue in peace how they may settle all differences other than by a recourse to war.

We are not to wait until all are converted to pure non-resistants, any more than we had to wait for all to be made purely anti-slavery in heart. We are not to wait until there shall be no disposition to take revenge, but to declare that revenge shall not be acted out in the barbarous ways of the present.

I know I am speaking long, perhaps entirely too long; but these subjects, as they occasionally come before me I cannot leave without endeavoring to impress them in a way that shall lead others to take up the subject and consider it, and be prepared to act.

You middle-aged men and women of this Society of Friends to whom I have been speaking, what are you doing that you are not advancing our principles more earnestly and more effectively? We are asked quarterly and yearly whether we maintain a public testimony against bearing arms, against all war in any form, and against military preparation. How are we to answer this inquiry if we are sitting quietly down satisfied with the conviction that we ourselves will not consent to it? But how are we bearing our testimony before the world? What influence are we exerting in our day to remove this greatest of evils that now afflicts humanity? The evils of slavery and of religious persecution have been now, to a great extent, brought to a close. War, the leading evil, has yet to come before the people. Be ye prepared. The Kingdom of God is at hand. "The light which lighteth every man that cometh into the world" has shone into the hearts of the people, to give them a knowledge of the glory of God, in the faith of the divinity of this principle.

Stenographic Report, Sermons, Mott Manuscripts, FHL

1. From Channing, "Honour Due to All Men."
2. LM may have read reports in the Philadelphia newspapers on Sunday school students raising funds for missions, or students benefiting from the charity of other parishioners ("City Intelligence: Religious Matters," *Philadelphia Inquirer*, March 6, March 13, 1869).
3. Members of the "Association of the Independent German Congregations" affiliated with the Free Religious Association. Their president, Fred Schuenemann-Pott, published a monthly organ "Blaetter fuer freies Religioeses Leben," or "Leaves for Free Religious Life," which LM may have seen (*Index*, February 26, 1870).
4. The *New York Times* (July 11, 1869) wrote favorably of German reformers' proposals for military drills in schools. Some public schools, such as Boston's Latin and High School, had already implemented them (*The Satchel*, May 15, 1866). At their second annual meeting, the Pennsylvania Peace Society called "the arsenal and military academy adjoining the church and school-house . . . a mockery and a disgrace," and recommended children "abstain from military training" and "learn the arts of peace" (*Banner of Light*, December 14, 1867).

Women's Suffrage Meeting,[1] Academy of Music, Brooklyn, New York, May 14, 1869

Lucretia Mott, the venerable pioneer in the cause of woman's rights in this country, was introduced, and stepped forward in her plain Quaker dress and removed her bonnet. This distinguished lady is now far beyond her threescore and ten years,[2] but her intellect and her memory remain as clear as in the prime of life. She spoke as follows:

It is very little that I have to say to you, both from inability to make my voice heard as well as from the failure of my strength to speak. But I feel comforted in the assurance that there are many here who will not suffer you to go away without being properly instructed. I must dissent from part of the address which we have just heard[3]—with the idea that it ill-becomes us to answer all these flings by newspaper articles that are presented to us, by which we are ridiculed and satirized in various ways. When we were in Washington, some time since, we had an excellent convention. Some objection was made to some of the peculiar costumes in which some of the members chose to appear on the platform.[4] But it was not the business of that Convention to take into consideration any such objections. I do not believe that the success of this cause is dependent upon any such considerations. I believe in women having such self-respect and such dignity of demeanor every where as shall commend her speeches to the acceptance of all right-thinking persons. I desire much that this cause may be advocated on the true ground. We must understand the great needs of the human race; we must have such clear insight as to be prepared to speak more from the inspiration of the time—with dignity rather than with levity. I would not be understood as wishing to bind any one to such serious and prosy addresses that shall not occasionally bring forth the mirthfulness of the congregation, to a certain extent; but I do desire that we may all regulate ourselves, and direct our meetings in a way that shall not bring reproach upon us. An occurrence which happened this afternoon, I think, is calculated to throw some ridicule upon this movement.[5] In taking up *The Herald*, a paper I do not often see, I perceive an intent to ridicule this movement; and *The World* is also rather questionable on the subject.[6] But depend upon it the cause is rising so fast, popular sentiment is rising so rapidly that it will not need that we should combat arguments or vituperations of any kind. We need not despair of ultimate success. When I consider what Lucy Stone did when she was at the Oberlin College, and the Faculty discouraged her reading the Thesis which she had prepared, and endeavored to persuade her to allow a man to read it, when she felt that it would not be consistent with her ideas of right and read it herself, then, indeed, I felt that there was room for hope and congratulation.

PD "Woman Suffrage," *New York Tribune*, May 15, 1869

1. Organizers hoped to use this meeting, held the day after an acrimonious meeting of the American Equal Rights Association, which debated the Fifteenth Amendment giving all men the right to vote, to form a "Woman's Suffrage Association." No action was taken, but the following day Elizabeth Cady Stanton organized the National Woman's Suffrage Association at a smaller gathering at the Woman's Bureau in New York City (*New York Tribune*, May 15, 1869; see LM to Martha Coffin Wright, in Palmer, 418–19; Gordon, 2:241–43).
2. LM was 76.
3. According to the *New York Tribune*, the previous speaker, Olive Logan (1839–1909), from Elmira, New York, "dealt numerous severe blows at the other sex. Her many sarcastic and humorous hits elicited great applause" (Palmer, 419–20).
4. Stanton called this meeting, hosted by the Universal Franchise Association on January 19–20, 1869, the "first National Woman Suffrage Convention ever held at the Capitol" (Gordon, 2:205–6). One of the speakers was Dr. Mary Walker, who dressed in male clothing (*New York Times*, January 21, 1869; Gordon, 2:254).

5. During the afternoon session, Minnie Merton, a "victim of a monomania," demanded to speak. Several women tried to persuade her to leave, and a policeman attempted to escort her off stage. Finally, the audience supported her right to address the assembly. Her "wild harangue" argued that it was the "duty of Government to take care of the women" (*New York Tribune*, May 15, 1869).

6. The *New York Herald* reported, "the Equal Rights women want to be free in everything but love . . . they piously affirm and passionately declare they do not want 'free love.' When they began their agitation the great oppression was the tyranny of marriage" (*New York Herald*, May 15, 1869).

Pennsylvania Peace Society, Friends' Meeting House, Abington, Pennsylvania, September 19, 1869

I feel greatly comforted in seeing such a large gathering here. There has been evidence ever since our late war, that the subject of peace is taking a deep hold on the minds of many persons, especially those who were engaged in that contest, many of these came home more opposed to war than ever before, and those in our society who enlisted in the war because they felt that it was necessary to overthrow the great evil of slavery which threatened the destruction of the government. These friends have been willing to go as far as they could in acknowledging the evils of war, and the great regret that the country was thus involved. I rejoice that there is this evidence of interest in the cause of Peace.

The treatment of the Indians may seem, by some, not to be strictly relevant to the subject of peace, and one for the Peace Society to take up, but we know as in the great crime of human slavery, that it never could have gone to the extent it has, but for war, so with the Indians they never could have arrived at the state of revenge and cruelty towards the white inhabitants of this land, if they had not set the example by taking the sword.[1]

Our friend mentioned that one great object of this society, was the education of the people of this country.[2] I knew not what branch of this subject would be considered at this meeting.

Greatly interested as I am in this question of Peace, it occurred to me as I was coming to this meeting, that what ought to be considered was the condition of our country and our State. I know there is an effort to have a portion of the education in the Public Schools of the country of a military character.

I do not know how far military tactics, training, and preparations have been introduced among the little children in our public schools. It seems to me that it is a duty that we owe to ourselves and to our children, to our State and to the world, as a Peace Society, if this practice is still continued to bear our testimony against it,—to enter some protest against it, and urge that States shall not introduce anything of this kind. I met a few days ago a Roman Catholic father, and in speaking of the education of that society, he said the Catholics never have given attention to the education of their people, said he, how could that be carried on in our country, when the popular education was not in accordance with their most conscientious belief—they could not send their children to Public schools.[3]

I believe there never was more willingness and openness in the minds of the people, to hear appeals made for peace in a way that can be carried out, than at present. I know that we cannot availingly advocate peace principles, until we are prepared to carry out the spirit of peace,—that spirit which delights not in anything like revenge, and indulging in any feeling towards the wrong doer, but a spirit of forgiveness. That this is attainable the testimonies on record go to show, and very desirable is it that there should be a sufficient number of the advocates of peace, so grounded and settled in the principles of peace, that they may know of what they speak, and thus be enabled to labor to prepare the minds of the people, for a better way of settling their disputes.

It may not be necessary to hold up the idea that all must attain to this state before Peace can be established. I believe as it was in the past, the righteous on the subject of slavery redeemed the country.

It was by the means of the moral warfare that was carried on that slavery was brought to an end, long before the slaveholding spirit was put an end to.

It was the great moral warfare that made our Congress anti-slavery, that made our Country ready to plead for, and hold up the great duty of abolishing slavery. So I fully believe with regard to war, and those who are grounded in the principles of peace, and have the subject near and dear to their hearts.

First I believe that those who are interested in this Peace Society, will be blessed in their labors, and be able to induce many, even though they may not have attained to the full spirit of Peace within themselves, to see how barbarous the spirit of war is, and how comparatively easy it would be for nations to settle their difficulties by the same means that individuals do, and that would do away with the barbarism of the sword and of war.

Some of the best writers of the age have pronounced war to be a barbarism, second only to the great evil of religious persecution. It seems to me that the continual holding up to the people, of the evil consequences which result to all who are engaged in warfare, the great expense to the country, the evils which result from exciting the passions of men, will tend to the instruction of the people, and that war may be presented to the intelligent minds of the country in such a manner as to induce the Government to abandon it. If the council of the political men (and women I trust too) will ere long be induced to look at this subject in all its aspects, we will be able to show how greatly to be desired is peace, and other means of settling all difficulties, and bringing to an end the evils which result from war.

Our friend has spoken of the barbarities which have been practiced toward the Indians, and of their present condition of degradation in contrast with their condition when William Penn landed on this continent. It occurred to me to ask if Friends were truly alive to their situation, and to the fact of the treatment they have received from the agents that have been employed by the Government, and who have wronged them so shamefully, whether there would not have been more frequent and more earnest protest and appeals to the Government on their behalf. I know there have been individuals who have been willing to sacrifice their time and leave their families, to devote themselves to the amelioration of the condition of the Indians. I remember Adin T. Corey, Griffith M. Cooper, Halliday Jackson and more recently our friend Joseph Walton and many others who were disposed to do what they could in their limited way.[4]

We have never considered the wrongs of the Indian as our own. We have aided in driving them further and further west, until as the poor Indian has said, "You will drive us away, until we go beyond the setting sun."[5] I would ask if, with the profession that we as Friends have made, of care for the Indians, we have been active enough in our labors. I believe they were saved by the Indian Committees appointed among Friends, from being driven entirely away from the Cattaraugus and other reservations in New York.[6] So far as we have labored by means of Committees, we have in various ways done great good to the Indians.

So also on the subject of Peace, it is a question that has often been with me whether as a religious body we have borne our testimony faithfully enough; whether it would not have prevented so many of our "young men and strong"[7] from being induced to enter the army. I know it is a very delicate subject, and many most conscientiously entered into the strife with the hope of doing what they might to bring peace in the right way, without slavery in the land, for they knew that the war which had been waged was against the colored people, was far greater than any war we could have where there was an equal conflict. Considerations of this kind were apologies, as they deemed, for entering upon this. But all that has passed, and there certainly has been a leniency on the part of the meetings where they have brought these members under dealings and there has been a disposition to pass all by; but I trust not with anything like a compromise of the principle. I do hope we are all as a body, more desirous to promote "peace on earth and good-will among men" than ever before, for now that slavery is done away, we may see how in many ways the spirit of war may be opposed, and appeals made for peace that would not have been while we were engaged in such a barbarous warfare as slavery. I want we should all be willing to look at this subject of war in its true light, and not feel because it is sanctioned as yet by all the nations of the earth, and there is so much glory given to those who are the leaders in warfare, that therefore we should not seek to expose its barbarities. It seems to me that it should be the especial duty of those who love and honor the name of Jesus to be opposed to war. I marvel when I see so much in his life and character in favor of Peace, that in his testimonies he so clearly pointed out these things, when he declared: "Ye have heard it said an eye for an eye and a tooth for a tooth, but I say unto you resist not evil—love thine enemy." How he taught that they should do good for evil, that they should put up the sword, for he that taketh the sword shall perish by the sword—which means if they indulge in this spirit it will return to them, and one of the apostles asks: From whence come wars and fightings; come they not from the lusts that war in the members?

I want to hold up the highest principles for our consideration and see how far we can act them out. Even in the Old Testament we find many prophecies in regard to the coming of a better era, when there should be no more war and bloodshed upon the earth. I know there are those who have quoted these Scriptures as authority for war. It was so in regard to slavery. It is so now in reference to the Temperance movement. It has been retarded doubtless by the appeals that have been made to the Scriptures placing them as authority for the wrong, rather than to present the many beautiful examples that are in favor of the right. Although it is true that we have done wrong, that nations have not obeyed the Lord, and they have been given over to their own destruction, as was said formerly, I proclaim that I leave you to your wars, to famine, to pestilence, but this was never uttered by the Highest Powers, the principles of Divine Love have never led any to war. We must go so far as not to be afraid to speak of war or any other evil that has ever existed in the world.

With God there is neither variableness nor shadow of turning. Let us have faith in this, and we shall find it is much easier to carry out every principle of right.

I was glad to hear how this peace principle was progressing. If we can once do away with the practice of taking life, it will be a great advance in the world. I have been glad that in the Peace Society a strong protest has been made against capital punishment. That we have petitioned to remove the death penalty on the ground of right.[8] Let us never be afraid to take hold of the right, however error and wrong may be sanctioned by usage, and by some quotations from Scripture. We know that the general run of these is for the right, else they would not be so valuable, if it were not that we found the testimonies of eternal truth in them. We must not take the examples of semi-barbarous nations as authority for our action.

PD *Bond of Peace*, October 1869, 88–89

1. In his opening remarks, Dr. Henry T. Child (ca. 1814–90) noted they had "reason to rejoice over the success which has attended the labors of Friends among the Indians . . . as a triumph of the principles of peace" (*Bond of Peace*, October 1869, 88). Philadelphia newspapers regularly reported on "Indian Depredations," for example, the *Philadelphia Inquirer*, September 17, 1869, 1.

2. Child stated that the object of the Society was "the education of the people in the great principles which have ever characterized this people [*Friends*]" (*Bond of Peace*, October 1869, 88).

3. The *Philadelphia Inquirer* (May 10, 1869) reported that a meeting of the Plenary Council of the Roman Catholic Church advised the "withdrawal of Catholic children from public schools, and the formation of schools of their own."

4. Adin T. Corey (1780–1845), an agent of New York Yearly Meeting, was honored with the name "Oatnus" by the Onondaga (see Halliday Jackson, *Civilization of the Indian Natives* [New York: Isaac T. Hopper, 1830], 92–94). Griffith M. Cooper (1790–1864) of New York, and Halliday Jackson (1771–1835) and Joseph Walton (1792–1876) of Pennsylvania, participated in Quaker missions to New York Indians.

5. LM may be paraphrasing Black Hawk (1767–1838), leader of the Sauk Indians: "From the day when the palefaces landed upon our shores, they have been robbing us of our inheritance, and slowly, but surely, driving us back, back, back towards the setting sun" (W. C. Vanderwerth and William R. Carmack, *Indian Oratory* [Norman: University of Oklahoma Press, 1971], 88).

6. With Cooper, LM had been a member of the Joint Indian Committee, an 1839 effort by Genesee, New York, Philadelphia, and Baltimore Yearly Meetings to help the Seneca fight removal efforts in New York State (Faulkner, 134).

7. From John Bunyan, *Pilgrim's Progress* (1758).

8. In 1868 the Pennsylvania Peace Society planned to petition the state legislature to abolish capital punishment (*Bond of Peace*, March 1, 1868).

Opening of Swarthmore College, Swarthmore, Pennsylvania, November 10, 1869[1]

LUCRETIA MOTT followed, expressing her deep interest in the College,[2] and her hope that it would never degenerate into a mere sectarian school, but that its teachings would be so comprehensive and free from theological bias, that those who receive them will be prepared to recognize good wherever found. The voice of Truth is so plain, and so universally applicable, that all may hear it in their own tongue in which they were born. She also referred to the skepticism which sometimes grows out of the study of Science when unaccompanied by religious faith, and feelingly recited the following lines of Cowper:

> . . . Never yet did philosophic tube
> That brings the planets home into the eye
> Of observation, and discovers, else
> Not visible, His family of worlds,
> Discover Him that rules them; such a veil
> Hangs over mortal eyes, blind from the birth,
> And dark in things divine. Full often, too,
> Our wayward intellect, the more we learn
> Of Nature, overlooks her Author more;
> From instrumental causes proud to draw
> Conclusions retrograde and mad mistake.
> But if His word once teach us, shoot a ray
> Through all the heart's dark chambers and reveal
> Truths undiscovered but by that holy light,
> Then all is plain. Philosophy, baptized
> In the pure fountain of eternal love,
> Has eyes indeed; and viewing all she sees
> As meant to indicate a God to man,
> Gives Him his praise, and forfeits not her own.[3]

PD "Inauguration of Swarthmore College" (Philadelphia: Merrihew & Son, 1869), 16–17

* * * *

William Dorsey[4] also spoke, who was followed by Lucretia Mott. The brief notice of her remarks in the *Press* account of the proceedings,[5] ascribes to her a phraseology which formed no part of her utterance. In that portion of her address specially addressed to the pupils, she counseled proper and watchful heed to the "inner light" as an inestimable source of instruction, at the same time directing their attention to the value of the teachings of such good men as Elias Hicks, and the beautiful and simple truth taught by Jesus of Nazareth. In the course of her happy remarks she quoted a passage from Cowper, appropriately adapted to the spirit and tenor of her remarks, in which these lines occur: —

> "Philosophy, baptiz'd
> In the pure fountain of eternal love
> Has eyes indeed; and viewing all she sees
> As meant to indicate a God to man,
> Gives *him* his praise, and forfeits not her own.
> Learning has born such fruit in other days
> On all her branches; piety has found
> Friends in the friends of science, and true pray'r
> Has flow'd from lips wet with Castilian dews."[6]

PD "Our Philadelphia Correspondence," *National Anti-Slavery Standard*, November 20, 1869

1. Two separate, conflicting accounts of LM's remarks follow.
2. When it opened, the co-educational Swarthmore College had 180 students. LM's daughter, Anna Hopper, was on the board of managers. At the ceremony, LM planted two oak trees in memory of JM, who had died on January 26, 1868 (Palmer, 424).
3. From Cowper's "The Task" (1785).
4. William Dorsey (1811–1874) was a Philadelphia Hicksite and merchant.
5. "The venerable Lucretia Mott exhorted those present to carry out the objects of the college, so plainly set forth; spoke of the necessity of institutions like Swarthmore; rejoiced in the simplicity of the course of studies proposed, and hoped that truth would ever prevail; and the divine mission of the Lord Jesus Christ would never be forgotten" (*Philadelphia Press*, November 11, 1869).
6. From "The Task."

Philadelphia Female Anti-Slavery Society, Assembly Buildings, March 24, 1870

The President Lucretia Mott opened the Meeting with a few appropriate remarks. She said that at this, the last meeting, an address to the people assembled might be expected; but her heart was so full that there was room only for a feeling of thankfulness. Remembering the time when this Society was formed she rejoiced to see among the persons assembled, some who had assisted in its organization & others who had joined at a time when their names were therefore cast out as evil.[1] In our most sanguine moment we never then expected to see the consummation now attained. Truly the Lord had triumphed gloriously, & in view of all that had been accomplished she could only say "Now lettest Thou thy Servant depart in peace—for mine eyes have seen thy Salvation."

* * * *

Lucretia Mott remarked, with reference to the course pursued by the Anti-Slavery Society that they had always relied upon appeals to the moral sense and the intelligence of the people, never counselling the overthrow of Slavery by violence. This example, she trusted might be useful in succeeding enterprises of similar kind.

AD Gulielma M. S. P. Jones, Recording Secretary, "Proceedings of the Thirty-Sixth Annual Meeting of the Phila. Female Anti-Slavery Society" (Reel 30, Pennsylvania Anti-Slavery Papers, Historical Society of Pennsylvania)

1. In addition to LM, three founding members were present: Margaretta Forten, Sidney Ann Lewis, and Sarah Pugh. Others who spoke at the meeting included Mary Grew, Gulielma Jones (1824–10), Edward M. Davis, Aaron Powell, and Robert Purvis (Faulkner, 197–98).

American Anti-Slavery Society, Apollo Hall, New York City, April 9, 1870

Mrs. LUCRETIA MOTT upon advancing to the stand was greeted with loud applause. Although perhaps the oldest person present, she rejoiced that she could still lift her feeble voice with those with whom she had been so long associated, upon that platform. When an opportunity was offered at the opening of the meeting for prayer, silence had seemed to her the most effective prayer of praise that could be offered. She agreed from her heart with the resolution of gratitude to Almighty God for this wonderful victory.[1] It was natural upon an occasion like this to look back to the beginning and to remember how they had gone on from year to year, never discouraged, through a good report and evil report, until the evil report became to them a very small matter. But with all their faith and confidence in the overruling power of justice and love, they had never anticipated a victory like the present. After so many years, there was no thought of ceasing their work. Their motto was still onward. With this in view, there was nothing sad in being called together for a final meeting. She looked upon this occasion, not as a funeral, but rather as a resurrection. We have realized to a great extent a fulfillment of the prophecy, "And I, if I be lifted up, will draw all men unto me." It was natural for the old to like to look back to the early days, and to contrast the small beginning with the great result. In season and out of season, they raised a feeble voice; but it proved a strong voice; for the seed sown in weakness was raised in power.

Mrs. MOTT proceeded to review the early history of the Anti-Slavery Agitation, from the time when THOMAS CLARKSON labored for the arrest of the slave trade, relating incidents in those early efforts; in inducing WEDGEWOOD to put the picture of the kneeling slave upon his porcelain;[2] in publishing prints of the slaveships; in introducing into schoolbooks descriptions of the slave trade; educating the people, so that the next generation would lay the axe nearer to the root of the tree. It was about the year 1825 that ELIZABETH HEYRICK came forward with her work on "Immediate, not gradual Emancipation." The old abolitionists of Pennsylvania had formed a Society with FRANKLIN at its head, the object of which was "to protect the rights of those unlawfully seized and held in bondage, as well as to promote the best interests of the colored people around us"; but this was of little avail, when slavery was legalized.[3] The abolition of slavery in the West Indies grew out of ELIZABETH HEYRICK'S book; and she mentioned it the more because she was a woman. At that time BENJAMIN LUNDY was Editor of the *Genius of Universal Emancipation*; and he took a copy of that book to WILLIAM LLOYD GARRISON who resolved thenceforth to devote his labors to that great work. She hoped that there would be prepared a history of the progress of the movement from its inception to its consummation. It seemed fitting, on an occasion like this, to make some allusion to the steps by which we have reached this great event.

* * * *

MRS. MOTT remarked that she had always taken pleasure in listening to remarks from ROBERT PURVIS, FREDERICK DOUGLASS, and other half-colored men, but she thought the blacker the speaker the better she liked it.[4] (Laughter and applause.) She believed that the overthrow of slavery had been accomplished, not by carnal weapons, but through moral means which have been mighty through God for the pulling down of the stronghold. She alluded to discussions by THEODORE D. WELD and others in the Lane Theological Seminary,[5] and the continued agitation which had so instructed the nation that when rebellion broke out the nation became one great Anti-Slavery Meeting and demanded the Proclamation of Emancipation. And although the nation was long in reaching the full results, we may have strong confidence that Truth is mightier than the sword, and should be careful how we admit the consummation was through the battle-field.

* * * *

MRS. MOTT proposed to offer a resolution of thanks to some of those who had spent their lives in this cause; but was reminded of the words of THEODORE D. WELD: "Let us as Abolitionists strike a level above which no one shall raise his head. Let us drop a curtain behind which every one shall work"; and would therefore forbear to offer the resolution.

PD "American Anti-Slavery Society: Commemorative Session," *National Anti-Slavery Standard*, April 16, 1870, 1–2.

1. With the ratification of the Fifteenth Amendment, which enfranchised African American men, the AASS disbanded. One of the resolutions thanked God "for the marvelous and unexampled quickness with which it had pleased him to do this great work," promising to continue their fight against all occurrences of " hateful prejudice" (*National Anti-Slavery Standard*, April 16, 1870).
2. Josiah Wedgewood (1730–95), British manufacturer of pottery, who produced this abolitionist medallion with the phrase "Am I not a Man and a Brother?"
3. From 1787 to 1790 Benjamin Franklin (1706–90) was president of the Pennsylvania Society for Promoting the Abolition of Slavery, founded in 1775. The state passed a gradual abolition act in 1780.
4. LM refers to the previous speaker, the Reverend Henry Highland Garnet (1815–82), who recalled that when he first appeared at an antislavery meeting in 1837, "MRS. MOTT was in the prime of her womanhood" (*National Anti-Slavery Standard*, April 16, 1870).

5. In 1834 Weld, a student at Lyman Beecher's seminary in Cincinnati, organized a series of debates on slavery that launched the careers of a number of abolitionists (Gordon, 1:xxix).

Reform League, Steinway Hall, New York City, May 9, 1871

I am much gratified that I have a little remaining strength to meet you here to-day, and to have had the opportunity of hearing your excellent report, presenting to us, as it does, a view of so much that is to be done.[1] Let us recollect that this meeting is called not merely for the purpose of entertainment, but to see how far we can unite our individual exertions for the benefit of our fellow-creatures. We want the Republic to be established on a permanent foundation; and I think we can well hope to attain that result by aiding this movement. But I want to ask our friend Wendell Phillips about one of the resolutions offered. I think I could not support the resolution that advocates the killing of human beings. Our friend Phillips has spoken with approval of Gen. [Benjamin F.] Butler's hanging of Munford.[2] Now it seems to me that the bravest of those men and women who went forth in the great battle against Slavery, went forth armed with moral power only; and I think that it would not be proper for us to advocate the use of any other power now. Let us have faith in our arguments.

If we had fixed opinion right when the Rebellion broke out, all need not have met it with the sword; we might have met it with intelligent argument.

PD "The May Anniversaries," *New York Tribune*, May 10, 1871

1. Former abolitionists had founded the organization to remove "other great wrongs," including racial prejudice, women's inequality, the oppression of workers, and intemperance, and for the promotion of "peace, religious freedom, and enlightenment" (*New York Tribune*, May 10, 1871). They fought for black civil rights and published a newspaper, the *National Standard* (see James M. McPherson, *The Abolitionist Legacy: From Reconstruction to the NAACP* [Princeton, N.J.: Princeton University Press, 1975], 13).
2. Phillips read a resolution that declared the Ku Klux Klan, an organization whose violence against African Americans had recently been the subject of congressional hearings, a "new form of rebellion" and called for martial law: "Let its first fruit to them be the drum-head conviction and the gibbet." Phillips declared, "I believe that the nation stands to-day just where Gen. Butler stood in New-Orleans when he arrested Mumford" (*New York Tribune*, May 10, 1871). In June 1862 Butler hanged William Mumford for removing an American flag from a government building.

Fifteenth Street Meeting, New York City, May 26, 1872

With the close of the sermon,[1] every word of which was fervently uttered, silence again falls upon the assemblage. A woman stands up in her place on the rostrum. She is attired in drab, with a face that shows the signs of patient struggles, softened by an expression of steadfast inspiration and of hope. There are few more remarkable women of the time than Lucretia Mott. As she stands looking at the large audience, fancy contrasts her with other women who have taken upon themselves missions which they prosecute with more of impudent, unseemly demagogueism than, like hers, of perfect womanliness. Every humane movement for the last forty years has known something of her aid. She is now very old. During her discourse she is frequently obliged to take a glass of water to enable her to proceed. After the first sentence she slowly unties the strings of her bonnet, and, removing it, places it in the lap of the Quakeress who sits next to her. She unfolds a white handkerchief, which is spread upon the rail of the rostrum before her.[2]

ALABAMA CLAIMS

Beginning in a low, tremulous tone, her thoughts seemed to gather strength and pour upon her like a summer flood, so that her voice grows at length more distinct, clear and loud. One cannot well picture an audience with such a woman standing before it, whose words it hangs upon with intense entrancement. Her words have the grace and sweetness of a Tillotson and the strength and significance of a Kempis.[3] It would be impossible to give a just sketch of an unwritten sermon such as the one of yesterday. She spoke with great feeling and eloquence, and her subject was the peace of nations, touching upon the Alabama claims in a strong appeal for the perpetual continuance of harmony between England and America.[4] She deprecated

THE SHEDDING OF BLOOD

in an age like this, when civilization and culture are so advanced and so rapidly advancing. The intellectual should be allied with the spiritual to govern and guide the physical nature—the intellectual should not league with the physical. Warring is retrograding toward barbarism. Since the beginning of the trouble between the two countries in relation to the Alabama claims she had ever hoped and prayed for the settlement by peaceful means, which were fixed in the Treaty of Washington. She hoped still that it would end in that way, and she felt thankful that during the labors of

THE JOINT HIGH COMMISSION

at Washington other means of settlement than such as were peaceful had never been spoken of in that body.[5] The principle of settling differences between nations by arbitration was what was to lead to the success of the cause which the Quakers had advocated for so many years. She thought it was the only way by which harmony could be preserved in the world. She urged that the influence of the Society of Friends should be used at the present time to further

THE PEACEFUL ARBITRATION

of the claims by advising the President of the United States in relation thereto. In former instances, however weak their efforts had seemed to themselves, they had brought forth fruit. If the Society of Friends kept firmly to that defense and advocacy of peace which had so distinguished it, it could not be long ere the principle would triumph in the world. Now, when the consummation of this labor was near at hand, they should use what aid the Divine Spirit should give them to bring it quickly about.

VANITY OF VANITIES

She closed her discourse by giving advice to young ladies on the subject of dress, the extravagance and showiness of which were evils of the time. The women's gallery, with its array of ribbons and head gear, *a la* Shetland pony, fluttered its multitudinous fans very nervously.

SILENCE

Lucretia Mott sat down for a moment, and then, rising, proposed a time of perfect silence, that they might "draw near to the Father." The stillness is at length broken by a stir through all the assemblage; the men and women on the "high seats" are shaking hands, the greeting passes all through the house, and then the meeting is over.

PD "The Quakers' Anniversary; Lucretia Mott Preaches on the Principles of Peace," *New York Herald*, May 27, 1872.

1. Samuel M. Janney (1801–80), a Quaker minister from Virginia, preached that "it was man who was to be reconciled to God, and not God to man" (*New York Herald*, May 27, 1872). This event likely preceded Yearly Meeting, which was held May 27–31.
2. LM disputed the *New York Herald*'s description of her placement of the bonnet and handkerchief as "not true" and "a thing I never do" (Palmer, 469).
3. John Tillotson (1630–94) was an influential Archbishop of Canterbury, whose sermons were widely read. He advocated reason, and expressed tolerance of non-conformists. Thomas à Kempis (ca. 1380–1471) was the author of *The Imitation of Christ*, a devotional text popular among Quakers.
4. The United States believed the British had aided the Confederacy by building ships like the CSS *Alabama* and demanded restitution for the damages the ship had wrought.
5. The Joint High Commission, composed of representatives from the United States and Britain, settled a number of disputes between the two countries. The resulting Treaty of Washington awarded monetary damages to the United States for its claims in the case of the *Alabama* (see also Palmer, 487–88).

Funeral of Mary Ann W. Johnson, Home of Oliver Johnson,[1] *New York City, June 10, 1872*

I think nothing more need be added. What the other speakers have said has been so true, so full, and so just, that to continue would only be to repeat. Cordially and emphatically do I approve the beautiful doctrine concerning death which has been enunciated here to-day—a view of this life and the other, of this world and the next, which I know was held by our dear friend whose earthly career has just closed in peace.[2] Too many of us indulge in heathenish views of death. The dissolution of the body, the passage of the spirit, the exchange of worlds—all this, which is in itself beautiful and sacred, and which is part of the benignant ordering of a kind Providence, and which we ought to look forward to with joy and not with fear; all this, I say, has been taken up by the old and severe theologies, and turned into a bugbear, and been held over the human soul like a rod of terror. But we have had no such inculcation in the remarks made to-day. Death is here, and we are met to celebrate it, and wherever there is death there is sorrow; but we sorrow not as they that have no hope; neither do we complain against God because of His chastisement. This event is no chastisement. It is the order of nature. It is natural and right. We look at it with solemnity and tenderness, but we do not shudder at it; nor do we think it a strange and ungentle thing. It is an occasion of much joyfulness—the inward peace of the soul.

Our sister and friend at whose face we are now looking for the last time before the earth shall hide it, was a true and noble woman. Although I was never on terms of the most intimate friendship with her, yet I was no stranger to her devotion to the sick and afflicted; and when I was last in her company, which was in Roxbury, Mass., one of my own family connection shared her kindly care.[3] My interest in her and her husband was enlisted many years since, not only in the anti-Slavery struggle but from the fact that, when a young man, he took thorough ground on the subject of war and peace. His appeals were then most searching. I watched his course with interest during the recent years of our civil war—remembering a conversation I had with him, and a comparison of views concerning the bloody methods which the North and the South had adopted for the settlement of their differences.[4] Now that an opportunity has been presented for the settlement of international disputes without resort to force [*Alabama Claims*], I hope our friend's early testimony against war will be borne anew—and not without fruits, for are not the fields almost white unto the harvest!

If these exercises—which to me have seemed so fit and proper—had not already been filled so full of tribute to our dear departed friend,[5] and if the time had not already been so profitably spent, I would say more. But there has been enough.

PD *In Memoriam, Mary Ann W. Johnson, Wife of Oliver Johnson* (New York: Printed, Not Published, 1872), 25–26

1. Mary Ann White Johnson (1808–72), lecturer on physiology and women's rights activist, and her husband Oliver Johnson (1808–89), former editor of the *Pennsylvania Freeman* and the *National Anti-Slavery Standard*.

2. Theodore Tilton, who preceded LM, noted that Mary Ann Johnson "had long accustomed herself to think of death as the culmination, the crown, the final joy of life. She looked forward to it, not as to a King of Terrors, but the Prince of Peace." Octavius B. Frothingham described her as "a Spiritualist in the sense of one who holds the belief that spirits exist, and that there is an open door of communication between them and the friends below" (*In Memoriam*, 22, 7).

3. Probably LM's niece Ellen Wright (1840–1931) and her husband, William Lloyd Garrison Jr., who lived in Roxbury, Massachusetts (Palmer, 482).

4. Oliver Johnson endorsed President Lincoln during the Civil War.

5. Giving the principal address, WLG discussed Mary Ann Johnson's "deep interest" in "the elevation and enfranchisement of her sex." Frothingham praised her work at Sing Sing Prison and the Isaac T. Hopper Home in New York City as "quite aside from the ordinary paths of human service" (*In Memoriam*, 16, 6).

Free Religious Association, Tremont Temple, Boston, May 30, 1873

As this is probably the last opportunity that I shall have of meeting with this Association, which has endeared itself to me from its beginning, I feel, late as the hour is, that I want to express the great delight and satisfaction that I have had in this session, and in the meetings of these two days, in the evidence they have afforded that the prayers of many for this Association have been heard, that their faith shall not fail them, and that they shall give evidence of a deep sense of religion, which will put an end to all the vain and false theologies and useless forms in Christendom and in Heathendom.

I have not many words to utter, but it is a great satisfaction to me to know that the science of theology has come to be considered so much now in these meetings, that I think there must be, another year, an amendment of our Constitution, which has been a great desire with me, for a year or two past; and instead of the science of theology being made a study, that it will come to be, as has been expressed today, the science of religion in liberty and truth, and of liberty and truth in religion; the science,—as was expressed in our first meeting by our beloved friends, John Weiss and Francis Abbot,—the science of the inspiration of the human mind; the science of truth, as manifested in the inmost soul.[1] This must come to be the only science of theology which it shall be necessary to study, or necessary to be taught. And, as regards the subject upon which so much has been written of late, the importance of faith in a personal God, we shall be content to let our limited knowledge remain where it is, while we have all that science can reveal, both that which is self-evident, which is natural, which is spiritual, and that which belongs to outward nature,—which it needs not that I enlarge upon, ignorant as I am, after all that has been said.[2] But I think that this will be found to suffice, and, as has just been expressed, that it shall pervade the universe of God, and bring us into the kingdom, which is nigh even at the doors;[3] and that we need not enter into any speculations as regards the future, as regards immortality, but that we all shall learn to rest content with the limited knowledge we have, and be confident, by fullness of faith, that that which is best for us shall and will be ours, while we do not endeavor by our speculations to make out or build up a heaven. I remember when Dr. [*William Ellery*] Channing, years ago, at our house,[4] attempted to advocate his views, and to show what everlasting progress there would be in the hereafter, I told him it was as interesting to me as any speculation to which I had ever listened on the subject, but he must allow me to say, that it was speculation still. I want we should tread under foot our speculations, and everything that will mingle aught that is uncertain with the religion which we have heard presented to us to-day—which is certain, which is sure; for that which is self-evident needs no argument. And so we come near to the beautiful truths and testimonies that rise out of this pure religion and undefiled, that need no scholastic learning, that need no pulpit explanations. They are clear truth, justice, love—highest, noblest, finest instincts of the human heart and mind, which we are to apply to all that we can imagine of the unseen and unknown. That divine power will be ours, if we seek it; and when these principles are stated they are self-evident; they need no learned oratory, and it is not employed in regard to them. You do not hear, in any of the pulpits, a definition of what love, and justice, and mercy, and right are. You know, and all know, that they are innate, self-defined. Therefore, I say, preach your truth; let it go forth, and you will find, without any notable miracle, as of old, that every man will speak in his own tongue in which he was born. And I will say, that if these pure principles have their place in us, and are brought forth by faithfulness, by obedience, into practice, the difficulties and doubts that we may have to surmount will be easily conquered. There will be a power higher than these. Let it be called the Great Spirit of the Indian, the Quaker "inward light" of George Fox, the "Blessed Mary, mother of Jesus," of the Catholics, or Brahma, the Hindoo's God—they will all be one, and there will come to be such faith and such liberty as shall redeem the world.

And yet, while thus delighting in what I have heard to-day, and feeling that I can go forth thanking God, and ready to leave the world now that mine eyes have seen His salvation, still, I would say, by way of friendly criticism, to my good brother who has just spoken, that, when he is elucidating his principle, he should be careful not to make too much use of the symbols of war.[5] I am afraid that some of our liberal friends are not quite sound enough on the subject of peace.

PD *Proceedings of the Sixth Annual Meeting of the Free Religious Association* (Boston: Cochrane & Sampson, 1873), 94–96.

1. John Weiss (1818–79), a Unitarian minister, had urged the audience to "empty all your minds clean of all belief in the miraculous; of all belief in the preternatural; of all past or present belief in any form of supernaturalism; and to remand yourselves back to the operations of your intelligence; to the strictly scientific movement of God's thought." Francis Ellingwood Abbot (1836–1903), a former Unitarian and editor of the Free Religious Association's newspaper *The Index*, argued that "equal and perfect faith in religion and in science, as natural friends and allies" distinguished Free Religion from other organizations (*Free Religion: Report of Addresses at a Meeting Held in Boston, May 30, 1867* [Boston: Adams and Co., 1867], 28, 38).

2. Speakers included Abbot, Samuel Longfellow, Thomas Wentworth Higginson, Robert Dale Owen, and Weiss. Longfellow argued, "What we want to get at, on every side, is reality,—facts: facts of physical nature, and of the spiritual world; facts of the emotions; facts of the soul." Abbot stated, "When you enter upon the search after truth, without limitation by any church or sect, and in the spirit of duty and of human love, I say you must be content to take then what Nature has to give" (*Proceedings*, 78, 92; Palmer, 485).

3. Speaking directly before LM, Abbot asserted, "I do believe that this effort to reproduce voluntarily within himself the unity of the universe and to help carry forward its laws and powers to their highest evolution in his own soul, has a direct tendency towards what I should name Theism" (*Proceedings*, 90–91).

4. LM had the "high privilege" of Channing's "society" in the summer of 1842. She wrote, "He never seemed more lovely than in our free interchange of sentiments at that time" (Palmer, 128).

5. Abbot had told a story about James Douglas, Lord of Douglas, "the Black Douglas" who cut out the heart of the dead Robert Bruce and used it to inspire his men to defeat the Saracens: "We must pluck out of our own hearts our dearest faith, hurl it into the ranks of the enemy, and then, without fear, without hesitation, without a thought of our own safety, plunge into their midst, and bring it back by the sword of thought" (*Proceedings*, 93–94).

Philadelphia Quarterly Meeting, Race Street, November 4, 1873

I do not feel quite prepared to have the meeting close without first expressing my gratification in listening to the several forcible appeals that have been made,[1] and at finding so strict an adherence to our great fundamental principles of individual teaching to the human mind through that true light which lighteth every man that cometh into the world. As this is often claimed to be our great fundamental doctrine it is very gratifying to me when I find so slight an admixture of sectarianism interwoven into the ideas of one and another upon it. We know how difficult it is for us mingled as we are in society, and observing as we do how these systems of faith have become incorporated in every organization so that the various sects are now trying to become one in faith; how difficult it is for us to be willing to stand thus alone, as it were, and be not considered as evangelical, or having the right faith. We know also how easy it is for the young to accept imperceptibly—as interwoven as they are in their religious faith—some of these theological ideas. I know the great pains that are being taken for the improvement of the young,[2] and the gathering together of our friends round about us for good purposes, endeavoring to train them in good habits and habits of industry, and also to instruct them, so far as they will be instructed, in that which is right and true, and my desire is that in thus gathering the young together there may be great care to preserve the simplicity of our faith as it is in Jesus; of the truth as it is in the divine will manifested to the will of man. I am anxious to express that desire, that hope that there may be great effort put forth to preserve our fundamental principles and that obedience to them may be manifested by increasing righteousness and good works. The spirit that is from above is always pure, peaceable, full of mercy, [*full?*] of good fruits. If our fathers were distinguished by any one thing more than another, it was in calling men, as Jesus called his disciples to him, to a higher righteousness, to a higher state of morality. We know that in the sectarian world morality is placed at too low an estimate, and good works at too little value. But when we feel ourselves called to higher works, [*ms damaged*] greater faith manifested by fruits, to do that which is truly humbling to [*ms damaged*] then it is that we are to be faithful [*ms damaged*] the shining of this true light and these clear intimations of duty. While our brother warned some not to be impatient for the time to come I felt as though I wanted him to add that they must not delay when the time did come. We know this, especially from our own experience. I feel there [are?] very many passing middle age of life who are suffering themselves, and their own power for good, to become dwarfed by expecting too much, looking for too high an evidence, for more than has been granted, not having sufficient faith to accept what has been given and obey it, and trust in the assurance that to be faithful thus in the little, will be an opening into that which is greater. While I was glad for all that our brother said on the one hand, I could not allow you to separate without urging you to be faithful, as you mingle in society, for in going in private to those whom you esteem above yourselves, in speaking the word of truth to them, or that you, the very young in your intercourse with your playmates that you may grow up willing to acknowledge the Master before men. It is a favorite expression with us, to say that we cannot conscientiously to do this or refrain from doing that. I want to bring this principle to the test of every-day life. We mourn at this present time to see so large a number of persons rushing into the extravagances of business, and now showing deficiencies by millions,[3] when failures of thousands were enough to alarm us only a few years ago. I have been led to ask whether the query so frequently before us as to Friends keeping within reasonable limits in trade or business should not be more strictly regarded. If this principle were more closely adhered to there would not perhaps be that incentive to large and extensive operations which are crushing so many in our community who have hitherto been looked upon as so worthy of confidence. My sisters, I have been led to rejoice as I looked over this assembly this morning, to see the general air of plainness and simplicity there is amongst us—no high-towering hats, covered with plumes and none of the useless and showy extravagances of the age, though from our contact with society, we are being led into them more and more, but judged as a whole, I do believe there is greater simplicity in our lives than with the world at large. Let us be willing to cultivate this simplicity, this plainness, and let us dress the dear little children more simply.

I felt that this was a little word to add while we are thus assembled, to what has already been so well said, and I trust it may not take from the weight of solemnity which I believe has been over this meeting.

PD Undated, unidentified newspaper clipping, Marianna Wright Chapman Scrapbook, FHL

1. The Quarterly Meeting briefly noted "a number of Friends from other meetings" and the "presence of so many young people and their quiet attention were strengthening and encouraging." A "valued friend from a distance" offered a "forcible and awakening" address (*Friends' Intelligencer*, November 15, 1873).

2. *Friends' Intelligencer* had published a series on the educational efforts of Philadelphia Monthly Meeting. By 1870 the meeting supervised five schools with 375 students. In 1871 the schools committee declared that Friends' Central School would be free to "the children who are members of this Monthly Meeting" ("Progress of the Educational Cause in Philadelphia Monthly Meeting," December 21, 1872).

3. Financier Jay Cooke, LM's neighbor, had closed his namesake firm in September, sparking an economic panic across the country (Palmer, 363).

Pennsylvania Society for Promoting the Abolition of Slavery, Concert Hall, Philadelphia, April 14, 1875

I came here without the least expectation of saying a word, understanding the meeting to be at the call of the Society for Promoting the Abolition of Slavery, as organized long before the Anti-Slavery Society, headed by William Lloyd Garrison. In this, the first society, women were not expected to take part. I therefore, should feel very much out of place were there not a union at this time of both societies. Then again, owing to a severe cold, my hoarseness is such that I cannot be heard probably many feet from me; but my interest in this cause makes me willing, at the suggestion of your chairman, to occupy a few moments.

The speaker [LM], after expressing the hope that what had been said would have the effect to stimulate her hearers to greater zeal in the support of schools for the education of people of color, and in the many similar directions in which they had been engaged, proceeded to correct an erroneous statement that Elizabeth Heyrick was a member of the Society of Friends.[1]

Referring to what had been said concerning the gratitude of the negro, she gave some instances from her personal experience, and remarked that much yet remained to be done in order to put a stop to outrages upon the colored people such as were still perpetrated in the South. She referred to the moral influence of the anti-slavery sentiments in bringing about the emancipation of the colored race.

PD "Centennial Anniversary of the Pennsylvania Society for Promoting the Abolition of Slavery" (Philadelphia: Grant, Faires and Rodgers, 1875), 27

1. Though she was not born into the faith, Heyrick converted to the Society of Friends.

Free Religious Association, Beethoven Hall, Boston, May 28, 1875

It seems to me very kind in an audience to be willing to stay and listen to the humble words of an old Quaker woman, after feeling how forcible are ripe words as we have heard them expressed this morning. When the beautiful bouquet was brought in, I thought perhaps it was meant to be a symbol of the words fitly spoken to which we have listened, which in the old Scripture were compared to apples of gold in pictures of silver. I have listened with the greatest interest to the essay that has been read, and to all your proceedings.[1] Indeed, since my first attendance at this Free Religious meeting, I have been a constant reader of the productions of the pens of those interested in the promotion of its objects, and very often have entirely responded to what has there been presented.

After relating many interesting personal reminiscences, she continued, with reference to the power of superstition even in enlightened circles: —

When in England, in 1840, I saw one of the Egyptian idols in the British Museum. Some one of our company said, "Well, they don't admit that they worship such ugly images as this; they look through and beyond this to one great Supreme Power." "They were scarcely more idolatrous," I answered, "than our Quaker friends when they read their Bible with such reverence last evening."[2] They brought it out with great solemnity, and laid it on the lap of the one who was to read it, and he bowed before it, and then opened it and read it in what we Friends call the preaching tone. The passages read were those that had no particular bearing upon the lives and conduct of those then present, nor upon the special occasion which had brought us together; but it was "the Bible" and "Scripture," and a chapter of it must be read in order, and in a solemn tone. I said to the friend who was pointing out this idol to me in the Museum, that the worship of that image was like the worship of the Bible as we had observed it the evening before. To me that was the worship of an idol.

So, too, in regard to many of the prayers that have been offered in many of the meetings I have attended, since I dared go without the limited enclosure of the Friends to attend Reformatory meetings. They have been so superstitious and childish, and so at variance with the idea that Jesus inculcated with regard to prayer, that I have been rejoiced since these meetings of yours have been organized that there has not been felt the necessity of calling on anyone to offer prayer. It is years since I have felt free to rise in time of prayer—as the custom is in our meetings,—so entirely have I concurred with the recommendation of Jesus, who said, "When thou prayest, enter into thy closet, and shut the door, and there pray to thy Father in secret; and thy Father, which seeth in secret, shall reward thee openly." This kind of prayer is as natural to man as the air he breathes,—the aspiration for divine aid, for strength to do right, the inward desire after truth and holiness, the yearning to be led to the rock that is higher than he. But when it comes to praying for rain in dry weather, or for the removal of evils that have been brought upon us by our own violations of the laws of health and nature, then it is most absurd and superstitious.

She closed by quoting some passages from Dr. [*William Ellery*] Channing, on the grandeur of the inward principles of duty, and on the growing power of human love, adding: —

These are sayings that commend themselves to the inmost heart of every reader and of every hearer. And we may so speak of the operation of this principle in the mind, if we divest ourselves of the influence of the traditions we have received from the superstition and ignorance of the past, and from the prejudices of our education, that as notable a miracle as that wrought in the days of old shall occur, and "every man shall hear in his own tongue wherein he was born," and all shall understand alike.

PD *Proceedings at the Eighth Annual Meeting of the Free Religious Association* (Boston: Cochrane & Sampson, 1875), 38–40.

1. Meeting attendees had heard remarks by Thomas Wentworth Higginson and an essay entitled "The Present Constructive Tendencies in Religion" by Unitarian clergyman William Channing Gannett (1840–1923). Higginson opened the meeting, describing the Free Religious Association as offering "the hospitality of the world of thought,—it is the religious sympathy of the world." Gannett characterized the tendencies of the current religious era as both "destructive" and "constructive," but highlighted the constructive "expansion of Church dogmas into nobler truths, and the grander aspect of the universe which Science opens to us, with its effect upon religious feeling" (*Proceedings*, 17, 26, 36).

2. Before her first visit to the British Museum on June 26, 1840, LM had tea at the home of Quaker minister William Ball (1801–78). She commented, "many more beside all our company—everything in style—servants in livery—shewn upstairs by a plain Quaker servant —tea handed—much conversation—reading scripture" (Frederick B. Tolles, ed., *Slavery and the "Woman Question": Lucretia Mott's Diary of Her Visit to Great Britain to Attend the World's Anti-Slavery Convention of 1840* [Haverford, Pa.: Friends' Historical Association, 1952], 48).

Women's Peace Festival, Institute Hall, Philadelphia, June 2, 1875

It is true, as our friend has well remarked, that the spirit of Peace must be cultivated in our own hearts, and the spirit of war eradicated before we can expect to make much progress.[1] I have often resisted the impression that woman differs so widely from man, and I think we have not the facts to substantiate it. I cannot believe that if woman had her just rights, which I desire she should have, that all these evils will cease. The efforts which have been made in the cause of Peace have been mostly from the pens and labors of men. Very few women have actively embarked on this question until very recently. We know that women have very generally encouraged war, and in the late strife in our country the women on both sides took an active part and encouraged the men. Some of us are old enough to remember when the rod was used in the school and in the family to keep children in order. Horace Mann thought it would not do to abolish it in the schools of Massachusetts, but after a visit to England, where he saw how cruelly this was used in the factories to compel little children to perform their hard tasks, he returned home and urged the banishment of this barbarous custom.[2]

There is a great deal to encourage us at the present time. Those of us who have been engaged in these labors for many years can look back to the time when but a few earnest men endeavored to awaken an interest in this subject—John Woolman, Jonathan Dymond, Elihu Burritt, and others.[3] The Society of Friends have always required their members to settle their difficulties by arbitration; they do not allow them to sue one another. We are too much in the habit of erecting partition walls between ourselves and others; have not associated with others as much as the early Friends did, but wherever there has been a mingling with them, there has been an advance of our testimonies. Within thirty or forty years there has been more remarkable success than ever before in all reforms. The people are learning that the weapons of our warfare are not carnal, but mighty because they are not carnal, to the pulling down of the strongholds. I was much interested in reading the account of the celebration of William Cullen Bryant's 80th birthday, in which he reviewed some of the events that had transpired during his life, and at the close of his remarks he referred to the subject of Peace. He hoped that the time was not far distant when standing armies would be disbanded, and the men would be returned to their farms and their workshops, from whence they should never have been taken, and that through international arbitration wars would cease.[4]

I remember as long ago as 1817 assisting my husband's brother[5] in stitching small peace pamphlets to the almanacs of that year. Everybody loves Peace better than war; everybody knows that war is wrong,—indeed it has to be decked out in all its paraphernalia to make it at all acceptable. It is a very encouraging fact that the working people of England and of this country are resolving that they will not be forced into fighting any more; some of them have gone so far as to say that they will have Peace if they have to fight for it.[6] I am glad to know that they are resolving that they will have no more wars; this has had its effect. We know that all oppressors are cowards more or less.

I believe there is a better feeling on the part of many of the rich. We see that many individuals are now distributing their property in their lifetime in a manner that must tend to lift up humanity far beyond anything of former times. Public education and the many opportunities that the people have to rise to higher conditions are removing many of the obstacles that have been in the way of the poor.[7] It will be in vain that there shall be any demands for anything agrarian; the people are gradually rising to higher conditions, and I think we may all rejoice in these things.

I attended the Unitarian Convention in Boston last week,[8] in which many subjects of a reformatory character were brought forward, and among them that of Peace. Reference was made to Noah Worcester, who was one of the pioneers. Many have been ready enough to cry, "Glory to God in the highest," but when they came to the words, "Peace on earth and good will to man," they were slower. I am much encouraged when I see from the fashionable circles in our country that many are ready to advocate the cause of Peace. Julia Ward Howe acknowledges that it would have been better if she had listened to the purifying angel in her breast earlier in life;[9] she would have come forward in this labor instead of devoting so much time to fashionable circles. She is now devoting herself nobly to this great work, and I am glad to know that these meetings are being held, as she suggested, in various parts of the world.

* * * *

Lucretia Mott referred to the same subject, the education of children, and related some cases in illustration of this.[10]

PD "Official Report of the Third Annual Meeting of the Woman's Peace Festival," *Voice of Peace*, vol. 2, no. 4 (July 1875), 51–52, 53

1. The previous speaker, Henry T. Child, had stated that "the work of Peace is in our own souls; we must realize it here before we can promulgate it among our fellow beings." He had also argued that "There is no field of labor in which woman can work more appropriately than that of peace; her habits of life, all her training and discipline should make for Peace" (*Voice of Peace*, 51).

2. Mann had traveled to Europe in 1843. In Prussia, where use of corporal punishment in schools had declined, he noted "a love of the teacher and a love of knowledge become a substitute—how admirable a one!—for punishment" (Horace Mann, *Annual Reports of the Secretary of the Board of Education of Massachusetts for the Years 1839–1844* [Boston: Lee and Shepard, 1891], 360).

3. In "An Epistle of Tender Love and Caution" (1755), American John Woolman (1720–72) encouraged other Quakers to withhold taxes used to fund war. In 1823 English Quaker Jonathan Dymond (1796–1828) published an "Enquiry into the Accordancy of War with the Principles of Christianity."

4. During his speech, newspaper editor and poet William Cullen Bryant (1794–1878) anticipated that "universal peace" would be "one of the next great changes" (Parke Godwin, *A Biography of William Cullen Bryant*, 2 vols. [New York: Appleton, 1883], 2:349–50).

5. Richard Mott (1804–88), a Toledo, Ohio, businessman and politician, had attended Nine Partners Boarding School with LM and JM.

6. The International Workingmen's Association, which sought to "unite the workers of all countries in one fraternal bond, irrespective of all differences of nationality, language, color, creed, or trade," advocated "the abolition of the standing army, as being a provocative to war." Forty members of the organization had attended the Pennsylvania Peace Society's 1871 meeting (*Woodhull and Claflin's Weekly*, January 13, 1872; Bacon, 236).

7. Public higher education had expanded since the 1862 passage of the Morrill Act, which provided land grants to sixty-nine universities.

8. LM probably refers to the meeting of the Free Religious Association, which she attended.

9. Suffragist Julia Ward Howe (1819–1910), who wrote "The Battle Hymn of the Republic," founded the Woman's Peace Festival (*Voice of Peace*, 49–50).

10. Previous speaker Frederic Heaton, a Shaker, lamented "the education of the children in regard to war. How many of their playthings, theirs books, the history that they are taught, are calculated to foster a love of war, to hide its terrible character, and make it attractive to the young mind" (*Voice of Peace*, 53).

Women's Peace Festival, Mercantile Hall, Philadelphia, June 2, 1876

I can but hope that the language of such a hymn[1] put in the mouths of little children in the Sabbath-schools, will be carried out by the conductors of these schools as well as by the children.

I fear very much that even now while there is this desire for the promotion of Peace and good will among men, by the intermingling of all nations, that many of these conservators of these sacred songs are really creating a warlike spirit in the community among the class of people that Jesus most acknowledged, in the effort to close the gates of the Centennial on the First day of the week,[2] and thus prevent the laboring classes of this city, and the country around from entering it on that day, not as a place of amusement, not as a place forbidden by any law, as has been shown by many of our ablest lawyers, but as a place of profitable entertainment, a place in which they and their families may have rational enjoyment, and such instruction as will be a lasting benefit to them. There is a spirit excited among these people that they have a right to go in there on the only day in which they can do it. The attempt of the Commission to keep the gates closed, it seems to me is a lamentable sign of the times; a warlike sign, and there are rumors that some of the people will demand their rights by force. I hope as lovers of Peace, for there is no true Peace that is not founded in justice and right,[3] we shall show our love for the whole people without any distinction, by using all proper means to have this opened and by a free and open recognition of the rights of all.

There is much to encourage us in the prospect of Peace, in the prospect of a disposition to settle all national differences by arbitration instead of a resort to arms. In going through these Centennial grounds we see many of the trophies of war exhibited,[4] so that some feel almost forbidden to enter, but this we must expect in the present state of mankind. I want that there should be a fullness of faith in the possibility of removing all these things before long. The fields are now white unto harvest, if we will only have faith enough. I don't mean a mere sectarian faith, that will keep Sundays and do wrong on other days. I want that there should be a belief, a faith in the possibility of removing mountains on the side of right. If we believe that war is wrong, and every one must, then we ought to believe that by proper efforts on our part it may be done away with.

When we consider what has been done in the last century, and especially within fifty years, I think we have great reason to hope that the time is drawing near much faster than many doubtful ones can believe.

I want that we should look back and see what a great evil war has been in every age of the world. When it was visited upon the Israelites it was considered as a judgment. The texts, "If thine enemy hunger, feed him; if he thirst, give him drink," were a quotation from the Old Testament. There are many beautiful testimonies scattered throughout the old Jewish history; to be sure they are not in such measure, not in the fulness with which Jesus uttered them, and for which he is properly called the Prince of Peace. I want to see his beautiful example carried out in our lives. There has been a great cry about coming to Jesus, but it will not amount to anything unless we get into His Spirit. It is in vain that we cry peace while this great wrong is done to our fellow beings. I have been much encouraged in seeing the determination of those that are called the workingmen to resist being drawn into war. They say that they are not willing to enter into wars that they have nothing to do in bringing on. Some have gone so far as to say that they would have Peace if they had to fight for it—they have been so much accustomed to fight for everything, that this seems to them to be the only way to obtain it.[5] Now it seems to me that our Peace principles require of us that we should take a firm stand against this priestly assumption of power that would close the Centennial on the first day of the week. It is altogether inconsistent with their own acts. Why, their ministers are paid for their labors on the first day of the week, and these have no difficulty in going through the week to the Exhibition, whilst they would keep out those who are obliged to labor every day, it is an assumption that I hope will be overcome by a strong public sentiment. I hope there will be more public meetings. I have great faith in the strength of a righteous public sentiment, the weapons of whose warfare are not carnal but mighty through God to the pulling down of strongholds. The public voice in this country, resulting from the intelligence and morality of the people is a power that must be felt and recognized. I claim to be religious, I have my view of the great Eternal Source of all things, I do not want to show my faith by my words, or by my Quaker bonnet, I want that we may all show our faith by our works, by our honesty and justice and mercy and love; I want love to begin with little children; they should all be governed by love, and love only. I am glad the rod is so far banished in the family circle and in the schools. We should never teach children that they have wicked hearts, or try to give them an idea of total depravity, or that it is easier to do wrong than right; they will soon learn that it is easier to do right than wrong. Children love Peace. The little child knows when it says, mother, I love everybody. There is a Divine instinct in them which prompts to this feeling. It is very natural for those advanced in years as I am to note with interest the progress of events within our times. I was much gratified in reading an account of the celebration of William Cullen Bryant's eightieth birthday. They had a banquet, and he made an address, referring to the changes that had occurred in his time, the progress of the temperance cause, of education, of the abolition of slavery, he said the next thing that I look for and hope for more than any other is success in the efforts to do away with war. I believe the time has come when arbitration shall supplant the spirit of warfare. This is already beginning, and many of us have been watching with deeper interest since the abolition of slavery, the spread of the principles of Peace. Since the Geneva arbitration there have been three international conventions; and we regret that Dr. Miles,[6] who was a delegate from this country, and who intended to give a report of these meetings in this city, was prevented from doing this, for soon after his return home his work was shortened by his death.

I think the signs of the times are encouraging to us, and I am glad that we have so many of the, so called, heathen nations amongst us.[7] I remember hearing one of these express that he was surprised on coming to this Christian country to find so much warlike preparations. We read in the Bible about Abraham when he returned from the wars, being met by Melchisedec, King of Salem, or *Peace*, and there is no mention of his going to war any more. You may remember it humbled Saul, when he said, "I know that while I have requited thee evil, thou hast requited me good." It is an ancient proverb that "wickedness proceedeth from the wicked, and righteousness from the righteous." Then it was prophesied that the time would come when the horse should be driven from Ephraim, and the battle bow from the gates, and Peace should reign, it should come in as a flowing river. I am religious enough to believe all these things; Jesus said if ye discerned the signs of the times, ye would see these things. I want that we should have faith, and know that if we make the sacrifice for Peace principles, we shall in our measure realize the day when "violence shall no more be heard in our land, wasting and destruction in her borders."

* * * *

While I am in favor of Peace, I am also very favorable to war, I mean the firmness and combativeness that marked us in the anti-slavery warfare. We all remember how earnest and determined William Lloyd Garrison was, no man stood more firm for Peace, and yet he was constantly fighting with his tongue and his pen.

PD "Woman's Peace Festival," *Voice of Peace*, Philadelphia, July 1876, 52–53, 54

    1. The hymn was "The Peace of the Hills," written by Universalist minister, prolific author, and member of the Universal Peace Union Phebe A. Hanaford (1829–1921), a distant relative of LM (*Voice of Peace*, 51).
    2. On May 10 the U.S. Centennial Commission had opened the exhibition of "Arts, Manufactures and Products of the Soil and Mine," in Fairmount Park in Philadelphia. The exhibition ran for six months, but it never opened on Sundays. On June 12 Philadelphia workingmen would hold a mass meeting, demanding Sunday hours and reduced admission cost (*The Socialist*, June 17, 1876). LM's grandson-in-law Richard P. Hallowell, Francis E. Abbot, and other members of the Liberal League also protested this closure as a violation of religious freedom and "a grievous practical wrong against the working classes" (*The Index*, July 13, 1876).
    3. A shorter version of this quote, "there can be no true peace without justice," is often attributed to LM.
    4. The exhibits included portraits of naval leaders, Paul Jones's cutlass, and a model of the USS *Antietam* (*New Age*, July 29, 1876).
    5. H. M. Hunt of the Workmen's Peace Society (United Kingdom) attended the Peace Festival, and stated that if the British government declared war, it "would be a signal for the uprising of the work[ing] people in order to put their foot upon such effort" (*Voice of Peace*, 54).
    6. James B. Miles (1823–75), Congregational minister and secretary of the American Peace Society and the Association for the Codification of the Laws of Nations. For the latter, he organized peace meetings throughout Europe (*American Advocate of Peace and Arbitration*, February and March 1889, 25; "International Law: Arbitration instead of War," *New York Times*, April 30, 1874, 8).
    7. LM may have meant the following nations that participated in the Centennial: China, Egypt, Japan, the Sandwich Islands, Tunis, and Turkey.

30th Anniversary of the Seneca Falls Convention, Unitarian Church,[1] Rochester, New York, July 19, 1878

    Lucretia Mott, under the weight of 85 years, but whose eye still gleams as of old, and whose heart is still young in the cause for which she has so long and persistently labored, was the next among those who addressed the Convention. Largely her address was given to reminiscences, which were very happily recounted and received with the heartiest manifestations of delight on the part of her auditors. After these remarks, pertaining to her connection with this great movement, she pled earnestly for not only woman's equal, civil, religious, educational and industrial rights, but an equality of political exertion, a right to use all the sources of this power equal with man. In substance she said, place woman in equal power, and you will find her capable of not abusing it! Give her the elective franchise, and there will be an unseen, yet a deep and universal movement of the people to elect into office only those who are pure in intention and honest in sentiment! Give her the privilege to co-operate in making the laws she submits to, and there will be harmony without severity, and justice without oppression. Make her, if married, a living being in the eye of the law—she will not assume beyond duty; give her the right of property, and you may justly tax her patrimony as the result of her wages. Open to her your colleges—your legislative, your municipal, your domestic laws will be purified and ennobled. Forbid her not and she will use moderation.

* * * *

Mrs. Lucretia Mott also spoke upon the same subject,[2] distinguishing between true Christianity and theological creed. True righteousness and goodness were the only right for the correction of wrong. She believed in the Scripture, "Behold, a new heaven and a new earth, for old things have passed away." The fields were ripened for the harvest now and the churches were becoming more and more ready to do away with verbal creeds, which were such an element of dissension among them. In her closing remarks and just previous to her departure for the east she said she wished to add her expression of gratitude to the Unitarian society who had so kindly given them the use of their edifice. She spoke of the fitness of this courtesy having been extended by just such a denomination.

The convention then arose in her honor, and in behalf of all of them Frederick Douglass said to her "Good-bye."

PD "National Woman's Suffrage Association—Anniversary Day," *The National Citizen and Ballot Box*, vol. 3, no. 5 (August 1878), WASM

1. This event was sponsored by the National Woman Suffrage Association, and took place in the same church that hosted the subsequent women's rights convention, which met in Rochester on August 2, 1848 (Lisa Tetrault, *The Myth of Seneca Falls: Memory and the Women's Suffrage Movement, 1848–1898* [Chapel Hill: University of North Carolina Press, 2014], 104–8).

2. The convention passed two resolutions on religion, asserting that to her detriment the church taught women self-sacrifice and obedience, and that women had the same right to individual conscience as men. Matilda Joslyn Gage, the editor of the suffrage newspaper *National Citizen and Ballot Box*, spoke in support of the resolutions: "The protestant reformation while freeing women from certain restrictions had still continued those of a corresponding nature, and what she now most needed was to take upon herself the right inherently belonging to her, of her own private interpretation of Scripture." Frederick Douglass urged an amendment, arguing that "the doctrine of self-sacrifice was the soul of Christianity, and the soul of everything good" (*National Citizen and Ballot Box* [August 1878]).

Acknowledgments

First, we want to thank Dana Greene for *Lucretia Mott: Her Complete Speeches and Sermons* (1980). Her edition formed the essential framework for this project. Greene located, transcribed, and published a number of the addresses we have selected for our volume. Additionally, we have been inspired by the work of the late Margaret Hope Bacon, most notably her biography of Mott, *Valiant Friend* (1980, 1999).

At the Friends Historical Library, Swarthmore College, archivists Susanna K. Morikawa, Patricia C. O'Donnell, and Celia Caust-Ellenbogen located necessary documents to complete annotations. Also at Swarthmore College, our advisory board members Bruce Dorsey, professor of history, and Ellen Ross, professor of religion, shared their wisdom at key moments in the project. Patricia C. O'Donnell, with the assistance of Kate Carter at McCabe Library, Swarthmore, skillfully designed the illuminating website "Lucretia Mott Speaks: A Timeline of her Spoken Ministry," which lists all of Mott's known speaking engagements.

The History Department at Pomona College provided office space, computer support, photocopying, and printing. Thanks to Gina Brown-Petty, administrative assistant, and Todd Shimoda, Information Technology Services, for their help. Benjamin Cohen (Pomona 2016) ably contributed to proofreading a portion of Mott's addresses.

The Syracuse University History Department, especially chair Michael Ebner, Syracuse University Libraries, particularly Interlibrary Loan and Library Delivery, and James Steinberg and Michael Wasylenko of the Dean's Office of the Maxwell School of Citizenship and Public Affairs, supported this project in numerous ways. We are grateful to Molly Jessup for assistance with proofreading and verification, and to Tammy Hnat for her computing expertise.

We thank the following repositories for allowing us to include documents from their collections: Friends Historical Library, Swarthmore College, for printed and manuscript sermons and speeches from various collections; Special Collections, Haverford Library, for an excerpt from the Julia Wilbur Diaries; Historical Society of Pennsylvania, for a meeting record from the Pennsylvania Anti-Slavery Papers; and Massachusetts Historical Society, for excerpts from the Dana Family Papers.

Laurie Matheson, director of the University of Illinois Press, efficiently guided our proposal to publication. We have benefited from the hard work of Jennifer Comeau, who supervised the publication process, and Maria denBoer, who copyedited the book with precision and care. Special thanks to Anne Boylan and Thomas Hamm for their careful and perceptive reading of our manuscript.

Finally, we deeply appreciate the support of our families as we prepared this book for publication.

Index

Lucretia Mott's statements on various topics are indexed under the topic (e.g., antislavery, equal rights). Numbers in **bold** indicate pages with identifications.

Abbot, Francis Ellingwood, 203, **204n1**, 205n3
abolition. *See* antislavery movement
activism, 42–43, 46, 53, 84–87; antislavery, 102–3; and religion, 63, 129, 136, 154–55; and women, 71–72, 87–89, 97, 122, 126
African Americans, 42; and antislavery, xvi; education of, 15, 24; and equal rights, xxii–xxiv, 161; and suffrage, 162, 166n9, 175–76. *See also* equal rights
Alabama (ship), claims arbitration, 200, 201n4, 202, 213
American and Foreign Anti-Slavery Society, 104n6
American Anti-Slavery Society: Declaration of Sentiments, 1833, xvii, 40, 43–44, 89, 92n6, 101, 140–41, 144, 147n3; 1833 meeting, xvii, 140–41, 144, 147n1; 1848 meeting, xviii; 1864 meeting, xxii; 1870 meeting, 198n1
American Equal Rights Association, xxiii, 166n1, 190n1
American Freedmen's Aid Commission, 146, 147n13
American Indians, xvii, xix–xx, 24, 156, 160n1, 191–93, 194n1
American Moral Reform Society, 16
American Woman Suffrage Association, xxiii–xxiv
Anglican Church, Thirty-Nine Articles, 159, 160n4, 172, 185

Anthony, Susan B., xxii, xxiii, 150–51, **151n7**, 152, 162, 166n2
Anti-Slavery Convention of American Women, 1838, 4
antislavery movement, 11–12, 40–43, 44n7, 100–104, 137–42, 148–50; fairs, 101–2, 138, 139n1; press coverage of, 139–40; progress in, 56; Scottish women's petition, 41, 44n5; women in, xvii, 40, 144–45, 146, 207. *See also* emancipation

Barker, Joseph, 118–19, **120n18**
Beecher, Catharine, 91; *Suggestions Respecting Improvements in Education*, xxi, 72, **80n5**, 126
Beecher, Henry Ward, 135, **137n5**, 146, 147n10, 151
Beecher, Lyman, 126, **127n8**
beliefs, religious. *See* religion
Benezet, Anthony, xiii, 40, **44n3**
Bible: authority of, xiv–xv, 29, 31–32, 56–64, 98–99, 113–14, 118–19, 120n18, 120n20, 130–32, 208; as inspiration, 61; and slavery, 134; and women, 88–90, 92n8, 96, 98, 100n13, 108–9, 110n9, 124–25. *See also* religion
biblical figures: Aaron, 70; Abraham, 213; Anna, 70, 124; Barak, 70, 124; Deborah, 9, 70, 96, 112, 124, 132; Huldah, 9, 70, 112, 132; Jael, 70, 96; Jesus, 17–18, 32, 51, 58, 83, 85, 90, 132–33, 158, 168–69, 182, 186, 212; Job, 116; Joel, 22, 114; John of Patmore, 35; John the Baptist, 83–84; Luke, 9; Miriam, 70; Paul, 8, 12, 22, 47, 63, 70, 85, 90, 92n8, 96, 108, 113, 124–25, 181; Peter, 114; Phebe, 9, 22, 47, 70, 113, 132;

Index

biblical figures (*continued*): Philip's four daughters, 22, 47, 70; Priscilla, 47, 70; Samarian woman, 9, 114, 124, 132; Simeon, 147; Sisera, 70; Solomon, 113, 119; Tryphena, 22, 47, 70; Tryphosa, 22, 47, 70
Black Hawk, 193, **194n5**
Blackstone, William, 77, 81n16, 110, 151, 177; *Commentaries on the Laws of England*, 44, **45n3**, 164
Blackwell, Elizabeth, 79, **81n21**
Blackwell, Henry, xxiv
Blair, Hugh, *Sermons*, 61, **64n2**
Blanchard, Henry, 166, **170n2**, 171n7
Blanchard, Joshua, 178, **180n3**
Bloomer, Amelia, 110, **119n1**
Bloomer costume, 115, 119n9
Bonheur, Rosa, 152, **153n6**
Bowring, John, 94, **95n4**, 123, 152
Brigham, J. B., 96, **99n3**
Bright, John, 149, **150n3**
Britain. *See* Great Britain
Bronte, Charlotte, 152; *Jane Eyre*, 91, **92n10**, 124
Brooks, Phillips, 146, **147n13**
Brougham, Henry Peter, 76, **81n14**, 127n5
Brown, Antoinette (later Blackwell), 90, **92n8**, 96–98, 99n5, 100n13, 105–6, 109n1, 113, 118, 119, 120n15, 120n20
Brown, Euphronia, 74, **80n9**
Brown, John, xxii, **139n1**; and Harper's Ferry Raid, 140–41, 142n3
Brown, William Wells, xi, **44n8**
Bryant, William Cullen, 209–10, **211n4**, 213
Buckle, Henry, 152, **153n4**; *History of Civilization in England*, 158, 160n3
Bunyan, John, 193, **195n7**
Burleigh, Charles C., xviii, 163, 165; "The Sabbath Question," 33, **39n3**
Burleigh, Cyrus M., 102, **104n2**, 109n5
Burleigh, Rinaldo, 170, **171n11**
Burritt, Elihu, 53, **55n5**
Bush, Abigail, xxi
Butler, Benjamin F., **144n3**, 199n5

Calhoun, John C., 23, **26n2**; "On the Slavery Question," 86, 87n2
capital punishment, 179, 194, 195n8, 199
Carey, Samuel Fenton, 117–18, **120n15**
Catherine the Great of Russia, 114, **119n7**
Centennial Exposition of 1876, 211–12, 214n2, 214n4
Chambers, John, 112, 113, 118, **119n4**
Channing, William Ellery, xxv, **14n2**, 22–23, 29, 73, 91, 106, 170, 203–4, 205n4, 208; *An Address Delivered at Lenox*, 157, 160n2; *Discourses on War*, 176, 177n6; "Honour Due to All Men," xvi, 10, 14n2, 50, 176, 177n7, 180, 189n1
Channing, William H., 106, **109n6**
Chapin, Edwin H., 135, **137n5**
Chapman, Maria Weston, 139, **142n1**
Cheever, George, 140, **142n2**
Child, Henry T., 191, **194n1**, 209, 210n1
Child, Lydia Maria, xviii, 167, **170n3**
Civil War (American), 143, 148, 193; and pacifism, xxii–xxiii
Clarke, James Freeman, 28, **30n3**
Clarkson, Thomas, xiii, 40, **44n3**, 135, 145, 197
Clarkson Anti-Slavery Society, xvii, 147n2
Cobbe, Frances Power, 152, **153n5**; *An Essay on Intuitive Morals*, 165, 166n7
Coe, Emma R., 117, **120n14**
Coffin, Anna Folger (mother), xiii, xvii
Coffin, Martha (sister, later Martha Wright), xvii, xx, xxv
Coffin, Thomas (father), xiii
Colenso, John William, 167, **170n6**, 172, 184
Colton, Mr., xx, 46, 47n2
Combe, Andrew, 88–89, **91n4**
Combe, George, xxv, **39n11**, 88–90, 134–35; *Constitution of Man*, 37, 39n11; *Phrenological Journal*, 91n4
Confiscation Act of 1861, 143, **144n1**
Congregational Friends, Yearly Meeting, xix, 68
Considerant, Victor, 111, **119n2**
Cooper, Griffith M., xix, 193, **194n4**, 195n6
Corey, Adin T., 193, **194n4**
corporal punishment, 4–5, 6n3, 209, 213
corruption in politics, 175, 177n4
Cowper, William, xxi; "The Task," 48, **55n2**, 75–76, 112–13, 195–96
Cromwell, Richard, 122
Crystal Palace, 116, 119n10

Dana, Richard Henry, "Woman and Her Influence on Society," xxi, 69, 71, 73–74, 76, **80n1**, 81n13
Dangerfield, Daniel, 139n3
Darling, Grace, 73–74, **80n8**
Darlington, Smedley, 68, 87
Davis, Benjamin B., **26n5**
Davis, Edward M., xxii, 160, **162n1**
Davis, Paulina Wright, 87–88, **91n2**, 99, 109n5
death, 154, 188, 201–2
death penalty. *See* capital punishment
Deborah. *See under* biblical figures
De Garmo, Rhoda, xix
Dickinson, Anna, 141, **142n6**
"Discourse on Woman," xxi, 68–81
District of Columbia Emancipation Act of 1862, 143

Dix, Dorothea, 73, **80n6**, 117
Dorsey, William, 195, **196n4**
Douglas, James, Earl of Douglas, 205n5
Douglass, Frederick, xviii, xix, xx, xxiii, xxv, 15–16, **16n4**, 44, 198, 215
Dugdale, Joseph, 94, **95n2**
Durant, Thomas J., 165, **166n8**
Dymond, Jonathan, 209, **211n3**

Edgeworth, Maria, 124, **127n6**, 152, 165
Edgeworth, Richard, 124, **127n6**, 152, 165
education: equality in, xiii–xiv, 46, 72–73, 78–79; and militarism, 188, 189n4, 191, 211n10; and Quaker values, 205, 206n2; and women, 126
Edwards, Justin, 33, **39n4**
Eliot, George, 123, **127n3**
Eliot, Mr., 107, 110n8
emancipation, xxii–xxiii, 143, 160–63, 197–98; and moral suasion, 178–79, 192, 196–97, 198, 207. *See also* antislavery movement
Emancipation Proclamation, xxii, 150n4, 160–61, 175, 186
Emerson, Ralph Waldo, "Domestic Life," 61, **64n1**, 174, 177n3
England. *See* Great Britain
equal rights, 45–47, 68–81, 105–6, 109n3, 163, 165–66; and African Americans, xxii–xxiv, 161; economic, 54, 67, 83–85, 106, 156, 177, 178n8, 185, 206, 207n3; and women, 96, 125, 151–53. *See also* women's rights
Essays and Reviews (ed. Parker, 1860), 167, 170n5
Europe, revolutions in: 1789, 76, 81n13, 97, 111; 1848, 40, 43

fairs, antislavery, 101–2, 138, 139n1
Female College of Pennsylvania, 88, **91n3**
Female Moral Reform Society of Philadelphia, 46, **47n3**
Fifteenth Amendment, xxii, 190n1, 197, 198n1
Forten, James, 16
Forten, Margaretta, 197
Foster, Abigail Kelly, xviii, 89, **91n5**
Foster, Stephen S., 4, **6n2**, 145, 147n9
Fox, George, 115, **119n8**, 168, 172, 174, 183–84, 204
Foxton, Frederick Joseph, *Popular Christianity*, 127, **136n2**
France: abolishes slavery in colonies, 41, 44n7; 1789 Revolution, 76, 81n13, 97, 111; 1848 Revolution, 97, 100n8, 110–11, 152; women's rights in, 97, 100n8, 110–11, 122, 152
Franklin, Benjamin, 197, **198n3**
free produce movement, xv, 14, 23, 43–44, 134, 142

Free Religious Association, xxiv, 170n2, 173, 177n2; founding of, 171n12
free speech, 4, 6, 162
Frémont, John C.: Proclamation of 1861, 149, **150n2**
Friends Association for the Aid and Elevation of the Freedmen, 161, 162n3
Frothingham, Octavius B., 166, **170n1**, 202n2, 203n5
Fry, Elizabeth, 73, **80n6**, 117
fugitive slaves: Fugitive Slave Law, 100, 102n2; Pennsylvania abolishes law, 37, 38n10; and purchase of slaves, 103, 104n7
Furness, William Henry, **30n1**, 135, 146

Gage, Frances Dana, 151, **153n3**, 162, 164, 166n5
Gage, Matilda Joslyn, 215n2
Gannett, William Channing, "The Present Constructive Tendencies in Religion," 207, **209n1**
Garnet, Henry Highland, xxv, **198n4**
Garrison, Ellen Wright, 202, **203n3**
Garrison, William Lloyd, xviii, xxiii, 103, 109–10, 119n1, 135, 146, 148n14, 167, 198, 203n5, 207, 213–14; *Thoughts on African Colonization*, 149, 150n5
Genesee Yearly Meeting, xix, 68
Girard College, 98, 100n10
goodness. *See* inherent goodness in humanity
good works, 11–13, 25, 27, 66, 133, 154–55, 175–77, 182, 189n2
Great Britain: antislavery in, 41, 44n5, 103–4; British and Foreign Anti-Slavery Society, 103–4; pacifism in, 11, 24–25, 26n4, 53–54, 210, 211n6; and poverty, 23–24; religious dissension in, 7, 167; and West Indies emancipation, 24, 26n3; women's rights in, 123–24, 127n5
Greene, Dana, *Lucretia Mott: Her Complete Speeches and Sermons*, xi, xxvn2, xxix
Grew, Mary, 139, **142n1**

Hanaford, Phebe A., "The Peace of the Hills," 211, **214n1**
Harper, Frances Watkins, 151, **153n2**
Harris, George, **7n1**, 11
Hatch, Junius L., 98, **100n11**
Havens, R. N., 92, **93n1**
Haydock, Mr., 55, 56
Hedge, Frederic Henry, 28, **30n2**
heresy, 10, 18, 49, 140
Herschel, Caroline, 74, **80n10**
Heyrick, Elizabeth, 40, **44n4**, 197, 198, 207
Hicks, Elias, xv, xvi, **27n2**, 37, 40, 66, 135, 145; and Hicksite/Orthodox separation, xiv

Hicksite Quakers: and activism, 27, 66–67; and antislavery, xv–xvi; dissension in, 67–68; and Hicksite/Orthodox separation, xiv–xv, 6–8; inner light, xiv; Mott's commitment to, xxv, 166, 168–69, 185; Quarterly Meetings, 64–68; and women, xx, 112. *See also* Quakers

Higginson, Thomas Wentworth, 209n1
Hopper, Anna Mott (daughter), xiv, xvii, 196n2
Hopper, Isaac, xxv, **16n1**; tribute to, 92–93
Howard, John, 117, **119n11**
Howe, Julia Ward, xxiv, 210, **211n9**
Howitt, Mary, 91, **92n10**
Howitt, William, 123, **127n4**, 152
Hugo, Victor, 111, **119n3**
Hunt, Jane, xx
Hunt, Richard, xx
Hurlbut, Elisha Powell, *Essays on Human Rights*, 77, **81n16**, 110

Indians. *See* American Indians
inherent goodness in humanity, 16–26, 49, 51, 83, 116–17, 121, 127, 131, 136
inner light. *See under* Quakers
International Peace Congress, London 1843, 26
International Workingmen's Association, 210, 211n6

Janney, Samuel M., 199, **201n1**
Jefferson Medical College students, 48–49, 55
Jesus. *See under* biblical figures
Jewett, Daniel E., 144, **147n4**
Joan of Arc, 74
Johnson, Mary Ann White, 201, **202n1**
Johnson, Oliver, xxiv, **202n1**
Jones, Jane Elizabeth, 97, **100n9**, 106, 109n4, 145
Joslin, Levi K., 178, 180n2

Keeler, Mr., 117, 120n15

Lay, Benjamin, xiii, 145, **147n8**
"Leaves for Free Religious Life," 185, 189n3
Leftwich, Mr., 124, 125, 127n7
Leveson-Gower, Harriet, duchess of Sutherland, 103, **104n3**
Lewis, Sidney Ann, 197
Liberator, 101, 102n5
Lilenthal, Max, 167, **170n4**
Lincoln, Abraham, 149, 150n2, 175. *See also* Emancipation Proclamation
Logan, Olive, **190n3**
Lord, Martha Mott (daughter), xiv
Louisville Examiner, 56
Love, Alfred, xxiv, 161, **162n4**, 180n1

Lowell, James Russell, "The Present Crisis," 36, **38n8**
Lundy, Benjamin, 40, **44n3**; *Genius of Universal Emancipation*, 198
Luther, Katharina von Bora, 94, **95n2**
Luther, Martin, 94, **95n2**

Manhattan Anti-Slavery Society, 15–16
Mann, Horace, 73, **80n7**, 209, 211n2
marriage: inequality in, 77–79, 114–15; Quaker observance, xiv, 47, 90, 164–65, 166n6
married women's property acts, 78, **81n17**, 94
Marriott, Charles, 43, **44n10**
Martineau, Harriet, 91; *Society in America*, 76, **81n14**
materialism, 5, 6n5, 13, 184, 201, 206
May, Samuel, Jr., 34, **38n5**
May, Samuel J., 4, **5n1**, 144, 147n1, 163
McCrummell, James, 145, **147n6**, 180
McKim, James M., 137, **138n1**, 142n8
M'Clintock, Elizabeth, xx
M'Clintock, Mary Ann, xvii, xx
M'Clintock, Thomas, xvii, xix, xx, 44, **45n3**
Merton, Minnie, 190, 191n5
Miles, James B., 213, **214n6**
Mill, Harriet Taylor, "The Enfranchisement of Women," 94, **95n5**, 111, 123
Mill, John Stuart, 123, **127n3**, 152, 153n4
Milton, John, *Paradise Lost*, 69, **80n2**
Mitchell, Maria, 74, **80n10**
Morais, Mr., 167, 170n4
moral suasion, 89, 101, 137–38, 143, 176, 213; and slavery, 149–50, 178
Mott, Anna (daughter; later Anna Hopper), xiv, xvii, 196n2
Mott, James (husband), xiii, xiv, xix, xx, 44, 95, 105, 180n1; and Orthodox/Hicksite differences, 7–8
Mott, Lucretia: as minister, xiii, xix; as presiding officer, 95–99, 104–10, 163–66, 196–97; and reform movements, xi, xxv; travels of, xvii–xviii, xix–xx, xxix
Mott, Martha (daughter), xiv
Mott, Richard (brother-in-law), 210, **211n5**
Mott, Thomas (son), xiii
Mumford, William, 199n5

Nantucket, and women's role, 116, 163
National Anti-Slavery Standard, 139–40, 142n1, 163
National Era, 101, 102n5
National Woman's Suffrage Association, xxiii, 190n1, 215n1
Neall, Daniel, xviii
Nell, William C., xx, 45, **47n1**
Nevin, Edwin H., 118–19, **120n17**

[Newall, Mr.], 169, 171n10
New England Non-Resistance Society, 4
New School Presbyterians, 130, 137n3
New York Association of Friends for the Relief of Those Held in Slavery, 16
Nichols, Clarina H., 95, **99n1**
non-resistance, 4–6, 140–41, 142–43, 148. *See also* moral suasion

Oberlin College, 97, 99
O'Connell, Daniel, xviii, 94, **95n3**, 123, 127n4, 141, 142n5, 152
Orthodox Quakers. *See* Quakers
Owen, Robert Dale, 171n7; "The Needle Women of London," 78, **81n19**
Owenson, Sydney (Lady Morgan), 152, **153n7**

pacifism, xxiv, 53–54, 133, 157–58, 178–80, 188–89, 191–93; and arbitration, 200–201, 202, 209, 212–13; and Centennial Exposition, 212; and women, 209. *See also* moral suasion; non-resistance
Parker, Theodore, xviii, 31, 34, **38n1**
Parkman, Francis, 29, **30n5**
Parkman, Samuel, 29, **30n5**
Paul. *See under* biblical figures
Peabody, George, 177, **178n8**
Penn, William, 115, **119n8**, 183, 192
Pennsylvania Abolition Slavery, 197–98, 207
Pennsylvania Anti-Slavery Society, xxiii, 102n1; need for continuation, 160
Pennsylvania Hall, destruction of, xviii, 4, 42, 138, 147
Pennsylvania Peace Society, xxiv, 180n1
Peter, Sarah Worthington, 78, **81n19**
Peter, William, 78, **81n19**
Phebe. *See under* biblical figures
Philadelphia Female Anti-Slavery Society, xvii, 101, 102n8, 144–45; disruption in antislavery fair, 138, 139n1; final meeting, 196–97
Philadelphia School of Design for Women, 88, **91n3**
Philadelphia Yearly Meeting of Women Friends, and antislavery, 138n2
Phillips, Wendell, xxiii, **56n2**, 90, 92n7, 97, 100n7, 148, 149, 150n2, 165, 166n9, 199
phrenology, 89. *See also* Combe, Andrew; Combe, George
Pillsbury, Parker, **56n2**, 137, 138n1
political participation: and antislavery, 101, 102n7, 148–49; and women, 76, 101, 145, 214–15
Pope, Alexander, "Messiah: A Sacred Eclogue," 48, **55n3**
Post, Amy, xvii, xix, xx, xxiv, xxv, **27n3**, 46

Post, Isaac, xvii, xix, xxv
Potter, Alonzo, 79, **81n20**
Potter, Ray, 146, **147n12**
Powell, Aaron, 162, **163n6**
Prescod, Samuel J., 41, **44n6**
primogeniture, 111–12
progress, 12, 36, 39–44, 50–51, 91, 156–59; and antislavery, 137, 139; and women, 73–74, 88, 93–94, 96, 98, 110–12, 114, 116, 122–24, 127n1, 152, 215
Progressive Friends. *See* Congregational Friends
property, married women's, 78, **81n17**, 94
Pugh, Sarah, 103, **104n4**, 197
Pulszky, Terezia Walder, 146, **147n11**
Purvis, Harriet, xvii, xxv
Purvis, Robert, xii, xvii, xxv, 141, **142n4**, 163, 198

Quakers: activism in, 141, 184; dissension in, xii, 14, 174; and education, 205, 206n2; in Great Britain, xviii, 6–8; and Hicksite/Orthodox separation, xiv, xv, 6–8; and inner light, xiv, xvi, xxiv–xxv, 15, 64–65, 128, 180–82, 183–86, 188, 196, 204–5; and pacifism, 201; and slavery, 13, 137, 138n2. *See also* Congregational Friends; Hicksite Quakers

Reform League, 199n1
religion: creeds and rituals, 11–13, 17, 19, 21, 27, 31, 129–30, 159, 184–85; and divine spirit, 128, 131, 171–73, 176; freedom of belief, 8–14, 16–26, 28, 48–55, 65, 103, 118, 129–30, 132–33, 136, 158–59, 166–70, 173–75, 187, 195; and free speech, 14, 18; natural depravity, 17–19, 28–29, 131, 175; prayer, 154, 183, 208; priestcraft, 40, 62, 120–21; progress in, 64–66, 128–29, 135–36; and reform, 20–21, 120–21; role of reason, 50–51, 62, 158–59; sectarianism, 129–30, 182; and slavery, 56, 134–35; and women, xix, 8–10, 21–22, 29, 46, 63, 70–71, 75, 108, 112–14, 132. *See also* Bible; Hicksite Quakers; Quakers; theology; universal religion
revolutions in Europe, 1848, 40, 43
Richardson, Anna, 103, **106n6**
rights. *See* equal rights; women's rights
Roach, Isaac, 138, **139n2**
Rogers, Rachel, 64, **68n1**
Root, J. K., 108–9, **110n9**
Rose, Ernestine Sismondi Potowski, 97, **100n8**, 106, 109n7, 122

sabbath, observance of, xvi, 30–39, 60–62, 211–12
Sandiford, Ralph, xiii, 145, **147n8**
science. *See under* theology
Scotland. *See* Great Britain

slavery, 15–16; evils of, 52–53, 86–87; Kentucky retains, 56n3; and purchase of slaves, 103–4, 104n7; and religion, 21–24, 67, 101–2
Smith, Elizabeth Oakes, 96, **99n2**
Smith, Gerrit, 96, **99n3**
Society for the Promotion of Permanent and Universal Peace, 55
Society of Friends. *See* Hicksite Quakers; Quakers
Somerville, Mary Fairfax, 74, **80n10**
speeches and sermons: characteristics of, xi, xii, xxi, xxviin28, 43, 172; coverage of, xx–xxii, 91n1, 195–96, 199–200; reactions to, 26, 39n13, 52–53, 55n4, 121–22
Spencer, Herbert, 152, **153n4**
Stanton, Elizabeth Cady, xix, xx, xxii, xxiii, 150, **150n7**, 151, 152, 153n3, 190n1
Stebbins, Sumner, 141, **142n7**
Stewart, Alexander T., 177, **178n8**
Stone, Lucy, xxiv, 96, 97, **99n5**, 105, 105n7, 109n3, 122, 127n1, 145
Stowe, Harriet Beecher, 152; *Uncle Tom's Cabin*, 101, **102n5**, 117
suffrage. *See* African Americans; women's rights
Sulley, Richard, xx, **47n5**
Swarthmore College, opening of, 195–96

telegraph, 133, 137n4
temperance, 51, 67–68, 117–18
theology: limitations of, 135, 143, 155–56, 174–75, 183; science and, 143, 203
Thirteenth Amendment, xxiii
Thomas à Kempis, 200, **201n3**
Thompson, George, **150n7**
Tillotson, John, 200, **201n3**
Tilton, Theodore, 145, **147n7**, 151, 202n2
Townsend, Myra Sharpless, 117, **119n12**
transatlantic cable, 1857, 133, 137n4
Treaty of Washington, 1871, xxiv, 200
Truth, Sojourner, xxiv, 90, **92n9**, 109, 110n10
Tuckerman, Joseph, 29, **30n6**
Twelfth Street Monthly Meeting, xiii

Una, 99, 100n14
Unitarians, xxv, 167; in Great Britain, 6–7; Unitarian Christians Convention, Philadelphia, 1846, 28, 30n1
Universal Franchise Association Meeting, 1869, 190n4
universal religion, xxiv–xxv, 167, 172–73, 204
University of Pennsylvania Medical School students, 48–49, 55
U.S. Constitution, amendments to. *See* Fifteenth Amendment; Thirteenth Amendment

Vassar, Matthew, 177, **178n8**
Victoria, Queen of England, 96, **100n6**, 123
voting rights. *See* African Americans; women's rights

Walker, Mary, 190n4
Walker, Timothy, *Introduction to American Law*, 77, **81n15**, 110
Walton, Joseph, 193, **194n4**
Watts, Isaac, "Divine Songs," 81–83, 86, **87n1**
Wedgewood, Josiah, 197, **198n2**
Weiss, John, 203, **204n1**
Weld, Theodore D., 101, **102n3**, 198, 199n5
Westminster Review, "The Enfranchisement of Women," 94, 95n5, 111, 123
White, Joseph Blanco, 168, **171n8**
White, Lydia, xvii
Whitson, Thomas, xvii, 144, **147n2**
Wilberforce, William, 40, **44n3**, 135, 149
Wilbur, Julia, **27n1**
Willis, Nathaniel Parker: *Inklings of Adventure*, xxi; "Minute Philosophies," 80, **81n22**; "Unwritten Philosophy," 96, 99n4
Wollstonecraft, Mary, *Vindication of the Rights of Woman*, **153n8**
Women's Loyal National League, xxii, 150, 151n7
women's rights, 6–7, 44–47, 68–81, 87–100, 104–20, 122–27, 151–53, 189–91, 214–15; and inequality, 105; and progress, 164; publicity, 91n1, 95, 106, 109n5, 190, 191n6; and religion, 46, 108; and suffrage, xx, xxiii–xxiv, 106–8, 109, 163–64. *See also* equal rights
Women's Rights Convention, Rochester, 1848, xx, 215n1
Women's Rights Convention, Seneca Falls, 1848, xx, 93, 105, 151
Women's Rights Convention, Syracuse 1852, 163–64, 166n3
Women's Rights Convention, Worcester, 1850, 94, 95n5, 123
Women's Suffrage Meeting, Brooklyn, 1869, xxiii
Woolman, John, 209, **211n3**
Worcester, Noah, 29, **30n4**, 176, 177n5, 210
World's Anti-Slavery Convention, 1840, and women's role, xviii, 6–7, 94–95, 123, 145, 152
World's Temperance Convention, 1853, 112, 116–18, 119n4, 120n15
Wright, Henry C., xviii, 31–32, **38n1**
Wright, Martha Coffin (sister), xvii, xx, xxv

Young, Edward, "Night Thoughts," 103, **104n5**

CHRISTOPHER DENSMORE is the curator of the Friends Historical Library at Swarthmore College and the author of *Red Jacket: Iroquois Diplomat and Orator*.

CAROL FAULKNER is a professor of history at Syracuse University and the author of *Lucretia Mott's Heresy: Abolition and Women's Rights in Nineteenth-Century America*.

NANCY HEWITT is Distinguished Professor Emerita of History and Women's and Gender Studies at Rutgers University. Her books include *Women's Activism and Social Change: Rochester, New York, 1822–1872*.

BEVERLY WILSON PALMER is a research associate at Pomona College and the editor or coeditor of numerous documentary editions, including *Selected Letters of Lucretia Coffin Mott*.

WOMEN, GENDER, AND SEXUALITY IN AMERICAN HISTORY

Women Doctors in Gilded-Age Washington: Race, Gender, and Professionalization   *Gloria Moldow*

Friends and Sisters: Letters between Lucy Stone and Antoinette Brown Blackwell, 1846–93   *Edited by Carol Lasser and Marlene Deahl Merrill*

Reform, Labor, and Feminism: Margaret Dreier Robins and the Women's Trade Union League   *Elizabeth Anne Payne*

Private Matters: American Attitudes toward Childbearing and Infant Nurture in the Urban North, 1800–1860   *Sylvia D. Hoffert*

Civil Wars: Women and the Crisis of Southern Nationalism   *George C. Rable*

I Came a Stranger: The Story of a Hull-House Girl   *Hilda Satt Polacheck; edited by Dena J. Polacheck Epstein*

Labor's Flaming Youth: Telephone Operators and Worker Militancy, 1878–1923   *Stephen H. Norwood*

Winter Friends: Women Growing Old in the New Republic, 1785–1835   *Terri L. Premo*

Better Than Second Best: Love and Work in the Life of Helen Magill   *Glenn C. Altschuler*

Dishing It Out: Waitresses and Their Unions in the Twentieth Century   *Dorothy Sue Cobble*

Natural Allies: Women's Associations in American History   *Anne Firor Scott*

Beyond the Typewriter: Gender, Class, and the Origins of Modern American Office Work, 1900–1930   *Sharon Hartman Strom*

The Challenge of Feminist Biography: Writing the Lives of Modern American Women   *Edited by Sara Alpern, Joyce Antler, Elisabeth Israels Perry, and Ingrid Winther Scobie*

Working Women of Collar City: Gender, Class, and Community in Troy, New York, 1864–86   *Carole Turbin*

Radicals of the Worst Sort: Laboring Women in Lawrence, Massachusetts, 1860–1912   *Ardis Cameron*

Visible Women: New Essays on American Activism   *Edited by Nancy A. Hewitt and Suzanne Lebsock*

Mother-Work: Women, Child Welfare, and the State, 1890–1930   *Molly Ladd-Taylor*

Babe: The Life and Legend of Babe Didrikson Zaharias   *Susan E. Cayleff*

Writing Out My Heart: Selections from the Journal of Frances E. Willard, 1855–96   *Edited by Carolyn De Swarte Gifford*

U.S. Women in Struggle: A *Feminist Studies* Anthology   *Edited by Claire Goldberg Moses and Heidi Hartmann*

In a Generous Spirit: A First-Person Biography of Myra Page   *Christina Looper Baker*

Mining Cultures: Men, Women, and Leisure in Butte, 1914–41   *Mary Murphy*

Gendered Strife and Confusion: The Political Culture of Reconstruction   *Laura F. Edwards*

The Female Economy: The Millinery and Dressmaking Trades, 1860–1930   *Wendy Gamber*

Mistresses and Slaves: Plantation Women in South Carolina, 1830–80   *Marli F. Weiner*

A Hard Fight for We: Women's Transition from Slavery to Freedom in South Carolina   *Leslie A. Schwalm*

The Common Ground of Womanhood: Class, Gender, and Working Girls' Clubs, 1884–1928   *Priscilla Murolo*

Purifying America: Women, Cultural Reform, and Pro-Censorship Activism, 1873–1933   *Alison M. Parker*

Marching Together: Women of the Brotherhood of Sleeping Car Porters   *Melinda Chateauvert*

Creating the New Woman: The Rise of Southern Women's Progressive Culture in Texas, 1893–1918   *Judith N. McArthur*

The Business of Charity: The Woman's Exchange Movement, 1832–1900   *Kathleen Waters Sander*

The Power and Passion of M. Carey Thomas   *Helen Lefkowitz Horowitz*

For Freedom's Sake: The Life of Fannie Lou Hamer   *Chana Kai Lee*

Becoming Citizens: The Emergence and Development of the California Women's Movement, 1880–1911   *Gayle Gullett*

Selected Letters of Lucretia Coffin Mott   *Edited by Beverly Wilson Palmer with the assistance of Holly Byers Ochoa and Carol Faulkner*

Women and the Republican Party, 1854–1924   *Melanie Susan Gustafson*

Southern Discomfort: Women's Activism in Tampa, Florida, 1880s–1920s   *Nancy A. Hewitt*

The Making of "Mammy Pleasant": A Black Entrepreneur in Nineteenth-Century San Francisco   *Lynn M. Hudson*

Sex Radicals and the Quest for Women's Equality   *Joanne E. Passet*

"We, Too, Are Americans": African American Women in Detroit and Richmond, 1940–54   *Megan Taylor Shockley*

The Road to Seneca Falls: Elizabeth Cady Stanton and the First Woman's Rights Convention   *Judith Wellman*

Reinventing Marriage: The Love and Work of Alice Freeman Palmer and George Herbert Palmer   *Lori Kenschaft*

Southern Single Blessedness: Unmarried Women in the Urban South, 1800–1865   *Christine Jacobson Carter*

Widows and Orphans First: The Family Economy and Social Welfare Policy, 1865–1939   *S. J. Kleinberg*

Habits of Compassion: Irish Catholic Nuns and the Origins of the Welfare System, 1830–1920   *Maureen Fitzgerald*

The Women's Joint Congressional Committee and the Politics of Maternalism, 1920–1930   *Jan Doolittle Wilson*

"Swing the Sickle for the Harvest Is Ripe": Gender and Slavery in Antebellum Georgia   *Daina Ramey Berry*

Christian Sisterhood, Race Relations, and the YWCA, 1906–46   *Nancy Marie Robertson*

Reading, Writing, and Segregation: A Century of Black Women Teachers in Nashville   *Sonya Ramsey*

Radical Sisters: Second-Wave Feminism and Black Liberation in Washington, D.C.   *Anne M. Valk*

Feminist Coalitions: Historical Perspectives on Second-Wave Feminism in the United States   *Edited by Stephanie Gilmore*

Breadwinners: Working Women and Economic Independence, 1865–1920   *Lara Vapnek*

Beauty Shop Politics: African American Women's Activism in the Beauty
   Industry   *Tiffany M. Gill*
Demanding Child Care: Women's Activism and the Politics of Welfare,
   1940–1971   *Natalie M. Fousekis*
Rape in Chicago: Race, Myth, and the Courts   *Dawn Rae Flood*
Black Women and Politics in New York City   *Julie A. Gallagher*
Cold War Progressives: Women's Interracial Organizing for Peace and
   Freedom   *Jacqueline Castledine*
No Votes for Women: The New York State Anti-Suffrage Movement   *Susan Goodier*
Anna Howard Shaw: The Work of Woman Suffrage   *Trisha Franzen*
Nursing Civil Rights: Gender and Race in the Army Nurse Corps   *Charissa J. Threat*
Reverend Addie Wyatt: Faith and the Fight for Labor, Gender, and
   Racial Equality   *Marcia Walker-McWilliams*
Lucretia Mott Speaks: The Essential Speeches   *Edited by Christopher Densmore,
   Carol Faulkner, Nancy Hewitt, and Beverly Wilson Palmer*

The University of Illinois Press
is a founding member of the
Association of American University Presses.

Composed by Lisa Connery
at the University of Illinois Press
Cover designed by Jennifer S. Holzner
Cover illustration: Lucretia Mott, three-quarter length portrait, seated, facing right. Library of Congress Prints and Photographs Division (LC-USZ62-42559).
Manufactured by Sheridan Books, Inc.

University of Illinois Press
1325 South Oak Street
Champaign, IL 61820-6903
www.press.uillinois.edu